Working Time:
The Law and Practice

AUSTRALIA
LBC Information Services Ltd
Sydney

CANADA and USA
Carswell
Toronto, Ontario

NEW ZEALAND
Brooker's
Auckland

SINGAPORE and MALAYSIA
Sweet & Maxwell Asia
Singapore and Kuala Lumpur

Working Time:
The Law and Practice

General Editors

John McMullen, MA, PhD (Cantab), FCIPD, FRSA
National Head of Employment Law at Pinsent Curtis;
Professor of Labour Law, University of Leeds

Martin Brewer, BA
Partner, Pinsent Curtis

Contributors

Martin Brewer, BA, *Partner*
Christopher Mordue, BA (Oxon), *Associate*
Melanie Steed, LLB, *Associate*
Justin Marks, MA (Cantab), *Associate*
Helen Milgate, LLB, MA (Cantab) LLM, *Solicitor*
Kirsty Ayre, LLB, *Solicitor*
Sara Sawicki, LLB, *Solicitor*
Philip Titchmarsh, LLB, *Solicitor*
Jon Fisher, BA (Cantab), *Solicitor*

All of Pinsent Curtis

Leeds, Birmingham, London and Brussels

SWEET & MAXWELL

Published by Sweet & Maxwell Limited of
100 Avenue Road, Swiss Cottage, London, NW3 3PF
(http://www.sweetandmaxwell.co.uk)

Typeset by Mendip Communications Ltd
Printed by MPG Books Ltd, Bodmin, Cornwall

No natural forests were destroyed to make this product:
only farmed timber was used and replanted.

A CIP catalogue record for this book is available from the British Library

ISBN 0 752 005774

Foreword

Dr John McMullen

Nothing has perhaps been so remarkable in terms of E.C. Labour Law and its transposition in the U.K. than the E.C. Working Time Directive, now in force, through the Working Time Regulations 1998 (S.I. 1998/1833) as amended by the 1999 Regulations (S.I. 1999/3372). A proposed European Directive which would attack head on the British culture of long working hours was always bound to be controversial. Following an E.C. Council recommendation in 1975, the adoption of the Social Chapter in 1989, Commission proposals in 1990 and the final adoption of the Council Directive 1993/104/E.C. in November 1993, this controversy began to intensify in the U.K. In fact so opposed was it to the concept of the Regulation of working time, the then, Conservative, government launched a legal challenge in 1994 to the use of (what was then) Article 118A (now Article 138) of the E.C. Treaty (health and safety) as the legal basis of the new Directive. This was always doomed to failure. Surely enough, the European Court of Justice, in *U.K. v. Council of the European Union* C–84/94 [1997] I.R.L.R. 30 dismissed the U.K.'s challenge to the Directive in a sweeping and summary way save in only one minor aspect, in relation to Sunday working.

On the election of a Labour Government in May 1997 legislation had urgently to be put in hand (especially as the date by which the Directive had to be transposed had now passed). Notwithstanding, it was not until October 1998 that the Working Time Regulations of 1998 came into force. As such, they are immensely topical and emerging as a vital new legal practice area.

The Regulations have given rise to an almost irreconcilable clash between deeply regulatory social policy and freedom of contract. It is fascinating that even the Blair Government has succumbed to pressure to reduce red tape. And controversial limiting provisions in the Working Time Regulations 1999 have extended the unmeasured time exemption also to partially unmeasured working time applicable to those who work additional voluntary overtime and work extra hours at their own discretion. Striking as it does at the health and safety policy aims of the Directive, litigation on the validity of this amendment is bound to follow in due course. On June 22, 2000 the Council adopted Directive 2000/34 amending the 1993 Directive concerning the extension of certain aspects of the organisation of working time to cover sectors and activities previously excluded by virtue of the 1993 Directive. In the meantime, cases both in Ireland and in the U.K. abound, principally, on technical points about holidays.

But, on the other hand, three cases in U.K. courts have been highly significant on other, more strategic, issues, including *Barber v. RJB Mining (U.K.) Ltd* [1999] I.R.L.R. 308, which holds that the 48 hour rule is a free-standing right implied into every employment contract, *R. v. Attorney General for Northern Ireland, ex p. Burns* [1999] I.R.L.R. 315 on the subject of night workers and their rights; and *Gibson v. East Riding of Yorkshire* [2000] I.R.L.R. 598 where, perhaps disappointingly, the Court of Appeal, overturning the EAT, held that the provisions of the Directive relating to annual leave were insufficiently precise to have direct effect as against a public body. But there is more.

A number of European Court referrals from Member States to the ECJ (including *SIMAP* C–303/98), *BECTU* (Case C–173/99), *Confederation Intersindical Gallga (CIG) and Services Gallga Saude (Sergas)* (Case C–241/99) and *Bowden v. Tuffnells Parcels Express* (Case C–133/00) will also prove to be significant on the interpretation of the Directive and hence the Regulations.

This book is a team effort, written by the employment lawyers at Pinsent Curtis drawing on research and interpretation but also on practical problems experienced by clients in implementing the new Regulations. Jon Fisher wrote Chapters 1, 3 and 7. Melanie Steed wrote Chapters 2 and 14. Helen Milgate wrote Chapters 4, 11, 13 and 17, Martin Brewer wrote Chapters 5 and 16, Justin Marks wrote Chapter 6, Kirsty Ayre wrote Chapter 8, Christopher Mordue wrote Chapters 9 and 18, Philip Titchmarsh wrote Chapter 12 and Sara Sawicki wrote Chapters 10 and 15.

Whilst attempting to explain the convoluted law arising from the Working Time Directive and the 1998 Regulations and their amendments in the main text, we have included a number of practical appendices including the text of the Directives, the Regulations concerned, and practical guidance such as specimen opt-out formats, workforce agreements and a collective agreement.

Dr John McMullen
Leeds, 2000

POSTSCRIPT

After this book had gone to proof, the European Court of Justice issued its decision in *Sindicale de Médico de Asistencia Pública (Simap) v. Conselleria de Sanidad y Consumo de la Generalidad Valenciana* (Case C–3–3/98) [2000] I.R.L.R. 845.

The SIMAP reference was made in the course of proceedings brought by a Spanish medical union on behalf of medical staff providing primary care at health centres in Valencia.

The reference raised five broad issues regarding the application and effect of the Directive, the major issue for our purposes being the status of "on call hours". The doctors concerned worked a standard 40 hours per week, with a period of 17 hours "on call" every 11 days. Were these "on call" hours working time? Could "on call" hours qualify a worker as a night worker? Were the on call hours overtime and, if so, what were the consequences for the average weekly working time limit and the Regulation of normal hours of night workers?

While the SIMAP reference raised a number of key issues it quickly became apparent that the case was of potentially much wider significance. The ECJ would, for the first time, have to rule on the interpretation of "working time" itself. This is the most fundamental concept under the Directive and the U.K. Regulations and is central to the operation of the limits on working hours and the entitlements to daily and weekly rest. Critically, the reference raised the possibility that the working time definition—time when the worker is "working, at the employer's disposal and carrying out activities and duties"—was disjunctive in nature and not (as had been widely assumed, not least in the DTI's regulatory Guidance) conjunctive. In other words, only one element of the definition needed to be present for time to count as "working time". Such an interpretation would stand on its head the most basic assumptions behind the U.K. Regulations. The scope of "working time" would be much wider, with a consequent impact on the whole operation of the Regulations from the weekly working time limit through to compliance with daily and weekly rest periods. Would the relative tranquillity which followed the introduction of the Regulations—boosted by the pro-business 1999 amendments—prove to be a "phoney war"? Could working time return with added bite?

In December 1999, the Opinion of Advocate General Saggio[1] fuelled these fears. Not only did he conclude that the working time definition was disjunctive in nature, he considered the separate elements of the definition to be mutually exclusive. This raised real uncertainties as to what these terms meant. How was time when the worker was "working" different from time when "activities and duties" were being carried out? The Advocate General concluded that "on call" hours counted as working time where the worker was required to be present at the employer's premises. Where on call hours were spent away from work, only such time as the worker was actually called upon to work counted as working time. Interestingly, Advocate General Saggio's approach to the concept of working time was based on the degree of freedom which the worker has to carry out non-working related activities. More controversially, and at odds with the literal wording of the Directive,[2] he concluded that "on call" hours which were not working time could not count as a rest period and fell outside the entitlement to daily or weekly rest.

The Judgement of the ECJ[3] (given on October 3, 2000) is rather more conservative. It is rather short on analysis and eschews the interpretative subtleties of the Advocate General Saggio's opinion. For instance, the ECJ does not directly refer to the "disjunctive" versus "conjunctive" debate, its support for a conjunctive interpretation being implied in its conclusions in relation to "on call" hours. As such, the decision provides clarification rather than revolution. The main aspects of the decision for U.K. readers are as follows:

- "On call" hours count as working time in their entirety if the worker is required to be present at the place of work. In such circumstances, all three elements of the working time definition are satisfied. Where the worker is simply required to be contactable, the definition is not met, albeit that the worker is at the employer's disposal. In such cases, only time linked to the actual provision of services is working time. It follows that the conjunctive interpretation is correct.
- A Worker's freedom to carry out non-work activities appears to be a relevant consideration in the interpretation of "working time". The judgment does not, however, provide concrete guidance on what is "working time", either generally or in terms of the three parts of the definition.
- "On call" hours may (to the extent that they count as working time) qualify the worker as a night worker, depending on their frequency.
- All time which is not "working time" is rest. The Advocate General's controversial attempt to create a third category of time was rejected.
- A worker who works on call may be a "shift worker". This would bring into play the derogations which allow some flexibility in the granting of rest periods included in Article 17(2.3) and Regulation 22.
- The limit on average weekly working time in Article 6 is capable of direct effect against emanations of the State. On the facts of the SIMAP case, the derogation from Article 6 contained in Article 17(2.1)(c) applied as the doctors' activities related to the reception/treatment and/or care provided by

---

[1] Unreported, but available on http://europa.eu.int, the E.U. homepage.
[2] Art. 2(2) states "rest period shall mean any period which is not working time".
[3] [2000] I.R.L.R. 845.

hospitals or similar establishments. This derogation allows a Member State to set a maximum reference period of 12 months for the averaging of weekly working time. It was this minimum standard under the derogation which had direct effect on the facts of this case. However, it appears that in the absence of an applicable derogation, the "directly effective" reference period would be 4 months.

- By implication, this approach casts doubt on the Court of Appeal's decision in *Gibson v. East Riding of Yorkshire*[4] in which Article 7 (annual leave) was held not to have direct effect on the grounds of the vagueness of the "working time" definition in Article 2. The ECJ had no such difficulties in holding that Article 6 had direct effect. It is possible that the SIMAP decision makes it more likely that other provisions of the Directive can have direct effect.[5]
- The ECJ confirmed that a worker's individual consent is necessary opt out from the weekly working time limit. A collective agreement will not suffice.

As this book was written before the ECJ judgment was delivered, attention was properly given to the potential consequences of the ECJ adopting Advocate General Saggio's reasoning and approach. The ECJ decision should therefore be borne in mind wherever the Advocate General's Opinion is referred to, particularly in Chapter 3 The Concept of "Working Time", (especially pages 32–38) and Chapter 7 (Rest Entitlements).

---

[4] [2000] I.R.L.R. 598.
[5] See further, Chap. 2.

Contents

Table of Cases

Table of Statutes

Table of Statutory Instruments

Table of Primary and Secondary European Legislation

Abbreviations

ACAS	Advisory Conciliation & Arbitration Service
CA	Court of Appeal
CBI	Confederation of British Industry
DDA	Disability Discrimination Act 1995
DTI	Department of Trade & Industry
EAT	Employment Appeal Tribunal
E.C.	European Community
ECHR	European Convention on Human Rights
ECJ	European Court of Justice
EPCA 1978	Employment Protection (Consolidation) Act 1978
ERA 1996	Employment Rights Act 1996
E.U.	European Union
HC	High Court
HRA 1998	Human Rights Act 1998
HSC	Health & Safety Commission
HSE	Health & Safety Executive
HSWA 1974	Health & Safety at Work etc. Act 1974
IGC	Intergovernmental Conference
ILO	International Labour Organisation
OECD	Organisation for Economic Co-operation & Development
TUC	Trades Union Congress
TULRCA 1992	Trade Union & Labour Relations (Consolidation) Act 1992
TUPE 1981	Transfer of Undertakings (Protection of Employment) Regulations 1981 (S.I. No. 1794)
WHO	World Health Organisation

CHAPTER ONE

The History of the Working Time Directive

INTRODUCTION

1–01   The Working Time Directive[1] was adopted by the Council of Social and Labour Affairs Ministers of the E.C. on November 23, 1993. From its earliest beginnings, the Directive was steeped in controversy. This was particularly so in the United Kingdom, where the terms of the Directive conflicted with the traditional laissez-faire approach to labour relations[2] and, more directly, with the deregulatory philosophy of the Conservative administration of the time.[3] However, perhaps the most controversial issue of all was the legal basis upon which the Directive was proposed and adopted. The Council adopted the Directive as a health and safety measure under what was then Article 118a of the E.C. Treaty,[4] which enabled measures to be adopted by "qualified majority voting", rather than as a social policy measure under ex-Article 100,[5] under which the Directive would have required unanimous approval. The United Kingdom was thus unable to veto the Directive without support from other Member States, and although the United Kingdom ultimately abstained from the vote, this was a futile gesture given the Community-wide support for the Directive.

The contentious nature of this issue and the strength of the United Kingdom's ideological opposition to the Directive are evidenced by its subsequent attempt to have it annulled. Essentially, the Government argued that the Working Time Directive was not in reality a health and safety measure but rather represented both a social policy measure and an economic measure aimed at job creation and reducing unemployment. On this basis, the United Kingdom contended that the Directive should have been adopted under the unanimous voting procedures of either Article 100 or Article 235.[6] The challenge ultimately failed before the European Court of Justice.[7]

Unable to block the Directive's passage under Article 118a and having failed in its legal challenge, the United Kingdom was consequently bound to implement the Directive's provisions in United Kingdom law.

---

[1] Directive 93/104/E.C. concerning certain aspects of the organisation of working time.

[2] The common law approach to limitations on working time is discussed in Chap. 4.

[3] *e.g.* the reply given by the then Secretary of State for Employment, Michael Howard, to a Parliamentary question concerning British industry's attitude to the Directive; "British industry is virtually unanimous in its opposition to the proposals. I fully agree with the Confederation of British Industry that the directive would be a needless strain on our competitiveness, and a threat to jobs and earnings" (*Hansard* 1991–1992 Col. 563).

[4] The Treaty provisions were renumbered following the ratification of the Treaty of Amsterdam on May 1, 1999. The provisions of Art. 118a are now found in Art. 137.

[5] Now Art. 94.

[6] Now Art. 308. This is the residual power under which the E.C. may take action necessary to attain one of the objectives of the Community.

[7] *U.K. v. Council of the European Union* C–84/94 [1997] I.R.L.R. 30.

1–02   This chapter provides a brief history of the Directive and of the process by which it was implemented in the United Kingdom. However, the discussion is not just of historical interest. The issues discussed are also relevant in identifying the objectives behind the Directive, which will determine the manner in which the European Court of Justice and the United Kingdom courts construe its provisions and hence those of the Working Time Regulations.[8]

INITIAL PROPOSALS FOR THE REGULATION OF WORKING TIME

1–03   Article 117 of the seminal Treaty of Rome 1957 (commonly referred to as the E.C. Treaty) under which the European Economic Community was established stated that:

> "Member States agree upon the need to promote improved working conditions and an improved standard of living for workers, so as to make possible their harmonisation whilst the improvement is being maintained."[9]

Despite the express reference to the need to improve social and working conditions in the E.C. Treaty, it was not until 1975 that the Commission made its first venture into the Regulation of working time. This resulted in the adoption of a Council Recommendation[10] in which the Member States agreed on the principle of a 40-hour week and four weeks' annual paid holiday. However, the proposal was only adopted as a non-binding Recommendation and not as a Directive. Accordingly, whilst the Recommendation was a first tentative step in the Regulation of working time, it was little more than an aspirational statement.[11]

1–04   As unemployment rose sharply throughout Europe during the mid 1970s, many Member States came to the view that, in addition to the consequent improvements in working conditions, the introduction of new systems of working time, and in particular work sharing, could be the antidote to the economic problems they faced in the labour market.[12]

It was against this background that the Commission drew up a draft resolution on the adaptation of working time, which was subsequently approved by the Council of Ministers on December 18, 1979.[13] The preamble to this Resolution referred to the need for a systematic Regulation of working time because of demographic trends, structural problems of the labour market, including unemployment, and the progressive introduction of new technology which the Resolution predicted would exacerbate employment problems in the 1980s. However, the preamble also referred to the need for the measures taken to adapt working time to be conceived with a view to improving living and working conditions and contributing to improved protection at work. The Resolution focused in particular on the need to limit overtime and to introduce a principle of compensatory time off for employees working systematic

---

[8] See para. 2–23 for a summary of the purposive, or teleological, approach used by courts to interpret the provisions of a Directive.

[9] The revised E.C. Treaty incorporates ex-Art. 117 within the significantly broader Art. 136.

[10] 75/457/EEC.

[11] Working time was already the subject of several International Labour Organisation Conventions, including *C1 Hours of Work (Industry) Convention 1919, C14 Weekly Rest Convention 1921, C47 Forty-Hour Week Convention 1935* and *C52 Holidays with Pay Convention 1936, revised 1970.* In addition there are several ILO Conventions on night work, in particular *C171 Night Work Convention (1990).*

[12] Some Member States are still of this view. For example, in 1998 France introduced legislation imposing a maximum 35-hour working week.

[13] Council Resolution of December 18, 1979 on the adaptation of working time.

overtime. The Resolution also invited the Commission to consider how a Community approach for reducing annual working time could be formulated.

Economic growth continued to fall, and unemployment to rise, throughout the E.C. in the early 1980s. Worryingly, economic analysts believed that unemployment had acquired new structural aspects which could not be naturally absorbed by any future economic upturn. This reinforced the perceived need for an overall strategy to regulate working time to complement the economic measures necessary to encourage technological modernisation without jeopardising existing jobs.[14]

1–05 Accordingly, on September 23, 1983, the Commission submitted a new draft recommendation to the Council of Ministers on the "reduction and reorganis-ation of working time". This followed closely the aspirations of the 1979 Resolution in targeting systematic overtime as one of the underlying reasons behind the high levels of unemployment and as a variable which could be regulated, thus creating new jobs. However, the draft recommendation was vetoed by the United Kingdom at a meeting of the Labour and Social Affairs Council on June 7, 1984. The Conservative Government took the view that the draft recommendation, and indeed a number of other proposals on, for example, protection for atypical workers, was incompatible with its deregulatory philosophy.[15]

It thus became clear that a "twin track" Europe was developing, with the United Kingdom occupying the slow lane of social policy reform, at odds with a more socially orientated Commission and European Parliament.[16] The divergence between what the United Kingdom regarded as acceptable social policy and what the other Member States aspired to was graphically illustrated in December 1989 with the adoption by all Member States except the United Kingdom of the Community Charter of the Fundamental Social Rights of Workers, commonly referred to as the Social Charter. The Charter did not have legal status; it was merely a "solemn declaration" by the Member States to pursue the social policy objectives referred to in the Charter. In response to the European Council's invitation to the Commission to submit initiatives to implement the Charter's social objectives, the Commission proceeded to draw up a Social Action Programme.

1–06 In light of the failure to legislate on working time in 1984, it was not surprising that the Social Charter reiterated the Member States' commitment to the improvement of living and working conditions by way of further Regulations on the duration and organisation of working time.[17] The Charter also stated that all workers should have the right to a weekly rest period and to annual paid leave.[18]

In its Social Action Programme, the Commission stated that "the adaptation, flexibility and organisation of working time are crucial aspects as regard both working conditions and the dynamism of firms and play a not inconsiderable role in determining the situation of the labour market and the creation of employment". Whilst acknowledging the importance of flexibility of labour, which enabled firms to improve competitiveness, the Commission nevertheless stated that "care should be taken to ensure that these practices (*i.e.* basic conditions with regard to the flexibility

---

[14] A useful summary of the economic situation throughout the Community and the steps taken in individual Member States to reduce working hours is contained in Chap. 8 of the *White Paper on Growth, Competitiveness and Employment: The Challenge and Ways Forward into the 21st Century* COM (93) 700.

[15] Regulation governing the working time of drivers in the road transport industry were adopted in 1985, but these were adopted under ex-Art. 75, which relates to transport policy (Council Regulation 3820/85/EEC).

[16] See for example Shaw (1994) *Twin-Track Social Europe—the Inside Track* in O'Keefe and Twomey (eds).

[17] Social Charter, Art. 7.

[18] Social Charter, Art. 8.

of working time as laid down in Collective Agreements) do not have an adverse effect on the well-being and health of workers. For this reason, as regards the maximum duration of work, rest periods, holidays, night work, weekend work and systematic overtime, it is important that certain minimum requirements be laid down at Community level".

ADOPTION OF THE WORKING TIME DIRECTIVE

1–07   Accordingly, in August 1990, the Commission tabled new proposals for a Directive "concerning certain aspects of the organisation of working time".[19] On the face of it, the draft Directive did not differ in philosophy from the failed 1983 draft recommendation. The major difference was that, as a Directive, the measure would if adopted have legislative force.

As the European Economic Community (as it was then known) was a creation of the Treaty of Rome, it only had competence to act where the Treaty provided for it to do so. Therefore, when proposing the Directive the Commission had to determine which provision of the Treaty gave the Community jurisdiction to legislate to that effect. The relevant provision is referred to as the "legal basis" of the measure. The legal basis also determines which legislative process must be followed for the Directive to be validly adopted.

1–08   The proposed Directive was based on Article 118a,[20] which had been inserted into the E.C. Treaty by the Single European Act 1986. Article 118a(i) stated that:

> "Member States shall pay particular attention to encouraging improvements, especially in the working environment, as regards the health and safety of workers, and shall set as their objective the harmonisation of conditions in this area, while maintaining the improvements made."

More significantly, Article 118a(ii) provided that the Council of Ministers, acting by a qualified majority on a proposal from the Commission, could adopt minimum requirements for implementation by Member States by means of Directives. In other words, no single Member State's veto could block the adoption of a Directive proposed under Article 118a. Had the Directive been proposed as legislation concerning the rights and interests of employed persons on the basis of ex-Article 100a or under ex-Article 235, it could not have been adopted without the unanimous approval of all Member States.

1–09   In basing the Directive on Article 118a of the E.C. Treaty, the Commission was therefore proposing the Directive under the banner of health and safety legislation. This undoubtedly proved to be the most controversial aspect of the Directive, as the terms of the Directive strayed beyond the boundaries of what were conventionally regarded as health and safety concerns. Some regarded the use of Article 118a as a cynical attempt to circumvent the United Kingdom's opposition to the Directive.[21] Nonetheless, the validity of using Article 118a as the legal basis was subsequently confirmed by the European Court of Justice when it rejected the United Kingdom's request to have the Directive annulled.[22]

Perhaps in anticipation of this debate, the Explanatory Memorandum which

---

[19] COM (90) 317.
[20] Now Art. 137.
[21] See *e.g.* the social and economic motivations for the previous proposals for regulating working time.
[22] *U.K. v. Council of the European Union* C–84/94 [1997] I.R.L.R. 30.

accompanied the 1990 proposal went to great lengths to justify the health and safety rationale for the Directive. The proposal centred on four key areas:

(a) Minimum daily and weekly rest periods;

(b) Minimum annual paid holidays;

(c) Minimum conditions concerning shift and night work; and

(d) Protection of workers' health and safety in the event of changes in working patterns resulting from adjustments in working time.

1–10 Significantly, the 1990 proposal did not include provision for a maximum average working week of 48 hours. Nevertheless, the Commission was clearly adopting a very liberal view of "health and safety" for the purposes of Article 118a. The Explanatory Memorandum quoted from the World Health Organisation constitution which states that "health is a state of complete physical, mental and social well-being and does not consist only in the absence of disease or infirmity". In adopting this broad definition, the Commission was clearly embracing legal principles characteristic of Nordic law which recognises that the whole question of health and safety and the working environment is not confined to immediate hazards to the physical well-being of workers but extends to social and psychological factors such as the monotony of work, the lack of social contact between workers, or the pace of work.[23]

The Explanatory Memorandum went on to state that the measures proposed by the Commission in the Directive were designed to supplement the provisions already adopted in the existing health and safety Directives, notably the 1989 Framework Directive which deals with the safety and health of workers at the workplace.[24] The Explanatory Memorandum quoted from this Directive, stressing that "the incidence of accidents at work and occupational diseases is still too high and 'preventive measures must be introduced or improved without delay to safeguard the safety and health of workers and ensure a higher degree of protection'". Furthermore, and perhaps most significantly of all, the Explanatory Memorandum proceeded to quote extensively from surveys carried out since the Second World War into the effects on workers of working time. The Commission recognised that the disassociation of individual working time and plant operating hours was becoming an increasingly necessary feature of modern business. In other words, there was a trend towards longer and more varied opening hours, particularly amongst businesses in the services sector, with a commensurate increase in the flexibility of employees' working time arrangements. Empirical evidence suggested, however, that there was clearly a link between work fatigue and the duration of working hours. The physical and mental effort needed in work exceeding eight hours was found to become increasingly strenuous as fatigue set in. These problems were exacerbated where the job in question involved heavy or complicated tasks. Longer hours of work were therefore found to result in increased mistakes and a greater probability of accidents. Empirical evidence also suggested that more serious accidents and increased stress occurred towards the final hours of the working day as a result of fatigue. These problems were obviously heightened where the working day was longer than average. The Explanatory Memorandum also referred to studies carried out in France in the 1970s and 1980s

---

[23] This is explained by the fact that the text of the proposal emanated from Denmark.

[24] Directive 89/391/EEC on the introduction of measures to encourage improvements in the safety and health of workers at work. The European Parliament subsequently described the Commission's proposal as "a logical follow-up" to Directive 89/391/E.C.

which confirmed a positive correlation between working weeks of more than six days and the development of work-related medical problems such as stress, disturbed sleep and fatigue.

1–11 It was in the area of shift and night work, however, that the Commission highlighted the strongest empirical link between working patterns and a worker's health. Quoting from a number of surveys, the Explanatory Memorandum highlighted evidence that shift and night workers displayed a higher incidence of health problems, such as cardio-circulatory complaints, gastro-intestinal illnesses, appetite disturbances, sleeping problems, greater recourse to medicines, alcohol and tobacco and, during night shifts in particular, an increased risk of serious work accidents, especially around 3 a.m. to 4 a.m. when a "performance drop" could be identified. To compensate for this "performance drop", a worker was required to exert far greater physical and mental effort to achieve the same activity level. In many cases, evidence showed that the adverse health effects only became apparent after a number of years and that night shift workers often took stimulants during the night or sleeping pills during the day in order to cope with the reversed organic functioning which night work required. As a result of these problems, the surveys identified a high turnover of employees performing night work. Not only did this increase costs to the employer but an increased risk of accidents was apparent because of the comparatively large number of workers who had to be initiated into the given job before they were competent to perform the role safely. Further surveys were quoted which highlighted the negative social and cultural influences of night work, whilst the death rate and invalidity rate of night workers appeared to be higher than that of normal day workers.

1–12 The Commission used this evidence as the mandate for proposing rules concerning minimum rest periods to protect workers against long hours which were detrimental to health and safety and special protections for workers who worked during the night. The Commission's hand was strengthened by the fact that the Regulation of working hours proposed was not without precedent. Indeed, in nearly all the Member States apart from the United Kingdom, there were pre-existing legislative limits on working time and on minimum rest periods. The Explanatory Memorandum pointed out that it was health and safety considerations which had prompted Member States to lay down these minimum standards unilaterally. The Commission also pointed to existing legislative provisions regarding night work. In Belgium and the Netherlands, for example, night work was in principle prohibited for both male and female employees, subject to specified exemptions. In Germany, Greece, France, Italy and Portugal, night work was prohibited for female workers.[25] The Commission was quick to draw on such existing laws to add legitimacy to its claim that the Regulation of working time was a health and safety issue appropriate for treatment under Article 118a.

Many of the provisions of this proposal eventually formed part of the Working Time Directive[26] which was subsequently adopted in 1993. However, in stark contrast to the Directive, the proposal did not contain any provision regarding maximum weekly working hours. The reason for this omission probably rested in the precise wording of Article 118a, which referred to the adoption of "minimum requirements". Thus when challenging the adoption of the Directive under Article 118a, the United

---

[25] However, the European Court of Justice ruled in 1991 that the ILO's *C89 Night Work (Women) Convention (Revised) 1948*, which prohibited women from working at night, infringed the Equal Treatment Directive (Directive 76/207/EEC) (*France v. Stoeckel* C–345/89 [1993] C.M.L.R. 673). For a discussion of this and other issues surrounding night work, see Kilpatrick (1996) I.L.J. 25(3), 169.

[26] Directive 93/104/E.C. concerning certain aspects of the organisation of working time.

Kingdom argued that Article 118a, by definition, could only be used to impose *minimum* periods of rest and not to legislate on maximum hours of work. However, this was clearly just a matter of semantics and the argument was emphatically rejected by the European Court of Justice.[27]

1–13 The omission of any Regulation of weekly working hours sparked controversy and condemnation by the European Parliament. The text which it returned to the Commission in February 1991 contained a range of amendments, including new limits on the working week. The Commission, whilst amenable to a number of the Parliament's proposals, was not prepared to consider limitations on weekly working hours. An amended proposal was finally submitted by the Commission to the Council of Ministers on April 23, 1991.[28]

It was a further 2½ years before the Council finally adopted the Working Time Directive. The submission of the proposal was followed by a protracted period of horse-trading designed not least to secure the United Kingdom's acceptance of the Directive. The turbulent passage of the Directive in the Council did more to influence the final form of the Directive than any of the prior legislative stages. In particular, the Council resurrected the European Parliament's proposal to limit average weekly working time to 48 hours.[29] However, the Council conceded to demands for a derogation from the restriction on weekly working hours enabling workers to sign an "opt-out" agreement whereby they agreed to work hours in excess of the limit.[30] This derogation is to be re-examined before the expiry of a seven year period from the date of adoption of the Directive. In implementing the derogation, Member States are still required to respect the general principles of the protection of health and safety of workers.

1–14 In summary, in addition to the 48-hour limit on the average weekly working week, the Directive obliges Member States to take the measures necessary to ensure that every worker is entitled[31]:

(a) To a minimum daily rest period of 11 consecutive hours per 24-hour period[32];

(b) To a rest break where the working day exceeds six hours[33];

(c) To a minimum uninterrupted rest period of 24 hours in each seven day period[34]; and

(d) To four weeks' paid annual leave.[35]

Arguably one of the most significant amendments made to the draft Directive by the Council was the introduction of Article 13. This Article, which expressly adopts the principle of "humanisation" of work, is something more than a mere restatement of

---

[27] *U.K. v. Council of the European Union* C–84/94 [1997] I.R.L.R. 30, 48.
[28] COM (91) 130.
[29] Art. 6.
[30] Art. 18(1)(b)(i). See Chap. 6.
[31] The Commission subsequently stated in its submissions in the *U.K. v. Council of the European Union* case that these measures "guarantee workers effective protection against regular or frequent overtime detrimental to their health".
[32] Art. 3.
[33] Art. 4.
[34] Art. 5.
[35] Art. 7.

the original draft Article 11 which required employers to "take all measures necessary" to ensure that changes to working patterns took account of health and safety requirements. The new Article 13 went much farther, and espoused the Nordic principles of "adapting work to the worker but with a view, in particular, to alleviating monotonous work and work at a predetermined work rate ...". The significance of this new wording is discussed in Chapter 7.

1–15 The Council however bowed to pressure from the United Kingdom to limit the application of the Directive. Accordingly, specific categories of activity (air, rail, road, sea, inland waterway and lake transport, sea fishing, work at sea and the activities of doctors in training) were excluded from the scope of the Directive.[36] In addition, provisions were added permitting derogation by collective agreement[37] and permitting Member States to derogate from the provisions of the Directive in specific circumstances, such as in respect of workers whose working time is "not measured and/or predetermined or can be determined by the workers themselves".[38]

Finally, the United Kingdom secured a further grace period in respect of the implementation of the Article 7 provision for four weeks' paid annual leave. It negotiated a three year transitional period for the introduction of four weeks' holiday, during which time Member States would only be required to provide three weeks' paid annual leave.[39]

It was this emasculated draft Directive which was adopted as the common position by the Council of Ministers on June 30, 1993. The United Kingdom chose to abstain from the vote, which was otherwise carried unanimously. As the United Kingdom delegation hailed the newly forged Directive as a triumph, the Directive returned to the European Parliament for its second reading. In addition to proposing a further 19 amendments, most of which were aimed at clarifying the text of the Directive, the Parliament was concerned that the Directive could be used by Member States as a springboard for actually reducing the protection of workers in those Member States. In other words, there was a fear that Member States could equalise existing working time legislation downwards to bring it into line with the minimum requirements set out in the Directive. In the end, the mandatory non-regression clause proposed by the Parliament was rejected by the Commission,[40] as were 10 of the other proposed amendments.

The Directive returned to the Council of Ministers where it was finally adopted on November 23, 1993.[41] Once again, the United Kingdom abstained.

1–16 Reactions to the new Directive were mixed. The Commissioner for Social Affairs, Padraig Flynn, hailed the Directive as "a milestone on the road towards a creation of a European Social Policy", although he acknowledged that the Commission was not happy with some of the changes made in the course of the Directive's genesis. Nevertheless, he welcomed the fact that the Directive had been substantially strengthened by the introduction of the maximum 48-hour week which would benefit a significant number of workers. The French Employment Minister, however, was more conservative in his praise, describing the common position as "extremely minimalist". The Secretary General of the European Trade Union Confederation claimed that the Directive represented no more than a tiny step towards restoring the balance between economic and social components of the European Community and

---

[36] Art. 1(3). See Chap. 12 and the discussion of proposals to extend the Directive to some of these activities.
[37] Art. 17(3). See Chap. 13.
[38] Art. 17(1). See Chap. 12.
[39] Art. 18(1)(b)(ii).
[40] Art. 18(3) cannot be construed as prohibiting regression.
[41] Council Directive 93/104/E.C. concerning certain aspects of the organisation of working time. See Von Prondzynski (1994) I.L.J. 23(1) 92.

expressed dismay at the stubborn opposition shown by the United Kingdom to social progress and the improvement of working and living conditions for European employees. The Socialist Chairman of the Parliament's Social Affairs Committee, Wim Van Velzen, lambasted the United Kingdom, claiming that the United Kingdom should realise that "successful economies treat workers better". Nevertheless, from the United Kingdom trade union perspective, the General Secretary of the TUC, Norman Willis, did acknowledge that the Directive represented progress for British workers.

The Council subsequently also adopted Council Directive 94/33/E.C. on the protection of young people at work (on June 22, 1994), which was also adopted under Article 118a.[42] This Directive, *inter alia*, makes special provision for young persons in respect of working time, night work and rest and leave entitlements.

THE UNITED KINGDOM'S LEGAL CHALLENGE TO THE WORKING TIME DIRECTIVE

1–17 The apparent euphoria of the United Kingdom Government in blunting the Directive's edge was short-lived. No sooner had the Directive been adopted than David Hunt, the new Secretary of State for Employment, announced that he would be seeking the Directive's annulment before the European Court of Justice. The challenge was subsequently launched in March 1994.

The United Kingdom's primary argument was that the link between the areas governed by the Directive and health and safety was too tenuous for the Directive to be properly based on Article 118a. It contended that there was no scientific material justifying the link between safety and health on the one hand, and several aspects of working time dealt with in the Directive, such as average weekly working time, paid annual leave and rest periods, on the other.[43] Rather, the United Kingdom argued that in reality the purpose of the Directive was twofold: first, to continue the series of Community initiatives concerned with the organisation of working time in the interests of job creation and reducing unemployment and second, to improve the living and working conditions of employees. Therefore, it was argued that the Directive should have been based on either ex-Article 100 or ex-Article 235 of the E.C. Treaty, both of which would have required the unanimous approval of all Member States for the adoption of the Directive.

1–18 The Court gave its ruling on November 12, 1996, in which it firmly rejected these arguments.[44] The United Kingdom had been similarly unsuccessful before the Advocate General. The United Kingdom's sole success, which provided scant consolation for the otherwise resounding defeat, was that the Court agreed that the second sentence of Article 5, which provided that the weekly rest period should in principle include Sunday, should be annulled, as the Council had failed to explain why Sunday, as a weekly rest day, was more closely connected with the health and safety of workers than any other day of the week.[45]

It is unnecessary now to consider the detailed reasons for which the Advocate

---

[42] See Bond (1995) I.L.J. 24(4), 377 for a discussion of the terms of the Directive. The U.K. again raised arguments as to the choice of Art. 118a as a legal basis but did not pursue these in the form of legal proceedings.

[43] The preamble to the Directive contains only one reference to scientific evidence, in the tenth recital, and that relates only to night work and to breaks between periods of work.

[44] *U.K. v. Council of the European Union* C–84/94 [1997] I.R.L.R. 30.

[45] See para. 37 of the judgment.

General and the Court rejected the United Kingdom's submissions. However, as the Directive was upheld as being a health and safety measure, it is instructive to examine the broad interpretation given to that concept by the Court and, in particular, by the Advocate General.[46]

As set out above, Article 118a refers to improvements as regards the health and safety of workers, "especially in the working environment". The Advocate General stated that the interpretation of Article 118a must be guided by the Danish concept of regulating the working environment which:

"... is not limited to classic measures relating to safety and health at work in the strict sense, but also includes measures concerning working hours, psychological factors, the way work is performed, training in hygiene and safety, and the protection of young workers and worker representation with regard to security against dismissal or any other attempt to undermine their working conditions. The concept of 'working environment' is not immutable, but reflects the social and technical evolution of society."

1–19 The Advocate General concluded that, in keeping with the Danish view, the 'working environment' within the meaning of Article 118a must be construed in broad terms as including any factor affecting the worker in his work, and in particular any measure which promotes the health and safety of workers, in the sense discussed below. Thus he concluded that, "[U]ltimately, the only limits on the definition of the concept of 'working environment' which I have proposed are to be found in the term 'workers', which it underlies".

Having regard to this conception of working environment, the Advocate General considered that "health and safety" should also be given a broad interpretation. He thus adopted the World Health Organisation's concept of health and safety, which the Commission had quoted in the Explanatory Memorandum to its 1990 proposal, namely that:

"health is a state of complete physical, mental and social well-being and does not consist only in the absence of illness or infirmity".[47]

1–20 Hence the Advocate General concluded that the measures adopted were "undeniably applicable" to the "working environment" within the meaning of Article 118a and that:

"... it cannot be denied that the provision of rest periods and the limitation of the weekly working time in fact contribute to the 'health' and 'safety' of workers within the broad meaning of Article 118a. Without such guarantees, workers were exposed to the risk of frequently being required to work excessively long hours beyond their physical and psychological capabilities, thereby jeopardising their health and safety."

The Court similarly favoured a broad interpretation of these concepts, and also quoted the definition of health and safety from the preamble to the Constitution of the WHO. Having regard to the scope of Article 118a, therefore, the Court held that

---

[46] Both the U.K. and the Council acknowledged that the wording of Art. 118a itself represented a "compromise between divergent positions" and that "eliciting its scope and purpose is far from easy". This gave the Court scope to arrive at its broad interpretation.

[47] As the Advocate General pointed out, all the Member States belong to the WHO.

the measures laid down in the Working Time Directive reflected concern for the protection of the health and safety of workers. The Court considered that the evolution of social legislation at both national and international level confirmed the link between measures relating to working time and the health and safety of workers. Referring to the dispute between the United Kingdom and the various intervening Member States as to the validity of the scientific research demonstrating the link between working time and health and safety, the Court stated that legislative action in the Community sphere could not be limited exclusively to circumstances where such action was scientifically justified.

As discussed in Chapter 2, the breadth of the scope of health and safety and of the working environment will have a substantial influence on the manner in which the provisions of the Directive are interpreted, as the Court will have regard to the purpose of the Directive in construing its provisions.[48]

IMPLEMENTATION OF THE DIRECTIVE: THE WORKING TIME REGULATIONS 1998

1–21   The Conservative Government did not accept its defeat graciously. In a statement read out to both the House of Commons and the House of Lords following the failure of the legal challenge, the Government stated that:

> "The Directive was adopted by the Council at a meeting on 23rd November 1993 and was forced on the United Kingdom through the use of the qualified majority voting procedure by being adopted by the European Council under Article 118a of the Treaty ... This is not what was envisaged when we agreed to Article 118a as a health and safety provision. We shall therefore insist that the intergovernmental conference (IGC) addresses the issues which this ECJ judgment raises.[49] That means both ensuring that the Working Time Directive no longer affects the United Kingdom and securing measures to prevent any other social engineering directives being forced on the United Kingdom by similar manoeuvres. The use of Article 118a in this fashion wholly undermines the spirit of our opt-out from the social chapter agreed at Maastricht ... We reject the imposition on industry of unnecessary requirements which can only damage competitiveness and jobs and we consider that this directive would be the thin end of a wedge that would lead to more such burdens."[50]

Despite this sabre-rattling, it was apparent that the United Kingdom was obliged, however grudgingly, to transpose the Working Time Directive into national law by November 23, 1996 at the very latest. Given the proximity of this date, and the fact that the Government had manifestly not made contingency plans for the implementation of the Directive should its challenge fail, it is not surprising that it was unable

---

[48] Indeed, there was much discussion at the time that given its broad scope, Art. 118a could be used as the legal basis for other social provisions: see Dunkley and Whittle, (1997) *Business Law Review* 201. However, this debate was rendered otiose for the time being when the new Labour Government voluntarily "opted in" to the Social Charter, a process formalised by the ratification of the Treaty of Amsterdam on May 1, 1999.

[49] The Prime Minister John Major went so far as to say in the House of Commons that "I shall not accept what has been determined by the court today and, at the end of the IGC, I shall demand that change or there will be no end to the IGC". However, the IGC would be, as Tony Blair put it "conveniently, after the [general] election" (*Hansard*, November 12, 1996, Cols 151–152).

[50] *Hansard*, November 12, 1996, Cols 155–170.

(or unwilling) to take steps to ensure that implementing measures were brought into force before the deadline.

1–22　The Government did issue a consultation paper regarding the implementation of the Directive but, with a General Election looming in 1997, it did not vigorously pursue progress. With the election of a Labour Government on May 1, 1997 the climate changed. Although the implementation of the Working Time Directive was evidently not the Government's top priority, on April 8, 1998 it eventually produced a consultation document and a set of draft Regulations aimed at implementing both the Working Time Directive and the Young Persons' Directive in the United Kingdom. The consultation period ended on June 5, 1998 and the Working Time Regulations 1998[51] finally came into force on October 1, 1998. The equivalent Regulations for Northern Ireland did not come into force until November 23, 1998.[52] The legal consequences of this delay are discussed in Chapter 2.

The United Kingdom therefore finally had a degree of central Regulation of working time. However, the precise nature of this Regulation was in some instances unclear. Given that in many instances the Regulations simply repeat verbatim the rather ambiguous text of the Directive, the DTI also published non-binding Regulatory Guidance in an attempt to clarify the practical issues which could arise under the Regulations. However, this has still left many areas of uncertainty which are highlighted throughout this book.

The Working Time Regulations 1999

1–23　As discussed earlier in this chapter, the idea of Regulation of working time was initially perceived to be unpopular with United Kingdom industry. In order to address some of their concerns over the impact of the 1998 Regulations, in July 1999 the Government published a consultation paper setting out its proposals to reduce the "red-tape" surrounding the provisions allowing workers to opt-out of the limit on their average weekly working time,[53] and to clarify the position of "unmeasured" working time.[54] These proposals eventually crystallised into the Working Time Regulations 1999,[55] which came into force on December 16, 1999. They were followed by a revised version of the Regulatory Guidance.

It seems unlikely that this long legislative evolution of the Regulations is now at an end. As discussed in Chapter 12, there are various proposals at E.U. level to extend the scope of the Working Time Directive,[56] which will need to be incorporated into the Regulations, and throughout the book there are highlighted areas in which the Regulations may not properly implement the terms of the Directive. Should these provisions be challenged in the courts and be found to be incompatible with the Directive or to be incomplete, the United Kingdom will have to take further steps to secure compliance with its obligations under the E.C. Treaty.

---

[51] S.I. 1998 No. 1833. See Barnard (1999) I.L.J. 28(1), 61.
[52] The U.K. was not alone in its tardiness in implementing the Directive. The Commission has successfully brought infringement proceedings under Art. 226 of the E.C. Treaty against both Italy and France for failure fully to transpose the provisions of the Directive into national law within the prescribed period: *Commission v. Italy* C–386/98 (unreported) and *Commission v. France* C–46/99 (unreported).
[53] See Chap. 6.
[54] See Chap. 12.
[55] S.I. 1999 No. 3372. See Barnard (2000) I.L.J. 29(2) 167.
[56] Indeed, the Directive has already been extended to cover some of the sectors initially excluded from its scope (see Chap. 12 and the Foreword).

CHAPTER TWO

The Legal Position Regarding the Working Time Directive prior to the Regulations

INTRODUCTION

2–01 The process behind the adoption of the Working Time Directive and the subsequent United Kingdom challenge which eventually resulted in the promulgation of the Working Time Regulations 1998 is discussed in Chapter 1. As discussed in that chapter, the delay in transposing the Directive into United Kingdom law that followed the European Court of Justice's rejection of the legal challenge meant that for almost two years the United Kingdom was in breach of its obligation to secure for workers the protection required by the Directive.

Whilst this obviously had legal implications for the United Kingdom Government at a European level, in that it was vulnerable to infringement proceedings by the Commission under what is now Article 226 of the E.C. Treaty, there were also implications for the workers who were deprived of the protection they would have been afforded had the United Kingdom complied with its obligation and implemented provisions of the Directive in United Kingdom law.

This chapter therefore deals with the legal status of the Directive in United Kingdom law pending the coming into force of the Regulations. The principles discussed remain of relevance as it is arguable that in several respects the United Kingdom has still yet to properly implement the terms of the Directive.

THE NATURE OF A DIRECTIVE

2–02 Article 249 of the E.C. Treaty provides that:

> "A Directive shall be binding, as to the result to be achieved, upon each Member State to which it is addressed, but shall leave to the national authorities the choice of form and methods."

This is in contrast with Regulations made by the European Commission which have general application and are binding and directly applicable in all Member States without further action and Decisions which are binding entirely but only upon those to whom they are addressed.

Thus whilst it is open, in limited circumstances, for the Government of a Member State to seek to implement Regulations and Decisions by virtue of national legislation, it is not usual. By contrast, Directives always require the governments in the Member

States to take action to implement, unless the scope of the Directive is already satisfied by existing national legislation.

2–03　Directives are therefore what they say; they direct a particular result, but not the specific way in which that is to be achieved. The Member States therefore have flexibility in relation to the method by which Directives are implemented. Whilst in some cases existing legislation may be sufficient, the governments of Member States usually either need to introduce new legislation or amend existing legislation to accommodate the requirements of a Directive.

The implementation of a Directive is of vital importance for a number of reasons. Firstly, the failure of a Member State to properly implement a Directive can be just as serious as a Member State's failure to implement the Directive at all. The United Kingdom Government is more than used to this concept. A challenge was of course made in relation to the United Kingdom Government's implementation of E.C. Collective Redundancies Directive 75/129[1] when the existing provisions of the Trade Union and Labour Relations (Consolidation) Act 1992 were deemed unsatisfactory insofar as the provisions only provided for collective consultation in circumstances where there was a recognised Trade Union representing the affected employees.

Secondly, the European Court of Justice is often called upon to consider preliminary references from national courts concerning the interpretation of particular Directives.[2]

2–04　Thirdly, as will be discussed later in this chapter, there is the difficulty of whether the specific requirements of a Directive can be relied upon in national courts by individuals ("direct effect") or, alternatively, to what extent there is a duty upon the national court to interpret national legislation in such a way as to avoid possible conflict with the provisions of a Directive (the "purposive approach").

Fourthly, there is the issue of whether the government of a Member State could be liable to an individual for its failure to implement (or properly implement) the provisions of a Directive.[3] The issues arising from each of these approaches are discussed below.

Finally, Directives must be implemented within the prescribed period set out therein. It is for the Member States to choose a manner and form of implementation which ensures that the Directive can function effectively, particularly in the light of the Directive's purposes and aims. It is clear that the national governments are required to ensure that implementation achieves both clarity and legal certainty and therefore that the provisions of the Directive have been transposed into national provisions having effective and binding force. It is not sufficient for a Member State, for example, to rely upon the fact that, in certain circumstances, the provision of a Directive may be directly relied upon before a national court.

The majority of the provisions within the Working Time Directive came into effect on November 23, 1996. The Directive specifically provides that implementation should take place either through collective agreement or agreement between the two sides of industry or by national legislation by that date. The United Kingdom Government, during the negotiation process, had succeeded in negotiating a derogation by which the provisions for the maximum working week may not have full effect until 1999. This derogation however could not take effect until the Regulations were introduced.

---

[1] As amended by E.C. Directive 92/56 (now consolidated in Directive 98/59/E.C.).

[2] This has most notably been seen in relation to disputes arising from the implementation of the E.C. Acquired Rights Directive 77/187 by the Transfer of Undertakings (Protection of Employment) Regulations 1981 and issues arising from the E.C. Equal Treatment Directive 76/207 (which in the U.K. had been pre-empted by the equal pay and sex discrimination legislation).

[3] The so-called *Francovich* principle.

THE LEGAL EFFECT OF A DIRECTIVE

2–05 A number of issues were touched upon above regarding the importance of implementation and the consequences of the Government's failure to implement or indeed implement properly.

(a) Direct effect

(i) The conditions to be satisfied

2–06 Directives may contain directly effective provisions which can be relied upon by individuals. This was confirmed by the European Court of Justice in its judgment in *Van Duyn v. Home Office*.[4] Simply because a Directive gives a choice to Member States as to the way in which a given result is to be achieved did not necessarily mean that the provisions of a Directive would not be capable of enforcement.

There are however conditions which must be satisfied in order for the provisions of a Directive (or any other type of E.C. law) to be capable of enforcement by a national court. According to the European Court of Justice in *Francovich v. Italian Republic*[5] three matters must be considered:

- The determination of the beneficiaries of the guarantees provided;

- The content of the guarantee; and

- The identity of the institution liable for the guarantee.

2–07 Having said that, the obligations for clarity and precision should not exclude the possibility of direct effect where provisions are complex (*Costa v. ENEL*)[6] but if the provision leaves the Member State with a discretion as to application then such provision cannot have direct effect.

Further, the wording of the provision must make the obligation contained therein unconditional and unqualified. It is for this reason that where provisions are inapplicable for a certain period, the provision is conditional and there can be no direct effect. If a provision provides for the adoption of implementing measures by either one of the European institutions or by the Member State this is a condition which will be satisfied when the implementing measures are adopted. Only at that time can the relevant provision acquire direct effect. Having said that, the mere fact that a provision contains an obligation to adopt implementing measures does not necessarily mean that the obligation is dependent upon such measures for direct effect. It is only if the Member State has a discretion on implementation that the provision cannot have direct effect. Perhaps the best summary regarding the direct effect of a Directive is found in the ECJ's decision in *Marshall v. Southampton & South West Hampshire Area Health Authority (Teaching)*[7] as follows:

> "Wherever the provisions of a Directive appear, as far as their subject matter is concerned, to be unconditional and sufficiently precise, those provisions may be relied upon by an individual against the State where that State fails to implement the Directive in national law by the end of the period prescribed or where it fails to implement the Directive directly."

---

[4] C–41/74 [1974] E.C.R. 1337 at 1348.
[5] *Francovich I* (case C–6, 9/90 [1992] I.R.L.R. 84).
[6] C–6/64 [1964] E.C.R. 585 at 597–598.
[7] C–152/84 [1986] E.C.R. 723 at 748, [1986] I.R.L.R. 140.

2–08 Applying these principles to the specific provisions contained within the Working Time Directive, it had been suggested that the language of the Directive may be sufficiently precise and unconditional in parts. For example:

> Article 7—annual leave
> (1) Member States shall [take] the measures necessary to ensure that every worker is entitled to paid annual leave of at least four weeks in accordance with the conditions for entitlement to and granting of such leave laid down by national legislation and/or practice
> (2) The minimum period of paid annual leave may not be replaced by an allowance in lieu, except where the employment relationship is terminated.

Contrast this provision with the language of Article 4 regarding breaks:

> Member States shall take the measures necessary to ensure that where the working day is longer than six hours, every worker is entitled to a rest break, the details of which including duration and the terms on which it is granted, shall be laid down in collective agreements or agreements between the two sides of industry, or, failing that, by national legislation.

2–09 Gradually as employees began to realise the significance of the Directive, cases began to be brought as to whether or not the Directive was capable of having, for example, direct effect. In *Gibson v. East Riding of Yorkshire Council*[8] the Employment Appeal Tribunal (EAT) had to consider whether an employee employed by a local authority as a swimming instructor would be entitled to paid holidays. Mrs Gibson had been employed from April 1996 under the terms of a contract providing for hourly pay and no entitlement to paid holiday leave. Shortly before October 1, 1998, she brought two complaints before an employment tribunal. First, she asked the tribunal to make a determination under section 11 of the Employment Rights Act 1996 to the effect that she was contractually entitled to paid holidays. Her second claim was pursuant to Part II of the Employment Rights Act, namely her allegation that her employers had been making unlawful deductions from her wages by not paying holiday pay. For the claims to be successful Mrs Gibson had to establish that the provision for annual leave, Article 7, was capable of having direct effect against her employers. The employment tribunal had accepted that East Riding of Yorkshire Council was an emanation of the State but did not find that the Directive had direct effect. In the employment tribunal's view the Directive was not sufficiently clear and was conditional, the reason being the array of exceptions and derogations.

When Mrs Gibson appealed the EAT found that the fact that the Directive permits precise derogations does not of itself render the Directive conditional. However, the EAT acknowledged that the Directive allowed a degree of discretion and a good deal of flexibility, indeed the Member States had the ability to utilise collective bargaining as an alternative to the normal legislative process and extensive derogations could be applied. In particular the EAT noted that the definition of "working time" in Article 2(1) was not drafted with the precision that might be expected of a Directive that was capable of conferring rights on certain categories of workers.

2–10 Having said all that the EAT did not believe that the fact that some provisions of the Directive lacked certainty prevented others which were unambiguous from having direct effect. However the EAT noted that the matter could not be confined to consideration of Article 7. In this case in the EAT's view the fact that the

---

[8] [1999] I.R.L.R. 358 (EAT).

Directive provided for derogations might support the argument that its provisions were capable of direct effect. The EAT concluded that the structure of the Directive was consistent with it having direct effect as it was intended to confer minimum rights on workers in a way that could be described as unconditional.

Turning to Article 7, the EAT found that the provision was clear and precise and could not give rise to ambiguity or conditionality. It found that where there were doubts as to the start and end of a holiday year, custom and practice would usually fill the gaps. There were no derogations. The EAT therefore concluded that Article 7 had direct effect so that during the period between November 23, 1996 and October 1, 1998 a person employed by an emanation of the State could take advantage of the protection. Accordingly in this case Mrs Gibson's contractual rights had been varied by the Directive in the sense that had the Directive been implemented on time, she would have been entitled to be paid leave as at the date when she brought her tribunal claim. Further Mrs Gibson was entitled to the full four weeks' paid annual leave. Even though when the Regulations were introduced the United Kingdom Government opted for the three week period for the first year, it was not open to the State or to an emanation of the State to rely on that option if it had not been exercised. Accordingly, the EAT concluded therefore that Mrs Gibson had a right to four weeks' leave and it would continue to be a right to four weeks' leave until such time as her contract was varied.

2–11 By contrast, picking up the comments made by the EAT in *Gibson*, in the case of *Cawley v. Hammersmith Hospitals NHS Trust*[9] the EAT expressed concern as to whether Articles 3 and 8 (concerning daily rest periods and length of night work respectively) would be capable of having direct effect. The reason for that was because the provisions are contingent on the definition of "working time" set out in Article 2(1) of the Directive. In the EAT's view that definition was "patently ambiguous". The EAT at this time had the benefit of knowledge that the definition was the subject of a Spanish reference to the ECJ in the case of *Sindicato de Medicos de Asistencia Publica (SIMAP) v. Conselleria de Sanidad y Consumo de la Generalidad Valenciana.*[10]

To complicate matters yet further the *Gibson* case was appealed to the Court of Appeal and heard on June 21, 2000.[11] Mummery L.J. giving the leading judgment, confirmed that the analysis by Morison J. in the EAT had been an accurate and valuable exposition. Mummery L.J. recognised that the EAT had itself concluded that there had been much to be said in favour of the conclusion reached by the original employment tribunal to the effect that the provisions of Article 7 were not sufficient to provide for direct effect. However, in the Court of Appeal's judgment the EAT's ultimate conclusion that Article 7 had direct effect had been wrong. Mummery L.J. indicated that the provisions in Article 7 were not sufficiently precise to have direct effect. He considered three basic areas. First, he concluded that in the wider context of the Directive its purpose was to lay down minimum safety and health requirements of the organisation of working time, incorporating what Mummery L.J. described as an 'imprecisely framed' definition of 'working time'.

2–12 Further, the derogations included within the Directive, together with the option for three weeks' leave during the transitional period, had to be taken into account. On the second ground Mummery L.J. agreed with the submission of leading counsel on behalf of the Council that Article 7 left unanswered key questions affecting individual entitlement to annual leave. Whilst it was precise in the sense of the length of the minimum period, that did not mean that the national court could enforce it

---

[9] [EAT 20.1.99 (475/98)].
[10] C–303/98.
[11] [2000] All E.R.(D) 846, [2000] I.R.L.R. 598 (CA).

without more information. The fact that the concept of "working time" was not precisely defined was a substantial hurdle. Mummery L.J. did not agree that it would be appropriate for the national court to "fill the gaps" by reference to the views and experience of the lay members on the custom and practice of the workplace in this country. Indeed Mummery L.J. indicated that the "very existence" of gaps in Article 7, even if viewed in the "wider context" set out above, was a strong indication that the terms of the Article are insufficiently precise to have direct effect in the courts and tribunals of member states. He said:

> "The right which Mrs Gibson wishes to assert against the Council is quite simply not sufficiently defined in Article 7 to be directly enforceable by an individual in national courts and tribunals."

2–13 On the third issue however Mummery L.J. confirmed the EAT's earlier opinion that even if Mrs Gibson was entitled to rely on Article 7's direct effect then her claim would be for four weeks' annual paid leave as the Council was not entitled to rely on the United Kingdom's option initially to provide only for three weeks' paid annual leave as that option had not been exercised by the United Kingdom at the appropriate point.

In the light of this case (and bearing in mind what has already been said in relation to *SIMAP*) one would suspect that case law will not develop in this area in the short-term.

(ii) The benefit of direct effect

2–14 Having found that a Directive can have direct effect the issue is then one of scope, *i.e.* who is entitled to take the benefit of that direct effect and more particularly whether an individual is entitled to rely upon the provisions of the Directive against another individual (so-called "horizontal" direct effect). Once again *Marshall* set the ball rolling. The ECJ found[12]

> "With regard to the argument that a Directive may not be relied upon against an individual, it must be emphasised that according to [Article 189 of the EEC Treaty[13]] the binding nature of a Directive, which constitutes the basis for the possibility of relying on the Directive before a national court, exists only in relation to 'each Member State to which it is addressed'. It follows that a Directive may not of itself impose obligations on an individual and that a provision of a Directive may not be relied upon as such as against such a person."

2–15 In other words it appeared that the Court was willing to allow individuals to rely upon Directives to prevent Member States obtaining any benefit which they could otherwise derive from their failure to implement. Having said that the decision in *Marshall* was strictly *obiter dicta* (as the employer in that case was a public authority). The ECJ took an extremely cautious approach in Case C–91/92 *Faccini Dori*[14]:

> "The effect of extending [direct effect] to the sphere of relations between individuals would be to recognise a power in the Community to enact obligations for individuals with immediate effect, as it has competence to do so only where it is empowered to adopt Regulations."

---

[12] E.C.R. p. 749, I.R.L.R. para. 45.
[13] Now Art. 249 E.C. Treaty.
[14] [1994] E.C.R. I–3325 at p. 3356.

Some may say this is an arbitrary distinction. Given that Directives are often used in the fields where it is the E.U.'s aim ultimately to alter the conduct of individuals as well as Member States (*e.g.* labour law and social policy) the possibility of an injustice is obvious. The employee within the so-called "public sector", like Ms Marshall, may rely strictly upon the provisions of the Equal Treatment Directive whereas a colleague working in a "contracted out" post alongside her could not. Not surprisingly ways around this arbitrary distinction have been sought. These are discussed below.

(iii) An "emanation of the State"

2–16 Since *Marshall* it has been clear that the State includes the State as an employer as well as the State as a public authority. Clearly from the point of view of the Working Time Directive then it is the State's role as employer which is of relevance. Since the case of *Foster v. British Gas Plc*[15] there has been some guidance as to what may be an emanation of the State. *Foster* concerned six female former employees of British Gas (pre-privatisation) who had been dismissed in 1985 and 1986 when they attained British Gas' compulsory retirement age of 60 for women. The complaint was one of unlawful discrimination on the grounds of sex as male employees were not required to retire until 65. Whilst at the time the case was heard the issue had been resolved by the provisions of the Sex Discrimination Act 1986, it was common ground that those amendments could not be relied upon by the six employees. Their contention therefore was one that they could rely upon the terms of Article 5 of the Equal Treatment Directive. The original complaint to the industrial tribunal was dismissed on the grounds that British Gas was not an "organ of the State". Similarly, appeals to the Employment Appeal Tribunal and Court of Appeal were dismissed. The Court of Appeal took the view that under E.U. law the Directive gave rise to legal rights for employees of the State itself and of any organ or emanation of the State, an emanation of the State being understood to include an independent public authority "charged by the State with the performance of any of the classic duties of the State". As a matter of English law, the Court of Appeal found that a nationalised industry did not fall within this category as its powers were not within the province of government.

2–17 Perhaps not surprisingly when the case reached the House of Lords, their Lordships were unwilling to make a finding and referred the matter to the ECJ for a preliminary ruling on the following question:

> "Was the BGC [British Gas Corporation] (at the material time) a body of such a type that the Appellants are entitled in English courts and tribunals to rely directly upon Council Directive 76/207 of February 9, 1976 on the implementation of the principle of equal treatment for men and women as regards access to employment, vocational training and promotion and working conditions so as to be entitled to a claim for damages on the ground that the retirement policy of the BGC was contrary to the Directive?"

The United Kingdom Government argued that it was an issue for the national courts to decide (and not the ECJ) whether BGC was a part of the State in the context of the United Kingdom legal system. The ECJ disagreed and indicated that it did have jurisdiction in proceedings for a preliminary ruling to determine the categories of

---

[15] C–188/89 [1990] I.R.L.R. 353.

person who could rely upon the provisions of a Directive. The national courts' role was, on the other hand, to decide whether a party to proceedings actually falls within one of the categories so defined.

2–18 The Court went on to note its decision in *Marshall* and that subsequently on the basis of *Marshall* that the Court had held in a series of cases that unconditional and sufficiently precise provisions of a Directive could be relied upon against organisations or bodies which were subject to the authority or control of the State or had special powers beyond those which result from the normal rules or relations between individuals. Accordingly the Court had previously held that the provisions of a Directive could be relied upon against:

- Tax authorities[16];

- Local or regional authorities[17];

- Constitutionally independent authorities responsible for the maintenance of public order and safety[18]; and

- Public authorities providing public health services[19].

The Court went on to say[20]:

"It follows from the foregoing that a body, whatever its legal form, which has been made responsible, pursuant to a measure adopted by the State, for providing a public service under the control of the State and has for that purpose special powers beyond those which result from the normal rules applicable in relations between individuals is included in any event among the bodies against which the provisions of a Directive capable of having direct effect may be relied upon."

2–19 Accordingly therefore the non-privatised British Gas was "an emanation of the State".

Further, the category cannot be closed. Consider what then happened with post-privatisation utilities. This dilemma was resolved in the case of *Griffin v. South West Water Services Limited*.[21] Taking the three conditions in *Foster*:

- Provision of a public service pursuant to a measure adopted by the State;

- Service under the control of the State;

- Special powers.

and applying those to the facts in *Griffin*, it was common ground that the "public service condition" and the "special powers condition" were fulfilled. What was an issue of debate was "control".

2–20 South West Water Services Limited was a wholly owned subsidiary of South West Water Plc, the successor to the South West Water Authority which was privatised in 1989. The five plaintiffs in *Griffin* were employees of South West Water

---

[16] C–8–81 *Becker v. Finanzamt Münster-Innenstadt* [1982] E.C.R. 53.
[17] C–103–88 *Fratelli Costanzo v. Comune di Milano* [1989] E.C.R. 1839 and see also *Gibson* above.
[18] C–222–84 *Johnston v. Chief Constable of the Royal Ulster Constabulary* [1986] I.R.L.R. 263.
[19] *Marshall* above.
[20] At para. 20.
[21] [1985] I.R.L.R. 15.

Services Limited and also members of UNISON. In October 1993 South West Water Services had decided it would not afford recognition to UNISON (following the merger of NUPE, NALGO and COHSE) but instead introduced a staff council with elected representatives of staff employees together with a staff consultative committee. A large scale redundancy exercise was later undertaken and the plaintiffs contended that the provisions of E.C. Collective Redundancies Directive 75/129 (as revised by Directive 92/56) were directly enforceable against South West Water Services and, therefore, South West Water Services could be required to consult with UNISON over proposed redundancies notwithstanding that it did not recognise UNISON. South West Water Services denied that it was a body against which the Directive could be enforced. Alternatively it argued that the provisions of the Directive were not sufficiently precise and unconditional so as to be capable of direct effect.

2–21   In the High Court, Blackburn J. granted a declaration that South West Water Services was an emanation of the State against which the plaintiffs could rely upon the provision of E.C. Directives where those provisions were sufficiently precise and unconditional but found that in this case the provisions of the Directive were not so sufficiently precise and unconditional. Given that there was only one area of dispute in relation to whether South West Water Services was an emanation of the State (*i.e.* the issue of control), Blackburn J. considered that it was necessary to appreciate several points:

- The question was not whether the *body* in question is under the control of the State but whether the *public service* is under control of the State;

- The legal form of the body is irrelevant;

- The fact that the body is a commercial concern is also relevant;

- The fact that the body does not carry out any of the traditional functions of the State and is not an agent of the State is irrelevant; and

- The fact that the State does not possess day-to-day control over the activities of the body is also irrelevant.

2–22   Having analysed the nature of the service required to be provided by South West Water Services Limited and its relationship with its regulatory "watchdog", OFWAT, Blackburn J. had no difficulty in finding that South West Water Services Limited was an emanation of the State.

It is now more or less common ground that government departments, local authorities, health authorities, further education corporations, police authorities and NHS Trusts are likely to be emanations of the State. Following *Griffin* many public utilities are also likely to be emanations of the State.

(b) The purposive approach

2–23   The uncomfortable dichotomy created by the concept of horizontal direct effect may be overcome when the concept of the purposive approach is considered. That is the ECJ's promotion of the principle of construction which requires national courts, in conformity with their duty under Article 10 of the E.C. Treaty to give full effect to E.U. law, to interpret all national law in the light of relevant E.C. law, regardless of whether it has direct effect or not. This "indirect effect" was first discussed in *Von Colson v. Land Nordrhein Westfalen*.[22]

---

[22] C–14–83 [1984] E.C.R. 1891.

Von Colson concerned circumstances in which the ECJ was unable to hold that a particular provision of the Equal Treatment Directive was sufficiently precise and unconditional to support the plaintiff's case. Nevertheless the ECJ found that[23]:

> "The Member State's obligation arising from a Directive to achieve the result envisaged by the Directive and their duty under [Article 5 of the Treaty[24]] to take all appropriate measures, whether general or particular, to ensure the fulfilment of that obligation, is binding on all the authorities of Member States including, for matters within their jurisdiction, the courts. It follows that, in applying the national law specifically introduced in order to implement Directive 76/207, national courts are required to interpret their national law in the light of the wording and purpose of the Directive in order to achieve the result referred to in the third paragraph of [Article 189]."[25]

2–24   However this decision led to two uncertainties. First, did it only cover legislation specifically introduced to implement an E.U. obligation or did it extend to all national law? In Case 222/84 *Johnston v. Chief Constable of the Royal Ulster Constabulary* the ECJ suggested the latter. The second issue was how far national courts were required to go in order to ensure conformity between national and E.U. law. Would that for example include reading words into a statute or reconstructing the intention of the legislature? In Case C–106/89 *Marleasing SA v. La Comercial Internacional de Alimentación*[26] the ECJ said[27] that:

> "In applying national law, whether the provisions in question were adopted before or after the Directive, the national court called upon to interpret it is required to do so, as far as possible, in the light of the wording and the purpose of the Directive in order to achieve the result pursued by the latter and thereby comply with the third paragraph of [Article 189 of the Treaty]."

2–25   However, since *Marleasing*, European cases appear to suggest that there is a limit to this approach and that would appear to be that this interpretation can only be used if statutory language is not wholly distorted. Perhaps the best-known example of this approach in the United Kingdom is the House of Lords decision in *Litster v. Forth Dry Dock and Engineering Co Limited*[28] regarding the application of the E.C. Acquired Rights Directive 77/187 and the wording of the implementing legislation, the Transfer of Undertakings (Protection of Employment) Regulations 1981 (TUPE), and in particular the rule in Regulation 5(3) of TUPE that a person has to be employed in an undertaking or part of one transferred "immediately before" the transfer. The case arose because of the widespread practice of certain employers of dismissing staff en masse prior to a transfer, thus removing employees from the protection of TUPE only then to be selectively re-hired often on lower rates of pay after the transfer itself. On the face of it, the wording of TUPE allowed this but clearly it was contrary to the spirit and purpose of the Directive.[29] Accordingly therefore the House of Lords read

---

[23] p. 1909.
[24] Now Art. 10 E.C. Treaty.
[25] Now Art. 249 E.C. Treaty.
[26] [1990] E.C.R. I–4135.
[27] p. 4159.
[28] [1989] I.R.L.R. 161.
[29] See *P Bork International v. Foreningen A F Arbejdsledere I Danmark* [1990] 3 C.M.L.R. 701.

words into Regulation 5 so that it became a condition that an employee was employed in the undertaking immediately before the transfer *or would have been so employed had he not been unfairly dismissed contrary to Regulation 8* (*i.e.* unjustifiably discussed for a reason related to the transfer).

As indicated above the main advantage of this approach is that it avoids the public/private sector dichotomy inherent with direct effect. However again it is limited. For example TUPE originally contained an express exclusion of non-commercial ventures which later transpired to be in breach of the Acquired Rights Directive.[30] However in that situation the difference between TUPE and the Acquired Rights Directive could not be resolved by the purposive approach as it would have involved distortion of the language of TUPE. Amending legislation was therefore required.

2–26 The difficulty in respect of the Working Time Directive is that there is little existing legislation in this field.[31] Whilst there is general health and safety legislation which may be open to a purposive interpretation one suspects it will be the Regulations which come under the closest scrutiny.

(c) State responsibility for Defective or non Implementation

(i) Francovich I

2–27 *Francovich I* established the principle that an individual injured by a failure by a Member State to implement a Directive might have a claim for damages against that Member State. The ECJ in that case set out the principle rather succinctly (some may say rather too briefly). In that case the Directive concerned was Directive 80/987 on the protection of employees in the event of insolvency of their employer. The ECJ had, in February 1987, in *Commission v. Italy*[32] found that the Italian Government had failed to bring into force laws, Regulations or administrative provisions necessary to comply with the Directive by the date for implementation, October 23, 1983. When Mr Francovich (and others) sought to rely upon the terms of the Directive to obtain the payments guaranteed under the Directive the national court referred, *inter alia*, the following to the ECJ for a preliminary ruling:

> "Under Community law in force, can an individual who has suffered as a result of the failure by the State to implement Directive 80/987, which failure has been established by a judgment of the Court of Justice, require that State to comply with those provisions contained in it which are sufficiently precise and unconditional by relying directly on the Community rules against the Member State in order to obtain the guarantees which that Member State was to ensure and, in any event, is he entitled to claim damages suffered in respect of provisions which do not have that status?"

2–28 Under the principle of direct effect described earlier, the ECJ found that the provisions of the Directive relating to the identity of the institution liable for the guarantee were not sufficiently precise and unconditional to allow individuals to rely on them before a national court. In particular the failure to implement the Directive meant that the State had not chosen what form the guarantee would take and how it would be funded. The alternative remedy was therefore a right to damages for non-implementation. The Court based its judgment on two possible alternative bases.

---

[30] See *Dr Sophie Redmond Stiching v. Bartol* [1992] I.R.L.R. 366.
[31] See Chap. 1.
[32] Case number 22/87.

First it sought to derive a right to damages from the nature of E.C. law and its superiority, indicating:[33]

> "It should be stated that the full effectiveness of Community provisions would be affected and the protection of the rights they recognise undermined if individuals were not able to recover damages when their rights were infringed by a breach of Community law attributable to a Member State.
>
> The possibility of obtaining damages from the State is particularly essential where, as in the present case, the full effect of Community provisions is conditional on the State taking certain action and, in consequence, in the absence of such action being taken, individuals cannot rely on the rights accorded to them by Community law before the national courts.
>
> It follows that the principle of the liability of the State for damage to individuals caused by a breach of Community law for which it is responsible is inherent in the scheme of the Treaty."

2–29   The alternative basis is Article 10 of the E.C. Treaty[34]:

> "The obligation on Member States to make good the damage is also based on [Article 5 of the Treaty][35] under which the Member States are bound to take all appropriate measures, whether general or particular, to ensure fulfilment of the obligations arising under Community law. This includes the obligation to make good the unlawful consequences of a breach of Community law."

Accordingly[36]:

> "It follows from the foregoing that Community law lays down a principle according to which a Member State is obliged to make good the damage to individuals caused by a breach of Community law for which it is responsible."

2–30   The Court also did not go into any detail on the subject of the conditions for *Francovich* liability. In essence, the right to damages is based on a test similar to but not identical to, the test applied in order to determine whether a provision has direct effect. There are three conditions:

- The result required by the Directive includes the conferring of rights for the benefit of individuals;

- The content of those rights may be determined by reference to the provisions of the Directive; and

- The existence of a causal link between a breach of the obligation of the State and the damage suffered by the persons affected.

2–31   The Court then went on to say that[37]:

> "Accordingly, in the absence of Community rules on this subject, it is for the domestic legal system of each Member State to designate the courts having

---

[33] At paras 33–35.
[34] Para. 36.
[35] Now Art. 10 E.C. Treaty.
[36] Para. 37.
[37] Para. 42.

jurisdiction and to determine the procedural conditions governing actions at law intended to ensure the protection of rights which parties enjoyed under Community law."

And[38]:

"It must also be stressed that any conditions as to both substance and form for the recovery of damages laid down by the various national laws applicable thereto may not be less favourable than those relating to similar claims under national law and they may not be so framed as to render the recovery of damages excessively difficult or virtually impossible in practice."

The concept therefore of *Francovich* liability would apparently present a number of advantages. It avoids the need to adjudicate the provisions of the Directive before the national courts by virtue of direct effect or construing apparently irreconcilable provisions of E.C. and national law in a strained manner in order to effect indirect effect or pursue a purposive approach. Instead it appears to focus on the Member State's obligation to implement and seeks to penalise where that obligation has not been fulfilled.

(ii) Factortame/du Pêcheur

2–32 Given the brevity of the *Francovich* guidance, welcome clarification came in *Brasserie du Pêcheur SA v. Federal Republic of Germany* and *R. v. Secretary of State for Transport ex p. Factortame Limited.*[39] The ECJ began by clarifying the scope of the *Francovich* principle and de-limiting any relationship with direct effect. It made it clear that this form of reparation was not only applicable in cases where there was no direct effect but that it could equally be used as a complementary remedy. The Court also went on to reconsider the three conditions for liability given in *Francovich I* and concluded that the three conditions for liability should be reformulated as follows:

- The rule of law infringed must be intended to confer rights on individuals;
- The breach must be sufficiently serious; and
- There must be a direct causal link between the breach of the obligation resting on the State and the damage sustained by the injured party.

2–33 Whether the breach is sufficiently serious is a matter for the national court but the decisive test is whether the Member State manifestly and gravely disregarded the limits on its discretion. The factors which the national court could take into consideration include:

- The clarity and precision of the rule breached;
- The measure of discretion left by that rule to the Member State;
- Whether the infringement and the damage caused was intentional or not;
- Whether any error of law was excusable or not;
- Whether the position taken by a Community institution may have contributed towards the omission;

---

[38] Para. 43.
[39] [1996] I.R.L.R. 267.

- The adoption or retention of national measures or practices contrary to Community law.

2–34   The Court however then went on to indicate that, on any view, a breach will clearly be sufficient if it has persisted despite a judgment establishing an infringement or a preliminary ruling on settled case law of the ECJ on the matter from which it is clear that the conduct in question constitutes an infringement. Having said that, a prior finding in this respect is not essential for the conditions to be satisfied.

These factors may make the employee's position in the case of *defective* transposition rather more difficult than might otherwise have been thought.

(iii) Dillenkofer

2–35   With the Working Time Directive, where the United Kingdom Government (both the outgoing Conservative Government and the incoming Labour Government) failed to take any measures to transpose the requirements of the Directive into United Kingdom law within the period of implementation, arises an interesting issue. In the case of *Dillenkofer v. Federal Republic of Germany*[40] the Court confirmed that failure by Member States to take such measures in itself constitutes a serious breach of E.C. law for the purposes of *Francovich*. In other words a failure to implement at all (before the expiry of the period for implementation) means of itself that a Member State manifestly and gravely disregards the limits on its discretion. In this case the Court rejected any argument that the failure to transpose may be because the Member State claims the implementation period is too short or would cause economic difficulties or, even, that transposition required the collaboration of third parties. The Court said that it is "settled case law" that a Member State may not rely upon provisions, practices or situations prevailing in its own internal legal system to justify its failure to observe the obligations and time limits laid down by a Directive.

In other words therefore there would appear to be ample scope for claims being brought by employees in respect of the period of non implementation between November 23, 1996 and October 1, 1998 in Great Britain.[41] Any arguments sought to be raised that introduction before the due implementation date was practically impossible as a result of the United Kingdom's legal challenge, the change of United Kingdom Government or, indeed, the necessary consultation process would, it is likely, obtain little sympathy.

(iv) ex p. Burns

2–36   The first reported *Francovich* claim in relation to the Directive is the case of *R. v. Attorney General for Northern Ireland, ex p. Burns*.[42] Miss Burns was employed by AVX Limited in Coleraine, Northern Ireland, as a production operative. In 1992 she was asked to change to a rotating shift system which would involve her working a night shift between 9 p.m. and 7 a.m. one week in every three. From September 1995, she worked on cycles of 15 shifts each of eight hours' duration. During five of these at least three hours of her working time fell between 11 p.m. and 6 a.m. Over a period of time Miss Burns unsuccessfully applied for day shift posts and she began to complain to her doctor of difficulties with night shift working. Ultimately in February 1997 she wrote to her employer stating that she wished to terminate her employment on medical advice. She later purported to withdraw her resignation if she could be

---

[40] C–178/94 [1997] I.R.L.R. 60.
[41] Until November 23, 1998 in Northern Ireland.
[42] [1999] I.R.L.R. 315.

considered for day work but the employers were not able to provide day work. Miss Burns brought a complaint by way of judicial review seeking

- A declaration that the United Kingdom was in breach of its obligations under the Directive;

- A declaration that she should be deemed a "worker" within the terms of the Directive;

- A declaration that she should be deemed a "night worker" within the terms of the Directive;

- A declaration that the United Kingdom's breach of European law in failing to transpose the Directive into domestic law was sufficiently serious to give rise to liability for any damage she suffered; and

- A declaration that she was entitled to exemplary damages.

2–37   Miss Burns claimed that because the United Kingdom Government had failed to implement the Directive then she had been deprived of the opportunity to be transferred onto day work and that had resulted in her losing her job. The Government argued that she was not a night worker within the meaning of the Directive and that even had they implemented the Directive that would not have conferred any effective right on her.

The Northern Ireland High Court found that the definition of "night worker" in Article 2(4) of the Directive did apply to Miss Burns and that she would have been deemed a night worker had the Directive been transposed into domestic law during the time that she was employed. The Court confirmed that where a Member State did not transpose the Directive within the prescribed period that gave rise to an automatic and serious breach of Community law and made the Government therefore liable for an injury suffered by an individual who suffered loss and damage in consequence. This was a straightforward application therefore of the decision in *Dillenkofer*. Accordingly the failure of the Government to transpose the Working Time Directive was an actionable breach of Community law.

2–38   However, on the facts of this particular case the Court did not consider that Miss Burns had established that she had suffered loss as a consequence of the failure of the Government to transpose the Working Time Directive. They considered that they did not have sufficient evidence before them to establish that she would have been able to require her employer to transfer her to day work and thus allow her to maintain her employment. Accordingly therefore the Court made the declarations sought, save that it refused to make the declaration that she was entitled to exemplary damages. However the Court did add that on production of the necessary evidence to establish that she would have been reassigned to day work had the Directive been transposed into domestic law that Miss Burns may well have been entitled to recover compensation for the loss of her employment.

So it would appear that there is ample scope for the application of the *Francovich* principle, at least in relation to those parts of the Directive which are clearer in their terms.

THE NATIONAL COURT'S ROLE

2–39   Whilst the high profile challenges to United Kingdom law based on the purposive approach/indirect effect or the direct effect of the provisions of European law have often reached the European Court of Justice, it is settled that it is by no means necessary for that to be the case. This is demonstrated by the challenges in *Cawley* and *Gibson* and *ex p. Burns* referred to above. English courts have jurisdiction to deal with those issues, whether or not they seek guidance from the ECJ by way of a preliminary ruling. The difficulty is the role which the domestic employment tribunal (formerly industrial tribunal) has to play. A useful authority to consider is the case of *Secretary of State for Employment v. Mann*.[43] The applicants in that case were union members who were summarily dismissed by reason of redundancy when their employer became insolvent. The trade union made an application for a protective award pursuant to section 189 of the Trade Union and Labour Relations (Consolidation) Act 1992 given the employer's failure to comply with the consultation requirements. They also sought payments from the Secretary of State for Employment in accordance with what was then section 122 of the Employment Protection (Consolidation) Act 1978.[44]

When making payment the Secretary of State had deducted wages paid in lieu of notice and payment for work done during the protected period in accordance with the then provisions of section 190(3) of the TULR(C)A 1992. The Secretary of State also applied a limitation period of eight weeks to the duration of the award and applied the statutory ceiling on a week's pay provided for in what was then section 122(3) and (5) of the EP(C)A.

The applicants complained that the deductions and limitations were contrary to E.U. law and, alternatively, that the Secretary of State was liable in damages to the applicants for failure to transpose into United Kingdom law Council Directive 80/987 which provided for protection for employees in the event of an employer's insolvency. In other words they made a *Francovich* claim.

2–40   The tribunal found that it was incompatible with E.U. law for the Secretary of State to make the set off and to apply statutory limitations to the award and held, as a preliminary issue, that it did have jurisdiction to determine the *Francovich* claim. For the purposes of this chapter the other findings are not relevant but the EAT found that its jurisdiction and that of the tribunal was defined solely by statute and therefore no jurisdiction had been conferred on a tribunal to hear and determine damages claims against the State for default in performing an obligation under E.U. law to transpose provisions of E.U. law into United Kingdom domestic law. Further, the EAT found that an effective remedy for such claims was already available in the High Court and the county court and that, as there was an effective remedy available, the United Kingdom was permitted to specify the courts and procedures whereby that claim could be enforced. Accordingly therefore the tribunal had no jurisdiction to entertain the applicants' claims for damages. In his judgment, Mummery J. found as follows:

> "(1) Industrial tribunals were established by Regulations made by the Secretary of State "to exercise the jurisdiction conferred on them by or under" the Employment Protection (Consolidation) Act 1978 or "any other Act, whether passed before or after this Act:" Section 128(1)).[45] The jurisdiction of industrial tribunals is therefore defined by statute. An industrial tribunal has no inherent, general or residual jurisdiction. There is no United Kingdom statute or Regulations made under primary legislation which confers on the industrial tribunal jurisdiction to hear and determine damages claims against a non-employer state for default in the performance of an obligation under

---

[43] [1996] I.C.R. 197 EAT.
[44] Now s.184 of the Employment Rights Act 1996.
[45] Now see s.2 of the Employment Tribunals Act 1996 (formerly Industrial Tribunals Act 1996).

Community law to transpose provisions of Community law, *e.g.* a Directive into United Kingdom domestic law.

(2) There is no provision of Community law which confers jurisdiction to determine Community law claims on industrial tribunals or requires such claims to be determined by an industrial tribunal. Community law only requires that such claims are capable of being entertained before an appropriate court of a Member State. The general principle of Community law is that provided that an effective remedy is granted, Member States are permitted to specify the courts and procedures whereby Community law claims are to be enforced.

(3) An effective remedy for damages under *Francovich* is available in the High Court which is well-equipped to deal with complex questions of State liability, causation and quantum liable to arise in these claims. The county court also has jurisdiction in civil proceedings against the Crown and could entertain a claim within the statutory limits; sections 13 and 15 of the Crown Proceedings Act 1947 and R.S.C Order 77 Rule 13.[46] There is provision in section 20(1) of the Act of 1947 to remove such proceedings to the High Court from the county court. There is no similar provision for removing proceedings from the industrial tribunal to the county court or to the High Court."

2–41 However, Mummery J. went to some lengths to clarify that his ruling only related to claims being brought within the *Francovich* principle and not to other ways in which employees could seek to take the benefit of Community law through the national courts. Indeed he indicated as follows[47]:

"In order to avoid any misunderstanding we should add that nothing we have said casts any doubt on the jurisdiction of an industrial tribunal to hear claims within the limits of its statutory jurisdiction in the course of which arguments are based on Community law relevant to the construction and the validity of the provisions of domestic law. Thus, there is no doubt that the industrial tribunal has jurisdiction in the present case to hear and determine the questions arising and the construction of the provisions of the Employment Protection (Consolidation) Act 1978 and the Trade Union and Labour Relations (Consolidation) Act 1992, in the light of the provisions of the Insolvency and Collective Redundancies Directives and also on the invalidity of domestic law provisions should they fail to accord with the directly effective provisions in the Directives."

In other words, where the provisions of a Directive are directly effective or, alternatively reference is being made to a Directive in order to construe United Kingdom law justiciable in the industrial tribunal (the purposive approach/indirect effect) then the tribunal is perfectly entitled to hear the arguments and make a finding. Of course claims based upon other directly effective provisions of Community law (*e.g.* Article 141 of the E.C. Treaty) have been pursued in the employment tribunals now for many years.[48]

2–42 Finally on this point Mummery J. indicated[49]:

---

[46] Now superseded by the revised Civil Procedure Rules.
[47] p. 205.
[48] See *Pickstone v. Freemans plc* [1987] I.C.R. 867.
[49] p. 207.

"An industrial tribunal has no jurisdiction to determine a claim against the State or an officer of the State for failure to perform a public legal duty. That is usually a matter for the High Court in judicial review proceedings. The same applies to a claim under Community law. The effectiveness of such a claim is not impaired by allocation of the power to determine such claims to the High Court. As already mentioned, the Attorney General is the proper respondent. Liability under the *Francovich* doctrine is that of the State, not of any particular department of the State."

EARLY DEVELOPMENTS

2–43 Shortly after the failure of the United Kingdom's legal challenge and the United Kingdom's failure to implement legislation in advance of the November 23, 1996 deadline there was much press speculation about the possibility of private sector claims being brought by the larger unions, in particular UNISON. Indeed the *Financial Times* on November 23, 1996 quoted Roger Lyons, General Secretary of the MSF Technicians Union, as saying that his union would "use the law to enforce those rights" granted by the Working Time Directive. Mr Lyons further indicated that his union had alerted its health and safety representatives to the possible grievances of individual members employed within the public sector wanting to take the benefit of the Directive's provisions. UNISON perhaps took a more dramatic approach by lodging a petition with the President of the European Parliament requesting the Parliament to refer its complaint to the Commission to take infraction proceedings against the United Kingdom Government.

It is true to say that the European Commission was not impressed. Whilst the United Kingdom was not singled out for action in relation to the Working Time Directive, the Commission did contemplate sending a reasoned opinion to France, Greece, Italy, Luxembourg, Portugal and the United Kingdom with regard to the late transposition, in other words the first step of infraction proceedings under Article 226 of the E.C. Treaty.[50] Such proceedings reached a conclusion in respect of Italy's failure to fulfil its obligations[51] but proceedings in connection with the United Kingdom were not pursued after the United Kingdom Government's response appeared to be satisfactory. Whether this will be reconsidered in due course remains to be seen at the time of writing.

2–44 Latterly however the change of Government appears to have softened the approaches of the various unions. Indeed by January 1998, the Legal Department & Policy and Research Unit of UNISON was confirming that UNISON were not supporting any claims by public sector employees against the Government for non-implementation. Having said that of course there have been some claims by public sector employees[52] and two cases in Northern Ireland. The case *R v. Attorney General for Northern Ireland ex p. Burns* has already been discussed. Another case *R. v. Attorney General for Northern Ireland ex p. McHugh* resulted in a settlement. However, further evidence of the use of the principles of direct effect or the purposive approach is extremely thin on the ground.

---

[50] Previously Art. 169 Treaty of Rome.
[51] Case C–386/98 *Commission of the European Communities v. Italian Republic*, March 9, 2000.
[52] *Cawley, Gibson.*

CHAPTER THREE

The Concept of "Working Time"

INTRODUCTION

3–01 The concept of "working time" is central to the operation of both the Working Time Directive and the Working Time Regulations. In particular, the following aspects of the Regulations are based upon it:

(a) The weekly working time limit[1];

(b) The definitions of "night work" and "night worker",[2] and consequently the protections afforded to night workers;

(c) The limit on the working time of night workers whose work involves special hazards or heavy physical or mental strain[3]; and

(d) The entitlement to receive rest breaks and minimum daily and weekly periods of rest.[4]

It is also relevant to the record keeping obligations under Regulation 9, for example in respect of the weekly working time limit.

3–02 One would think that a clear and unambiguous definition of "working time" was therefore imperative. Unfortunately, however, the definitions used in both the Directive and the Regulations leave many areas of ambiguity which tribunals and the courts will have to resolve in order to determine the precise scope of the entitlements and limitations listed above. The rapid growth in "atypical" working[5] presents particular problems in this regard; as working patterns become less standardised, it becomes increasingly difficult to deal adequately with each of them within one all-encompassing definition of "working time".

The lack of clarity of the definition found in Article 2(1) of the Directive has already prompted a reference from a Spanish labour court to the European Court of Justice seeking the Court's guidance as to the proper interpretation of that definition.[6] This chapter discusses the definitions of "working time" contained in the Directive and the Regulations and highlights the residual areas of uncertainty, together with the potential impact the resolution of that uncertainty could have on employment practices in the United Kingdom.

---

[1] Regulation 4. See Chap. 6.
[2] Regulation 2(1). See Chap. 9.
[3] Regulation 6(7). See Chap. 9.
[4] Regulation 2(1), 10 & 11. See Chap. 7.
[5] See Chap. 5.
[6] *SIMAP v. Conselleria de Sanidad y Consumo de La Generalidad Valenciana* C–303/98. This chapter should be read in the light of the postscript to the foreword to this book, which details the European Court of Justice's decision in this case.

DEFINITION OF "WORKING TIME"

3–03   Article 2(1) of the Directive provides that "working time" means:

"any period during which the worker is working, at the employer's disposal and carrying out his activity or duties, in accordance with national laws and/or practice".

It then goes on to define a rest period as meaning: "*any period which is not working time*".[7]

In *SIMAP*[8] Advocate General Saggio stated that Article 2(1) "did not read clearly". This sentiment was echoed in *Gibson v. East Riding of Yorkshire Council*[9] by both Mummery and Pill L.JJ., who referred to the Article 2(1) definition as being "imprecise". The principal question is whether, in order for time to constitute working time under the Directive, it must be time during which the worker satisfies *all* or *only one* of the following conditions:

(a) He is working;

(b) He is at his employer's disposal; and/or

(c) He is carrying out his activities and duties.

In other words, the crucial question is whether Article 2(1) should be construed conjunctively or disjunctively. Although, given the use of the word "and", the former is the natural reading, the EAT considered in *Cawley v. Hammersmith Hospitals NHS Trust*[10] that the wording of Article 2(1) is "patently ambiguous as to whether the requirements are conjunctive or disjunctive". This question is one of those referred to the European Court of Justice in the *SIMAP* litigation,[11] which is discussed later in this chapter.

3–04   In addition, each of the three criteria used in Article 2(1) are themselves imprecise. It is not immediately obvious, for example, what the difference is between "working" and "carrying out his activity or duties".[12] It is unclear whether the latter criterion refers to all the worker's contractual duties or only to those central to the activity which he is employed to perform. Nor is the phrase "at the employer's disposal" easy to construe with any degree of certainty. However, it is to be noted that there is no requirement that the worker be paid for the period in question, and nor is there any express requirement that the worker be contractually required to work during that period.[13] Therefore, a worker's "working time" may or may not coincide with the time for which he receives pay, or with the time which he may be required to work under his contract.

Despite the lack of clarity in Article 2(1), the United Kingdom Government chose

---

[7] Identical definitions appear in Art. 3 of the Young Persons Directive (Directive 94/33/E.C.).

[8] C–303/98. This and the other comments on the Advocate General's opinion in this chapter are based on an unofficial translation of the French transcript.

[9] CA, [2000] I.R.L.R. 598. They therefore concluded that Art. 7 of the Directive, concerning annual leave, was insufficiently precise to have direct effect. See Chap. 2.

[10] EAT/475/98, unreported.

[11] *SIMAP v. Conselleria de Sanidad y Consumo de La Generalidad Valenciana* C–303/98.

[12] Although see the view of Advocate General Saggio expressed in *SIMAP* discussed below at para. 3–12.

[13] As to this latter point, see the discussion of Regulation 20 below and in Chap. 12.

directly to transpose that wording to form the core part of the definition of "working time" in the Regulations. Regulation 2(1) provides that:

> " 'working time' in relation to a worker means:
>
> (a) Any period during which he is working, at his employer's disposal and carrying out his activity or duties;
> (b) Any period during which he is receiving relevant training; and
> (c) Any additional period which is to be treated as working time for the purpose of these Regulations under a relevant agreement and "work" shall be construed accordingly."

3–05 Whilst this obviously means that paragraph (a) of the definition is equally lacking in clarity,[14] it at least means that the Regulations cannot be said to be incompatible with the terms of the Directive in this respect. Given the ambiguity of Article 2(1), there would have been a substantial risk that, had the Government chosen to attempt to formulate a more precise definition of "working time", that definition would have excluded periods which the definition in the Directive is subsequently interpreted by the European Court of Justice to include. As it is, there should be little difficulty in tribunals and courts applying the evolving jurisprudence of the European Court of Justice on Article 2(1) in construing paragraph (a), save to the extent that this causes difficulties in interpreting other provisions of the Regulations.

In one respect, paragraph (a) increases the ambiguity already inherent in Article 2(1). As discussed above, the Directive contains no definition of "working". However, Regulation 2(1) rather circularly provides that any activity performed during working time is "work", despite the fact that the requirement that a worker be "working" itself forms only part of the definition of "working time". On the conjunctive approach, this would mean that a worker could be working without doing "work", and on the disjunctive approach he could be doing "work" without actually working.

3–06 It is clear from the DTI's original guidance to the Regulations that it considered paragraph (a) to be conjunctive, or cumulative,[15] so that a period would only constitute "working time" if the worker satisfied all three of the criteria therein during that period. The accuracy and practical significance of this is discussed below.

SIGNIFICANCE OF THE CONJUNCTIVE OR DISJUNCTIVE DEBATE

3–07 As stated above, the United Kingdom Government took the view in both the Consultation Paper which preceded the promulgation of the Working Time Regulations 1998[16] and the Regulatory Guidance which followed it that "[W]hether time is "working time" will depend upon all the elements of the definition being satisfied in a given situation".

The significance of using this conjunctive interpretation is best illustrated by using "on-call" hours as an example. There are a variety of ways in which workers may be on-call. They may be required simply to be contactable by the employer within a

---

[14] See the discussion of the differing approaches taken in respect of this definition in various industries in an interim report produced for the DTI by Fiona Neathey and James Arrowsmith entitled *Early Implementation of the Working Time Regulations* (October 1999), pp. 38–39, 47–48.

[15] The statement in *Cawley v. Hammersmith Hospitals NHS Trust* EAT/475/98, unreported to the contrary is clearly erroneous.

[16] URN: 98/645.

defined period of time and to be available to attend work at the employer's request or on the occurrence of a specific event. Alternatively, a worker on-call may be required to be in attendance at the employer's premises. Indeed, the worker could be required to sleep on the employer's premises in order that he be ready to carry out his duties if required.

3–08   If the worker was called upon to work during the on-call period, the hours spent carrying out his activity would clearly be working time. However, the status of the time during which the worker is available for work but not actually carrying out his activity is less clear.[17] It would appear that whilst on-call a worker is at his employer's disposal, in the sense that the employer may require him to work and he could not contractually refuse. The employer has the right to decide whether the worker should work and, if so, for how many hours. If one adopted the strict disjunctive construction of paragraph (a) of the definition in the Regulations, the satisfaction of that criterion alone would be sufficient to render on-call hours "working time" for the purposes of the Regulations. This time would therefore count for the purposes of determining whether the worker had exceeded the weekly working time limit over the applicable reference period. Assuming a consistent construction of working time throughout the Regulations, as a "rest period" is defined to mean time which is not working time, this interpretation of "working time" would mean that on-call hours could not count towards the daily or weekly rest periods to which workers are entitled under Regulations 10 and 11. Moreover, if the worker was, as a normal course, on-call for at least three hours during the period between 11 p.m. and 6 a.m., he would be a "night worker" within the meaning of Regulation 2(1). Consequently, Regulation 6 would apply and his average normal working hours could not exceed eight hours for each 24 hours.[18] In addition, the provisions of Regulation 7 relating to health assessments would bite. Employers would have to keep adequate records of all time spent on-call for the purpose of showing that these obligations had been complied with.[19]

3–09   However, during the on-call hours, it would seem to be stretching the natural meaning of the word to suggest that the worker was "working" unless the employer exercised the right to require the worker actually to perform the activity for which he is engaged.[20] For example, it is difficult to see how a worker who is asleep when on-call can be said to be "working". Equally, it is difficult to see how that worker is "carrying out his activity or duties", unless one adopted a broad interpretation of "duties" to include the duty to remain contactable. As explained above, it is irrelevant for these purposes that the worker is paid an hourly rate for the time spent on-call.[21]

Therefore, using the conjunctive interpretation initially favoured by the Government, time spent on-call would not be working time save to the extent that the worker was called upon to work during those hours. Thus, the original version of the Regulatory Guidance issued by the DTI stated that:

> "Time when a worker was 'on-call' but otherwise free to pursue their own activities would not be working time, as the worker would not be working. Similarly, if a worker is required to be at the place of work 'on-call' but was

---

[17] See for example the differing practices discussed by Neathey and Arrowsmith, *Early Implementation of the Working Time Regulations* (October 1999), p. 47.

[18] Regulation 6(1). See Chap. 9.

[19] Regulation 9.

[20] cf. the view of Advocate General Saggio on the meaning of "working" in the *SIMAP* case.

[21] The Guidance issued by the DTI in relation to the National Minimum Wage legislation states that workers should be paid for time "spent on standby or on-call at or near the place of work".

sleeping though able to work if necessary, a worker would not be working and so the time spent asleep would not count as working time."

3–10   This in itself disclosed uncertainty. On both the strict conjunctive and the strict disjunctive constructions there is no distinction to be drawn between hours spent on-call at the employer's place of work and time spent at home. However, the guidance implied that there was a distinction to be drawn if the worker was on-call at his employer's place of work but was not asleep. This would in effect be the equivalent of a "zero-hours contract". On a strict reading of paragraph (a) of the definition in Regulation 2(1), applying the conjunctive approach, the question of whether or not the worker was asleep would be irrelevant—time spent at his place of work but not working would not constitute "working time". It would not therefore count towards the weekly working time limit, and could constitute a rest period. Nor would it raise the problems for employers in respect of night work discussed above.

However, when one considers the purpose behind the Directive, the results produced by the conjunctive approach appear inappropriate.[22] As discussed in Chapter 1, the Directive was adopted under Article 137[23] of the E.C. Treaty and is designed primarily to ensure a better level for the health and safety of workers, especially in their working environment. If one adopts a purposive approach to the provisions relating to weekly and daily rest periods, for example, it is difficult to see how time during which a worker is required to be physically present at his place of work and is at his employer's disposal could be deemed to count as rest periods (any time which is not working time constituting a rest period within the meaning of Article 2(1)), given the restrictions on the worker's freedom to use that time and the close connection such time has with work even if it is not spent actually working. This is particularly so when one considers that the broad definition of "health and safety" adopted by the European Court of Justice in *United Kingdom v. Council of the European Union*[24] includes a worker's psychic and social well-being.

3–11   The arguments are not as strong in relation to time spent on-call away from the worker's place of work. Although a worker is strictly at his employer's disposal during those periods, he has a degree of flexibility as to how to manage his time and the connection with work and his working environment is weaker.[25] If on-call time spent away from the workplace were counted for the purposes of determining observance with the weekly working time limit, for example, a worker could exceed the limit simply by being on-call for an average of over 48 hours per week even though he is never actually called into work. This would substantially reduce the ability of employers to achieve flexible working patterns.

Both the strict conjunctive and disjunctive approaches, whilst giving the benefit of legal certainty, do not admit of such refinements. In order fully to achieve the objectives of the Directive, a more flexible approach is required. How to formulate such an approach was the problem facing the European Court of Justice in the *SIMAP* case.

---

[22] As early as 1990, the European Parliament, in its opinion on the text for the Working Time Directive initially proposed by the Commission, stated that "Consideration should be given to the introduction of special arrangements covering on-call periods, particularly where such periods regularly include substantial periods of working time. A formula should be introduced to ensure such workers also have adequate rest periods".

[23] ex-Art. 118a.

[24] C–84/94 [1997] I.R.L.R. 30. See Chap. 1.

[25] Although on the broad definition of "working environment" adopted by the Advocate General in *U.K. v. Council of the European Union*, it seems that for such a worker his home and the need to be contactable would all form part of his working environment.

The SIMAP Case

3–12   The *SIMAP* case[26] was brought by the Valencia Medical Association (SIMAP) against the Valencia Health Authority over the terms of a collective agreement regulating doctors' terms and conditions of employment. In the Spanish labour court, various questions arose as to the compatibility of Spanish working time legislation with the Directive, which the court referred to the European Court of Justice under Article 234 of the E.C. Treaty.[27] For these purposes, the most important of these questions concerned whether periods during which the doctors were required to be on-call, either in the sense that they were required to be contactable or that they were required to be physically present at health centres, constituted "working time" within the meaning given to that term in Article 2(1).

Before the Advocate General, all the intervening States and the Commission argued that in both cases only those periods of on-call time during which the workers actually worked should count as working time. In particular, the United Kingdom Government argued that Article 2(1) should be construed conjunctively. It referred to the preamble to the Directive, which states that:

> "Whereas, in order to ensure the health and safety of Community workers, the latter must be granted minimum daily, weekly and annual periods of rest and adequate breaks; whereas it is also necessary in this context to place a maximum limit on weekly working hours."

3–13   According to the United Kingdom, "working time" should therefore be construed as a period of time the limitation of which was needed to secure the health and safety of workers. As workers may rest during on-call periods, the United Kingdom argued that these should not count as working time. It also argued that the words "in accordance with national laws and/or practice" in Article 2(1) militated against a broad interpretation of working time which would excessively restrict the ability of Member States to legislate in this regard.

The Commission also argued for a conjunctive definition, and was thus of the view that, since on-call time satisfies only the second requirement of Article 2(1) that the worker be at the employer's disposal, such time could not constitute working time within the meaning of the Directive, although Member States could legislate to expand the definition if they so wished.

SIMAP, on the other hand, pointed out that to adopt this interpretation would in effect mean that under the terms of the agreement in question doctors could be made to be at the employer's disposal for 30 consecutive hours.

3–14   Having commented on the lack of clarity in Article 2(1), the Advocate General agreed that its wording invited the conclusion that all three of the criteria must be met if time is to constitute working time. Interestingly, he considered that "working" means that the worker must be physically present at work. This therefore distinguished that criterion from that of "carrying out his activity or duties". It also in effect compels the use of the disjunctive approach, since the conjunctive interpretation argued for by the Commission and the intervening states would exclude from the definition of "working time" both time during which the worker carried out his duties but not at his place of work (*e.g.* a business meeting at a client's offices) and time during which the worker was physically present at his place of work but did not carry

---

[26] *SIMAP v. Conselleria de Sanidad y Consumo de La Generalidad Valenciana* C–303/98. This section should be read in the light of the postscript to the foreword to this book, which details the ECJ's decision.
[27] ex-Art. 177.

out his activity, even if in either case the worker was also at his employer's disposal.[28] The Advocate General considered that this interpretation did not correspond with the principal reason for the Directive, being to guarantee workers a reasonable period of rest. Not to take account of periods during which the worker is not carrying out his activity but is nonetheless at his employer's disposal, and not therefore truly resting, would thwart this objective.

He was therefore firmly in favour of the disjunctive interpretation of Article 2(1). He considered the three criteria to be autonomous and that it was not necessary for time to satisfy all three of them in order for it to constitute working time. In so deciding, he took note of the fact that to decide to the contrary would be to consider that the Council, in adopting the Directive, had decided to put in place a level of social protection lower than that already in place in many Member States.[29] He made reference to the notion of "travail effectif", which is used to define working time in for example French and Italian law, and commented that this definition comprised of only one of the criteria included in Article 2(1) (that of "carrying out his activity and duties"). He also made reference to the International Labour Organisation's Hours of Work (Commerce and Offices) Convention 1930,[30] Article 2 of which defines "hours of work" to mean:

> "the time during which the persons employed are at the disposal of the employer; it does not include rest periods during which the persons employed are not at the disposal of the employer."

3–15 Clearly this also comprises of only one of the criteria present in Article 2(1). The preamble to the Directive expressly states that account should be taken of the principles of the ILO with regard to the organisation of working time.

In the light of these considerations, the Advocate General opined that time during which a worker was on-call and required to be physically present at his place of work was working time, which would therefore count towards the weekly working time limit and could not constitute a rest period. If carried out at night time, such hours would also constitute night work within the meaning of the Directive, thus introducing a further layer of Regulation.

However, he did not think that on-call time during which the worker was required to remain contactable but need not be present at the place of work could be treated in the same manner.[31] As stated above, such time has a weaker connection with work and consequently is less of a threat to the health and safety of the worker. The Advocate General therefore concluded that such periods did not constitute working time save to the extent that the worker actually carried out his activity during that period. Nor could periods during which the worker is not called in to work constitute night work. However, he could still be a night worker if he is called in for at least three hours during night time "as a normal course".[32] It is not clear from the Advocate General's opinion whether the working time clock would start ticking as soon as the worker set

---

[28] Previously, Fairhurst (1999) has argued that "the only workers to be affected by a conjunctive/disjunctive distinction are those on call". This can no longer stand if the ECJ adopts the Advocate General's interpretation of the word "working".

[29] This is despite the fact that, as discussed in Chap. 1, a non-regression provision was deliberately excluded from the Directive.

[30] C30.

[31] cf. Barnard, (1999) I.L.J. 28(1), 61, 70, who considers that "if read disjunctively, time spent at home waiting for the phone to ring would constitute working time".

[32] Regulation 2(1).

off for his place of work or not until he arrived and began to carry out his activity. It is submitted that the latter is the better view, for reasons discussed later in this chapter.[33]

3–16   The Advocate General did not refer to the passage in *United Kingdom v. Council of the European Union*[34] in which the European Court of Justice argued for a broad interpretation of "working environment" and referred to health and safety as being "a state of complete physical, mental and social well-being", although the factors which he took into account when determining whether a worker could effectively rest during the on-call periods, such as the ability to spend time with family, indicates that he supported this broad view of the concept of health and safety.

On this basis, it is to be inferred that during such periods the Advocate General considers that a worker is not working nor at the employer's disposal nor carrying out his duties.[35] Thus the concept of being at the employer's disposal cannot coincide exactly with the contractual obligations of the worker to obey his employer's instructions. The distinction drawn by the Advocate General seems to envisage that one should instead look at the freedom the worker has in practice to pursue his own interests during a given period of time.

Having said that on-call time spent away from the place of work was not working time, the Advocate General went on to say that this did not mean that it counted as a rest period. Given that the Directive defines a rest period as being "any period which is not working time", this is surprising. The Advocate General in effect envisages a threefold classification of time: working time, rest periods and time which does not constitute either of these. On this basis, if a worker is on call at home for a period of 13 hours, but is not called in to work, he will still then be entitled to an 11-hour rest period.[36] The Advocate General reached this conclusion despite the fact that a worker is entitled to a rest period of 11 consecutive hours in every 24-hour period[37] and to an uninterrupted rest period of 24 hours in every seven day period,[38] so that if the worker is called in to work during his on-call period the time for which he has previously been on-call cannot count towards these entitlements unless it has already exceeded them.[39]

Summary of Conclusions of Advocate General Saggio

3–17   According to the Advocate General, the definition of "working time" in Article 2(1) should be construed disjunctively. Time is therefore working time if during it the worker is either at his place of work or at his employer's disposal (which is not a purely contractual test) or carrying out his activity or duties.

On-call time during which the worker is required to be physically present at his place of work is therefore working time. However, according to the Advocate General, this is not the case for on-call time spent away from the workplace. Nevertheless, on this basis, such time cannot count towards a worker's rest period entitlements.

The consequences of this approach outside the context of on-call working are discussed below. First, however, the interface between this approach and the derogations contained in Regulation 20 of the Regulations is examined.

---

[33] Fairhurst (1999) inclines to the former view because from the point of the call onwards the worker is "at the employer's disposal".

[34] C–84/94 [1997] I.R.L.R. 30.

[35] Fairhurst (1999) suggested before the Advocate General gave the opinion that the ECJ could use the concept of *de minimis* to disregard this time.

[36] Regulation 10. See Chap. 7.

[37] Regulation 10(1); emphasis added.

[38] Regulation 11(1); emphasis added.

[39] This threefold classification was subsequently rejected by the ECJ. See the postscript to Foreword.

Interface Between the Definition of "Working Time" and Regulation 20

3–18   Article 20(1) of the Directive permits Member States to derogate from the provisions relating to the maximum weekly working time limit, the maximum duration of night work, weekly and daily rest periods and rest breaks when:

> "on account of the specific characteristics of the activity concerned, the duration of the working time is not measured and/or predetermined or can be determined by the workers themselves, and particularly in the case of:
>
> (a) Managing executives or other persons with autonomous decision-taking powers;
> (b) Family workers; or
> (c) Workers officiating at religious ceremonies in churches and religious communities."

As discussed in Chapter 12, the United Kingdom transposed this text in more or less the same form into what is now Regulation 20(1). This appears to be a derogation in respect of particular activities, and therefore particular workers, rather than a derogation from the meaning of working time itself. If the duration of a worker's working time is unmeasured then the specified provisions do not apply to that worker; the unmeasured time is still however working time.

3–19   However, in the Working Time Regulations 1999,[40] the United Kingdom Government went further and inserted a new Regulation 20(2) which provides that:

> "Where part of the working time of a worker is measured or predetermined or cannot be determined by the worker himself but the specific characteristics of the activity are such that, without being required to do so by the employer, the worker may also do work the duration of which is not measured or predetermined or can be determined by the worker himself, Regulations 4(1) and (2) and 6(1), (2) and (7) shall apply only to so much of his work as is measured or predetermined or cannot be determined by the worker himself."

In contrast to Regulation 20(1), a worker involved in an activity having the characteristics described in Regulation 20(2) is not wholly excluded from the operation of the provisions specified therein. Rather, the portion of his working time that is unmeasured is not taken into account in determining whether the weekly working time and night work limits have been complied with in respect of him. Viewed in this way, Regulation 20(2) in fact forms part of the definition of "working time" for these limited purposes. Indeed, the revised Regulatory Guidance issued by the Government states that "[Regulation 20(2)] applies to working time—it is not confined to any particular category of worker". Given that there is no express provision for such an exclusion in the Directive, it must therefore be determined whether Regulation 20(2) only serves to exclude from working time time which would not in any event constitute working time within the meaning of Article 2(1). If it goes further than this then United Kingdom law is in breach of the Directive. On this basis,

---

[40] S.I. 1999 No. 3372. These came into force on December 16, 1999. See Barnard (2000) I.L.J. 29(2) 167.

it is to be noted that if Regulation 20(2) is compatible with the Directive then it is superfluous; such periods as it would exclude from working time would not in any event constitute working time within the meaning of paragraph (a) of Regulation 2(1) for any purpose, and not just in relation to the provisions to which Regulation 20(2) applies.

3–20 Similarly, it is to be noted that Regulation 20(2) is also superfluous if one adopts the conjunctive interpretation of Article 2(1) argued for by the United Kingdom since during the periods which it would exclude from working time the worker would not be at his employer's disposal. Indeed, the very inclusion of Regulation 20(2) could be used to support the argument for a disjunctive interpretation.

It is clear from the revised Regulatory Guidance that the Government intends Regulation 20(2) to be construed narrowly. From the examples given in the Guidance,[41] it appears that "the key factor for this exception is choice without detriment". Hours during which the worker is implicitly required to work, because of the requirements of the job, workload or even because colleagues habitually work long hours and the worker is led to believe that his employer considers it unacceptable to work shorter hours, do not fall within Regulation 20(2). Equally, voluntary overtime would not. However, time voluntarily spent reading about work or in doing work where in practice the worker has a true choice to leave that work until it can be done during his contracted hours, will not count as working time under Regulation 20(2).

Naturally, this restrictive interpretation enhances the probability that Regulation 20(2) is compatible with the Directive. However, on the disjunctive approach, if one examines the periods of time which Regulation 20(2) in fact excludes from the definition of working time then it is more restrictive than Article 2(1) and would therefore be an unlawful derogation from the protections conferred by the Directive. During time voluntarily spent working at home, for example, a worker would be clearly carrying out his activity which, on the disjunctive approach used by the Advocate General, would be sufficient to render that time working time. This interpretation is consistent with the objective of securing the health and safety of workers. If the worker truly wishes voluntarily to work in excess of the weekly working time limit, he may sign an opt-out,[42] and the concerns over the detrimental effects of night work could justify intervention to prevent a worker jeopardising his health and safety through his own actions.

3–21 However, if the conjunctive approach prevails then, as stated above, Regulation 20(2) would be a lawful, if superfluous, derogation.

DEFINITION OF WORKING TIME: SPECIFIC EXAMPLES

3–22 In addition to on-call time, there are various other periods and working practices which present particular problems in this regard.

(a) Lunch breaks

3–23 It is tolerably clear that in the usual course lunch breaks will not be working time. Certainly, this is the view taken by the Government in its Regulatory Guidance.

---

[41] Discussed further in Chap. 12.
[42] Regulation 5.

However, as recognised in the Guidance, "working lunches" (*e.g.* where the worker is required to attend a business meeting or to entertain clients) will count as working time. Similarly, other client entertainment functions which the worker is required (whether explicitly or implicitly[43]) to attend would constitute working time, although purely social events would not. The distinction will in practice be very difficult to draw.[44] Where people choose to work during their lunch break, it is submitted on the basis of the discussion of Regulation 20(2) above that this will be working time.

If the worker is required to take his lunch break at work in order to be able to resume work if required, then his position will be analogous to that of an on-call worker who is required to be physically present at his place of work, and the lunch break will count as working time. If it is merely the case that due to the length of the break or the location of the place of work the worker has no option but to spend the lunch break at work, but is not obliged to be available for work in that period, then the better view would seem to be that this is not working time because the worker is not required to be at work, even though in a broad sense he could be said to be at the employer's disposal. If in practice the worker is sometimes called upon to work during his lunch break, then this could tip the balance in favour of all lunch breaks being working time.

This last example demonstrates that it is perhaps too broad to interpret "working" to mean a physical presence at the place of work. Rather, in these circumstances, in order to be classed as "working", it is submitted that the worker must be required (whether explicitly or implicitly) by his employer to be physically present.

Other rest breaks, including those to which a worker is entitled under Regulation 12, should be treated in the same way as lunch breaks.

(b) Travelling time

3–24 The Guidance states that working time does not include routine travel between home and the workplace. However, if a worker is required to travel as part of his work (*e.g.* a mobile repairman) then time spent so travelling will be working time. This will also be the case if a worker is required to travel home during the working day, for example to retrieve an item needed by the employer.

If the worker travels home at the end of the usual working day intending to work further at home, then it is submitted that such time will not be working time unless in the particular circumstances the worker is at the employer's disposal during that time and on the conjunctive approach, is also working and carrying out his activity. It has been suggested[45] that when a worker is on-call at home and is called in to work then his travelling time counts as working time. However, with respect it is difficult to see what distinction could be made between this time and the time spent travelling when a worker is required to be at work by a certain time of day; the worker is no less at the disposal of the employer in the latter scenario. The fact that in the former he is paid for his travelling time does not mean that such time must be working time.

Different considerations arise if the worker travels by train or bus and works during the journey. If he is carrying out his activity, and not for example merely reading about his field of work as a matter of personal interest, this should constitute working time on the disjunctive approach but would not do so on the conjunctive approach unless

---

[43] See the discussion of the scope of Regulation 20(2) above.
[44] Neathey and Arrowsmith, *Early Implementation of the Working Time Regulations* (October 1999), cite one organisation which distinguishes between corporate hospitality at the employer's direction, which is working time, and that resulting from a third-party invitation, which the employer does not count as working time. This distinction would appear to be wrong in law.
[45] Fairhurst (1999).

he can be said to be at the disposal of his employer. The above discussion of Regulation 20(2) will be relevant in these circumstances.

(c) Working at home

3–25   Where a worker is a "homeworker"[46] or carries out work at home with the agreement of the employer, this time is likely to count as working time. However, more difficult issues arise in the case of a non-homeworker if the worker works at home outside his or her normal working hours and without prior arrangement with (or, indeed, the knowledge of) the employer.[47] Such time will not be working time on the conjunctive approach as the worker is not at the employer's disposal.

(d) Working away from home

3–26   As discussed above, time spent travelling will be working time where the worker is required to travel as part of his job.[48] Problems arise in relation to situations in which the worker is required to travel from home to somewhere other than his usual place of work. Suppose for example a solicitor usually starts work at 9 a.m., which means that he must set off from home at 8.30 a.m. If one day he must attend a business meeting at a client's premises at 9 a.m. and must travel for two hours to get there, does this travelling time constitute working time? The Guidance states that "time spent travelling outside normal working time" is not working time. However, there would seem to be no legal basis for such a distinction. Therefore, it is submitted that the Guidance is wrong in this respect and that the whole of such period should count as working time, since during that time the worker can be said to be carrying out his duties. It would seem artificial, not to mention very difficult in practice, simply to count the extra travelling time as working time.

In addition, difficulties of interpretation arise in circumstances when a worker is required to undertake a long journey, for example by air, and may sleep during that journey. Although it seems strange to suggest that time spent sleeping may constitute working time, it is submitted that in this case it would be, since the worker would be at the employer's disposal and carrying out his duties. Such time could not therefore constitute a rest period.

3–27   However, once at a destination at which the worker is required to stay overnight in order to work the following day, it is submitted that on a purposive view only those periods during which the worker carries out his activity actually constitute working time. Therefore, time spent in a hotel would only be working time to the extent that the worker worked there. Even though in a broad sense the worker could be said to be at the disposal of the employer and carrying out his duties in staying away from home, to deem the entirety of such time to be working time would be an unduly broad interpretation of the Regulations and is not necessary in order to give effect to their objectives.[49]

The Regulatory Guidance states that time spent working abroad does constitute working time, even though Regulation 1(2) provides that the Regulations extend to Great Britain only.

---

[46] "Homeworkers" will generally fall within the definition of worker in Regulation 2(1).

[47] The original DTI Regulatory Guidance stated that "time worked [at home] would only count as working time where the work was performed on a basis previously agreed with the employer".

[48] Workers in the transport sector may be excluded from the operation of the Regulations; see Chap. 12.

[49] It is to be noted that Art. 137 expressly provides that Directives made under it are to "avoid imposing administrative, financial and legal constraints in a way which would hold back the creation of small and medium-sized undertakings". See however the discussion of the potential impact of the Human Rights Act 1998 at the end of this chapter.

(e) Salaried staff

3–28 These staff may well be employed on contracts of employment which state that, perhaps in addition to a specified minimum number of hours per week, they are required to work "such hours as are required by the needs of the business". Such staff may, for example, work through their lunch hours and work outside any normal working hours laid down in the contract or work at home. It is primarily these staff at whom the Regulation 20(2) exclusion is aimed. On the conjunctive approach, whether time during which such staff carry out their activity or duties will be working time will depend on whether when doing so they are at their employer's disposal.

(f) Sick leave

3–29 Time spent on sick leave is not working time. Such time does not fulfil any of the three criteria in Article 2(1) and there would appear to be no health and safety reason why it should be governed by the Regulations or Directive. This was the conclusion reached by the London (North) employment tribunal in *RC Warnes v. Situsec Contractors Limited.*[50]

(g) Statutory rights to time off

3–30 Employees (and not, at present at least, workers who are not employees[51]) have a number of statutory rights to take time off work. In practice, the most important of these are for:

(i) Time off for trade union duties and activities[52];

(ii) Time off for employee representatives[53];

(iii) Time off for ante-natal care[54]; and

(iv) time off to care for dependants.[55]

As already discussed, the fact that in some of the above cases the employee also has a statutory right to be paid in respect of such time is not determinative of the question as to whether the time off is working time. Nor would the various rights appear to admit of a uniform treatment. Rather, it would appear that an analysis of the purpose behind each of the rights and the nature of the activities to be performed during the time off is necessary in order to resolve the question of whether such time is working time.

Generally, the question should boil down to whether during the time off the employee could be said to be "carrying out his activity or duties". In relation to time off for ante-natal care or time off to care for dependants, it seems clear that such periods would not be working time within the meaning of paragraph (a) of Regulation 2(1). The duration of such time off will in practice be agreed with the employer so that the employee is free to devote that time wholly to the relevant task without being

---

[50] Case No. 6003949/99. See Chap. 8, para. 8–36.
[51] The Government has the power under s.23 of the ERA 1999 to extend these rights to workers other than employees.
[52] Trade Union and Labour Relations (Consolidation) Act 1992, ss.168–170.
[53] ERA 1996, s.61, and in respect of employee safety representatives Safety Representatives and Safety Committees Regulation 1977 (S.I. 1977 No. 500) and Health and Safety (Consultation with Employees) Regulation 1996 (S.I. 1996 No. 1513).
[54] ERA 1996, s.55.
[55] ERA 1996, s.57A. Other rights to time off under the ERA 1996 include time off for public duties (s.50), time off to look for work or arrange training after receipt of notice of dismissal for redundancy (s.52), time off for pension scheme trustees (s.58) and to time off for young persons for study or training (s.63A).

concerned with the need to return to work. Thus it would not appear necessary to include such time within working time in order to protect the health and safety of the employee, even adopting the broad understanding of that term used by the European Court of Justice.

3–31   However, it is strongly arguable that when taking time off for the purpose of carrying out duties relating to collective bargaining or to undertake duties as a union or employee representative in relation to collective redundancies or business transfers, an employee is in fact "carrying out his activity or duties". Given the close nexus of such activity with work, a purposive approach would support this interpretation. Otherwise, an employee could throughout a reference period spend a full day per week involved in intensive meetings with the employer and work an additional 48 hours per week and yet not exceed the weekly working time limit in respect of that period. Where the employee is required to attend the employer's premises in order to participate in the meetings, as is commonly the case, he may be deemed to be "working", but the classification of this time should not turn on his physical presence at work or otherwise. The arguments for including time off for trade union activities taken pursuant to section 170 TULR(C)A 1992 as working time are weaker, as they may be unconnected with work (although they may constitute "relevant training"[56]).

In practice, such time may be deemed to be working time by means of a relevant agreement, as permitted by paragraph (c) of the definition of working time in Regulation 2(1), given that as union or employee representatives the employees concerned will be in a position to conclude such an agreement. This would benefit the employer as it would provide certainty. As discussed below, however, if such time falls within either of the other two paragraphs of the definition, a relevant agreement may not exclude such time from the scope of working time.

RELEVANT TRAINING: PARAGRAPH (B) OF THE DEFINITION

3–32   Although paragraph (a) is clearly the core part, and indeed the most contentious part, of the definition contained in Regulation 2(1), there are two other aspects of the definition.

Paragraph (b) provides that "working time" in relation to a worker includes:

"any period during which he is receiving relevant training".

"Relevant training" is defined to mean:

"work experience provided pursuant to a training course or programme, training for employment, or both, other than work experience or training:

(a) The immediate provider of which is an educational institution or a person whose main business is the provision of training; and
(b) Which is provided on a course run by that institution or person".

3–33   Thus the Regulatory Guidance states that "job-related training that is directly related to [the worker's] job" is working time. Although there is no express requirement in the definition of "relevant training" that it be directly related to the worker's job, in practice a worker who works in addition to undergoing training is unlikely to be provided with any non-job-related training by his employer; and the worker is unlikely to receive training from anyone other than his employer or an

---

[56] See the discussion of para. (b) of the Regulation 2(1) definition below.

educational institution or training body. Training that is not job-related will therefore rarely constitute working time.

Although this provision does not appear in Article 2(1), this may not represent an extension of the definition in the Directive, as seemingly during work experience with an employer or job-related training provided by the employer, the worker is "at the disposal of his employer" or is carrying out his duties. However, given the conjunctive construction placed by the Government on paragraph (a), it perhaps felt the need expressly to include paragraph (b) to ensure that training time did count as working time.

TIME TREATED AS WORKING TIME BY VIRTUE OF A RELEVANT AGREEMENT: PARAGRAPH (C) OF THE DEFINITION

3–34 By virtue of paragraph (c) of the definition of working time in Regulation 2(1), it includes:

> "any additional period which is to be treated as working time for the purpose of these Regulations under a relevant agreement".

Employers and their workers may therefore resolve any ambiguities in the definition by reaching a legally binding agreement.[57] This might be achieved, for example, through a workforce agreement or by a provision of the worker's individual contract of employment. However, it seems clear from the use of the word "additional" that such an agreement may only serve to render as working time periods of time which would not otherwise be working time within paragraphs (a) and (b); the parties cannot derogate from the definition of working time used in the Regulations by virtue of a relevant agreement. Therefore, the ability to define certain time as working time in a relevant agreement can only be used either to clarify any grey areas by expressly including these in the definition of working time or, by way of concession to a trade union, employee representatives or workers generally, to expand the definition of working time to include time which would not otherwise fall within the definition.

Given that working time is the basic unit by reference to which many of the entitlements and limitations contained within the Regulations are defined, and that the existing definition is potentially very broad, it is clear that employers should proceed with caution before concluding an agreement under paragraph (c), as this may expose them to criminal sanctions.[58]

SOLUTIONS ADOPTED IN OTHER MEMBER STATES

3–35 It is instructive briefly to examine the definitions of working time adopted in other Member States particularly since, as discussed in Chapter 1, many of these states have legislation concerning the organisation of working time which predates the adoption of the Directive. It was noted above that one of the grounds on which Advocate General Saggio based his interpretation of Article 2(1) in the *SIMAP* case was that to adopt a disjunctive interpretation would be more restrictive than the approach taken by some Member States prior to the Directive's adoption.

---

[57] See Chap. 13 for a discussion of what constitutes a "relevant agreement".
[58] See Chap. 14. Fairhurst (1999) cites as an example of such an agreement the General Whitley Council Agreement, in which, prior to the *SIMAP* case, it was agreed that time spent on-call at the employer's premises would constitute working time.

Traditionally, French law has defined "working time" to mean the time when work is actually performed. In 1998, however, when introducing legislation to implement an enforced 35-hour week, working time was re-defined to mean "the time during which the employee remains at the disposal of the employer and must comply with the instructions of the latter without being allowed to deal with his or her personal matters". It is debatable whether on the disjunctive view this definition fully implements Article 2(1), comprising as it does of only the second of the three criteria therein.

The Irish Organisation of Working Time Act 1997 defines "working time" as "any time that the employee is: (a) at his or her place of work or at his or her employer's disposal; and (b) carrying out or performing the activities or duties of his or her work". In the light of the Advocate General's opinion in *SIMAP*, it appears unlikely that this marriage of the disjunctive and conjunctive approaches has produced a legitimate offspring.

3–36 In the Netherlands, however, working time is very broadly defined to include any physical or mental effort required of a worker. This definition can be seen to accord with the broad concept of health and safety adopted in *United Kingdom v. Council of the European Union*.[59] In Germany, the relevant rules expressly provide that time during which a worker is present at the employer's workplace is working time and that any time spent travelling on the instructions of the employer is also working time.

Thus the approach to defining "working time" is far from uniform throughout the E.U. The variety of definitions used, and the many areas of ambiguity in the Directive, should produce a healthy number of referrals to the European Court of Justice to clarify the scope of Article 2(1).

COMPARISON WITH EUROPEAN PROVISIONS RESTRICTING DRIVING HOURS

3–37 The European Council has promulgated various Regulations limiting the working hours of drivers in the road transport industry and the recording equipment which must be used to ensure that such limits are complied with. A brief analysis of the concepts of rest and working time as they appear in those Regulations provides a useful insight into the E.U. notion of what constitutes working time.[60]

Article 1(5) of Regulation 3820/85, which lays down minimum rest entitlements for drivers, defines "rest" as "any uninterrupted period of at least one hour during which the driver may freely dispose of his time". It can be seen that the requirement that a worker must be able freely to dispose of his time is very similar to the test applied by the Advocate General in *SIMAP* in identifying what constituted a "rest period" for the purposes of the Working Time Directive, especially given the interpretation of Article 1(5) adopted by the High Court in *Prime v. Hosking*.[61] There, it was argued that voluntary overtime could still constitute rest as the worker was free to choose whether or not to work during that period. The High Court rejected this proposition:

"It may be that at the moment when the driver was taking the decision whether to

---

[59] C–84/94 [1997] I.R.L.R. 30.
[60] It should be noted however that these Regulation have a different legal basis to the Working Time Directive (see Chap. 1).
[61] [1995] I.R.L.R. 143.

work overtime or not he was free to dispose of his time. However, the moment that he opted to do the overtime, he then came within the control of his employer, was under their direction and was not then free to dispose of his time."

3–38   It is clear that voluntary overtime also constitutes "working time" for the purposes of the Working Time Directive and Working Time Regulations.

During rest breaks, Article 7(4) of Regulation 3820/85 provides that a driver may not "carry out any other work". Article 7(4) expressly provides that for these purposes the waiting time and time not devoted to driving spent in a vehicle in motion, a ferry, or a train shall not be regarded as "other work". This therefore differs from the situation where a non-driver is required by his employer to travel, but this is logical given the nature of a driver's work and the purpose behind Regulation 3820/85, which is to guarantee the health and safety of other road users as well as that of the drivers themselves.

There are detailed rules as to the recording equipment that must be put in place to ensure that the obligations imposed by Regulation 3820/85 are complied with.[62] This contrasts with the more limited record-keeping obligations imposed by Regulation 9 of the Working Time Regulations.

POTENTIAL IMPACT OF THE HUMAN RIGHTS ACT 1998

3–39   A detailed discussion of the provisions of this Act is beyond the scope of this book.[63] For these purposes, it is sufficient to note that, as from October 2, 2000, when the Act came into force, United Kingdom courts and tribunals are under an obligation, so far as possible, to interpret and give effect to primary and subordinate legislation in a way which is compatible with the rights conferred by the European Convention on Human Rights.[64]

Article 8(1) provides that:

"Everyone has the right to respect for his private and family life, his home and his correspondence."

Therefore, employment tribunals and courts will have to have regard to this right when interpreting Regulation 2(1).[65] Any working practices which have an adverse impact on a worker's private or family life could potentially infringe the right. For example, it is possible that the reference to family life could be construed as requiring restrictions to be placed on an employer's ability to require a worker to travel excessively or to work unreasonable hours.[66] This may lead to a more expansive construction of "working time", for example to include all time spent away from home on the employer's business, whether or not that time is actually spent working. There would be an even stronger argument for excluding such time from the scope of

---

[62] Council Regulation 3821/85 on recording equipment in road transport (as amended).
[63] See for example *Human Rights Law and Practice* (eds) Lord Lester Q.C. & Pannick Q.C.; Starmer, *The Human Rights Act 1998 and European Convention on Human Rights*; Ewing (1998) I.L.J. 27(4), 275.
[64] HRA 1998, s.3(1).
[65] It is also to be noted that the ECHR informs the content of Community law; *e.g. P v. S & Cornwall County Council* [1996] 2 C.M.L.R. 247.
[66] However, it would appear to be extremely unlikely that by requiring a worker to work longer hours or at weekends an employer would breach the prohibition on forced labour under Art. 4 of the ECHR.

"rest periods". It is noticeable in this regard that the inability to devote time to the family was one of the factors taken into account by Advocate General Saggio in *SIMAP* in reaching the conclusion that time spent on-call at the workplace should constitute working time.

However, at the time of writing no claim or argument based on interference with family or private life had succeeded before the European Court of Human Rights in relation to working hours.

Interpretation of the Working Time Regulations

3–40 The discussion in this chapter could potentially have other ramifications in the interpretation of the Regulations. For example, Regulation 2(1) defines a "worker" as:

> "an individual who has entered into or works under a contract whereby the individual undertakes to do or perform personally any work."

Since, following the definition of "working time" Regulation 2(1) states "and 'work' shall be construed accordingly", the debate concerning the concept of "working time" may impact on the definition of a "worker".

However, given that the same definition of worker is used in other employment protection legislation, such as the National Minimum Wage Act, such inconsistency would be undesirable.

As already discussed, the debate will also impact on the interpretation of "night worker".

This reinforces the pervasive importance of the definition of "working time" in the interpretation of the Regulations. It is therefore vital to bear in mind the points made in this chapter when reading the discussion of the Regulations in the remainder of this book.

CHAPTER FOUR
The Common Law Approach

4–01 One of the most significant aspects of the implementation of the Working Time Directive in the United Kingdom is that, for the first time, national minimum standards govern the way in which working time is organised. This is a novel concept for English law which has, until recently, played little part in the Regulation of patterns of work. Instead the traditional common law approach has been to allow such matters to be negotiated by the parties (either individually or collectively), leaving the final bargain to be recorded in either a collective agreement or the individual contract of employment.

Over the years, inroads have been made into this approach and legislation regulating working time in certain industries or for particular sectors of the workforce has found its way on to the statute book. However, the process has been a piecemeal one and no universally accepted standards have emerged. In addition the culture of deregulation fostered by the Conservative Government in the 1980s and early 1990s meant that much of the statutory Regulation which did exist was largely swept away in an effort to improve the efficiency and profitability of United Kingdom industry. (The demise and ultimate abolition of the Wages Councils during this period provide one example of this trend.)

Some developments in European law also contributed to deregulation. The combined effect of the Equal Treatment Directive with the European Commission's drive to remove sex discrimination in factories, mines, quarries and transport forced the repeal of many United Kingdom Regulations which had been designed to "protect" women, but which also restricted their employment. As a result, were it not for the Working Time Regulations, very little statutory Regulation of working patterns would now survive in the United Kingdom, the remaining restrictions being limited to a few occupations such as mining, sheet glass working and (as a result of E.C. transport policy) driving heavy goods vehicles.

4–02 The position in the United Kingdom is in stark contrast to that of continental Europe where national Regulation of working hours and paid annual leave has long been the norm. In Germany working hours and paid leave have been regulated since the First World War and in France it has been forbidden to work more than a 6 day week since 1906. In Spain the constitution itself imposes a duty on public authorities to guarantee "necessary rest, by limitation of the length of the working day ... [and] ... by periodic paid holidays".[1] The United Kingdom is therefore exceptional in failing to have any general statutory Regulation of weekly hours of work. It is not surprising therefore that long working hours remain an important part of the United Kingdom employment culture.

Comparisons such as these led many to predict that of all the E.U. countries, it

---

[1] For a summary of the relevant legislation in Member States see the Conservative Government's consultation document on measures to implement the provisions of the E.C. Directive on the organisation of working time, Annex D.

would be the United Kingdom which would feel the greatest impact from the Working Time Directive. Although this has to some extent been the case, it does not give the whole picture. In fact by the mid-1990s there was evidence that some judges were prepared to use the common law to create an embryonic set of rights and obligations relating directly to working time. This basic protection, developed in the context of cases concerning the employment contract and the employer's duty to protect the health and safety of his workforce, imposes substantial obligations on employers, particularly in cases where overwork has led to injury to health. Of course these common law rules now co-exist with the Working Time Regulations. However because of the increasing awareness of the health risks associated with workplace stress and a long hours culture they are likely to remain relevant and develop further in the future, particularly as courts and tribunals become more familiar with the standards set by the Regulations. This will give an additional means of redress to many workers now covered by the Regulations. In addition it will ensure that there is basic protection for those who are currently excluded from their scope. Employers therefore need to act with both the Regulations and the common law rules in mind.

THE TRADITIONAL COMMON LAW APPROACH

4–03   At first sight the development of any common law Regulation of working time seems unlikely. The traditional approach of the English judges has been to ignore any notions of fairness and reasonableness and determine disputes over working time solely by reference to the worker's individual contract. Whilst this has had the advantage of promoting certainty, so that if the contract is drafted unambiguously there is no room for challenge, it means that, whatever the relative bargaining strengths of the parties may be, the terms of the contract are decisive. So for example in *Tucker v. British Leyland Motor Corporation Limited*[2] the county court looked solely at the contract of employment to determine whether certain employees of British Leyland were entitled to take particular days over the Christmas period as paid leave. Although the court found in favour of the employees, it went out of its way to emphasise that if the relevant contracts had been clearly expressed in the employer's favour, the outcome would have been different.

4–04   An extreme example of this non-interventionist approach is provided by the case of *NCB v. Galley*.[3] In that case a contractual term required pit deputies to work "such days ... as may *reasonably* be required by the management to promote the safety and efficient working of the pit and to comply with statutory requirements" (emphasis added). The employee in question had worked 11 shifts on consecutive days. Nonetheless the employer required him to work a 12th consecutive shift on a Saturday morning, arguing that he was obliged to do so under his contract. The issue reached the Court of Appeal where Pearce L.J., giving the judgment of the court, avoided any reference to the employee's state of health or to the possible effects of exhaustion on his performance. Instead he was at pains to emphasise that, in construing the relevant term, the court was "in no way concerned with what constitutes reasonable hours in the abstract. Its task [was] to consider the agreement ... and to determine on the evidence whether or not the Defendant was being required to work in breach of this agreement". He therefore found in favour of the employer.

4–05   The decision of the Court of Appeal has been criticised as being unduly

---

[2] [1978] I.R.L.R. 493.
[3] [1958] 1 W.L.R. 16.

restrictive. After all the parties had themselves introduced the concept of reasonableness into the relevant contractual provision and it was therefore open to the court to construe the contract much more liberally, even under the traditional common law approach. Instead the court decided that the only situation which could amount to a breach of the working hours clause was where one pit deputy was required to work longer hours than everyone else. Otherwise the employer could apparently demand such hours to be worked as it thought fit. In light of this reasoning it is hardly surprising that Galley's counterclaim for a declaration that he should not have to work more than a 42½-hour week, except in emergencies, was unsuccessful.

A more recent example of the traditional approach is provided by *British Bakeries Limited v. Hoggans*.[4] In this case the contract provided for overtime to be paid if the employee worked more than 39 hours per week. However a dispute arose over whether meal breaks counted as part of the working week. The matter reached the EAT which decided that it could construe the agreement in its factual setting. However, its role was restricted to determining the objective intention of the parties and to giving "a fair meaning to the words used in the ... agreement". It could not under any circumstances rewrite the agreement by deciding what would be a reasonable term of the contract. On this basis the tribunal found in favour of the employees and decided that meal breaks were to be included in the calculation of the working week.

4–06 However even against this traditional, common law background some judges have been prepared to become more interventionist and to insist that basic obligations and responsibilities do exist in relation to working time, even if, on occasion, this means effectively rewriting express contractual terms. This new approach can be seen in three contexts. First in relation to the construction of the contract of employment, second in relation to the tortuous duty to provide a safe system of work and thirdly in the judicial interpretation of statutory employment rights. In each of these areas there is evidence that even before the implementation of the Working Time Regulations judges were prepared to jettison orthodox thinking and to accept that their role is to set basic standards in respect of working patterns.

THE NEW CONTRACTUAL APPROACH

4–07 The leading case in this area is *Johnstone v. Bloomsbury Health Authority*.[5] In that case the Plaintiff was a hospital doctor employed under a contract of employment that provided for a standard working week of 40 hours. In addition the contract stated that he would be "available" on call for a further 48 hours "on average" per week. He alleged that in some weeks he worked more than a 100 hours with inadequate sleep and with the result that he suffered from "stress, depression, lethargy, diminished appetite, insomnia, exhaustion and suicidal feelings". As a result he sued his employer, the Bloomsbury Health Authority, claiming amongst other things that he was entitled to a declaration that his contract did not require him to work so many hours in excess of his standard working week as would foreseeably injure his health.

The Health Authority argued that such a claim could not succeed because the Authority were entitled under the express terms of the contract to require the plaintiff to work up to 88 hours on average per week. Although this argument represents the orthodox common law approach discussed above, surprisingly it did not succeed. By a

---

[4] EAT 478/96.
[5] [1991] I.R.L.R. 118.

majority decision the Court of Appeal accepted that the doctor had an arguable case. The most radical judgment was that of Stuart Smith L.J.. He held that the contractual terms relating to hours of work "had to be exercised in light of the other contractual terms" and in particular the employer's duty to take care for the employee's safety which is implied into every contract of employment. In other words if the Health Authority knew they were exposing Dr Johnstone to a risk of injury to his health by requiring him to work long hours then they were in breach of contract—regardless of whether the hours were mandatory or discretionary. In coming to this conclusion the judge emphasised that the NHS was effectively a monopoly employer and that the only way for a doctor to qualify was to work for one year as a house officer in an NHS hospital. It could not be right that a junior doctor must either abandon his chosen profession or work so long that his health was undermined. He was therefore prepared to find that the employer could only exercise its express powers if it did so consistently with the duty to have proper regard to the employee's health and safety.

4–08   This judgment marks a fundamental shift from the traditional common law approach. By construing the express terms of the contract in light of an implied duty to protect the employee's health, Stuart Smith L.J. was effectively re-writing the contract and came very close to imposing a basic minimum standard in respect of working time on the employment relationship.

By contrast the Vice Chancellor, who also found in favour of the employee, took a much more restricted approach. In his view it was important that the Health Authority had a discretion, as opposed to a right, to call for overtime. That being the case there was no reason why that discretion could not be exercised in conformity with "the normal implied duty to take reasonable care not to injure their employees' health". However, the situation would have been very different if the contract had imposed an "absolute obligation to work 48-hours overtime and would have precluded any argument based on the implied term."

4–09   It was left to Leggatt L.J. in his dissenting judgment to assert the traditional common law approach. To him it was absolutely clear that "there can have been no breach, fundamental or otherwise, by the Defendants in calling on the Plaintiff to work the hours *for which he had contracted to be available*" (emphasis added). If the Plaintiff fell sick as a result of working long hours "he did not do so by reason of any relevant breach of duty on the Defendant's part".

One of the most interesting features of the *Johnstone* decision is that none of the judges would allow the applicant to argue that the working hours clause was contrary to public policy. So although the Vice Chancellor was prepared to acknowledge that "in any sphere of employment other than that of junior hospital doctors, an obligation to work up to 88 hours in any one week would be rightly regarded as oppressive and intolerable" all three judges—including Stuart Smith L.J.—refused to debate the policy issues head on and declare that the clause was unlawful on policy grounds.

4–10   The *Johnstone* case does not therefore impose a minimum working standard to be applied universally to all hospital doctors employed by a Health Authority. However it does at least suggest that any such Authority should look at each house officer separately and assess his or her physical stamina on an individual basis—an important result given that the doctors are currently excluded from the protection of the Working Time Directive. Of course, the notion of an individual assessment carries echoes of the principle of adapting work to the particular worker referred to in Article 13 of the Directive and it may well be that case law developed in relation to that Article (as well as Regulation 8 which purports to implement the principle into United Kingdom law) informs subsequent judicial development of the *Johnstone* decision. Equally it may be that cases interpreting other aspects of the Regulations are influential in this area of law. The High Court has already found, to the surprise of many commentators, that the 48-hour limit on weekly working time set out in Regulation 4(1) is implied into the contract of every worker who is covered by this aspect of the Regulations (see *Barber v. RJB Mining (UK) Limited*[6]). This gives such workers a free-standing contractual right to refuse to work in excess of the limit and raises the possibility of constructive dismissal if the employer breaches the contract by requiring a worker to exceed the limit. However the *Barber* decision appears to go beyond what was contemplated by the Regulations. These merely provide that workers who refuse to work in excess of the 48-hour limit can complain to an employment tribunal if they are dismissed or suffer detriment as a result. There is no express indication that a contractual remedy is also possible. The *Barber* decision, together with the judgment of Stuart Smith L.J. in the *Johnstone* case, may therefore be used to argue that, even where the Regulations do not apply, terms restricting weekly working time may well be implied into a worker's contract and will override any express terms to the contrary. Certainly where there is evidence that long working hours may be injurious to health, arguments in favour of such a clause will be particularly strong. Finally it is possible that some of the reasoning in the *Johnstone* case may also be relevant to workers covered by the Regulations. So, for example there is a passage in Stuart Smith L.J.'s judgment suggesting that if a worker becomes exhausted and has an accident then he would be entitled to sue his employer for breach of contract and "it [would be] no defence for the employer to say that the workman expressly agreed to work such hours". This argument could well be developed in the context of a worker who agrees to sign an individual opt-out and work more than 48 hours per week under the Regulations and who is subsequently injured at work. It remains to be seen if such reasoning will be adopted.

THE TORTIOUS APPROACH

4–11   It is well established that in addition to the implied contractual duty to take care of the employee's safety the civil law also imposes a tortious duty an employer to take reasonable care of the health and safety of employees whilst they work. This means that an employer will be negligent—and therefore potentially liable to the employee—if he fails to take reasonable steps to avoid a reasonably foreseeable risk of injury. The duty has always encompassed a number of features, including a requirement to provide a safe system of work. However it is only in recent years that the courts have started to use the obligation to provide a safe working system to impose liability when an employee suffers illness through overwork. This development—coupled with a recognition that the duty extends to cover both the physical and psychological health of employees—means that an employer now overburdens an employee at his peril.

Two recent cases illustrate how far the law has come in this area. In the first case, *Petch v. Commissioners of Customs and Excise*[7] a high flying employee suffered a nervous breakdown and was off work for a period. When he subsequently returned to work he developed further mental illness and the employer decided to transfer him to other less demanding duties. Petch sued the department and claimed that it had been negligent because it had overloaded him with work prior to the first breakdown. The employer conceded that it owed Mr Petch "a duty to take reasonable care to ensure that the duties allocated to him should not damage his health". It also agreed that this

[6] [1999] I.R.L.R. 308.
[7] [1993] I.C.R. 789.

included both the physical and mental health of the employee although it maintained that issues of foreseeability and causation were likely to be more difficult in mental injury cases. However, it argued that on the facts there had been no breach of that duty. The Court of Appeal agreed. In particular the court found that until the initial breakdown Mr Petch had appeared to be more than able to cope with his existing workload and it was therefore "absurd to suggest that the employer had negligently overloaded him with work". However, on different facts the Court of Appeal might well have found the employer liable.

4–12   In the second case, *Walker v. Northumberland County Council*,[8] a different outcome was reached with the result that, for the first time in English Law an employer was held liable for mental illness suffered by an employee as a result of workplace stress. The *Walker* case concerned a social services officer who suffered two nervous breakdowns, both of which were attributed to the demanding nature of his work. Following the second breakdown he was dismissed by his employer on the grounds of ill health. He sued the employer for damages in negligence, alleging that the Council had been in breach of its duty by failing to take reasonable steps to avoid exposing him to a health endangering workload. Colman J. in the High Court agreed. He found that, in the first place there was no "logical reason" why risk of psychiatric damage should be excluded from the scope of the employer's duty of care. Secondly, there was no reason why an employer in the public sector should be treated any differently from a commercial employer. As a result although the court might need to take account of budgetary constraints and the bureaucratic nature of decision making in the public sector when considering the Council's conduct, those factors in themselves did not absolve the Council from liability. He went on to hold that on the facts the Council had not been in breach of its duty in respect of the first breakdown, even though some risk of illness was foreseeable before that breakdown occurred.[9] However the Council were in breach of their duty in respect of the second breakdown. Once the employee returned to work after his first illness the Council should have foreseen that there was a real risk of repetition. They should have provided him with additional assistance and as they failed to do so were liable in damages for his resulting loss.[10]

4–13   One important feature of the *Walker* case is that it focuses on the individual and his particular circumstances, including his perceived ability to cope with pressure. To this extent it will give better redress to the employee who is prepared to complain about his working conditions than to the employee who silently accepts intolerable hours and then reaches breaking point. This was recognised by Colman J. when discussing the case of the ambitious professional (who if covered by the Regulations would no doubt agree to "opt-out" of the 48-hour limit). In such a case the Judge accepted that there were likely to be "difficult evidential problems of foreseeability and causation". However, he clearly did not rule out the possibility of liability in such circumstances and it would seem there must come a point where the employee is being put under such pressure that any reasonable employer would realise there was a risk of illness regardless of whether the employee complains or whether an opt-out agreement has been signed.

It is difficult to assess the impact of the *Walker* decision because successful claims of

---

[8] [1995] I.R.L.R. 35.
[9] The important point appeared to be that no other area officers had suffered illness and the employer could not have foreseen that the plaintiff was exposed to any greater risk than anyone else. However, this reasoning must be questionable. Liability in negligence is normally established if the risk of harm can be shown to have been reasonably foreseeable. There seems little justification for requiring a plaintiff to show that he or she was clearly at special risk of illness.
[10] For a recent case where the employer was held liable for physical injuries caused by negligence in failing to give proper rest breaks see *Alexander v. Midland Bank plc* [2000] I.C.R. 464.

this kind tend to be settled and their details kept private by means of confidentiality clauses in settlement agreements. Nonetheless the case clearly gives the worker who suffers illness as a result of workplace stress the possibility of substantial redress. The Council involved in the *Walker* case was reported to have paid out between £175,000 and £200,000 once liability was established.

4–14   There are however a number of features in the *Walker* case which may be peculiar to it.

1. The trial judge did recognise that every case has to be put into context. He also recognised that professional work is intrinsically demanding and stressful and therefore never easy to ascertain at what point the employer's duty to take protective steps is engaged. Here though, clear warning signs had been given.

2. Working at the social services is inherently stressful.

3. Stress is likely to affect the field workers, particularly in relation to child abuse cases and also those like Walker who would have to make decisions in relation to field work cases.

4. The media expert witnesses all acknowledged that social work could be of a stressful nature; two had had experience specifically of social workers who had developed psychiatric illnesses as a result of their work.

5. The sheer volume of work in this context could cause stress to a normally robust person but the stress might also develop because the character of the work was especially stressful.

6. There were also particular features about the way Walker's job was operated in practice:

    (a) The case conference system was a difficulty, on the evidence, combining the note taking and decision making role that he had to play; and
    (b) The structure and manning of the management of the social services department in Northumberland is onerous to him.

7. The judge was also satisfied that Walker's superior was aware that social work is stressful; that childcare work in particular could cause considerable anxiety; and that staff in Blythe Valley Area were operating on a crisis management basis. He also realised that social services in Northumberland were both understaffed and inadequately organised and that Walker as a manager had a growing sense of grievance that nothing was being done; that he must have known that Walker believed that unless steps were taken which would have the effect of making more staff available within two years and removing the current problems from him, he would not be able to carry on managing the area.

4–15   In summary, the question of reasonable foreseeability makes the difficulties an employee faces in pinning the blame for his mental condition on his employer immense. The reason Mr Walker's employer was found liable for this was because Mr Walker had suffered a nervous breakdown in 1986 and had thereby put his employer on notice that he was predisposed to illness attributable to the impact of work on his personality.

The *Walker* case, therefore indicates it will be easier to show that a risk was reasonably foreseeable if the employee has previously suffered work-related psychiatric illness. However, given a growing awareness of the risks of stress at work, it cannot be assumed that this will always be the case. The case therefore emphasises again that employers must keep abreast of relevant statutory and advisory guidance.

The *Beverley Lancaster* Case

4–16 In a recently decided case, *Beverley Lancaster v. Birmingham City Council*,[11] Birmingham City Council admitted liability for a work-related psychiatric illness. Although there is an admission of liability in the case and therefore the case creates no law on the issue of merit, the court was allowed to assess damages for Beverley Lancaster's injury.

It was found that she had suffered and continued to suffer from a very unpleasant psychiatric condition specific to her work environment, necessitating her to take anti-depressants. It was held that the prognosis for recovery was good in the future, particularly as her home environment was satisfactory, but the court and therefore the general damages (for distress as such) were limited to £12,000. However, as far as loss of future earnings were concerned, it was found that but for ill-health, she would have continued to be employed at the housing officer grade, working part-time until September 2001 and full-time thereafter until the age of 60. Therefore she would have enjoyed the full benefits of working over that period including pension rights earned. The loss until August 2004 at which point childcare costs would cease was agreed at £13,908.03. A further award was made for loss of future pension rights. The total damages payable by the council were therefore £67,041.91.

The *Randy Ingham* Case

4–17 More recently, Mr Randy Ingham received £203,000 in an out of court settlement from Worcestershire County Council after he retired from his job as a relief warden on 16 gypsy sites. He left his job on the grounds of ill health caused by stress leading to a nervous breakdown. Apparently he was on one occasion shot at and frequently threatened and verbally abused by members of the gypsy community.

Walker in Context

4–18 However, it must be emphasised that the *Walker* case is the only case of significance where liability was actually decided by the court (as opposed to an admission being made (also in the last two cases mentioned, where settlements resulted)) and it is a special one. Unless the employer admits liability in these circumstances, it will be very much for the plaintiff to show very special circumstances such as existed in the *Walker* case.

In *Maryniak v. Thomas Cook Group Limited*[12] it was held that even a deliberate attempt by a regional manager to destroy a junior manager's career (had such an attempt happened, which it did not) would not have made an alleged consequential psychiatric illness foreseeable under the foreseeability test in *Walker*.

It was held that it was for the claimant to show that there was a duty of care; demonstrate the standard of care required; show that the standard had been breached; and, demonstrate foreseeability and causation. It was clear that an employer could be liable for damage to an employee's mental health and that there was a duty of care. But

---

[11] [1999] 6 Q.R. 4.
[12] Unreported, October 26, 1998.

there were always going to be extremely difficult evidential problems of foreseeability and causation in respect of psychiatric damage allegedly resulting from the volume or organisation of work. The injury that was likely to follow from a breach must be such as a reasonable man would contemplate. The existence of some risk was an ordinary incident of life even when all due care had been taken.

4–19 In *Petch v. Customs and Excise Commissioners*,[13] Petch, who joined the civil service in 1961, had a mental breakdown in 1974. In 1975, after his return to work, he was transferred as assistant secretary to the Department of Health and Social Security. In 1983 he fell ill again but was able to work until 1986 when he was retired from the civil service on medical grounds. He made a claim for injury benefit under the civil service pension scheme on the grounds that his breakdown had been caused by pressure of work. This was rejected. He then brought an action for damages for negligence. Part of his claim concerned allegations that the employer had not provided proper information to assess his claim. At the appeal stage his claim was rejected. Also, the Court of Appeal rejected his claim that he had a claim for damages concerning the employer's failure to prevent his illness. It was held that it had not been shown on the evidence that the customs and excise commissioners' senior management were aware or ought to have been aware in 1974 that the plaintiff was showing signs of his impending breakdown or that his workload carried a real risk of breakdown and had not acted negligently following his return to work, they had not been in breach of their admitted duty to take reasonable care to ensure that the duties allocated to him did not damage his health and therefore his action failed.

And there are other cases, apart from *Petch* (discussed above) where the employee's claim did not succeed.

4–20 In *Panting v. Whitbread plc*[14] (Gloucester County Court) the plaintiff claimed damages for psychiatric injury due to his employment as a pub manager with Whitbreads. He contended that his wife and his staff at the pub were subjected to violence, threats, theft, burglary, attempted burglary and other offensive conduct. He contended that such conduct caused him to suffer permanent psychiatric illness in the nature of reactive anxiety/depression akin to post-traumatic stress disorder as a result of which he was no longer able to work. He said that the brewery knew that the pub was difficult and did not give him special training or warning about this. Eventually his employment was terminated due to sickness.

The County Court dismissed his claim on the basis that his pre-morbid personality was not significantly more vulnerable than that of the average person; that he was sufficiently qualified to run the pub without formal training due to his experience running other licensed premises and his army background (his successful interview persuaded the brewery that no formal training was necessary); it was reasonable for the brewery to ask him to run the pub despite its difficulties; he was aware of the brewery's employee assistance programme and the grievance and other internal management programmes; he did not fully inform the brewery of the incidence of assault; he never made a formal request for transfer; there was insufficient notice to the brewery that he had a personal health problem. The brewery had in place a comprehensive set of arrangements aimed at protecting managers suffering as he was and therefore the brewery had not failed to take reasonable steps to prevent the onset of his illness. He had not put his concerns in writing at any time during his employment and therefore the brewery had done everything it reasonably could.

4–21 In the Australian case of *Gillespie v. Commonwealth of Australia* a claim by

---

[13] [1993] I.C.R. 789.
[14] Unreported, November 24, 1998.

an employee of the department of foreign affairs and trade whose health broke down after being sent to the a diplomatic mission in Caracas, Venezuela, failed. He was eventually repatriated to Australia after his breakdown and retired from the public service on medical grounds but he claimed that this was the responsibility of his employer in posting to Venezuela where living conditions caused him hardship and not informing him of the conditions he was likely to face in not relieving him of the various stresses.

What Gillespie complained about was failure to protect him from such hardships in Venezuela as the:

- Necessity to bribe customs officials;

- Necessity to face threats of personal violence from customs officials;

- Necessity to be subjected to long periods of personal abuse whilst dealing with public service officials including airport officials whilst waiting to clear air freight bags;

- Personal violence in the streets of Caracas;

- Difficulties in obtaining medical assistance in the case of emergency;

- Necessity to engage in arguments with hotel staff regarding reservations even after written confirmation of reservations has been obtained;

- Difficulty for members of his family in visiting friends in Caracas due to transport difficulties;

- High incidence of street assaults and robberies leading to the inability to allow his children to go outside the front garden of the house they lived in without an escort;

- Necessity to go long periods without water because terrorists bombed the Caracas water supply leading to the necessity to move from the house in which he lived with his family into a hotel until the water supply had been fixed;

- Inability to engage in many social functions because of the impossibility of obtaining satisfactory babysitters;

- Unavailability of inexpensive sporting and other recreational facilities; and

- High cost of living forcing him to live beyond his means.

This resulted in his anxiety state for which he claimed damages.

It was held by the court that regard must be had to whether it was reasonably foreseeable that the plaintiff or a person in the plaintiff's position might be subject to some sort of psychological decompensation beyond the difficulties and stresses which most officers would ordinarily be prone in the circumstance which prevailed in Caracas at the time of the plaintiffs service.

The discharge of the employer's duties to take reasonable care for the safety of its employees required that any such officer posted to Caracas be given some preparation beyond that which was appropriate to less stressful posts. It would therefore have been unreasonable to withhold from the plaintiff information that this was a new post with difficulties as great, if not greater, than any other Australian diplomatic post.

In view of the remoteness of the possibility that an officer would be subject to such an extreme reaction as that of the plaintiff however, reasonableness did not require the defendant to give more than the most general warning and a description of the circumstances which would render it difficult to cope with the conditions.

Anyway, such a warning or description was unlikely on the facts to have deterred the plaintiff from applying for or accepted the post in Caracas and hence was unlikely to have averted the damage of which he complained.

4–22 The final case in this series is perhaps the most robust. In a Scottish case *Rorrison v. West Lothian College*,[15] Rorrison, a welfare nurse employed by the College sought damages from the College on the grounds that she had suffered psychological damage comprising severe anxiety and depression, panic attacks and lack of self-confidence and self-esteem resulting from the conduct of her manager. She argued that her line manager and therefore her employer, should have known there was a serious risk of her mental and psychological health being damaged.

Dismissing her action, the outer house of the Court of Sessions held that there was no indication on the facts, that she had suffered from a recognised psychiatric illness or had to be treated by a psychiatrist. She had not proved any disorder recognised by the major diagnostic classification systems.

Robustly, Lord Reed said:

> "To suffer with such emotion and others such as stress, anxiety, loss of confidence and low mood from time to time not least because of problems at work was a normal part of human experience. It was only if they were liable to be suffered to such a psychological degree as to constitute a psychiatric disorder that a duty of care to protect against them could arise. That was not a reasonably foreseeable occurrence unless there was some specific reason to foresee it in a particular case. Such was not the case here."

4–23 Although the Working Time Regulations do not have any direct relevance to the *Walker* decision, they may nevertheless have an influence on the development of liability in this area. In the first place, the Regulations have helped to increase awareness of the health implications of long hours and for that reason alone the number of *Walker* type claims may rise. Secondly, the record keeping requirements imposed by the Regulations may actually assist an employee in proving that his illness was caused by his pattern of work (although the abolition of the requirement to keep detailed records where a worker agrees to opt-out of the 48-hour week is clearly a blow to claimants in this respect). Finally, employers may try to absolve themselves from liability by arguing that workers who have opted-out of the 48-hour week have voluntarily assumed the risk of injury. Whether such an argument would succeed is very doubtful, not least because in the *Johnstone* case referred to above, all three judges accepted that it was at least arguable that section 2(1) of the Unfair Contract Terms Act 1977 prevents an employer from relying on any contractual term to restrict liability in negligence. No doubt this reasoning could be applied equally to opt-out agreements at least where these are contractually binding.

STATUTORY EMPLOYMENT RIGHTS

4–24 The final way in which the courts have started to take account of the detrimental effect of long working hours is in connection with statutory employment rights. This is significant because in some cases this will provide the employee with a financial remedy *before* he succumbs to illness—which is not possible under the

---

[15] [2000] S.C.R.L. 245.

Walker approach. So for example in *Whitbread Plc v. Gullyes*[16] the Respondent was promoted to the position of store manager even though the employer knew she did not have the requisite experience. Her working week averaged 76 hours and she was not given enough staff to do her job properly. The final straw came when two of her most experienced staff were transferred to other branches. She resigned and claimed constructive dismissal. The EAT upheld the tribunal's decision that she had been unfairly dismissed. In their view the employers were in breach of an implied term not to behave in such a way as to make it difficult or impossible for the employee to carry out her contract. Alternatively, if they were mistaken on this point then the employers were in breach of the implied term of trust and confidence. Clearly the long hours worked by the employee were not the only relevant factors in this case. However, if the EAT were correct in their view that an employer is in fundamental breach of contract if it makes it extremely difficult, although not impossible, for the employee to fulfil the contract this raises the possibility that an employee required to work such long hours that he or she cannot function efficiently, may be able to claim constructive dismissal before he suffers any injury. It is not clear how any agreement to work long hours (such as an "opt-out" agreement) would affect this decision, although it is possible that such an agreement would be overridden by the implied terms in the contract including the duty to care for the employee's safety (as proposed by Stuart Smith L.J. in the *Johnstone* case).

4–25   An alternative approach was seen in *Thorn v. Agyei*.[17] In that case a security guard was found to be drunk on duty and was dismissed on account of being unfit for work. He claimed unfair dismissal, arguing that in the four of the five weeks prior to the incident he had worked an average of 18 hours a day, seven days a week. In the two weeks prior to the dismissal he had worked 20 hours a day. He therefore argued that the employer had acted unreasonably in dismissing him on the night in question. The employment tribunal agreed, stating that because of his exhaustion the employee would not have been fit for work even if sober. The EAT upheld that decision, emphasising that it had been appropriate to take into account the hours worked by the employee in the weeks leading up to the dismissal. Presumably if the applicant in *Thorn* had resigned and claimed constructive dismissal on the basis of his long hours there was a good chance that following the *Gullyes* case he would have succeeded. However, as *Thorn* shows even though he did not do this and actually aggravated the situation by being drunk on duty, the court was still prepared to recognise the serious impact of his working hours and to find his dismissal was unfair.[18]

CONCLUSION

4–26   Although the Working Time Regulations will have a major impact on the organisation of working time in this country, the role of the courts and the Employment Appeal Tribunal in adapting the common law and existing statutory remedies to prevent the exploitation of employees should not be underestimated. Judicial developments in these areas will continue to be important not least because in the short term many employees will not be covered by the Regulations. Such case law

---

[16] EAT 478/92.
[17] EAT 50/92.
[18] Oppressive working hours may also give rise to a discrimination claim. So, for example an employee may be able to show that a particular shift system amounts to indirect sex discrimination under the Sex Discrimination Act 1975 or disability discrimination contrary to the Disability Discrimination Act 1995. In neither case is it necessary to show that the pattern of work has led to physical or mental illness, although compensation may be awarded for such injury in appropriate cases.

will also be relevant to workers covered by the Regulations—particularly if abuse of opt-out agreements leads to health problems. Employers would therefore be unwise to assume that an opt-out agreement renders them immune from liability for long working hours and should try to address any problems of overwork long before injury to health occurs.

CHAPTER FIVE

Working Time and the Atypical Labour Market

INTRODUCTION

5–01   The Working Time Directive was introduced as a health and safety measure. It has been argued that the structure of work can be related to employees' health.[1] In this chapter we look at the patterns and growth of job market flexibility and consider the impact of flexible working patterns on the employment relationship.

One of the more notable trends in employment practice over recent years has been the increasing introduction of atypical working patterns. The drive for increasing competitiveness as companies become more global in scope has gone hand in hand with new human resource strategies resulting from a perceived need to increase employee flexibility through the introduction of working patterns which in some cases enable the employer to deploy its human resources in the most effective way.[2] Perhaps the most obvious example of this trend is the practice of introducing annualised hours which we discuss below. Not all flexible working patterns operate in the ostensible interest of the employer. For example flexi-time (also discussed below) would not, of itself, appear to directly benefit the employer because apart from certain core hours the employee is free to come and go as he or she pleases. It might be argued that the benefits of flexi-time and other employee driven flexible working patterns do, however, benefit the employer through producing more satisfied employees; employees who feel that they have some control over the way in which their work is undertaken and who therefore perceive themselves as more than merely a part of the employer's resources.

5–02   Some would say that the term "flexibility" has been used historically as a euphemism for a process under which the managers of an organisation have the ability (whether through the contract of employment or otherwise) to organise employees in a way which best suits the interest of the organisation at the expense of the interests (and possibly the well-being) of the employees. Management in the United Kingdom does not have a particularly good history of introducing flexible working patterns painlessly. On the other hand it is true to say that trade unions historically have been slow to accept the benefits of flexibility for employees and have often held out against flexible working arrangements as a matter of principle rather than being based upon any sound need for protection of their members' interests.

It is almost certainly true that some management practices have been purely exploitative but this is far from the entire picture. It is clear that in many organisations flexible working arrangements work to the mutual benefit of the employer and the employee. One has only to consider the widespread use of "flexi-time" in the public

---

[1] See for example: "New Rights, New Responsibilities for a New Safety World", TUC, November 1996.
[2] For a fuller discussion on globalisation see: 'The globalisation of human resource management', January 2000 E.I.R.R. 312, 21.

sector to realise the significant benefit some flexible working arrangements can provide, particularly for example for working parents.

5–03   In a study of labour market trends[3] the issue of flexible working arrangements was examined. Almost 20 per cent of respondents said that they were working under flexible arrangements. The flexible working arrangements identified were:

- Flexible working hours;

- Term-time working;

- Annualised hours;

- 4½-day week;

- Job sharing;

- Zero hours contracts; and

- Nine-day fortnight.

It is quite interesting to look at the split between male and female employees within these statistics. 15.4 per cent of men said that they were working flexible arrangements. This figure increases to 23.8 per cent for women. Some of the difference between the figures for men and women is undoubtedly accounted for by the fact that women still traditionally have the burden of childcare and are therefore more likely to request an atypical work pattern. However that cannot account for all of the difference because when looked at as separate categories the percentage of women with dependant children who work flexible arrangements is 28.6 per cent compared with 20.7 per cent for women without dependant children. The bulk of the difference is almost certainly accounted for by the very nature of the employment in which women find themselves.

5–04   Taking all respondents into account the figures for flexible working arrangements were as follows:

- Flexible working hours   9.5%;
- Term-time working   4.4%;
- Annualised hours   2.8%;
- 4½-day week   1.8%;
- Job sharing   0.9%;
- Zero hours contracts   0.5%;
- Nine-day fortnight   0.3%.

Perhaps the surprising statistic here is the fact that almost 3 per cent of respondents worked an annualised hours contract, nearly three times as many as working job sharing arrangements. Again the picture is complex but some of this will undoubtedly be explained by the fact that job sharing arrangements tend to be undertaken on a case by case basis whereas the introduction of annualised hours tends to be across whole sectors within a business or indeed across the whole of a business.

Here then is the first area of flexibility. It is the nature of the overall employment

---

[3] Labour Market, October 1999.

relationship which is "flexible". Here we mean anything which moves away from the traditional full-time five- or six-day working week where individuals work a set pattern of working hours. It is the structure of the employment relationship which is, to a greater or a lesser extent, flexible. We shall look at these flexible working arrangements in more detail below.

The second area of flexibility is flexibility within the employment contract itself. Here we shall be looking at clauses relating to flexibility in job descriptions, in working time where the standard pattern of full-time working applies and in other terms and conditions of employment. A detailed discussion of these issues appears below.

We turn first therefore to a brief examination of the reasons for the growth in flexible working and of different types of flexibility from an organisational perspective.

REASONS FOR GROWTH IN FLEXIBLE WORKING

The home/work balance

5–05   The flexible working arrangements described above have emerged as being the principal types of flexible working arrangements. There are many others. For example, different shift systems, different lengths of working week, allowing employees to choose whether they work only nights or only days or whether there is a rotating pattern, different annualised hours systems. All have been tried with greater or lesser success in a variety of different industries.

5–06   In the early years of flexible working arrangements it was undoubtedly true that the impulse to introduce flexible working patterns came from employers wishing to deal with such things as seasonal working. However more recently the introduction of flexible working arrangements has been used defensively by employers to head off claims for much shorter working weeks or different sorts of flexibility which, in particular, trade unions have been pressing for in order to help reduce what they see as the pressure on employees to balance home and work. This pressure has been given impetus by the Working Time Directive (and to some extent by the Working Time Regulations) where the concept of humanisation would seem to be important and where adapting work to the worker is the principle rather than asking the worker to be more adaptable.[4] One example is Rolls Royce in Bristol which introduced a shorter working week of 37 hours having first promoted a nine-day fortnight in order to head off demands for a 4½ day working week across the board. In the public sector and in certain hi-tech businesses homeworking is becoming more common, although that in itself creates tremendous difficulties from a management and administrative perspective.

Another example is Playtex in Port Glasgow which has introduced a 38½ hour working week spread over four days. All employees therefore have a three-day weekend, Friday to Sunday. Full-time workers start at 8.45 a.m. and work until 5.45 p.m. Part-time workers have different start and finish times. Apparently the system works well and is extremely popular even though the longer days are tiring. The set-off is a longer weekend which is extremely popular according to the GMB Union. There are many other examples of flexible working. In practice, however, one thing is clear:

---

[4] For a full account of the following examples see: "Flexible Friends?" Case studies of Positive Workplace Flexibility: TUC, April 1998. For a discussion of the "humanisation principle" and Regulation 8, see Chapter 7, paras 7–20 to 7–25.

that in order to introduce such flexibility there must be a business advantage and the employees must see some benefit.

Age

5–07   The difficulty of an ageing population has been exercising the minds of policy makers, both domestically and in Europe, and academics for some time.[5]

In 1999 the labour force numbered some 28.6 million. Those who were aged 55 and over amounted to 3.6 million. It is estimated that by the year 2015 more than 40 per cent of people of working age in the United Kingdom will in fact be over the age of 50.

Furthermore, in 1975 around 95 per cent of those aged between 55 and 65 were still working. In 1999 the figure is slightly less than 60 per cent.[6]

There would appear therefore to be a vast pool of resources consisting of men and women over the age of 50 who either have retired or who cannot get work because of arguably age discrimination. Flexible working for this group may be particularly attractive. Perhaps semi-retirement is the answer. If, as many predict, the early years of the new century will see skills shortages employers will have to consider first trying to keep or entice back to the work place workers who are more mature and couple that with an open mind about working arrangements for this group. This may be no small task. Something like 18.5 million people feel that they have been discriminated against on the grounds of age in one or more aspects of their life and some eight million people report age discrimination in employment. This cultural phenomenon will have to be met head on to meet the challenge of employment in an ageing population.

Job security

5–08   The question of job security (or perhaps job insecurity) is global. It is not just in the United Kingdom where employees feel insecure in their work. Recent work by the Organisation for Economic Co-Operation and Development (OECD) suggests that in fact there has been little change in the length of time which employees spend in a job although that time certainly does vary across countries, occupations, gender and industries. On the other hand, there is a general view shared amongst workers that the world is a less secure place than it used to be and in particular that jobs are less secure.

It would seem that employees perceive the security of their job as being related in some way to individual well-being and also related to how well they perceive the economy to be doing in general terms. Job security is also related to how quickly pay is rising and to related factors such as consumer spending.

For individual organisations job security is significant because it can impact upon human resource management. For example, if a work force feels insecure in their employment they may be less inclined to work hard, to train more and morale may suffer. It is accepted that there is a contrary view which is that workers who feel insecure are more likely to work hard in order to convince the employer to continue to employ them but studies tend to suggest that employees do not in fact operate in this way.

5–09   Does the perception of employees regarding job security reflect reality? Job security can be measured by looking at length of service and retention rates (although

---

[5] See for example: 'Ageing of the Labour Force in OECD Countries: Economic and Social Consequences: Peter Aver and Mariange's Fortyny, ILO 2000; 'Age Diversity in Employment', Helen J. Desmond, Industrial Law Journal, Vol. 28 No. 2, June 1999; E.U. Council Resolution on the employment of Older Workers, June 29, 1995, O.J.E.C. 228, 2.9.95 pp. 1–3 and E.U. Council Resolution of flexible retirement arrangements, June 30, 1993, O.J.E.C. 188, 10.7.93 pp. 1–2.

[6] Employers Forum on Age, 1999, obtainable at www.eja.org.uk.

it is stressed that the perception of security is more complex). An organisation which has low turnover and a high percentage of staff who have been employed for a relatively long time will certainly be perceived as being in an environment where job security obtains. Conversely, an organisation with a high percentage of recent recruits with high turnover is likely to be one where there is a pervasive feeling of insecurity. One only has to cast one's mind back to the financial boom of the 1980s where there was a general perception that people would be employed in very highly remunerated work in the City but would burn out after only two or three years to recall a period where there was apparent financial success coupled with a feeling of insecurity.

There seems to be no doubt however that over the last perhaps 20 years employment relationships have become much more fragile. This has almost certainly reflected a change in the structure of work from traditional manufacturing to a much more service-based economy where relatively low skills may be required (there are exceptions in the high-tech sector). The fact that skills are in short demand may also lead to lower retention rates as employees with high skills are in more demand and are therefore more likely to move employment on a regular basis. This in turn may have led to the increased use of agency workers, sub-contractors, casual workers, and so forth which may in turn have a knock-on effect for permanent staff numbers. In this downward spiral employees who perceive that their employer may not replace permanent staff but may sub-contract the work—who perceive that the employer is not necessarily loyal to the workforce—will themselves have reduced loyalty and commitment.

5–10 The OECD research suggests that there are wide variations in length of service between countries. In 1995 the average length of service in 23 countries was ten years but in some countries the length of service was considerably shorter. The OECD say that even when the statistics are weighted to take account of differences in labour markets there has been little change in the overall pattern.

It is also the case that retention rates do not seem to have changed significantly over the five years to 1995.

However, against the background of stable length of service and retention rates there is still a reported increase in perceptions of job insecurity. How can this be explained?

The explanation appears to be that the perception that a worker has about the security of their employment does not relate to overall statistics but to how they feel generally about the economy and how they perceive economic performance. Certainly in 1995 when this research was carried out there was a general increase in unemployment in the developed world and even though, in general terms, length of service and retention rates had not changed significantly, nevertheless the perception was that people were more than likely to lose their job than had been the case years before.

5–11 The analogy here is with the oil tanker; once the brakes have been applied it takes some time before the tanker stops. It will take a significant period of sustained economic success in any particular economy to change individuals' perceptions of job security. This of course may be to say no more than what is really important to the perception of job security is the "feel good factor".

FLEXIBLE WORKING HOURS ("FLEXI-TIME")

5–12 The standard model of flexi-time working requires an employee to undertake core hours: hours when he or she is required to be at work around which the employee is able to start and finish work as they choose within certain parameters.

So for example the employer may require the employee to be at work between the hours of 10 a.m. to 12 noon and from 2 p.m. to 4 p.m. Within that and subject to the employee working a standard week (35 hours, for example) the employee may start work at any time between say 7 a.m. and 10 a.m. and may leave any time after 4 p.m. The employee is entitled to take lunch of say one hour at any time between 12 noon and 2 p.m.

A slight variation on this is that if the employee works longer than a standard, say, 7½ hour day, the extra time is banked and can be used by the employee to take extra holiday. In some cases this is limited to a maximum of say one extra day per month, thus preventing an employee from building up vast amounts of holiday in the first half of a year only to then take three months off at the end of the year.

5–13 Flexi-time of this sort may be particularly important for those with childcare or similar responsibilities and because the individual is always obliged to work the standard week such a system tends not to be abused. No doubt this can create some difficulty. For example, colleagues may wish to have a meeting at 8 a.m. but they may not be able to guarantee that all of those who need to attend that meeting start work at the same time. In practice this would not appear to present any great difficulty. Employees working this system simply ensure that if they do have to start work earlier than they normally would they leave earlier than they normally would or bank the time. It is easy to see why flexi-time is attractive to employees. Furthermore, provided the employer manages the working time effectively and provided that it gets its core hours and standard working week correct, there should be no difficulty for the employer.

ANNUALISED HOURS CONTRACTS

5–14 Annualised hours contracts are a relatively recent phenomenon. Many employers who use or are considering annualised hours contracts believe that such an arrangement allows maximum flexibility with the workforce.

Traditional contracts of employment specify a normal working week in terms of numbers of hours and of course imposed upon that regime are the Working Time Regulations. This standard working week takes account of holiday entitlement with both annual holiday and statutory holidays.

However, there are many employments in which work is exceptionally seasonal. One has only to think of the tourism industry and those industries heavily dependant upon specific times of the year such as Christmas to realise that through no fault of the employer there can be periods of exceptionally high demand and indeed exceptionally low demand for their goods and services.

5–15 Where business fluctuates (but not *in extremis)* it is possible to cater for variations by adopting a standard working pattern but allowing for overtime or perhaps shift working during peak periods. In such a case contracts of employment would be drafted to enable the employer either to insist upon overtime or to offer it with the assumption that sufficient staff will wish to work overtime to cover periods of excess demand.

Annualised hours contracts operate on the basis that employees are given a total number of hours to be worked in one year. Employees are paid on the basis of a national standard week but otherwise the employer is free to organise the working hours (this may be subject to imposing a maximum and one must always bear in mind the Working Time Regulations here[7]) as it sees fit.

5–16   Such working arrangements are not without contractual difficulty. What, for example, would the position be in an annualised hours contract which was silent on the question of overtime pay?[8] Say for example an individual has to work 1,400 hours per year and the contract states merely that if they work longer than 1,400 hours per year they will receive pay at an overtime rate of 1.5. What happens to people who join or leave the organisation part way through the year? They may work on average longer than the standard week but may not exceed (indeed are very unlikely to exceed) the maximum working hours in the year. As we shall see below courts have in recent years been quite keen to impose terms and conditions on the employment relationship where contracts are silent. In such a case a court may well decide it can imply a term either that overtime is not payable unless and until the 1,400 hours threshold has been reached or, alternatively, that an employee is entitled to notionally average out the number of hours they have worked and if on average that comes to more than the standard working week (in terms of hours) during any particular week, they are entitled to the appropriate overtime rate for the number of excess hours worked. It is much better for the contract to cover the point. For example the contract could state expressly that workers who leave or join partway through a year are not entitled to overtime unless and until they reach the annual threshold. Alternatively the contract could state that the employees in such circumstances have a pro rated threshold or any other variation which suits the employer. What the employer should not do is leave it to chance because, as discussed above, over the past few years the courts have been very keen to fill the gaps left by poorly drafted contracts of employment.

The same principles would apply to every employment benefit which accrued during the course of a year—for example holidays, perhaps bonuses and commissions, rights in relation to sickness benefits and so on.

5–17   It is also incumbent upon the employer to consider the effect of annualised hours on such matters as health and safety. It is clear that the prime motivation for shifting to annualised hours is to avoid overtime payments where productivity tends to arrive in peaks and troughs based on perhaps seasonal demand. Inevitably one of the consequences will be long working hours during peak periods. This may involve long shifts with the inevitable claims about employee stress and fatigue. An employer has a duty both at common law and under health and safety legislation to ensure that the system and methods of work are safe and this will include working patterns. An employer will disregard these at its peril.

Furthermore, employers must consider the impact of changing work patterns on certain employees. It is possible that particular employees will prefer to work regular hours in order that, for example, they can properly organise childcare arrangements. It will not be a simple matter in such circumstances simply to impose changes to work patterns because there will be an inevitable tension between the employer's needs and those of the particular employees.[9]

---

[7] Note that Regulation 23(b) Working Time Regulations allows the average weekly working time limit under Regulation 4 to be applied over a reference period of 52 weeks, for objective or technical reasons or reasons concerning the organisation of work, by means of a collective or workforce agreement. See Chapter 4 and 13.

[8] See for example: *Ali v. Christian Salvesen Food Services Limited* [1995] I.R.L.R. 624 EAT and [1997] I.R.L.R. 17, CA.

[9] See for example *London Underground v. Edwards* (No. 2) [1998] I.R.L.R. 364, CA.

TERM-TIME WORKING

5–18 This is exactly what it says. Employees work only during term-time. During holiday unpaid leave is taken although pay is spread across the year. This is of course particularly helpful to those with childcare responsibilities.

JOB SHARING

5–19 This is one of the oldest forms of flexible working and very often arises in circumstances where a maternity leave returner wishes to come back to work but not on a full-time basis. In some cases the employer, because of the nature of the work, cannot accommodate one part-time worker in the job. The employer here argues that there is a full-time job which requires to be done on a full-time basis. However in many cases that full-time job can be undertaken by more than one person (usually two people) and therefore someone can share the job with the maternity leave returner. Again it is suggested that these arrangements are most prevalent in the public sector.

Provided that the handover from one employee to another in these circumstances is managed there would appear to be no significant difficulty, particularly with regard to the terms and conditions of employment which are simply pro rated (and would have to be both in terms of sex discrimination—most part-time employees are of course female—and because of the effect of the Part-Time Workers (Prevention of Less Favourable Treatment) Regulations[10]).

FOUR-AND-A-HALF DAY WEEK

5–20 Typically this involves a normal working week. However the employees finish early on one of those days (usually Friday).

NINE-DAY FORTNIGHT

5–21 Under these arrangements individual employees take one day off per fortnight (usually every other week) leading to an alternating pattern of five day and four day working.

ZERO HOURS CONTRACTS

5–22 This is one of the most controversial flexible working patterns to emerge in recent years where a new shift pattern was held to amount to unlawful (indirect) sex discrimination. The principle is simple—employees are not contracted to work any particular hours but are merely contracted to work as and when the employer requires it over a set pattern. Here the employee only actually gets paid when they in fact work. This may sound fine in principle. However, in the most extreme form of zero hours contracts, the employer makes employees attend at the workplace for the whole of the working day (or the relevant shift period) but only pay them when they are actually called into work. For example, if restaurant staff were idle during a slack period, notwithstanding the fact that they were at work, they were not paid. If they were busy during lunch and actually had to be cooking or serving or clearing tables they were paid. This led to people being at work for very long periods but being actually paid for

---

[10] S.I. 2000/1551, in force from July 1, 2000.

relatively short periods (and, indeed, at low rates of pay) and caused something of an outcry.

5–23   In a recent survey[11] of 173 respondents to a questionnaire about zero hours working some 21 per cent of employers who responded reported employing people on a zero hours basis which, as the report points out, is a substantial minority.

The survey confirmed what is the commonly held view in this area, that zero hours contracts are apparently restricted in the main to the service sector. Flexibility in manufacturing tends to relate to shift working, annualised hours, and so forth. The majority sector was retail and wholesale in which 52 per cent of the employees on zero hours contracts were employed. The survey suggested that the range of employment covered by zero hours contracts was everything from low-skilled clerical work through to sales representatives, delivery drivers and packing staff. However in some cases (particularly in the health sector and local government) zero hours contracts were filled by skilled and professional employees including doctors, dieticians, physiotherapists, library assistants, teachers, and so on.

For the employer the zero hours contract was ultimately flexible. Employees were on tap but did not cost anything unless and until work was undertaken by them. Indeed the most common reasons cited for introducing zero hours contracts included flexibility and planning and cost savings. Typically many zero hours contracts would contain no contractual rights or benefits beyond wages, for example including no right to sick pay or holiday pay.

5–24   Of course the National Minimum Wage Act 1998 and National Minimum Wage Regulations 1999 have effectively brought an end to the abuses of the most extreme form of zero hours contract, under which the worker was paid only for those hours during which actual duties were being performed but not for simply being in attendance at work. In these cases, workers would have to continually "clock" on and off and only be paid for the time when they were clocked on. This practice is no longer permissible as the employer must pay the worker the applicable minimum wage for all hours of unmeasured work. (See sections 1 and 2 of the Act and Regulation 18 and 27 of the National Minimum Wage Regulations.) Also, the national minimum wage is available to "workers" and not simply employees.

The legal issues are complex. It is clear that employers who use zero hours contracts and whose employees are on call believe that this gives the employer maximum flexibility because not only can that employer utilise his employees to his, the employer's, maximum financial benefit but it is also apparent that those same employers believe that the employees do not have and cannot obtain the normal rights and protections afforded to employees employed under traditional arrangements. Is this the case?

For some statutory rights (such as unfair dismissal, redundancy pay and so forth) it is crucial to determine whether the individual is employed under a contract of service or not. The first issue of course is whether there is in fact in existence a contract of employment between employees on zero hours and the employer.

Whether somebody working zero hours is in fact an employee may not be a simple matter to decide. It is possible that the individual is employed in the traditional sense but it is also possible that the individual is self-employed. A more subtle variation on the employment contract would suggest that the individual only becomes an employee when performing work.

5–25   Over the years the courts have identified a number of tests to determine the status of individuals *vis-à-vis* an employer. Suffice it to say that the court in assessing

---

[11] See: Flexible Working—Vol. II March 1997.

an individual's employment status will look at the totality of the relationship between employer and individual and will assess whether on the balance of probabilities the individual is an employee or not. Some of the crucial factors include how much control the employer has over the individual during work time, whether there is any mutuality of obligation between the employer and the individual, whether the individual is integrated into the employer's undertaking sufficiently to enable the individual to be called an employee (and a comparison with the employer's employees proper is inevitable) and whether the individual is under any economic risk in his or her relationship with the employer (the argument being that if the individual does have some element of economic risk imposed upon them, then there is a distance between that individual and the employer which does not appear to be the case with traditional employment where the individual is paid irrespective of whether work is available). In the context of employment agencies and temporary workers the Court of Appeal has held[12] that a temporary worker was entitled to be treated as an employee of an employment agency in respect of each assignment actually worked even if under the general arrangement between the worker and the agency, the worker was not entitled to be classified as an employee. In particular when the worker carried out his assignments the agency could dismiss, stipulate the hourly rate of pay and deduct pay for poor timekeeping, work, attitude or misconduct.

Another form of zero hours contract is the use of "casual" or "as required" labour, typically drawn from a "pool" or a "bank" of workers. These working relationships have been the subject of much case law in relation to the question of employment status. While it is possible (see *McMeechan v. Secretary of State for Employment* [1997] I.R.L.R. 353) to base employment status on the actual performance of work under these relationships—*i.e.* a single engagement—that will not assist in relation to those key employment rights (such as statutory redundancy payments and unfair dismissal) where length of service is a factor. The applicant would have to establish employment status under the general or global arrangement with the alleged employer. This can be difficult, as the following two cases demonstrate.

5–26   In *Carmichael v. National Power Plc*[13] Carmichael and Lees were employed as guides at a power station. They had worked for up to 25 hours per week for a period of six years. The relationship between Carmichael and National Power was on a casual basis and they worked "as required". The employment tribunal found as a matter of fact that National Power could not require the ladies to work; the ladies had the right to refuse. Whilst the employment tribunal found that the ladies were not self-employed they found also that they were not employed because there was a lack of mutuality of obligation. The issue before the tribunal was a narrow one and the tribunal was not asked to consider what was the status of the ladies, merely whether they were employed. In fact, the tribunal concluded that there was no evidence of a contract between the parties at all, since neither side had entered into any legal commitment to the other in particular, National Power were not obliged to offer work, nor were the applicants obliged to carry out any work offered to them. For example the employment tribunal did not consider whether the ladies were employees when they were in fact carrying out work although such a finding would have been of considerable interest. Indeed, it is inevitable that many such cases will leave crucial questions undecided because tribunals will be asked to determine as a preliminary issue the status of individuals *vis-à-vis* the employer and if the finding is that they were not employees that is sufficient to take any complaint out with the jurisdiction of the employment tribunal and it need concern itself no further with any outstanding issues.

---

[12] See *McMeechan v. Secretary of State for Employment* [1997] I.R.L.R. 353, CA.
[13] [2000] I.R.L.R. 43, HL.

In *Clark v. Oxfordshire Health Authority*[14] Mrs Clark a "bank" nurse was employed between 1991 and 1994. This employment was on what was referred to as a casual basis and no work was guaranteed. Mrs Clark did receive a statement of employment which set out some of the terms of her relationship with the Authority, including a grievance and disciplinary procedure. There were also terms relating to confidentiality and details of trade union membership.

5–27   In *Carmichael*, the tribunal, the EAT and the House of Lords considered that on the facts of the case the Company was not obliged to offer work, nor were the guides obliged to accept and perform any work offered to them. The Court of Appeal in that case reached a different conclusion, overturned by the House of Lords, that there was an obligation on the part of the company to offer a reasonable level of the available work to the two guides. This issue—whether there is mutuality of obligation to provide work on the one part and to perform it on the other—is often at the heart of these employment status disputes. In *Clark*, the tribunal concluded that there was no such obligation on either party on the facts of the case. Again, it must be stressed that the status of the worker when she actually performed work was not in issue. The EAT in *Clark* held that the lack of mutuality of obligation was a significant factor but was not decisive—it had to be seen in the context of the other terms of the contract. These other terms included repeated use of the word employment; superannuation scheme; a grievance and disciplinary procedure and a specific provision concerning dismissal. On these grounds the EAT found that a global employment contract existed. However, the Court of Appeal reversed the decision on the grounds that the facts as found by the tribunal could not support the existence of a global contract of employment covering the whole period of engagement as a bank nurse. There needed to be, as a minimum, an obligation on one side to accept and perform any work offered and on the other an obligation to pay a retainer during such period as work was not offered. The case was however resubmitted to the employment tribunal to determine whether there was at the time of dismissal a specific engagement, amounting to a contract of employment, of sufficient duration on which to base a claim of unfair dismissal.

Of these two cases, *Clark* is the most problematic, and illustrates best the inherent difficulties in combining flexible working patterns with social protections based on employment status. The relationship in *Clark* was much clearer than that in *Carmichael*, and on the face of it contained many of the features of an employment contract proper. But the very flexibility of the arrangement—the lack of any obligation when no work was actually being carried out—was fatal to the global employment contract argument. On this approach are left only with the slim hope of being able to show that they are employees when actually working and, even then, of assembling the necessary continuity of service under such specific engagements to gain access to statutory employment rights.

In the meantime employers cannot assume that individuals who work for them on the basis of a zero hours contract (even if that is not the label given to the relationship) or who are on-call or part of a bank of workers will not be employees and will need to ensure fair treatment in implementing for example dismissal or action short of dismissal.

5–28   Looked at from the perspective of flexibility versus security, one can see that in certain circumstances such an arrangement could benefit both the organisation and the worker. In other circumstances however the story may be quite the opposite.

Where individuals are relatively high earners with relatively scarce skills it may be

---

[14] [1998] I.R.L.R. 125, CA.

that because they are very likely to get regular well-paid work, because they are well-paid enough to organise their own pension and other "fringe benefits" and because they may enjoy the flexibility of not being tied to one employer, there may be significant advantages to having such self-employed status. On the other hand, where the work may be relatively low-skilled and where those skills are not scarce, circumstances may arise where although the organisation benefits from such a flexible arrangement (it simply can decide whether or not to call on the individuals to do work) the reality is that when called upon the individual is very likely to need work and therefore will have to do it. They may actually be dependent upon work from the organisation but have none of the benefits of employee status. Hence the argument that there is a group of second-class employees who have neither the benefits nor the security of permanent staff.

Out-working and Tele-working

5–29   This is the form of atypical work where the individual works from their home. The E.U. has already turned its sights on this form of atypical work and has proposed a directive regulating employers relationships both with contract workers and tele-workers. The Information Society which was set up to assess the impact of new technology on work patterns has urged the E.U. to take a closer look at protections for workers who are affected by technological change.

Of course, not all out-working or tele-working has resulted from technological change. Individuals have always worked from their home whether they be crofters or people filling envelopes. However, it is clear that new technologies and in particular of course remote communication via the telephone system and the internet is allowing increasingly sophisticated work to be carried out from home and the perception which is apparently becoming more common currency within the E.U. is that since such working relationships are on the increase, clearly such relationships need Regulation.

Indeed, and this refers to all of the types of atypical work which we have looked at in this chapter, the recent E.U. Green Paper "People First in the Information Society" stated that "waged employment and self-employment are converging, rendering the scope of labour law unclear and reducing its effectiveness [for] non-standard contracts, tele-work and outsourced work...".

5–30   Of course where tele-workers are providing easily measurable productive work, such as indeed stuffing envelopes, and where they are paid in relation to the amount of work produced, then to the largest extent the employer very much controls the relationship. Payment is provided for work done, the obligation on the employer being to provide the work. The position is more difficult where the nature of the work provided is less easily quantifiable—for example where traditionally office-based work is undertaken from the home. What then are the principal issues in respect of out-working?

5–31   The first issue is of course the exact nature of the relationship between employer and individual. We have already seen above that there is a considerable debate raging about whether individuals who are working on zero hours contracts or similar contracts are employees. The same argument applies in relation to outworkers. The significance of this cannot be over-emphasised. The definition of the relationship between the employer and the individual is crucial because of its impact upon not only the matters referred to above (rights to unfair dismissal and so forth) but also the individual's tax status and of course the employer's obligations *vis-à-vis* health and safety, another matter which, over the recent past the E.U. has become involved to a much greater degree.

Of course the relationship between the outworker and the employer can and ought to be determined by a reference to the contractual relations between them and it is incumbent upon the employer to ensure that the relationship is properly evidenced in appropriate documentation. Some of the matters to consider are set out below.

Place of Work

5–32   In an out-working arrangement, the employees normal principal place of work will of course be his or her home. However, the employer should consider including a requirement on the individual to attend the employer's normal place of work should the employer require it. This may be for a number of purposes, including training, disciplinary matters, general reporting purposes, and so forth. An employer must of course always be aware that such a requirement is not implemented in a manner which causes the employee difficulty in complying with the requirement, otherwise the employer may be accused of breaching mutual trust and confidence. Therefore, the employer may wish to implement such a requirement only on reasonable notice.[15]

Hours of Work

5–33   The individual tele-worker will have tremendous flexibility in determining his or her work pattern. Indeed, it may be extremely difficult for the employer to monitor the hours of work worked by the tele-worker, which may create tremendous difficulties in relation to the requirements of the Working Time Directive. Clearly the employer must ensure that contractually the employee does not work too many hours in relation to the Directive and Regulations but inevitably this will be difficult to monitor.

Furthermore, the employer may wish to include obligations on the employee to be available for telephone calls during certain times or perhaps for visits by the employer to the individual's home on a regular basis.

Employers' Property

5–34   In relation to what we might call traditional office-based work, the employer may be providing the out-worker with expensive equipment including computer hardware, software, modems, printer, and so forth. The employer must have the right to take this property back as and when required and the employer will want to ensure that it can enter the individual's home to retrieve that property. It should therefore be a contractual requirement that the employee allows the employer access on reasonable notice for these purposes. Furthermore, the employer will want to ensure that the equipment is properly insured at the employee's home and also that the home is properly secure. Clearly this may need to be at the employer's expense.

Health and Safety

5–35   All of the usual health and safety requirements apply to tele-workers as they do to the employer's employees who work at the employer's principal place of work except that there is no duty on the employer to maintain the place of work if that place of work is not under the control of that employer. On the other hand, the employer is still required to maintain safe equipment, safe systems of work, a safe working environment and so forth. Therefore any equipment which is provided at the employee's home must be properly installed, maintained and appropriate for the

---

[15] See: *United Bank Limited v. Akhtar* [1989] I.R.L.R. 507, EAT.

purpose. The employee must be trained sufficiently well to be able to use the equipment safely. It is also a requirement under the management of Health and Safety at Work Regulations 1992 (see also the Health and Safety (Display Screen Equipment) Regulations 1992) for the employer to carry out a risk assessment and assess risks to the employee's health and safety whilst at work and of those who may be affected by the conduct of the employer's undertaking. Where tele-working is concerned, this may, perhaps surprisingly, include the tele-worker's family.

Use of premises

5–36 Most homeworkers have mortgages or a tenancy agreement and most of these agreements prevent the use of the home for business purposes. It may therefore be necessary to obtain someone's permission to undertake work at home. This should be checked. Use of the home for work may have an impact upon both capital gains tax in respect of the exemption on the sale of the individual's main residence.

There are other issues in relation to employees working from home which will need to be considered, including whether such individuals will receive different pay and/or benefits compared to employees who are obliged to turn up for work each day. However, the employer will need to be aware of the potential for indirect sex discrimination because it is likely that the vast majority of individuals working from home are currently women although no doubt with the apparent increase in more technological based work being undertaken from the home this will change.

THE RELATIONSHIP BETWEEN FLEXIBLE WORK PATTERNS AND THE CONTRACT OF EMPLOYMENT

5–37 We considered above that there were two aspects to job flexibility. The first (discussed above) relates to the entire nature of the employment relationship, the structure or pattern of the work.

The second aspect, discussed here, relates to flexibility within the contract of employment itself, flexibility within the terms and conditions of employment. Some key areas are considered.

Employers have tried over the years to push the boundaries of the employment contract to such an extent that in some cases employment has been abandoned altogether and organisations have adopted sub-contracting for significant parts of their organisation. For permanent employees, organisations have tried to create contractual arrangements which allow the employer to manipulate the workforce or to create contracts which are flexible enough to cater for future changes so that, for example, where there is to be development in the pattern of work or in the nature of work or even in the place of work it is not necessary for the employer to negotiate new contracts of employment with the employees but to simply utilise flexibility in the pre-existing contractual arrangements. How successful can this strategy be?

5–38 One of the problems in this area is the tension which exists between the drafting of contractual terms and the apparent increased willingness of courts to impose in effect what amount to rules of law on to the employment relationship. One has only to think of the obligation of mutual trust and confidence which is never drafted into a contract of employment but which would appear clearly to exist in every single contract of employment as an imposed term (or in effect a rule of law). The importance of this can be seen if one considers the possibility of contracting out from the implied or imposed term of mutual trust and confidence. Would it be possible? Many commentators would suggest not. It would be contrary to public policy to allow an employment relationship to exist without an obligation of mutual trust and confidence. The difference here may be between terms which are implied *in fact* and terms which are implied *in law*.[16] The argument is that a term which is imposed in fact can be contradicted by an express term of contract but a term imposed in law cannot. That is not to say that this is a simple matter but perhaps an example will assist.

We considered above contracts of employment in the context of annualised hours. We considered what the position might be with regard to overtime in relation to employees who joined or left an organisation part way through an annualised hours year where the contract is silent on the matter. We said that in those circumstances the court could imply a term that, for example, such an individual could average out the hours they worked over the part of the year in which they were employed and if on average they worked longer than the average working week which applied across the year the court could imply a term that they received overtime pay for that excess time. This is clearly a term which is implied in fact and could easily be overwritten by an express term to the effect that employees who did not work for a whole year did not get overtime. That is a million miles away from the term of mutual trust and confidence which, it is argued, is a term implied in law: it is a matter of public policy.

Before we consider further the implied terms in a contract we shall look briefly at express terms.

EXPRESS TERMS

5–39   A contract of employment is a bargain made between the employer and, usually, the prospective employee. What goes into it therefore is between the parties. A court can at a later time interpret and apply what was agreed but, subject to the discussion on implied terms, it is not open to a court to determine whether a particular term was fair. It is important therefore that the express terms are set out clearly and with certainty so that the contract says what the parties mean it to say and reflects what they agreed.

It is not uncommon for lawyers who draft lengthy contractual clauses to hear the complaint that there are too many words, the clause is too complicated and it should be turned into "normal" English. There is clearly a tension between the need to draft for the sake of certainty and the commercial need to have contracts which are easily digestible by the parties. However, it cannot be stressed enough that quite often putting things into "normal" English means creating vagueness and ambiguity leaving the matter open to the court to interpret. Quite often lengthy, detailed and complex drafting does have the significant benefit of leaving nothing to chance.

Of course there is also a tension between certainty and flexibility. To reduce everything to writing may be to limit flexibility because much of what makes the employment relationship tick is what happens in practice. However with careful drafting it should be possible to take account of much of the employer's need for flexibility (which usually relates to things like working time, job duties and so on). In general the benefits of certainty outweigh the disadvantages of any loss of flexibility.

5–40   Express terms may be incorporated into the contract of employment from other sources, most usually a collective agreement. However it is not at all uncommon these days for a particularly large organisation to have both a document which purports to be the contract of employment and also a company handbook. That

---

[16] For a full discussion of this see "Beyond Exchange: The New Contract of Employment" by Douglas Brody, Industrial Law Journal Volume 27 No. 2 June 1998, p. 79.

handbook may contain any number of pieces of information, terms of employment, policies, and so forth. The question in each case will be whether the whole or any part of the handbook constitute terms and conditions of employment.

In some cases that will be made clear in the contract and/or the handbook itself. The contract may for example say that the disciplinary procedure is contained in the handbook but that the procedure itself does not constitute a term of employment. That will be sufficient to take the disciplinary procedure outside of the contract of employment itself. This is important because if there is any failure to follow the procedure it will not give rise to a claim for breach of contract. However, in the absence of such a clear statement it is quite possible that a tribunal will infer that the disciplinary procedure is contractual.

There are many examples where this can be a problem and again this relates to the issue of certainty versus flexibility. Take for example the question of company cars. It is not uncommon to see in the contract the fact that the employee has the right to a company car "in accordance with the company's car policy in force from time to time and as contained in the company handbook". The company handbook will then contain a lengthy and detailed policy setting out what the entitlements are to the particular car, petrol, usage, repair, maintenance, taxation, insurance, and so on. Does the fact that this is in the handbook and called a "policy" mean that it is or is not a term of employment? The point is arguable and will depend on all the circumstances but to be certain it should be stated clearly in the contract that the only contractual entitlement is the entitlement to a car. Everything else is governed by a non-contractual company policy. It is strongly arguable that in the absence of such a clear statement the "policy" will in fact be incorporated into the terms of the contract.

5–41 The above example is a relatively straightforward one given the nature of the benefit being discussed—a company car is a fairly common benefit of employment and is usually considered, of itself, to be a term of employment without more. There are however some grey areas. One classic example is the question of a redundancy policy.

It is not uncommon, particularly where there is collective bargaining, for there to be in existence a policy dealing with a redundancy process which may include details of enhanced redundancy pay and so on. Collective agreements are not legally binding contracts unless stated to be so and the vast majority are not. If the collective agreement is of itself not legally binding can an individual nevertheless say that anything which is contained in it is incorporated into the individual's contract? Again much will depend on the circumstances of each case. If the collective agreement deals with collective bargaining for pay purposes and the union agrees a pay increase which is reduced to writing in a collective agreement it is extremely likely that an individual employee would be able to argue that that is incorporated into their own contract. But what of a redundancy selection procedure and an enhanced redundancy pay policy contained in a collective agreement? Will an individual be able to argue that that is incorporated into their contract so that if they are selected for redundancy on a different basis to that contained in the collective agreement they could argue that there has been a breach of contract? So far the courts have fallen short of accepting that this is merely a matter of interpretation of the facts and circumstances surrounding the question of incorporation itself. In the leading case the courts have said that there is in fact a two-stage test. The second stage is indeed to look at whether, on the facts and circumstances of the particular case, the term was indeed incorporated into the individual's contract of employment. However, the first step is to establish whether the term itself is "apt" to be incorporated into a contract of employment. In this particular case the issue was indeed the redundancy selection procedure and the judge in the High Court said that a redundancy selection procedure was not appropriate to be a term of employment at all and therefore the question of whether it was incorporated never arose. The same reasoning can of course be applied to many matters which are more appropriate for being "policies" including, we would have thought some time ago, things such as equal opportunities policies.[17] But as we now know it is possible for even an equal opportunities policy to be incorporated into a contract of employment and to become a term of employment. By this we can see that what was "apt" to be a term of employment some ten or so years ago may have developed and broadened so that as we reach the new millennium courts may be more than willing to find that all sorts of things which previously would not have been considered to be entirely inappropriate to form legally binding terms of employment can now be considered to be so. Such development is entirely in line with the general trend principally emerging from European sources giving employees more rights during and at the end of the employment relationship.

IMPLIED TERMS

5–42   In the discussion above on express terms we considered the need for certainty against the desirability of flexibility within the contractual relationship. Both certainty and flexibility can, to a greater or lesser extent, be undermined by courts who may, in certain circumstances, imply terms into contracts of employment. In this section we look at the basis on which courts may imply terms into a contract of employment and the main implied terms.

There are three bases on which it may be found that a term of employment is implied into the contract.

The presumed intention of the parties

5–43   Under this heading the courts can apply two tests. These are the so-called "officious bystander" test or the so-called "business efficacy" test. It is necessary to look at what the parties would have agreed if they put their minds to the particular matter at hand when the contract was made.

The officious bystander test may be characterised as applying in circumstances where a third party had looked at the contract and suggested the need for a particular term. The parties would have said "oh, of course". The business efficacy test is perhaps slightly narrower but applies where it is necessary to imply a term into the contract in order to make the contract workable. In both cases however it must be stressed that terms will be implied under either of these tests on the presumed intent of the parties.

Conduct and custom

5–44   One will often hear the phrase "custom and practice" referred to in industrial relations. This is to say no more than the conduct of the parties over a period of time may suggest that certain practices (whether it be in relation to timekeeping, pay or anything else) have become implied into the contract as a result of what has in fact happened irrespective of what seems to have been agreed in writing or not referred to at all.

---

[17] *Taylor v. Secretary of State for Scotland* [1999] I.R.L.R. 362, Court of Session; [2000] I.R.L.R. 502, HL.

Reasonableness

In some limited cases courts or tribunals may imply terms because it is reasonable to do so in the circumstances. The courts do so on the basis that they have to be satisfied that the implied term is one on which the parties would probably have agreed if they were being reasonable. This should be distinguished from cases where the court implies into a term itself that it can only be operated reasonably (discussed below).

IMPOSED TERMS

5–45 We can see then that the creation of the contract of employment should be express. The parties should turn their minds to all matters relating to the employment relationship and reduce those to writing. We have also seen however that terms may be implied by the courts for various reasons whether on the basis that to imply such a term would be reasonable, or reflect custom and practice or in order to make the contract effective. There is however a growing body of case law within which courts have imposed terms into the employment relationship. The most obvious imposed term is the term of mutual trust and confidence. *In many respects these are not so much terms of employment as rules of law which attach to every employment contract irrespective of what the parties say.* This is a powerful judicial tool because the terms have nothing to do with what the parties intended and everything to do with legal Regulation.

5–46 Some of the key imposed terms are as follows:

- Mutual trust and confidence (referred to above);

- The obligation of the employee to keep confidential the employer's trade secrets;

- The employer must exercise reasonable care to safeguard the health and safety of employees; and

- Obeying lawful and reasonable instructions: An important implied term in contracts of employment is that employees must carry out their employer's lawful and reasonable instructions. This implied term entitles an employer to make rules for the conduct of its employees at work within the scope of their contract of employment. For example in the case of *Dryden v. Great Glasgow Health Board*[18] the EAT held that the Board's introduction of a ban on smoking in all its employees' workplaces did not breach the contract of employment of one of those employees who was a smoker. It found that there was no express or implied term of her contract to the effect that she was entitled to or would continue to enjoy facilities for smoking during working hours. Where an employer's rules are not the terms of its employees' contracts of employment but merely instructions to them as to how they are to do the work, the employer is entitled unilaterally to change its rules.

- Working practises: Another implied term is that employees are expected to adapt themselves to new methods and techniques introduced during the course of their employment subject to three qualifications. First, the particular method or technique should not alter the work which the

---

[18] [1992] I.R.L.R. 469, EAT.

employees do to such an extent that it is no longer the kind of work that they were employed to do. Secondly, their employer must provide any training or re-training necessary. Thirdly, such training or re-training must not involve acquisition of such esoteric skills that it would not be reasonable to expect the employees to acquire them. For example in the case of *Cresswell v. Board of Inland Revenue*[19] the High Court held that the Revenue was entitled to require civil servants whom it employed to administer the PAYE system to do their jobs using computers instead of manually. In the Court's view their job was essentially the same as it was before computerisation. Although partly done in a different way the job content was not altered anything like enough to fall outside the original description of the employees' proper functions. The Board had also provided the necessary instruction in the use of the computerised system and there was no suggestion that the employees had found any difficulty in accepting it and putting it into practice. Asking them to acquire basic skills so as to retrieve information from or feed it into a computer could hardly be said to be in the slightest esoteric or unusual.

In the same way that implied terms restrict the scope of express terms which purport to allow an employer unilaterally to vary a contract, implied terms which purport to do the same may similarly be restricted by other implied terms. In *Dryden* the EAT said "it is necessary to exercise caution before holding that there are implied contract terms which restrict the employer's power to control what happens in the workplace by making and altering from time to time rules for the conduct of the work and the employees". But it added "it may not be difficult to envisage implied terms that the employer will not change the rules of the workplace in a way which adversely affects an employee or group of employees without reasonable notice or without consultation or perhaps without some substantial reason". In *Prestwick Circuits Limited v. McAndrew* the Court of Session held that the (on the facts of the case) "implied right to order a transfer from one place of employment to another must be subject to the qualification that reasonable notice must be given in all the circumstances of the case".[20]

5–47   There are two final matters to consider under this heading. The first is that courts have also been willing to imply certain limitations to an employer's ability to act apparently in accordance with the contract in certain cases. There have been a string of cases involving permanent health insurance and other health insurance type benefits in which a general principle seems to have emerged that an employer cannot dismiss an employee in order to prevent, or where such dismissal would, in any event prevent the employee from obtaining the benefit of such insurance. Finally we should not forget that statute can also imply terms into the contract. For example, the Equal Pay Act 1970 implies into every contract an equality clause requiring that men and women are treated equally in relation to remuneration. Most recently of course the Working Time Regulations create detailed and complex rules regarding the organisation of working time which case law suggest can be implied into the contract of employment (see the discussion of *Barber v. RJB Mining (U.K.) Limited* in Chapter 6).

---

[19] [1984] I.R.L.R. 190, HC.
[20] [1990] I.R.L.R. 191.

CHAPTER SIX

The 48-Hour Working Week and the Individual "Opt Out"

INTRODUCTION

6–01 Of all the measures in the Working Time Regulations, it is the provisions dealing with the so called "48-hour maximum working week" that have perhaps attracted the most controversy. Actually, this expression is rather misleading because the Regulations limit *average* weekly working time to 48 hours, the average being calculated on the basis of a specific reference period. The Regulations do not limit the duration of working time in any particular week to 48 hours. Under Regulation 4, a worker may enter into a so called "individual opt out" agreement whereby he agrees with his employer that the 48-hour maximum working week will not apply to him. With effect from December 17, 1999 by virtue of the Working Time Regulations 1999 there have been significant changes to Regulations 4 and 5 in respect of "opted-out" workers, as will be explained later in this chapter. Regulations 4 and 5 apply to all workers except those in "excluded sectors of activity"[1] or those who fall within the Regulation 20 "unmeasured working time" derogation.[2]

REGULATIONS 4 AND 5 (AS AMENDED BY THE WORKING TIME REGULATIONS 1999)—THE PROVISIONS

6–02 These Regulations concern the limit on average weekly working time. They provide:

"(1) Unless his employer has first obtained the worker's agreement in writing to perform such work, a worker's working time, including overtime, in any reference period which is applicable in his case shall not exceed an average of 48 hours for each seven days.

(2) An employer shall take all reasonable steps, in keeping with the need to protect the health and safety of workers, to ensure that the limit specified in paragraph (1) is complied with in the case of each worker employed by him in relation to whom it applies and shall keep up-to-date records of all workers who carry out work to which it does not apply by reason of the fact that the employer has obtained the worker's agreement as mentioned in paragraph (1).

(3) Subject to paragraphs (4) and (5) and any agreement under Regulation 23(b), the reference periods which apply in the case of a worker are—

---

[1] See Chap. 12.
[2] See Chap. 12.

(a) where a relevant agreement provides for the application of this Regulation in relation to successive periods of 17 weeks, each such period, or

(b) in any other case, any period of 17 weeks in the course of his employment.

6–03   (4) Where a worker has worked for his employer for less than 17 weeks, the reference period applicable in his case is the period that has elapsed since he started work for his employer

(5) Paragraphs (3) and (4) shall apply to a worker who is excluded from the scope of certain provisions of these Regulations by Regulation 21 as if for each reference to 17 weeks there were substituted a reference to 26 weeks.

(6) For the purposes of this Regulation, a worker's average working time for each seven days during a reference period shall be determined according to the formula—

$$\frac{A + B}{C}$$

where—

A is the aggregate number of hours comprised in the worker's working time during the course of the reference period;

B is the aggregate number of hours comprised in his working time during the course of the period beginning immediately after the end of the reference period and ending when the number of days in that subsequent period on which he has worked equals the number of excluded days during the reference period; and

C is the number of weeks in the reference period.

(7) In paragraph (6), "excluded days" means days comprised in—

6–04   (a) any period of annual leave taken by the worker in exercise of his entitlement under Regulation 13;

(b) any period of sick leave taken by the worker;

(c) any period of maternity leave taken by the worker; and

(d) any period in respect of which the limit specified in paragraph (1) did not apply in relation to the worker by reason of the fact that the employer has obtained the worker's agreement as mentioned in paragraph (1)."

6–05   Agreement to exclude the maximum

"(2) An agreement for the purposes of Regulation 4—

(a) may either relate to a specified period or apply indefinitely; and

(b) subject to any provision in the agreement for a different period of notice, shall be terminable by the worker by giving not less than seven days' notice to his employer in writing.

(3) Where an agreement for the purposes of Regulation 4 makes provision for the termination of the agreement after a period of notice, the notice period provided for shall not exceed three months."

COMPLIANCE WITH THE WORKING TIME DIRECTIVE

6–06 Regulation 4 seeks to implement Article 6 of the Working Time Directive which provides:

"*Maximum weekly working time*
Member States shall take the measures necessary to ensure that, in keeping with the need to protect the safety and health of workers—

(1) the period of weekly working time is limited by means of laws, Regulations or administrative provisions, or by collective agreements or agreements between the two sides of industry;
(2) the average working time for each seven-day period, including overtime, does not exceed 48 hours".

Article 16 of the Directive provides that Member States may lay down for the application of Article 6 a reference period not exceeding four months. This broadly equates with the standard 17 week reference period specified in Regulation 4. According to the Government, 17 weeks is the period of whole weeks that is closest to four months and the 17 week period was selected in order so far as possible to simplify the calculation of average hours worked. In the Government's view a four month period could also potentially distort the average depending on whether the consequent additional fraction of weeks comprised working days or rest days.

Article 17 of the Directive deals with derogations from the provisions of its other Articles. Under Article 17 derogations may be adopted by means of laws, Regulations or administrative provisions or by means of collective agreements or agreements between the two sides of industry provided that the workers concerned are afforded equivalent periods of compensatory rest or that, in exceptional cases in which it is not possible, for objective reasons, to grant such equivalent periods of compensatory rest, the workers concerned are afforded appropriate protection in the case of various specified activities. Under Article 17.4 the option under Article 17 to derogate from Article 16 may not result in the establishment of a reference period exceeding six months. However, Member States have the option, subject to compliance with the general principles relating to the protection of the safety and health of workers, of allowing, for objective or technical reasons or reasons concerning the organisation of work, collective agreements or agreements included between the two sides of industry, to set reference periods in no event exceeding 12 months.

6–07 Regulation 4 provides that the 17-week reference period in relation to the 48-hour week may be replaced by a 26-week reference period in circumstances specified in Regulation 21. These circumstances mirror those specified in Article 17.2 of the Directive. Regulation 24 then implements the "compensatory rest" and "adequate protection" provisions of Article 17.2. Further, the provision in Regulation 23 whereby the reference period may be extended for up to 52 weeks by a collective or workforce agreement seeks to give effect to the above provision of Article

17.4. Apparently the Government considers that the workforce agreement is an agreement concluded "between the two sides of industry".

The opt-out under Regulation 4 seeks to apply Article 18 of the Working Time Directive. Under Article 18(b)(i):

> "However, a Member State shall have the option not to apply Article 6, while respecting the general principles of the protection of the safety and health of workers, and provided it takes the necessary measures to ensure that:
>
> – No employer requires a worker to work more than 48 hours over a seven day period, calculated as an average for the reference period referred to in ... Article 16, unless he has first obtained the worker's agreement to perform such work;
>
> – No worker is subjected to any detriment by his employer because he is not willing to give his agreement to perform such work;
>
> – The employer keeps up to date records of all workers who carry out such work;
>
> – The records are placed at the disposal of the competent authorities, which may, for reasons connected with the safety and/or health of workers, prohibit or restrict the possibility of exceeding the maximum weekly working hours; and
>
> – The employer provides the competent authorities at their request with information on cases in which agreement has been given by workers to perform work exceeding 48 hours over a period of seven days, calculated as an average for the reference period referred to in ... Article 16.

6–08   Before the expiry of a period of seven years from [November 23, 1996], the Council of the European Union shall, on the basis of a Commission proposal accompanied by an appraisal report, re-examine the provisions of this point (i) and decide on what action to take".

6–09   Following the amendments introduced by the Working Time Regulations 1999, the opt-out provisions are in line with the Directive in that the records to be maintained by employers in respect of opted-out workers are up-to-date records of all workers who are opted-out. Prior to the 1999 Regulations, the record keeping obligations imposed by the 1998 Regulations on employers in respect of opted-out workers were more onerous than those specified under Article 18: in particular employers had to maintain records of hours actually worked by opted-out workers.[3] This disparity was heavily criticised and led to the amendments introduced by the 1999 Regulations. Interestingly, however, the 1999 Regulations have deleted the provisions of the 1998 Regulations which had sought to implement the provisions of Article 18(b)(1) which require employers' records of all opted out workers to be at the disposal of "the competent authorities" and employers to provide such authorities on request with information in respect of opted-out workers. The Government appears to decide that the original obligations in the 1998 Regulations went further than the

---

[3] See later in this Chapter and also Chap. 18.

actual requirements of the Directive. Moreover, Article 18(b)(1) differs from Regulations 4 and 5, even as amended, in that it does not stipulate that opt-out agreements should be in writing or be subject to any specific notice of termination provisions.

Article 8.2 of the Directive on the Protection of Young People at Work provides:

"Member states shall adopt the measures necessary to limit the working time of adolescents to eight hours a day and 40 hours a week".

Article 17(1)(b) of that Directive provides:

"The United Kingdom may refrain from implementing. . . Article 8(2) . . . for a period of four years from the [June 22, 1996].
The Council, acting in accordance with the conditions laid down by the Treaty, shall decide whether this period should be extended."

Article 3 of that Directive defines "adolescent" as:

"Any young person of at least 15 years of age but less than 18 years of age who is no longer subject to compulsory full-time schooling under national law."

THE AVERAGE 48-HOUR WORKING WEEK

6–10 Under Regulation 4(1) the working time, including overtime, of each worker to whom the Regulation applies[4] in the applicable reference period shall not exceed an average of 48 hours for each seven day period unless the worker enters into an individual written agreement with his employer "opting out" of the 48-hour limit[5] (discussed later in this chapter). It should be noted that the 48-hour limit is an average calculated over a reference period.[6]

Regulation 4 applies to workers, including "young workers" as defined in Regulation 2.[7] In the Government's view the 48-hour limit provisions set out in Regulation 4 give sufficient protection for all workers; the Government has accordingly taken advantage of the derogations in the E.C. Directive on the Protection of Young People at Work which disapply the requirements in that Directive for a maximum of 40 hours working time per week for adolescent workers. Strictly, under Article 17 of that above Directive the Government could refrain from implementing these limits for adolescent workers (that is those of at least 15 years of age but less than 18 no longer subject to compulsory full-time schooling) for a period of four years from June 22, 1996. Although the four year period expired last June, the Government has still refrained from implementing the Article 17 limits for adolescent workers so the 48-hour limit still applies to them.

6–11 Under Regulation 4(2) the employer is under a duty to take all reasonable steps in keeping with the need to protect the health and safety of workers, to ensure that the 48-hour limit is complied with in the case of each worker employed by him to whom it applies.

In the case of *Barber v. RJB Mining (UK) Limited*[8] the High Court held that the

---

[4] Exceptions are discussed below.
[5] See below para. 6–21.
[6] See paras 6–14 to 6–17.
[7] See Chap. 15.
[8] [1999] I.R.L.R. 308.

average 48-hour weekly working time limit has contractual force and effect and is therefore capable of direct enforcement by workers. The facts of the case are set out below. It is important to bear in mind, however, that the *Barber* case was decided before the amendments to Regulations 4 and 5 under the 1999 Regulations were implemented; that is *Barber* dealt with the form of opt-out agreement originally prescribed by the Regulation 5 disapplying the 48-hour limit, rather than with the revised form of opt-out agreement introduced by the 1999 Regulations which is an agreement to work in excess of the 48-hour limit. Consequently as will be explained the practical ramifications of *Barber* may no longer be as far reaching where revised form opt-out agreements are in force.

6–12   Mr Barber and colleagues were pit deputies who had worked for RJB Mining in excess of an average of 48 hours per week during the 17 weeks from when the Regulations came into force on October 1, 1998. This was contrary to Regulation 4(1), none having entered an individual opt-out agreement under Regulation 5 as it then was. They continued to work in excess of the weekly working time limit but reserved their legal rights. Mr Barber and his colleagues brought claims based on a breach of Regulation 4 against the company in the High Court. They claimed a declaration that having exceeded the average of 48 hours per week in that reference period, they need not work until such time as their average weekly working time fell within the 48 hours limit. Their argument was that Regulation 4(1) was part of their contact of employment. They also claimed an injunction restraining the company from requiring them to work until such time. The company argued that the Court had no jurisdiction to hear the claims or grant the relief sought. It argued that employees could not enforce the weekly working time limit. The limit in Regulation 4(1) was a statutory duty placed on the employer, enforceable only by the health and safety authorities. Employees had no direct ability to enforce it, although they could complain to an employment tribunal if they were dismissed or suffered a detriment as a result of refusal to work in excess of the weekly working time limit or to sign an opt-out agreement. Note that the issues centred on whether the employer was in breach of contract by requiring the workers to continue to work in excess of the 48-hour limit. There was no express discussion of whether the fact that the workers had already worked more than the average 48 hours per week in the 17-week period since the Regulations were introduced was itself a breach of contract.

The High Court therefore had to determine whether it had jurisdiction to hear these claims which depended on, whether Regulation 4(1) conferred a contractual obligation and entitlement on the employer and worker respectively; if it held the Regulation did so then the High Court would have jurisdiction to deal with the claims. The High Court held that Regulation 4(1) is mandatory and is incorporated into every contract of employment; that Regulation 4(1) is to be read separately from Regulation 4(2) (which provides that an employer should take all reasonable steps to ensure that the 48-hour limit is complied with); and that breach of Regulation 4(2) is enforceable by criminal proceedings by the Health and Safety Executive and local authorities under the Regulations, and so may not be dealt with by the High Court.

6–13   The High Court held that in the absence of an opt-out agreement (then under Regulation 5(1) a requirement by an employer that any of his workers) work in excess of the 48 hour weekly average is a breach of that worker's contract; consequently the court had jurisdiction to hear the claims arising from such a breach (regardless of the other enforcement mechanisms in the Regulations) and to grant appropriate relief. In this case the High Court went on to grant the declaration sought but refused to grant the injunction because Mr Barber and his colleagues would have remedies under the Regulations should they be dismissed or subjected to a detriment for refusing to work in excess of the 48-hour limit.

The *Barber* decision that Regulation 4(1) gives rise to a free-standing legal right which takes effect by way of an implied term in the contract of employment clearly has important consequences. (Although it is debatable whether the decision is correct). Giving contractual effect to the 48-hour limit in Regulation 4(1) gives rise to the possibility of claims for breach of contract and/or constructive dismissal by a worker whose employer breaches this limit in the absence of an opt-out agreement. Although the High Court's decision suggests that the implied term is an obligation on the employer not to *require* a worker to work more than the lawful number of hours per week, it may be that if Regulation 4(1) takes effect as an implied contractual term it does so on its wording verbatim. If so, the implied term would be breached, giving rise to liability for breach of contract, simply by the worker actually exceeding this limit and not just where the employer specifically requires him to do so. However, it may possibly be that a breach of the limit, hence breach of contract, which occurs inadvertently or by mistake, may not be regarded as sufficiently fundamental to enable the worker concerned successfully to claim constructive dismissal. In any event, in practice workers would appear to be well-protected under the Regulations already, without having to resort to the rather drastic steps of resigning and claiming constructive dismissal. Also, given the amendments to Regulations 4 and 5 regarding opt-out agreements introduced by the 1999 Regulations, the *Barber* decision may since their introduction be of rather more limited significance in practice, as we explain later in this chapter.

Reference Periods

6–14 Some flexibility is available under the Regulations over the terms of the reference period over which the average is taken. Regulation 4(3) sets a reference period of 17 weeks. This is effectively a "rolling" period of 17 weeks, unless a Relevant Agreement[9] provides for successive 17 week periods. In practice the worker may actually work up to 816 hours in that rolling 17 week period without exceeding the 48-hour weekly average. Also, in some instances, the reference period may be longer than 17 weeks. Under Regulation 4(5), in the case of a worker who is excluded from the scope of certain provisions of the Regulations by Regulation 21 (special cases),[10] a reference period of 26 weeks applies. Further, under Regulation 23(b) a Collective or Workforce Agreement[11] may "for objective or technical reasons or reasons concerning the organisation of work" extend the 17-week period in respect of particular workers for up to a maximum of 52 weeks. This expression is not clarified in the Regulations. Note that if the 26- or 52-week reference periods apply the average 48-hour weekly working time limit still applies; it is just that the reference period is longer and capable of "absorbing" more weeks in which more than 48 hours are actually worked (of course there would have to be weeks within the extended reference periods during which the number of hours actually worked were proportionately less than 48).

6–15 Regulation 4(4) provides that where a worker has worked for his employer for less than 17 weeks, the reference period applicable in his case is the period that has elapsed since he started work for his employer. This means that worker's working

---

[9] See Chap. 13 and Regulation 2(1).
[10] See Chap. 16.
[11] See Chap. 13.

hours will be averaged over the number of hours actually worked. The Government introduced this provision because it believed that it was necessary to protect and secure the rights of temporary workers. Otherwise, these workers would find that it was lawful for their employer to require them to work longer than the limits envisaged by the Working Time Directive, because the employer would know that they would do so only for the few weeks for which they worked. Accordingly, the effect of Regulation 4(4) is that for the first 17 (or 26, where Regulation 21 applies) weeks of employment, the new worker's actual working time is more tightly constrained. For example, a worker who works for only 24 hours in his first week of employment might work 72 hours in the second week. This would produce an average of 48 hours over the fortnight of actual employment. In that case, the third week could involve no more than 48 hours' working time. Note that this restriction would not apply where the new worker enters into an individual agreement opting out of the working time limit.

In the absence of a Relevant Agreement on the point, the start date for the 17-week reference period is either October 1, 1998, that is the date when the Regulations came into force, or if later, the date on which a worker starts work for the particular employer.

6–16 Consequently, in summary the possible reference periods that may be applied in order to determine average weekly working time are basically as follows:

- in the case of a worker who has worked for his employer for less than 17 weeks, it is the actual period since he started work;

- in the case of a worker who has worked for his employer for 17 weeks or more, it is either:
  - a rolling period of 17 weeks, or
  - successive periods of 17 weeks if so provided by a Relevant Agreement.

- in the case of a worker to whom Regulation 21 applies and who has worked for his employer for less than 26 weeks, it is the actual period since he started work.

- in the case of a worker to whom Regulation 21 applies and who has worked for his employer for 26 weeks or more, it is either:
  - a rolling period of 26 weeks, or
  - successive periods of 26 weeks if so provided by a Relevant Agreement

- in the case of objective or technical reasons or reasons concerning the organisation of work, a collective or workforce agreement may set a rolling reference period or successive reference periods of up to 52 weeks.

Calculating the Average

6–17 Having ascertained the appropriate reference period applicable to a particular worker, it is then a case of calculating his or her average weekly working hours. Regulations 4(6) and (7) provide a formula for this purpose. Essentially, it is a matter of identifying the number of weeks in the relevant reference period, the number of hours of working time actually worked in that period and dividing the latter by the former to provide an average. In detail, the calculation for the average hours worked is determined according to the formula:

$$\frac{A + B}{C}$$

Where A is the total number of hours of working time worked during the applicable reference period; B is the total number of hours worked, immediately after the reference period, during the number of working days equivalent to the number of "excluded days" in the reference period; and C is the number of weeks in the applicable reference period.[12]

6–18   "Excluded days" are those days on which the worker is absent for one of the reasons given below. To ensure that the reference period is a "full" one and that the average weekly working time is not distorted by these days of absence, the calculation under Regulation 4 (6) requires the worker's working time in the number of working days equivalent to the number of excluded days immediately following the actual reference period to be taken into account. Note, however, that the time in the excluded days will still need to be taken into account in respect of the reference period to which the excluded days themselves actually belong. Days that qualify as "excluded days" comprise days included in any annual leave under Regulation 13, sick leave and maternity leave and in any period in respect of which the opt-out agreement regarding the 48-hour week has been obtained by the employer. Essentially, if during a reference period a worker does not work on one or more excluded days, the equivalent number of days subsequent to that reference period are treated as being brought into that reference period in substitution for the excluded days. Effectively, the reference period is extended by that number of subsequent days. Such subsequent days would still however be counted for the purposes of the reference period in which they would otherwise appear. For the purposes of the calculation, the hours worked in the number of working days immediately after the reference period, equivalent to the number of "excluded days", is added to the total working hours.

To some extent this is of benefit to employers because otherwise they may find that unexpected sickness during the reference period distorts the number of hours worked in the average working week. Obviously periods of sick leave and maternity leave may be quite lengthy and employers must take care to adjust the applicable reference period when the worker returns to work by the relevant number of excluded days.

6–19   Note that absences on days other than excluded days are not excluded from the reference period in question. For example, a worker's absence from work by virtue of any contractual leave entitlement effectively "over and above" the entitlement under Regulation 13 should not be excluded from the reference period concerned. Consequently, during that reference period the "contractual absence" will reduce the average hours worked so that the worker may in appropriate circumstances be required to work correspondingly more than 48 hours during another week or weeks.

The following examples should serve to illustrate how the calculation works. Assume a worker works 60 hours per week, for the first 12 weeks of a 17-week reference period, and then has one week's sick leave and then returns and works 35 hours per week during the remaining four weeks of the reference period and 40 hours during the following week.

$$A \text{ is } (60 \times 12) + (0 \times 1) + (4 \times 35) = 860$$
$$B \text{ is } (40 \times 1) = 40$$
$$C \text{ is } 17$$
$$\frac{A + B}{C} = \frac{860 + 40}{17} = \text{an average of 52.94 hours per week}$$

6–20   Now assume that instead of one week's sick leave in week 13 the worker

---

[12] The concept of "working time" is explained in Chap. 3.

takes one week's contractual leave, having already taken his annual leave entitlement under the Regulations:

A is $(60 \times 12) + (0 \times 1) + (4 \times 35) = 860$
B is 0
C is 17

$$\frac{A + B}{C} = \frac{860}{17} = \text{an average of 50.58 hours per week}$$

THE INDIVIDUAL OPT OUT

6–21 Under Regulations 4(1), it is possible for an employer to agree with each and any of his workers that the worker will work in excess of the average 48-hour limit on the working week. Note that as underlined by the High Court in the *Barber* case,[13] any agreement by a worker to exceed the 48-hour limit will be irrelevant and ineffective unless it is in the form of an opt-out agreement in accordance with Regulations 4 and 5.

To be valid and effective an opt-out agreement must be an individual written agreement with the worker concerned, and by implication it has to be signed by the worker.

6–22 This requirement is substantially less stringent than those relating to opt-out agreements under the original 1998 Regulations before they were amended by the 1999 Regulations. Under Regulations 5(1) and (4), as originally implemented, provided:

(a) There had to be an individual written agreement with each worker who agreed with his employer to disapply the 48-hour limit;

(b) The employer had to maintain up-to-date records identifying each of the workers employed by him who agreed that the 48-hour limit would not apply. These records had to set out the terms on which the worker agreed to disapply the 48-hour limit. The employer had to record the number of hours of working time worked by that worker during each reference period since the agreement came into effect;

(c) The records had to be available for inspection by Officials of the Health and Safety Executive or Local Authority and the employer had to co-operate with the officials of such bodies and give them any relevant material on the individuals who had agreed to disapply the 48-hour limit.

6–23 The employer's obligation to maintain a record of the actual hours worked by each opted out worker was found to be onerous by employers; it was certainly more onerous than the record keeping obligations that apply in respect of non opted-out workers. Employers were therefore faced with a dilemma—did they want to be bound by the 48-hour weekly working time limit or by a more onerous obligation to maintain records of daily working time? The record keeping obligation in respect of opted-out workers was consequently heavily criticised by employers, who argued that it was not required by the Working Time Directive itself. The Government responded to these criticisms and introduced amendments to Regulation 5 under the Working Time Regulations 1999.

---

[13] *Barber v. RJB Mining (UK) Limited* [1999] I.R.L.R. 308—see earlier in this Chapter (para. 6–12).

Consequently, Regulations 5(1) and (4) have been deleted and employers no longer need to maintain records of working time for opted-out workers; Regulation 4(2), has been amended so that employers simply have to keep a record of those of their workers who have opted out. This change may result in a greatly increased use of opt-out agreements since there is now no major disincentive to their use. Indeed employers may even seek to use opt-out agreements not just to avoid the weekly working time limit but also to avoid any obligation to maintain records of working time (under Regulation 9 employers have to keep records that are adequate to show compliance with the 48-hour limit in respect of their non opted-out workers).[14] The opt-out agreement may therefore become the means whereby employers seek to avoid the practical record keeping problems created by the Regulations.[15]

6–24 Moreover, the amendments to Regulations 4 and 5 seem to result in a change to the nature of the opt-out agreement itself. Under the original provisions in Regulation 5(1), the opt-out agreement was an agreement in writing between worker and employer that the weekly working time limit was not to apply to that worker. This required an agreement specifically relating to the Working Time Regulations and consequently employers could not rely on a contract of employment that set a working pattern that would breach the weekly working time limit (for example if the contract specified a normal working week of 60 hours per week) as amounting to an opt-out agreement. In other words employers could not rely on hours of work clauses in their employment contracts as constituting an opt-out agreement under the Regulations as originally implemented.

Prior to the 1999 Regulations, in light of the *Barber* decision, it appeared that in consequence if a worker's contract already contained provisions requiring him to work in excess of an average of 48 hours per week over the applicable reference period, such provisions would nevertheless be invalid unless the worker additionally entered an individual opt-out agreement under Regulation 5(1) as it then was. However, since the 1999 Regulations came into force a provision in a worker's written contract requiring him to work in excess of 48 hours per week would constitute a valid "revised form" opt-out agreement (so long as "genuine" and the employer complies with the record keeping obligations).[16] Consequently, in this regard *Barber* may cease to be of practical significance.

6–25 Since December 17, 1999, however, the limit specified in Regulation 4(1), applies unless the worker has agreed to work longer hours. This seems to imply that the agreement between the employer and worker no longer needs to be a specific agreement to disapply the limit specified in Regulation 4, but may consist simply of an agreement to work longer hours than those permitted by the weekly working time limit. This would seemingly allow for a written agreement for example in a written contract of employment to work 60 hours per week to count as an opt-out agreement. Also, previously mentioned, this would mean that the decision in *Barber* regarding the original form of opt-out agreement may well no longer be of practical significance (provided that the record keeping obligation under Regulation 4(2) is complied with). If a term in the contract to work, *e.g.* 60 hours per week, is a valid opt out, there would be no room for implying any term based on Regulation 4(1). Only where the contract did not contain a term allowing the unit to be exceeded, could the *Barber* analysis apply.

However, the fact that the weekly working time limit applies unless the worker agrees to work longer hours may mean that under the amended Regulations the

---

[14] See Chap. 18.

[15] But see the discussion later in this Chapter.

[16] As discussed later in this Chapter.

revised form of opt out cannot be used as a means of avoiding the obligation to maintain records of working time unless the employer can demonstrate a genuine agreement on the part of the worker to work hours beyond those permitted by the weekly working time limit. For example, the employer might not be able to demonstrate that a worker has genuinely opted out of the working time limit if his hours of work are usually only 20 per week.

6–26   It is unclear whether original form opt-out agreements entered into before the amendments to Regulations 4 and 5 were implemented, that is before December 17, 1999, remain valid. On a strict interpretation of the wording of Regulations 4(1) and 5(1) before and after the amendments introduced by the 1999 Regulations, it could be argued that under an original form opt-out agreement the worker had not necessarily agreed to work longer hours than those permitted by the Regulations; rather, that he had simply agreed that the limit itself does not apply (which is not necessarily the same thing). Also, the amendments introduced by the 1999 Regulations do not specify whether in respect of original form opt-out agreements employers still need to comply with the original more onerous record keeping obligations (see above) in order for such opt-out agreements to remain valid. We suggest that the better view is that as from implementation of the 1999 Regulations, the validity of original form opt-out agreements should no longer be subject to the original record keeping obligations.

6–27   Under Regulation 5(2) each individual opt-out agreement to disapply the 48-hour limit must allow the worker to bring it to an end. The opt-out agreement may either be for a specified period or apply indefinitely, but subject to any provision in the agreement for a different notice period, the worker may terminate it by giving not less than seven days' written notice. If there is provision in the agreement for a different notice period, this notice period may not exceed three months.

Finally, it should be borne in mind that the availability of the individual opt-out agreement should be reviewed by the Council of the European Union before November 23, 2003. It is therefore uncertain for how long the opt-out agreement will remain available to employers and workers. However, given the views of the European Commission and the fact that only the United Kingdom has implemented the individual opt-out agreement, the individual opt-out agreement may well not be available following the Council review.

PROBLEM AREAS

6–28   The impact of the amended Regulations 4 and 5 means that employers should focus on the following issues:

- Whether any of their workers works or is likely to work more than 48 hours per week on average over the relevant reference period;

- Any worker who does or is likely to do so will need to sign or already to have signed a valid written opt-out agreement; otherwise the employer must take all reasonable steps to ensure that the 48-hour limit on the average working week is being complied with;

- The administrative burden of keeping records in respect of non opted-out workers adequate to demonstrate that the 48-hour limit on the average working week is being complied with—there is no such burden in respect of an opted-out worker; and

- Not all workers may be prepared to sign opt-out agreements and those that do may terminate them at any time by giving the requisite notice (a worker cannot be fairly dismissed or subjected to detriment for refusing to sign or for terminating an opt-out agreement). The prudent employer would therefore be prepared as may be or become necessary to be able to demonstrate compliance with the 48-hour limit and the associated record keeping obligation.

6–29 Looking at these issues in more detail, the employer's first step should be to analyse what constitutes "working time" for each worker as defined in the Regulations.[17] Then it will be necessary to analyse how much time each worker spends working within the meaning of the Regulations. For example, a worker may have more than one job, working for one or more other employers. The employer should therefore take steps to ascertain whether his workers have second jobs because each employer has either to take reasonable steps to ensure that his workers do not exceed the 48-hour average, whether for that employer or others, or must enter individual opt-out agreements.

According to the DTI Guidance, in order to comply with the 48-hour limit an employer may reasonably ask his workers if they are working for anyone else and/or request that they inform him if and when they so do. The employer would then be in a position to adjust working arrangements accordingly. Presumably this covers any such worker giving the employer details as to the number of hours worked for somebody else, so that working arrangements may be adjusted. Consequently, if an employer is informed that a worker does work a certain number of hours for another employer or employers then the employer will have to assess whether the 48-hour limit is being or may be exceeded. If so, the employer would either have to seek an individual opt-out agreement from the worker concerned or reduce that worker's working hours for him such that the 48-hour limit would not be exceeded. Other options could be for the employer to stipulate that the worker correspondingly reduces the hours worked for the other employer or employers or to stipulate in the contract of employment that the worker may only work for him. There will be potential breach of contract/unfair dismissal/Working Time Regulations issues for the employer to bear in mind and advice should be sought before proceeding to implement any of these options.

6–30 Having taken the above steps (taking account of those who work for other employers), the employer should identify his planned work and/or shift patterns. In respect of each working pattern, the employer needs to check the precise length of "working time" involved, including overtime. It may be apparent from this exercise that, in fact, certain workers are unlikely ever to exceed an average of 48 hours per week over a 17-week reference period. Whilst account needs to be taken of any overtime, it may be apparent that employees' defined start and finish times mean that the 48-hour limit will not be exceeded so they will obviously not exceed the average.

Employers may also consider whether or not a rolling 17-week reference period is preferable given the needs of their businesses. If an employer's workers infrequently but still regularly work more than 48 hours per week, then the employer may consider adopting, by means of a Relevant Agreement,[18] successive reference periods rather than the rolling 17-week reference period. That way the occasions on which the 48-hour week are exceeded may be offset by catering for corresponding reduced hours in the fixed reference period. On the other hand if an employer's workers invariably

---

[17] See Chap. 3, para. 3–04.
[18] See Chap. 13 and Regulation 2(1).

work less than 48 hours per week the employer may be content to stick with the rolling reference period.

6–31   Another option would be to extend the reference period over which the average weekly working hours are assessed. As we have seen, the rolling reference period is 26 weeks in the case of a worker who is excluded from the scope of certain provisions of the Regulations by Regulation 21, the special case exemptions. The reference period may be extended up to 52 weeks by a collective or workforce agreement in the circumstances set out in Regulation 23. This may be appropriate if working hours vary greatly week to week or seasonally, that is, "for objective or technical reasons conceiving the organisation of work". However, as it is not clear what this means, employers may be reluctant to risk availing themselves of this option until clarification is provided through the courts or tribunals.

As discussed, it is in respect of each of those workers who exceed or are likely to exceed the 48-hour limit (remembering that this is based on an average) that the employer must consider entering into an individual opt-out agreement.

The individual opt-out agreement has to be in writing and signed by the worker concerned. It is itself likely to be a fairly short document and could be incorporated into a written contract of employment. Indeed, given its nature since implementation of the 1999 Regulations it may readily be part of an appropriately drafted "hours of work" clause in the contract. However it must be remembered that the agreement may be terminated on appropriate notice being given by the worker so any subsequent opt-out agreements may have to be set out in separate documents or new written employment contracts.

6–32   The main administrative burden facing employers is that they will need to consider how they will comply with the obligations to keep sufficient records for the purposes of these Regulations, as regards workers to whom the 48-hour working limit applies. Pursuant to Regulation 9, employers have to keep records which are adequate to demonstrate that the 48-hour working limit has been complied with.[19]

Employers should carefully consider how to comply with the record keeping obligations under Regulations 4 and 9. It is for each employer to determine what records need to be kept for compliance purposes. As regards records adequate to demonstrate compliance with Regulation 4, an employer is not necessarily required to keep a running record of each worker's average weekly working time. Working patterns and contractual terms will be relevant considerations. If, for example, the contract of employment stipulates standard daily working hours such as 9 a.m.–5 p.m. it may be sufficient to meet the requirement by using management assistance from time to time to monitor and ensure that the specified hours are kept. The employer would need to ensure that his means of monitoring workers' working time would be adequate to highlight instances of any workers working in excess of the standard working hours. That said, the employer may need to monitor the hours worked by such workers more closely or adjust the work they are asked to do to ensure compliance, particularly if they appear to be close to the 48-hour limit.

6–33   Note the consequences if the rolling 17-week reference period applies. The employer will, each week, have to mention records to show that his workers (other than any who have opted out by individual agreement) have not exceeded the 48-hour weekly average in that week and the previous 16 weeks (similar considerations apply in respect of the Regulation 21 rolling 26-week reference period).

Finally, employers may give consideration to introducing disciplinary offences, for example, as follows:

---

[19] See Chap. 18.

(a) The failure to provide any information necessary for the employer to maintain adequate records to show that the 48-hour limit is being complied with; and

(b) Any deliberate falsification of relevant information by an employee.

6–34   As we have seen, under the amended Regulation 4(2) as regards workers who have entered written opt-out agreements and agreed to work more than 48 hours per week on average, the employer's record keeping obligation is only to keep an up-to-date record of those workers who have done so. It is far less onerous than the record keeping obligation in respect of non opted-out workers under Regulation 9. For this reason, the opt-out agreement may also appeal to employers, and as we have indicated, may also contribute to a significant increase in their use. Of course, many employers will have entered the original form opt-out agreements with workers and set up systems in compliance with the original more onerous record keeping obligations. Employers will have to take a view as to whether or not they should continue with such systems in respect of original form opt-out agreements given that the more onerous record keeping obligations under the Regulations have been deleted. As discussed earlier in this chapter, we suggest that as such record keeping obligations have been deleted, this is no longer necessary.

That said employers should remember that they cannot lawfully force workers to enter opt-out agreements—dismissing a worker for refusing to do so will be "automatically" unfair and subjecting him to a detriment for refusing to do so will render the employer liable to him.[20] Likewise, employers should bear in mind that a worker who has entered an opt-out agreement may at any time terminate it by giving the requisite notice (not less than seven days and not more than three months, as discussed earlier in this chapter). Again, dismissing a worker or subjecting him to a detriment for terminating an opt-out agreement will give rise to similar liability on the employer's part as in relation to the worker refusing to enter an opt-out agreement.[21]

6–35   With that in mind, the prudent employer will anticipate the possibility that his workers may not enter or may terminate opt-out agreements, thereby giving rise to the relevant record keeping obligations under Regulation 9. Employers would be well advised therefore still to be prepared in respect of any such worker and scenario to demonstrate they have taken all reasonable steps to ensure compliance with the 48-hour limit and with the relevant record keeping obligations—it would be unwise to assume either that all workers will opt-out or that they will remain opted out.

The Abolition of the "Opt Out"?

6–36   The Government has negotiated with the E.C. the provision in the Working Time Directive for the individual agreement between employer and worker disapplying the 48-hour limit. This provision is set out in Article 18(b)(i) of the Directive and as we have seen is implemented in Regulation 4. However, it should be noted that Article 18(b)(i) also goes on to stipulate that the availability of the individual agreement should be reviewed by the Council of the European Union before November 23, 2003. It therefore remains to be seen whether and for how long the individual opt-out agreement will still be available in future.

---

[20] See Chap. 14.
[21] See Chap. 14.

CHAPTER SEVEN

Rest Entitlements

INTRODUCTION

7–01   The provisions relating to rest breaks and daily and weekly rest periods together form one of the principal health and safety protections afforded to workers by the working time legislation. As discussed in Chapter 1, the Explanatory Memorandum which accompanied the initial proposal by the Commission for a Directive regulating the organisation of working time referred extensively to scientific studies which demonstrated a positive correlation between fatigue (and in particular the length of the working day) and the risk that a worker's health and safety may be endangered.[1]

Thus the eleventh recital to the preamble to the Directive states that "in order to ensure the health and safety of Community workers, the latter must be granted minimum daily, weekly and annual periods of rest and adequate breaks".

Although prior to the adoption of the Directive there was in the United Kingdom no specific statutory Regulation of rest breaks and rest periods on a general basis, it is arguable that, given the scientific evidence referred to above, employers are in certain circumstances under an obligation to ensure that employees[2] have sufficient rest as part of their general duty under section 2(1) of the Health and Safety at Work etc Act 1974 to "ensure the health, safety and welfare at work" of their employees.[3] As it is an implied term of every contract of employment that an employer will take reasonable care of his employee's safety, an employee may be able to enforce this obligation as a matter of contract.[4] For example, in *Pickfords v. ICI plc*[5] the House of Lords accepted that in principle an employer could in certain circumstances be under a duty in tort (and probably therefore also in contract as part of the implied term described above) to warn employees to take rest breaks to minimise the risks of injury in the performance of their job. The corollary of this must surely be that an employer would be obliged to permit the worker to take appropriate breaks for the same purpose.

---

[1] See also *Validation and Development of a method for assessing the risks arising from mental fatigue*, published by the Health and Safety Executive, July 2000, which includes rest periods, breaks and cumulative fatigue as factors in a "fatigue index" designed to measure fatigue.

[2] Unlike the Regulations, this would not apply to workers who were not engaged under a contract of employment.

[3] s.2(2) refers in particular to "the provision and maintenance of ... systems of work that are, so far as is reasonably practicable, safe and without risks to health ... [and] the provision and maintenance of ... a working environment for his employees that is, so far as is reasonably practicable, safe, without risks to health and adequate as regards facilities and arrangements for their welfare at work". However it may still be relevant to those employees who are excluded from the scope of the Regulation but who are covered by the Health and Safety at Work etc Act 1974.

[4] See *Johnstone v. Bloomsbury Health Authority* [1991] I.R.L.R. 118. See Chap. 4, para. 4–07.

[5] [1998] I.R.L.R. 435. Similarly, in *Gandy, Herrick and Gerrard v. Mattessons Wall's Ltd* (unreported) the Oldham County Court held in a case concerning repetitive strain injuries to workers working on an assembly line that the employer was liable (seemingly in tort) for having failed to warn the plaintiffs regarding the risk of strain injury and having operated a system of work in which production rates were too high and job rotation *and rest periods* were inadequate.

7–02 In addition, an employer may also be under an obligation to provide additional rest breaks to an employee who is disabled within the meaning of the Disability Discrimination Act 1995. Section 6(3) of the Act specifically gives altering a person's working hours as an example of an adjustment which it may be reasonable to make if the employer's arrangements in that regard place a disabled person at a substantial disadvantage in comparison with persons who are not disabled.

In the Consultation Document which preceded the Regulations,[6] the Labour Government provided an additional rationale for the introduction of rest entitlements: "If a worker is over-worked or tired, they are less likely to be productive. Appropriate periods of rest will combat tiredness from long hours and contribute toward a better motivated workforce which should enhance competitiveness".

Broadly, the Regulations provide that an adult worker is entitled to:

(a) A rest break of at least 20 minutes if his working day exceeds six hours[7];

(b) A daily rest period of at least 11 uninterrupted hours in each 24-hour period during which he works for his employer[8]; and

(c) A weekly uninterrupted rest period of at least 24 hours in each seven day period during which he works for his employer, or, if his employer so determines, to two uninterrupted rest periods of at least 24 hours or one uninterrupted period of 48 hours in any 14-day period during which he works for his employer.[9]

7–03 The entitlements of young workers are more generous, as specific provision was made in respect of them in the Young Persons Directive,[10] which the United Kingdom also purported to implement by means of the Regulations.

The full title of the Working Time Directive itself betrays the practical effect of these provisions. Although expressed as entitlements for workers, in practice, together with the limitations on weekly working time and night work, they serve to restrict an employer's discretion to organise working time as he sees fit. This curtailment of the managerial prerogative is not however as extensive as it might at first appear, as there are several derogations from the entitlements.

7–04 As with the other provisions of the Directive and the Regulations, there are many areas of ambiguity in this area which will ultimately have to be resolved by tribunals and the courts. Given the proven link between rest and health and safety identified above, it is probable that the wide concept of "working environment" and health and safety supported by the European Court of Justice in *UK v. Council of the European Union*,[11] which encompasses the mental and social well-being of the worker, will be of particular relevance in resolving these ambiguities using the teleological approach to statutory construction discussed in Chapter 2.

It is also vital to note the particular application of Article 13 of the Directive to the area of rest breaks. This provision, which has been referred to as the "principle of the humanisation of work",[12] is potentially of the broadest scope and should strongly influence the interpretation of the Directive and the Regulations in this area.

---

[6] URN: 98/645.
[7] Regulation 12.
[8] Regulation 10.
[9] Regulation 11.
[10] Council Directive 94/33/E.C. on the protection of young people at work.
[11] C–84/94 [1997] I.R.L.R. 30.
[12] Bercusson, *European Labour Law*, p. 311.

ENTITLEMENT TO REST

7–05   It is to be noted at the outset that the provisions relating to rest periods and rest breaks are *entitlements*.[13] This contrasts with the provisions relating to average weekly working time and duration of night work, which are expressed as *limitations*.[14] The distinction will be significant in practice as effectively it means that although an employer cannot lawfully require a worker to work during any period in which he is entitled to rest, it is not unlawful for an employer to permit a worker to choose to work during such a period. As the revised Regulatory Guidance puts it "[E]mployers must make sure that their workers *can* take their rest, but are not required to make sure that they *do* take their rest".[15]

Therefore workers may voluntarily forego their rights to rest, whereas the limits on the average weekly working time and the duration of night work can only be modified or excluded by specific types of agreement in the circumstances allowed in the Regulations. However, if in practice the rights to rest were regularly foregone by a worker, an employer would be well-advised to remind the worker of his entitlements to safeguard against possible claims by the worker that he was not permitted to take them.

This distinction also impacts upon the issue of enforcement. A refusal to grant a worker his entitlement is not a criminal offence under Regulation 29 of the Regulations, whereas breach of the limitations referred to above may be. Rather, a worker has the right to complain to an employment tribunal under Regulation 30.

7–06   In any event, it should be noted that in many cases contracts of employment specify certain periods of rest, whether in the form of lunch hours or breaks or by the definition of contractual working hours. The entitlements provided by the Regulations are not additional to any which are set already by the contract, but create minimum entitlements which override any less favourable entitlement already created in the contract.[16]

In the light of the High Court's decision in *Barber v. RJB Mining (UK) Ltd*,[17] it is almost certainly the case that a worker's entitlements under the Regulations form part of the contract under which he works, so that a worker may in any event bring an action for breach of contract against an employer if he is not allowed to take his full entitlement. If such a breach were regarded as a fundamental breach of contract, an employee[18] who resigned in response to that breach would be deemed to have been constructively dismissed for the purposes of Part X of the Employment Rights Act 1996.[19] Arguably, the principal reason for the employee's resignation, and hence the dismissal, will be that the employee has "refused to forego a right conferred on him by the Regulations". The dismissal would therefore automatically be deemed unfair by virtue of section 101A of the ERA 1996, and consequently in such circumstances an employee would be able to bring a complaint of unfair dismissal regardless of whether he had completed one year's continuous service or whether he was over the normal retiring age for that job.[20]

---

[13] Both the Directive and the Regulation express these provisions in terms of entitlements.

[14] cf. *Barber v. RJB (UK) Mining Ltd* [1999] I.R.L.R. 308, H.C.Q.B. See Chap. 6.

[15] This is subject to the argument raised above about an employer's potential *duty* to provide rest breaks and rest periods to its employees under the Health and Safety at Work etc Act 1974. It is also debatable to what extent a worker may be permitted to endanger his own health and safety by working excessive hours without rest.

[16] Regulation 17.

[17] [1999] I.R.L.R. 308, H.C.Q.B.

[18] But not a worker who was not an employee within the meaning of the Employment Rights Act 1996.

[19] See *Western Excavating Ltd v. Sharp* [1978] I.C.R. 221.

[20] ERA 1996, ss. 108(3)(dd) and 109(2)(dd).

ENTITLEMENT TO REST BREAKS

Legislative provisions

7–07   Article 4 of the Directive provides that:

"Member States shall take the measures necessary to ensure that, where the working day is longer than six hours, every worker is entitled to a rest break, the details of which, including duration and the terms on which it is granted, shall be laid down in collective agreements or agreements between the two sides of industry or, failing that, by national legislation."

It can be seen therefore that whilst the Directive lays down the fundamental principle that workers are entitled to a rest break where their working day exceeds six hours, the duration, nature and timing of that break are to be determined by Member States. Given the absence of collective bargaining at sector-level and the comparative rarity of collective bargaining at any level in the United Kingdom, in practice the legislative minima laid down in the Regulations are likely to be of more importance than the equivalent provisions in other Member States.

In keeping with the general practice adopted in drafting the Regulations, Regulation 12 repeats almost verbatim the wording of the Directive and provides that:

"where an 'adult worker's'[21] daily working time is more than six hours, he is entitled to a rest break ... [the details of which], including its duration and the terms on which it is granted, shall be in accordance with any provisions for the purposes of this Regulation which are contained in a collective agreement or a workforce agreement."[22]

7–08   However, Regulation 12(3) provides that, subject to any provisions of such an agreement, the rest break is to be:

"an uninterrupted period of not less than 20 minutes, and the worker is entitled to spend it away from his workstation if he has one."

The term "rest break" is not defined in either the Directive or the Regulations.

In relation to "young workers",[23] where their daily working time is more than 4½ hours, Regulation 12(4) provides that they are entitled to a rest break of at least 30 minutes away from their workstation. Interestingly, Regulation 12(4) also states that the 30 minutes are to be "consecutive if possible", rather than that the period must be uninterrupted. This reflects the wording of Article 12 of the Young Persons Directive. There is no equivalent provision in respect of an adult worker's rest break entitlement in the Working Time Directive.

7–09   Regulation 12(5) also makes specific provision in respect of young workers for circumstances where the young worker is working for more than one employer. In

---

[21] *i.e.* a worker aged 18 or over (Regulation 2(1)). See Chap. 15.

[22] Regulation 12(1) and 12(2). For a discussion of what constitutes a collective or workforce agreement for these purposes, see Chap. 13.

[23] *i.e.* a worker who is at least 15 years old and in any event is over compulsory school age but not yet 18 (Regulation 2(1)). See Chap. 16.

such cases, the worker's daily working time for the purposes of Regulation 12(4) is to be determined by aggregating the number of hours worked by him for each employer. Again this difference in treatment is due to the differential legal basis for the provisions relating to adult workers and those relating to young workers; Article 8(4) of the Young Persons Directive specifically provides that "where a young person is employed by more than one employer, working days and working time shall be cumulative" but there is no express provision to similar effect in the Working Time Directive.

Duration of rest breaks

7–10 As discussed above, Article 4 of the Working Time Directive does not specify the minimum duration of a rest break. The preamble to the Directive does however state that workers should be granted "adequate" breaks.

The Conservative Government initially proposed an entitlement to a five minute break in order to comply with its obligations under the Directive. The Labour Government extended this to an entitlement to a break of at least 20 minutes in the absence of any collective or workforce agreement, which it described in its Consultation Document as a "fair minimum".[24] Ultimately the question of whether this period is sufficiently long properly to implement the terms of Article 4 will be for the courts to determine. As discussed below, in addition to the need to protect a worker's health and safety in its widest sense, Article 13 of the Working Time Directive may have a major impact on the determination of this issue in any particular case. It is also to be noted that the Young Persons Directive itself specifies the 30 minute period referred to in Regulation 12(4), which a court may consider when deciding what would constitute an "adequate" break.

7–11 For an adult worker, the entitlement is to an "uninterrupted" break of at least 20 minutes.[25] On the other hand, for young workers the entitlement is to a break of 30 minutes which must be "consecutive if possible".[26] As discussed above, the latter requirement stems from the wording of the Young Persons Directive. However, Article 4 of the Working Time Directive does not expressly state that a rest break should be uninterrupted. Whether in fact it would be so construed would depend on a court's view as to whether one uninterrupted period of rest was more beneficial to worker's health and safety than several fragmented breaks.

It has been argued, because of the difference in wording between Regulations 12(3) and 12(4), that in respect of adult workers there is no obligation for the 20 minutes to be consecutive.[27] This would mean that "uninterrupted" would simply mean that a worker was entitled to a total of 20 minutes' rest during which he was not required to work. With respect, this must be wrong. The Regulations clearly envisage an entitlement to one break of the defined duration, a view supported by the Regulatory Guidance.

However, there is nothing to prevent provision being made in a collective or workforce agreement for a worker's entitlement to a break to be taken in segments. It should also be noted in this regard that on the face of it a young worker's break may be split where it is not possible for the whole entitlement to be taken at once. However, given the general tenor of the protection afforded in the Regulations, which is more generous in respect of young workers than adult workers, it is likely that a court would

---

[24] URN 98/645. In the Republic of Ireland, for example, s.12(2) of the Organisation of Working Time Act 1997 provides for a minimum break of at least 30 minutes.
[25] Regulation 12(3).
[26] Regulation 12(5).
[27] Tolleys *Working Time*, C2.2.

adopt a restrictive view of the circumstances in which it could be said that it was not possible to grant a single break of at least 30 minutes.

When should rest breaks be granted?

7–12 Neither the Directive nor the Regulations stipulate the time during the worker's daily working time at which the break should be granted, although it appears that, subject to the terms of any collective or workforce agreement, this is for the employer to decide. However, the Government stated in the Consultation Document which preceded the Regulations that "it is implicit in the word 'break' that it cannot be taken either at the start, or at the end, of a period of working time", a view subsequently repeated in both versions of the Regulatory Guidance. It therefore follows that a break cannot overlap with a worker's daily or weekly rest period.[28]

Nor, on a purposive view of Regulation 12, should an employer be able to insist that the entitlement to a break be exercised within a certain period of a worker commencing work, as this would not be as effective in combating fatigue as a break granted in the middle of the working day. However, it is difficult to see how a court would be able to formulate any precise test as to when a break should be granted. Perhaps the best approach, where the matter has not been dealt with by agreement, would be to require an employer to act reasonably in determining the times at which a break must be taken. Arguably an employer would be obliged to do so in any event pursuant to his implied contractual duty to take care of his employees' safety.[29] If an employer leaves the question of when breaks should be taken to his workers' discretion, he should consider what notice of their intention to take such a break he will require.

It is not immediately clear whether the Regulations require a break to be granted during the first six hours of work. This is connected to the question of whether a worker is entitled to more than one rest break in any given day, which is discussed below.

Multiple rest breaks

7–13 An adult worker is entitled to a rest break where his daily working time exceeds six hours; he is not entitled to a rest break under Regulation 12 if his working time is less than six hours. However, as a worker is entitled to only 11 hours' rest in any 24 hour period,[30] a worker may work for up to 13 hours in any day. It is unclear whether in these circumstances, in the absence of a collective or workforce agreement, a worker is entitled to two rest breaks, as he has worked for two periods of six hours. Having regard to Article 13 of the Directive, and to the broad notion of health and safety in European law, it can certainly be argued that more than one break should be provided.

Equally, the same considerations would support the conclusion that in order to comply with the Directive a worker is entitled not to have to work for six consecutive hours without a rest break.[31] This impacts on the question discussed above of when rest breaks should be granted. On this view, if a worker works less than 12 hours but

---

[28] See the definition of "rest period" in Regulation 2(1). S.12(4) of the Irish Organisation of Working Time Act 1997 also expressly states this.

[29] *Johnstone v. Bloomsbury Health Authority* [1991] I.R.L.R. 118 . See Chap. 4.

[30] Regulation 10. See para. 7–28.

[31] Again this may be the position in any event as a result of the worker's contract, whether by reason of an express term, custom and practice or the employer's implied duty to take reasonable care of his employees' safety. S.12(2) of the Irish Organisation of Working Time Act 1997 would seem to have adopted this construction of Art. 4.

more than six, the break will have to commence during the first six hours of his working day. If a worker works in excess of 12 hours, he would be entitled to a break in each half of his working day.

7–14 Subject to the requirements of Article 13 and Regulation 8, an adult worker will only be entitled to one rest break if he works for less than 12 hours. Article 4 would not appear of itself to require a pro-rated entitlement in respect of hours worked in excess of six in any day. However, the construction of Article 4 adopted above would mean that the single break to which a worker would be entitled in these circumstances would have to be scheduled in such a way as to ensure that the worker nevertheless did not have to work more than six hours during that day without having an "adequate" rest break.

In relation to young workers, it is submitted that the above discussion is equally applicable, although references to six hour units should be replaced with reference to units of 4½ hours. Although there is no direct equivalent of Article 13 in the Young Persons Directive, it is unlikely that young workers would be afforded less protection than their adult counterparts.

Nature of a rest break

7–15 Regulations 12(3) and 12(4) stipulate that a worker should be entitled to spend such breaks away from his workstation if he has one. Although strictly the question of whether the worker is "at his employer's disposal" is not relevant here, as the term "rest break" is not defined by reference to the definition of "working time", it may be inferred from the Advocate General's opinion in the *SIMAP* case[32] that on a purposive view of Article 4 it is relevant to determining whether a break is "adequate". Thus it appears that a worker must be able freely to dispose of his time, and not be at his employer's disposal, during a period in order for it to constitute a rest break within the meaning of the Directive and Regulations.

However, given the length of the break and the fact that it will be taken during the working day, it seems that the concept of when a worker is "at his employer's disposal" which should be applied here should be more restrictive than that used in determining whether a period may constitute working time or a rest period.

Do rest breaks constitute working time?

7–16 This question is discussed in detail in Chapter 3. Broadly speaking, rest breaks during which the worker is entitled to do as he pleases, so that he is not at the disposal of his employer, will not constitute working time for the purposes of the Regulations. If one does not accept the view put forward above concerning the more restrictive interpretation of the phrase "at the employer's disposal" in this area, however, it would still be possible for a rest break to constitute working time.

Is a worker entitled to be paid in respect of rest breaks?

7–17 Both the Regulations and the Directive are silent on this issue. There is therefore no express obligation on an employer under either of these instruments to pay a worker in respect of time during which the worker was on a rest break, although there may be under the worker's contract. Nor would a purposive construction of the Regulations appear to demand that such a right should be implied, unless it was

---

[32] *SIMAP v. Conselleria de Sanidad y Consumo de La Generalidad Valenciana* C–303/98. See Chap. 3.

thought that the fact that a worker was not paid in respect of a rest break would act as a very real disincentive to taking such a break, hence jeopardising the worker's health and safety.

Thus the view taken in the initial Regulatory Guidance that this matter will be determined by the provisions of a worker's contract would appear to be correct.[33]

Multiple Employers

7–18　As stated above, Regulation 12(5) specifically provides that where a young worker works for more than one employer, his daily working time for the purposes of Regulation 12(4) is to be determined by aggregating the number of hours worked by him for each employer. This implements Article 8(4) of the Young Persons Directive. There is no similar provision in either the Regulations or the Working Time Directive in respect of adult workers.

Thus, where a young worker works for one employer for two hours and then immediately commences work for another employer for three hours, he will be entitled to a rest break. In practice this may occur only rarely since generally the worker will have to travel between jobs, or will not begin work on his second job immediately, and these periods will in themselves constitute a rest break if they are of sufficient duration.[34] If they are not, the second employer could grant the worker such a break as was necessary to bring him above the 30-minute threshold at the beginning of his shift, as this would still be a break in his (aggregate) working time.

7–19　If it is an issue, this may cause problems for employers as they will of necessity have to rely on the word of the worker as to how long he has worked that day. The original version of the Regulatory Guidance stated that "[I]t would be reasonable for an employer to make enquiries of any adolescent worker to ascertain whether an entitlement to a rest break is being observed, taking account of the adolescent's total working time". Employers may take comfort in the fact that there are no criminal penalties for failing to grant a worker his entitlement, and that a worker who does not disclose that he is owed a rest break may be taken to have foregone his entitlement if he is aware of his rights.

It would appear that, despite the absence of any express provision to that effect, the position is the same in respect of adult workers, as the right is defined by reference to working time and the definition of "working time" does not distinguish between periods worked for different employers.[35] This is equally applicable in the context of rest periods.

ARTICLE 13: THE PRINCIPLE OF HUMANISATION

7–20　Article 13 of the Working Time Directive, which was inserted by the Council at a late stage in the legislative evolution of the Directive, requires Member States to take the measures necessary to ensure that:

"... an employer who intends to organise work according to a certain pattern takes account of the general principle of adapting work to the worker, with a

---

[33] The National Minimum Wage Regulations 1999 (S.I. 1999 No. 584) provide that a "time worker" is not entitled to be paid in respect of rest breaks (Regulation 15(7)).

[34] Even if these breaks are for less than 30 minutes, they may still count towards the worker's entitlement to a rest break if it is not possible for the worker to be granted his entitlement in one consecutive period.

[35] See Chap. 3.

view, in particular, to alleviating monotonous work and work at a pre-determined work rate, depending on the type of activity, and of safety and health requirements, especially as regards breaks during work."

Thus Article 13 lays down that when organising the pattern of work, and in particular when organising rest breaks, an employer must have regard to:

(a) The general principle that work should be adapted to the worker; and

(b) The requirements of health and safety.

This Article has been described as embodying the principle of "humanisation of work" and is regarded by some commentators as being of considerable significance.[36] It is generally considered that although it appears in the section of the Directive dealing with night and shift work, Article 13 will be of general application.[37]

7–21 In the United Kingdom, the Labour Government stated in its Consultation Document that "[T]he intention of Article 13 is unclear, but appears to replicate and, to an extent, add to Article 6(2)(d) of the Health and Safety Framework Directive"[38]. Article 6(2)(d) provides that employers must, as part of the measures which they are obliged to take to prevent occupational risks to the health and safety of workers, have regard to the principle of:

"... adapting the work to the individual, especially as regards the design of work places, the choice of work equipment and the choice of working and production methods, with a view, in particular, to alleviating monotonous work and work at a pre-determined rate and to reducing their effect on health."[39]

It is to be noted that Article 1(4) of the Working Time Directive expressly provides that, without prejudice to any more stringent and/or specific provisions contained in the Directive, the provisions of the Framework Directive are fully applicable to a worker's entitlement to rest and patterns of work. The implication of this is that employers may have to conduct risk assessments before fixing their working patterns.

7–22 It can be seen that both of the provisions quoted above are concerned especially with the risks to health and safety presented by monotonous work and work at a pre-determined rate, which may be taken to include work on an assembly line or the performance of repetitive tasks. This in turn supports the broad interpretation of health and safety referred to above, as such work will primarily affect a worker's mental and social, rather than physical, well-being. However, neither provision is limited in its scope to such work.

The United Kingdom has purported to transpose Article 13 in Regulation 8, which provides that:

"[W]here the pattern according to which an employer organizes work is such as

---

[36] Bercusson, *European Labour Law*, p. 311.
[37] However, Art. 6 (weekly working time limits) refers only to the need to protect the health and safety of workers.
[38] Council Directive 89/391/EEC on the introduction of measures to encourage improvements in the safety and health of workers at work.
[39] In U.K. law employers must have regard to the principle of humanisation of work when implementing any preventive and protective measures (see the Management of Health and Safety at Work Regulations 1999 (S.I. 1999 No. 3242), Regulation 4 and Sch. 1).

to put the health and safety of a worker employed by him at risk, in particular because the work is monotonous or the work-rate is predetermined, the employer shall ensure that the worker is given adequate rest breaks."

It is doubtful whether this fully transposes Article 13 into United Kingdom law. First, it refers only to health and safety, whereas Article 13 also obliges employers to have regard to the parallel principle of "adapting work to the worker". The significance of this omission is, however, reduced if one adopts the WHO concept of health and safety, which incorporates mental and social well-being as well as physical health.

7–23   Secondly, Regulation 8 applies only where a worker's health and safety is at risk, whereas Article 13 requires an employer to have regard to the principle of health and safety in organising working patterns. Article 13 therefore envisages that working patterns should be formulated in such a way as is as beneficial as possible to the health and safety of a worker, whether or not the worker's health and safety can be said to be at risk. On this basis, Bercusson has suggested that if it could be shown that working time could be re-organised in such a way as to ameliorate health and safety, it would be for an employer to justify its failure to do so on objective grounds.[40]

Finally, Regulation 8 stipulates that the only remedial step that an employer must take if a worker's health and safety is at risk is to ensure that the worker is given "adequate" rest breaks. Although Article 13 suggests that rest breaks will be the primary remedial step which employers should take, it may also be inferred that it envisages that in some cases employers will have to take other steps to implement the principle of adaptation and to secure the health and safety of its workers. In the context of working time, these may include, for example, limiting the duration of the working day, providing additional periods of leave or weekly rest or only requiring workers to work at night where the employer is justified in doing so. Article 13 regards the granting of additional rest breaks as only one illustration of the general principle embodied within it. It has been argued that the most obvious way of ensuring that work is adapted to the worker is for employers to consult with workers on the organisation of working time.[41] Regulation 12, in keeping with the other provisions of the Directive and of the Regulations, emphasises the role of collective bargaining in determining the detailed nature of the rights it confers. In this regard it is noticeable that Article 13 refers to an employer who *intends* to organise work according to a certain pattern, which would enable bargaining to take place before any new pattern of work was implemented.[42]

7–24   Although the precise scope of Article 13 in uncertain, it is nevertheless clear that, notwithstanding the point made above, it will be in the area of rest breaks that Article 13, and indeed Regulation 8, will be of most relevance. As discussed above, it is likely to influence a court's interpretation of the nature, duration and timing of the rest breaks to which a worker is entitled under Article 4 and Regulation 12.[43] In addition, where the pattern of work is such as may put a worker's physical, mental or social well-being at risk, the employer will be obliged to give that worker "adequate" rest breaks, regardless of whether the worker has worked in excess of six hours during that day.

---

[40] Bercusson, *European Labour Law*, p. 313. He also suggests that the test of objective justification may be imported from sex discrimination law.

[41] Bercusson, *European Labour Law*, p. 343.

[42] It is arguable that an employer is in any event *obliged* to consult employee representatives in these circumstances under the Safety Representatives and Safety Committees Regulations 1977 (S.I. 1977 No. 500) and Health and Safety (Consultation with Employees) Regulations 1996 (S.I. 1996 No. 1513).

[43] See Chap. 2 for an explanation of the principle of purposive interpretation.

As an example of the application of Regulation 8, the Government's Consultation Paper suggested that where work was monotonous or at a pre-determined rate, employers should consider awarding workers more short breaks as opposed to a longer continuous break. Similarly the original version of the Regulatory Guidance suggested that an employer should consider granting regular breaks in order to reduce the risks to health and safety. However, Regulation 8 is not a derogation from the entitlement conferred by Regulation 12. It may therefore only be used to argue that a worker is entitled to a rest break in addition to any break to which he is entitled under Regulation 12. If, as submitted above, Regulation 12 entitles a worker to a continuous break of 20 minutes if his daily working time exceeds six hours, an employer will not therefore be able to implement the suggestion in the Consultation Paper unless one of the breaks lasts for at least 20 minutes. However, other breaks will not have to be of this duration although, in their totality, they must be "adequate" to secure the health and safety of the worker.

7–25   One final point to bear in mind is that both Article 13 and Regulation 8 are framed in terms of a requirement on the employer, rather than an entitlement of a worker. Breach of Regulation 8 is a criminal offence,[44] which seems anomalous considering that breach of Regulation 12 is not. However, given that it is an employer's statutory duty to comply with Regulation 8, it would appear that the corollary is that a worker is entitled as a matter of contract to enforce the right.[45] Again, this may be under the implied term that an employer will take reasonable care of his workers' health and safety. If this is correct, workers would be able to bring court proceedings seeking a declaration of their contractual right to additional rest breaks. Equally, the point made above in respect of possible unfair dismissal claims will be applicable if the right is breached.

REST PERIODS

7–26   Article 2(1) defines "rest period" to mean "any period which is not working time". An identical definition is used in the Young Persons Directive.[46]

For the purposes of the Regulations, "rest period" is defined to mean:

> "... a period which is not working time, other than a rest break or leave to which the worker is entitled under these Regulations."[47]

Thus additional rest breaks and leave to which a worker is entitled under his contract, which exceed his entitlements under the Regulations, will count as a "rest period".[48]

7–27   However, as discussed in Chapter 3, if the European Court of Justice follows the approach taken by Advocate General Saggio in the *SIMAP* case,[49] this definition may require amendment if the Regulations are to transpose the Directive properly. The Advocate General opined that not all time that is not working time constitutes a rest period. Rather, time during which a worker is not working, at his employer's disposal nor carrying out his activity or duties, but during which there is still some

---

[44] Regulation 28 and 29. See Chap. 14.

[45] *Barber v. RJB Mining (UK) Limited* [1999] I.R.L.R. 308, H.C.Q.B. See Chap. 6.

[46] Art. 3(2)(f).

[47] Regulation 2(1).

[48] Although Regulation 17 preserves a worker's more favourable contractual rights, it cannot be said that a worker is therefore entitled to those rights under the Regulations.

[49] *SIMAP v. Conselleria de Sanidad y Consumo de La Generalidad Valenciana* C–303/98. See para. 3–12.

psychological connection with work because he is not free to dispose of his time as he wishes, and is therefore unable properly to rest, would (on this view) fall into an intermediate category which is neither working time nor a rest period.[50] The example given by the Advocate General was time during which a worker is on call but is not required to wait at his employer's premises.

Daily Rest Periods

7–28   Regulation 10(1) provides that:

"An adult worker is entitled to a rest period of not less than 11 consecutive hours in each 24 hour period during which he works for his employer."

A worker works for his employer during a period if any of his time during that period is working time.[51]

A young worker is entitled to a rest period of not less than 12 consecutive hours in the same reference period,[52] although Regulation 10(3) provides that this may be interrupted in the case of "activities involving periods of work that are split up over the day or of short duration". There is no similar provision in respect of adult workers; again this is due to the different origins of the provisions.[53]

7–29   Due to the reference to a 24-hour period, the entitlement is not to 11 or 12 hours' consecutive rest during a calendar day. The applicable period which must exceed 11 or 12 hours is essentially that between the time at which working time ends on a particular day and the time at which it starts on the next working day. For example, if a worker works between 09.00 and 17.30 between Monday and Friday, then the worker will have 15½ hours rest between each period of work, and thus will have had his entitlement under Regulation 10. Regulation 10(1) does not require 11 consecutive hours' rest in any rolling period of 24 hours.

If Advocate General Saggio's views are adopted, if a worker works for a period and then returns home for a further period during which he is on-call, his rest period would start only when his on-call period ended. If none of the derogations apply, therefore, this may lead to considerable difficulties in ensuring that such a worker receives his full entitlement to daily rest. However, as discussed above, the worker may voluntarily forego this entitlement if he so wishes. Thus if the worker voluntarily continued to work at home, although this time would be working time, if the work was truly voluntary then a worker could not subsequently complain that he had been deprived of his entitlement under Regulation 10. Similarly, it would appear that a worker who does overtime when he is not required by his employer to do so will be deemed to have foregone his full entitlement to a rest period.[54]

7–30   Subject to the various derogations discussed later in this chapter, therefore, an adult worker may not be compelled to work in excess of 13 hours in a day, less his rest break entitlement. However, this does not give employers an absolute right to compel workers to work a 13-hour day, as this may infringe Article 13.

---

[50] See the discussion of the definition of "rest period" in Art. 1(5) of Council Regulation 3820/85 in Chap. 3.

[51] Regulation 2(1).

[52] Regulation 10(2).

[53] Art. 10(4) of the Young Persons Directive permits Member States to derogate in the manner utilised in Regulation 10(3).

[54] *Sed quaere* whether a worker can lawfully agree to work in unsafe conditions.

Equally, subject to any derogations which may apply, if for the purposes of Regulation 10(1) a 24-hour period is taken to start when a worker's working time begins, all of an adult worker's working time must be confined to the 13-hour period following that time, as otherwise he would not receive 11 *consecutive* hours' rest.

This will not be the case for young workers carrying on "activities involving periods of work that are split up over the day or of short duration", as their rest period may be interrupted.[55] As with any derogation from a basic Community right, this should be restrictively construed. The Government's Consultation Paper stated that the Government believed that "it should not be difficult to establish whether periods of work are reasonably described as being "split up over the day". The characteristics of such a split might be distinguishable from a mere temporary break by its duration in relation to any such break and/or the freedom given to the worker during the time away from work". It is suggested that cleaning work, where a worker was required to work for example two hours before opening hours (*e.g.* 6 a.m. to 8 a.m.) and then for four hours following closing (*e.g.* 6 p.m. to 10 p.m.) would fall within this category. The Consultation Paper went on to say that "whether work might be aptly described as of "short duration" introduces consideration of relativity which might produce different conclusions if one working arrangement is compared to another. The Regulations therefore leave this expression undefined". In these circumstances, Regulation 10(2) will be satisfied as long as the worker is entitled to a total of 12 hours of rest in each 24-hour period.

7–31   However, the Regulations do provide some degree of flexibility in respect of an adult worker in this area as well. Regulation 22(c) provides that Regulation 10(1) does not apply to "workers engaged in activities involving periods of work split up over the day, as may be the case for cleaning staff".[56] However, as discussed below, in such circumstances the employer must provide compensatory rest pursuant to Regulation 24.

WEEKLY REST PERIODS

7–32   Article 5 of the Working Time Directive provides that Member States must take the measures necessary to ensure that:

"... per each seven-day period, every worker is entitled to a minimum uninterrupted rest period of 24 hours plus the 11 hours' daily rest referred to in Article 3."

Thus Regulation 11(1) stipulates that:

"an adult worker is entitled to an uninterrupted rest period of not less than 24 hours in each seven-day period during which he works for his employer."

However, this is expressed to take effect subject to Regulation 11(2), which provides that:

"If his employer so determines, an adult worker shall be entitled to either:

---

[55] Regulation 10(3).
[56] See Chap. 10.

(a) Two uninterrupted rest periods each of not less than 24 hours in each 14-day period during which he works for his employer; or

(b) One uninterrupted rest period of not less than 48 hours in each such 14-day period,

in place of the entitlement provided for in paragraph (1)."

7–33 There is some doubt as to whether this derogation from a worker's strict entitlement under Article 5 is lawful. Article 16(1) of the Directive does permit Member States to lay down a reference period of not exceeding 14 days for the application of Article 5, but this does not necessarily give Member States the right to give employers sole discretion as to the nature of a worker's entitlement.

By virtue of Regulation 11(4), a 7- or 14-day period begins at the time specified in a relevant agreement[57] or, where there are no provisions of a relevant agreement which apply, at the start of each week or (as the case may be) every other week. A week starts at midnight between Sunday and Monday.[58] If an employer opts for a 14-day reference period under Regulation 11(2), this period will begin at the start of every other week, the first such week beginning on October 5, 1998 or, where the worker was not employed with his employer at the time when the Regulations came into force,[59] at the start of the week in which his employment began.

The reference periods are fixed in time rather than rolling. Therefore, subject to any provisions of the worker's contract and to the employer's implied duty in respect of health and safety, an employer could comply with the Regulations by granting a worker 48 hours' rest at the beginning of a 14-day period and then 48 hours' rest at the end of the subsequent period, so that the worker is required to work for 24 consecutive days. Originally the Directive may have resolved this problem, as Article 5 provided that the minimum rest period should in principle include Sunday. However, as discussed in Chapter 1, this phrase was deleted from the Directive following the European Court of Justice's ruling in *United Kingdom v. Council of the European Union*[60] that there was no health and safety justification for such a provision.[61] In any event, as the Government pointed out in its Consultation Document, this requirement was no more than "exhortatory".

7–34 There is no requirement for employers to nominate in advance the days on which workers may take their rest entitlements nor, subject to the terms of a worker's contract, is there anything to prevent an employer chopping and changing between a 7-day and 14-day reference period.[62]

The areas of discretion reserved to employers in this regard, which are additional to the flexibilities afforded to them by the derogations in the Regulations, weaken both the limitations on their ability to organise working time and the protection afforded to workers. It is therefore likely that an employer's implied contractual duties will be of particular relevance in securing adequate protection for workers in respect of the scheduling of weekly rest. Article 13 may also confer additional protection on workers if the courts have regard to it when interpreting Regulation 11.

---

[57] This may therefore be dealt with in a worker's contract of engagement.
[58] Regulation 11(6).
[59] *i.e.* October 1, 1998.
[60] C–84/94 [1997] I.R.L.R. 30.
[61] Although an identical provision may still be found in Art. 10(2) of the Young Persons Directive, it is probable that this would also be struck out if challenged.
[62] However, the Government did state in its Consultation Paper that it would be good practice for employers and workers to agree beforehand whether workers are to be granted two periods of 24 hours' rest or one period of 48 hours.

Young Workers

7–35   A young worker is entitled to a rest period of not less than 48 hours in each 7-day period in which he works for his employer.[63] This minimum weekly rest period must be provided each week; it cannot be averaged out over two weeks.

It is to be noted that, unlike Regulation 11(1), Regulation 11(3) does not specify that the period should be uninterrupted. However, it may be inferred from Regulation 11(8)(a), which provides that, as in the case of a young worker's daily rest period under Regulation 10(3), the minimum weekly rest period may be interrupted in the case of activities involving periods of work that are split up over the day or are of short duration, that it is only in those circumstances that the 48 hours may be non-consecutive.

7–36   Regulation 11(8)(b) provides that the minimum period may be reduced where this is justified by "technical or organization reasons", subject to a minimum period of 36 consecutive hours. The revised Regulatory Guidance states that such a reduction may be made "if the nature of the job makes it unavoidable". This may be the case, for example, where the worker's activities involve the need for continuity of service, such as in the media industry. However, the extent to which circumstances which in relation to adult workers constitute special cases justifying a derogation from the rest entitlement under Regulation 21 may justify a reduction in a young worker's weekly rest entitlement must be doubtful, as Regulation 21 expressly does not apply to young workers.

It is noticeable that Article 10(2) of the Young Persons Directive provides that "[W]here justified by technical or organization reasons, the minimum rest period may be reduced, *but may in no circumstances be less than 36 consecutive hours*".[64] In the light of this it is possible that Regulation 11(3) should be read as requiring a minimum period of 36 *consecutive* hours' rest even if an employer is entitled to interrupt the worker's rest period under Regulation 11(8)(a).

INTERFACE BETWEEN DAILY AND WEEKLY REST PERIODS

7–37   As discussed above, Article 5 provides that a worker is entitled to "a minimum uninterrupted rest period of 24 hours plus the 11 hours' daily rest referred to in Article 3". However, it goes on to state that:

> "[I]f objective, technical or work organization conditions so justify, a minimum rest period of 24 hours may be applied."

This reference to a rest period omits two of the conditions specified in respect of rest periods in the first part of Article 5; first that it be uninterrupted, and secondly that it be in addition to a worker's daily rest period. However, the better view is that this means that in the specified circumstances a worker's daily rest period may be incorporated into his weekly rest period rather than that it qualifies a worker's right to an "uninterrupted" period of rest.

Thus, Regulation 11(7) stipulates that:

> "The minimum rest period to which an adult worker is entitled under paragraph

---

[63] Regulation 11(3); Young Persons Directive, Art. 10(2).
[64] Italics supplied.

(1) or (2) shall not include any part of a rest period to which the worker is entitled under Regulation 10(1), except where this is justified by objective or technical reasons or reasons concerning the organization of work."

7–38   In general, therefore, an adult worker will be entitled to 35 consecutive hours of rest every week (or 59 consecutive hours' rest once a fortnight) unless the employer is able to justify the amalgamation of his daily and weekly rest periods on objective or technical grounds or grounds concerning the organization of work. It is submitted that an employer must also be able to justify on objective grounds the extent of the amalgamation, so that the fact that a reason of the specified nature exists is not of itself sufficient automatically to justify the reduction of the 35-hour period to 24 hours.

It is not clear what circumstances would in fact justify the incorporation (whether partial or full) of the daily rest period within the weekly rest period. The original version of the Regulatory Guidance stated that "such reasons would have to be inherent in the nature of the work or its desired purpose, rather than merely to avoid the effect of the Regulations". Given that Regulation 11(7) is in effect a derogation from a worker's entitlement under Regulation 10(1), it should be restrictively construed, particularly where Article 13 of the Working Time Directive is in issue.

Many of the circumstances in which an employer might be justified in availing himself of the power reserved in Regulation 11(7) are in any event listed as special cases in Regulation 21, so that Regulations 10(1) and 11(1) would not in fact apply to those workers. However, in such cases employers must provide the workers with "compensatory rest".[65] By contrast, there is no provision for compensatory measures if the conditions specified in Regulation 11(7) are met.

7–39   It is submitted that the proper reading of the Regulations is that if any of the circumstances specified in Regulation 21 arise, an employer cannot elect to avoid the compensation requirements by taking advantage of Regulation 11(7). However, in such circumstances Regulation 11(7) may be read as limiting the amount of compensatory rest which the employer is required to grant the worker. Indeed, this may prove to be the principal function of Regulation 11(7).

The limit on average weekly working time will also have an impact on the application of Regulation 11(7) unless that limit does not apply to the worker in question.

Neither weekly nor daily rest may in any circumstances be amalgamated with annual leave granted pursuant to Regulation 13.[66]

DEROGATIONS FROM REST ENTITLEMENTS

Adult workers

7–40   These are discussed in more detail in Chapters 12 and 15. For these purposes, it is sufficient to note that the rest entitlements do not apply to workers within the excluded sectors[67] or to workers whose working time is not measured or predetermined or who can determine their own working time.[68]

The following further derogations, however, take effect subject to the provisions of Regulation 24:

---

[65] Regulation 24. See below.
[66] See the definition of "rest period" in Regulation 2(1).
[67] Regulation 19.
[68] Regulation 20(1).

(a) Regulation 10(1), 11(1) and (2) and 12(1) do not apply to a worker who falls within any of the special cases listed in Regulation 21, for example where the worker's activities are such that his place of work and place of residence are distant from one another;

(b) Regulation 10(1) and 11(1) and (2) do not apply to a "shift worker" when he changes shift and cannot take a daily or weekly rest period between the end of one shift and the start of the next one[69];

(c) Regulation 10(1) and 11(1) and (2) do not apply to workers engaged in activities involving periods of work split up over the day, as may be the case for cleaning staff[70]; and

(d) Any or all of Regulation 10(1), 11(1) and (2) and 12(1) may be modified or excluded by a collective or workforce agreement.[71]

Young workers

7–41   The derogations from rest entitlements are much more restrictive in relation to young workers. Briefly, the derogations are as follows:

(a) Regulation 10(2) and 11(3) do not apply in relation to a young worker serving as a member of the armed forces[72];

(b) Regulation 10(2), 11(3) and 12(4) do not apply in relation to a young worker whose employment is subject to Regulation under section 55(2)(b) of the Merchant Shipping Act 1995[73];

(c) Regulation 10(2) and 12(4) do not apply in relation to a young worker where his employer requires him to undertake work which no adult worker is available to perform and which:
  (i) is occasioned by either an occurrence due to unusual and unforseeable circumstances, beyond the employer's control, or exceptional events, the consequences of which could not have been avoided despite the exercise of all due care by the employer;
  (ii) is of a temporary nature; and
  (iii) must be performed immediately.[74]

Compensatory rest must be provided in cases (a) and (c). In case (c), this rest must be provided within three weeks.[75] This latter requirement stems from Article 13 of the Young Persons Directive.

COMPENSATORY REST

7–42   It can be seen from the discussion above that although there are fairly extensive derogations from a worker's entitlements to rest, a worker's health and safety is still protected in many cases by an employer's obligation to provide the worker with compensatory rest or other appropriate protection. This requirement

---

[69] Regulation 22(1)(a) and (b).
[70] Regulation 22(1)(c).
[71] Regulation 23(a).
[72] Regulation 25(2).
[73] Regulation 26.
[74] Regulation 27.
[75] Regulation 27(2).

originates from Article 17(2) of the Working Time Directive, the key provisions of which have been transposed almost verbatim into Regulation 24 and are discussed fully in Chapter 11.

RECORD KEEPING[76]

7–43   There is no requirement for employers to record the rest breaks and rest periods granted to their workers. However, it is clearly advisable for them to do so in order to be in a position to defend any claim by a worker that they were not granted their entitlement, or a criminal prosecution due to, for example, an alleged breach of Regulation 24.

---

[76] See Chap. 18 for a full discussion on record keeping.

CHAPTER EIGHT

Annual Leave

INTRODUCTION

8–01 Prior to October 1, 1998, workers in the United Kingdom had no entitlement to holiday (whether paid or unpaid) under either statute or common law. In contrast with many of its European neighbours U.K. holidays were traditionally a matter to be agreed between employer and employee in the contract of employment and the issue was almost entirely free of Government intervention. This was true even for those whose hours of work were otherwise governed by statute, such as young workers and HGV drivers. The common law tradition of freedom of contract gave employers and workers great flexibility over the issue of holiday pay and associated rights such as the carrying forward of untaken holiday and payment of holiday pay on termination of the relationship.

Until the Working Time Regulations came into force therefore, it was not unlawful for an employer to require a worker to work 52 weeks a year, without any time off, even on bank holidays. In practice of course, most employers did grant employees contractual rights to paid leave which included the right to be paid for bank holidays. However a substantial minority of non-employee workers were not entitled to any paid leave, with the highest concentration of such workers being found, perhaps not surprisingly, amongst temporary, casual, part-time and agency workers who have traditionally benefited from less favourable terms and conditions and employment protection than permanent and full-time employees. The consultation document issued by the Conservative Government before the last election[1] cited the Labour Force Survey of Spring 1995 which estimated that there were 1.8 million employees in the United Kingdom with annual holiday entitlement of less than three weeks, of which 0.8m were full-time and more than one million were part-time; and approximately 2.7 million employees who had less than four weeks' paid holiday a year, with 1.1 million of those being full-time and 1.6 million part-time.

8–02 Regulations 13–16 therefore represent a significant break with common law tradition by creating a new statutory entitlement to paid holiday and laying down a detailed statutory framework governing the way in which the entitlement operates in practice. This new statutory right appears simple enough on the face of it, with Regulation 13 granting all workers the right to three weeks' paid leave a year until November 23, 1999 and four weeks' paid leave thereafter. In practice, however, the annual leave provisions are proving to be amongst the most complex of the Regulations and appear to be giving rise to more difficulties in implementation and resultant litigation than any other. Whilst this could be due to the complexity of the Regulations themselves, it may also be a reflection of the lack of familiarity of the tribunal system in dealing with the concepts of paid leave, and the myriad of holiday

---

[1] "A Consultation Document on measures to implement provisions of the E.C. Directive on the organisation of working time."

schemes that exist in practice and which have had to be intertwined with the statutory provisions.

When the Labour Government published its consultation document on the Working Time Regulations,[2] it estimated that the cost of complying with the new annual leave provisions would be £0.47 billion during the period to November 1999 (when the right was only to three weeks' paid leave) and £0.87 billion thereafter when the entitlement increased to four weeks' paid leave per year. This out of a total estimated cost of £1.9 billion (to 1999) and £2.3 billion thereafter.

In its interim report on the implementation of the Regulations published in October 1999[3] the Employment Market Analysis and Research Department of the DTI found that the right to paid holiday had been "*the least problematic aspect of the WTR for our case-study organisations*" and that the main issue raised was "*the provision of leave for casual workers, especially 'as and when casuals', such as 'bank' workers in NHS trusts and other organisations ... this issue is yet to be resolved in a number of establishments.*"

8–03 The Report indicated that most employers already provided contractual holiday that was equal to or in excess of the statutory entitlement save in respect of casual and temporary staff for whom the issue had not yet been entirely resolved. Notwithstanding this fact, it did report a number of changes that had been made to the operation of existing holiday schemes, and notably the abolition of the practice in some organisations of "buying-out" paid leave from employees, and reducing the qualifying period after which leave can be taken.

ARTICLE 7 OF THE WORKING TIME DIRECTIVE

8–04 The origin of the statutory right to paid annual leave is contained in Article 7 of the Directive, which provides that:

> "1. Member States shall take the measures necessary to ensure that every worker is entitled to paid annual leave of at least 4 weeks in accordance with the conditions for entitlement to, and granting of such leave laid down by National legislation and/or practice.
> 2. The minimum period of paid annual leave may not be replaced by an allowance in lieu except where the employment relationship is terminated."

The Directive therefore specifically provides for Member States in implementing the right to annual leave to set their own conditions governing the way in which annual leave will be granted and this open invitation has not gone unheeded! In the United Kingdom the Government has made considerable use of this option and in contrast with other areas such as, for example, the definition of working time[4] where the Regulations copy verbatim whole passages from the Directive, the Government has expanded greatly upon the Directive by translating this simple paragraph into more than two pages of detailed rules on annual leave in the Regulations themselves.

8–05 On the face of it the provisions of the Directive appear simple enough and this simplicity has been relied upon by public sector employees seeking to rely upon them directly to establish a right to annual leave in the period between November 23, 1996, when the Directive should have been implemented in the United Kingdom, and

---

[2] Measures to Implement provisions of the E.C. Directives on the organisation of working time and the protection of young people at work URN 98/645.
[3] Implementation of the Working Time Regulations.
[4] See Chap. 3.

October 1, 1998 when the Regulations came into force. However, it now appears that Article 7 is not sufficiently precise and unconditional to have direct effect.[5] In the unreported case of *Shevlane v. Mid-Kent College of Higher and Further Education*[6] a lecturer who was dismissed prior to the implementation of the Directive in the United Kingdom was held by an employment tribunal not to be entitled to paid holiday under Article 7 of the Directive because the Article was not sufficiently precise and unconditional to be capable of having direct effect. In March 1998 the EAT at a preliminary hearing of his appeal against the first instance decision of the tribunal considered that he did have an arguable case and his appeal could therefore proceed to a full hearing. Although there was initially some doubt as to whether Article 4 did have direct effect, the issue now appears to have been resolved by the Court of Appeal in the following case.

THE EAST RIDING OF YORKSHIRE COUNCIL V. GIBSON[7]

8–06   In June 2000 the Court of Appeal gave judgment in the first case to come before it on the Regulations. The case concerned Mrs Gibson who worked for the Council of the East Riding of Yorkshire as a part-time swimming instructor at Haltenprice Leisure Centre in Hull. Under her contract she was required to work 11½ hours per week. She also had another contract with the Council under which she worked an additional 14 hours a week during school time as a school swimming instructor. She was paid an hourly rate and under neither contract was she entitled to any paid leave. On the contrary, clause 12 of her school instructor contract expressly stated that *"there is no annual leave entitlement attached to this post"*.

In July 1997 Mrs Gibson issued proceedings against her employer, including a claim that she had not received any payments for annual leave since November 1996 when the Directive should have been implemented in the United Kingdom. The parties agreed that the Council was an emanation of the State and that Mrs Gibson was a "worker" within the meaning of the Directive. In order to succeed in her claim however, Mrs Gibson had to establish that the provisions of Article 7 were sufficiently precise and unconditional as to have direct effect in the European Member States and therefore grant individual rights to workers in the public sector. The employment tribunal rejected her claim and held that Article 7 was not directly effective. She appealed and in January 1999 the EAT chaired by its then President, Morison J, held that Article 7 was precise enough to confer rights and therefore was capable of being directly effective. This was despite the fact that other areas of the Directive such as Article 2.1 defining "working time" were not capable of being directly effective. In giving judgment Morison J. stated that:

> "the structure of the Directive is consistent with it having direct effect. It is designed to require Member States to confer minimum rights upon workers in a way which can be said to be unconditional . . . Article 7 is clear and precise and, in our view, admits of no ambiguity or conditionality."

8–07   As a result, "Article 7 has direct effect so that during the period from November 23, 1996 to October 1, 1998 an employee of an emanation of the State may take advantage of its protection". According to the EAT therefore, Mrs Gibson was

---

[5] For a more detailed analysis of the principles of direct effect see Chap. 2.
[6] March 6, 1998 EAT 242/98.
[7] [2000] A.E.R. 846.

entitled to four weeks' paid annual leave during that period. The right was to four weeks' and not three weeks' leave because the British Government had not at that stage taken up the option in Article 18(i)(b)(ii) of the Directive to grant just three weeks' paid leave during the transitional period to November 1999, and therefore the full four week provision applied. The EAT recognised that there were some "gaps" in Article 7 which would need to be filled, such as, for example, the start and end of a "leave year". However it was the view of the EAT and in particular the lay members that any gaps would be filled by "custom and practice in the workplace".

The Council appealed to the Court of Appeal, which gave its judgment on June 25, 2000. In giving judgment Mummery L.J. (formerly President of the Employment Appeal Tribunal) reviewed the principles that should be taken into account in determining whether a provision has direct effect and went on to find that the provisions of Article 7 of the Directive were not sufficiently precise as to have direct effect. The Court of Appeal recognised that Article 7 was precise to the extent that it provided for a clear minimum period of four weeks' paid annual leave **but** there were a number of questions that remained unanswered, to the extent that a national court would not be able to enforce Article 7 without knowing the essential conditions of an individual's entitlement to paid holiday leave. A national court could not fill the gaps in the absence of these by reference to national practice or custom in the workplace and therefore national legislative measures were needed to define the precise entitlement to annual leave. Indeed Mummery L.J. stated that:

> "the very existence of gaps in Article 7 . . . is a strong indication that the terms of the Article are insufficiently precise as to have direct effect in the courts and tribunals of Member States."

8–08   The fact that the Government has taken two pages of detailed Regulations to lay down the conditions surrounding the right to annual leave in the Regulations is, it is submitted, an indication of the complexity of the issues surrounding the right. Indeed it would be fair to say that Article 7 has been the subject of more attention by the parliamentary draftspeople in the United Kingdom than any other single provision of the Directive.

Had the Court of Appeal upheld the decision of the EAT, the net result would have been that those who worked for an emanation of the State between November 23, 1996 and October 1, 1998 would have been entitled to four weeks' paid leave. This possibility now appears however to have been excluded.

THE SCOPE OF THE RIGHT TO ANNUAL LEAVE

8–09   Amongst all of the provisions of the Regulations, the right to annual leave is unique in that it is the only one which is not subject to any exception or derogation. Regulations 13 to 16 apply to all workers covered by the Regulations without any exception. Even those workers who are excluded from many of the other substantive provisions of the Regulations, such as for example those employed as domestic servants[8] or those whose working time is not measured or pre-determined[9] are covered by the annual leave provisions. Similarly the "special cases" exemptions set out in Regulation 21[10] do not apply and it is not possible to derogate from the annual leave

---

[8] Regulation 19. See Chap. 12.
[9] Regulation 20. See Chap. 12.
[10] See Chap. 12.

provisions by way of collective, workforce or other "relevant" agreement. However the employer by way of a relevant agreement can achieve some flexibility in implementing the annual leave provisions although the basic leave entitlement can not be reduced.

EXCLUDED SECTORS

8–10   The only workers excluded from the annual leave provisions are those who are excluded from the entire ambit of the Regulations, namely those employed in the excluded sectors of activity listed in Regulation 18.[11] These include those engaged in air, rail, road, sea, inland waterway and lake transport, sea fishing, other work at sea, the activities of doctors in training and specific activities of the Armed Forces, Police or other civil protection services. There has been considerable debate as to whether administrative and clerical workers involved in excluded sectors of activity should benefit from the provisions of the Directive or not.[12] However in relation to annual leave it is submitted that the better view is that all workers in the excluded sectors of activity are currently excluded from the right to paid annual leave, irrespective of the nature of the work they carry out within that sector. That was the approach adopted by the Leicester Employment Tribunal in the unreported case of *Coleman v. Eddie Stobart Limited*[13] where workers involved in loading and unloading products and raw materials from the delivery lorries operated by their employer were held not to be entitled to paid annual leave. The business of the employer was essentially that of a transport company and the tribunal considered that the work carried out by the workers in question was in effect part of those transport activities.

That case involved workers who were involved in transport activities but the question came before the EAT in the case of *Bowden v. Tuffnells Parcels Express Limited*[14] in the context of workers not involved in transport activities. Tuffnells operate as a parcel delivery company, which specialises in the delivery of parcels by road. They had a number of depots around the country and Mrs Bowden worked part-time as a "batcher" receiving and sorting consignment notices in an office above a loading bay. She was not entitled to paid holiday under her contract and claimed that under the Working Time Regulations she was entitled to statutory annual leave. All parties accepted that Mrs Bowden was a worker. The employment tribunal that initially heard the case made a finding of fact that she worked in the Company's offices and that she had no contact with the vans or other transport and could not contractually be required to work in actual transport. She was essentially employed in an administrative role in a transport company.

8–11   Mrs Bowden and two colleagues claimed that they were entitled to paid leave whereas Tuffnells argued that they were working within the transport sector and were therefore not entitled to any. The employment tribunal in Ashford held that all three applicants were excluded from the benefits of the Working Time Regulations and were therefore not entitled to paid leave. They appealed and the case came before the new President of the EAT, Lindsay J. In giving judgment, Lindsay J. recognised that the language of Regulation 18 refers merely to a sector of activity. He also recognised that it would be possible either in the Regulations or the Directive to have made provision to exclude clerical or administrative staff within a certain sector of

[11] See Chap. 12.
[12] For a more detailed analysis of this debate see Chap. 12.
[13] Case number 1900920/99 and others; October 11, 1999.
[14] [2000] I.R.L.R. 560.

activity or those within the sector who were not required to work away from home. However, he also went on to comment that the EAT had been unable to see any:

> "safety, health, social, economic or even rational reason underpinning the exception of, for example, all workers in the road transport sector of activity ... We have unfortunately been quite unable to see what, if any, rational or other material distinction could, in relation to annual holidays be required to exist between, say a clerk in a shipping office and a clerk at a solicitors, a telephonist to an airline and one in a department store."

He recognised that in a number of proposals to extend the Working Time Directive it was *"the opinion of responsible community bodies"* that *"non-mobile workers in the road transport sector of activity are, as yet, excluded from the benefit of the Working Time Directive and that a formal amendment is required before the Directive will be able to cover them."*

8–12 The EAT was not able to resolve this dilemma and decided to refer the matter to the European Court of Justice. The questions referred to the ECJ by the EAT were as follows:

1   Given the view being taken by responsible European bodies that an amendment to the Working Time Directive is needed, how far can it be inferred from non-legislative material such as the views of the European Parliament, the Commission and the Council's Common Position Paper either that:

   (a) as yet a proper construction of the wording of Article 1.3 of the Directive is one which excludes all such persons; or
   (b) that such a reading would not represent a just and purposive construction of the Article?

2   Is the court entitled (and if so, by reference to what principles) to apply national law to the facts of a particular case so as to give effect to the broad purpose of the Directive to give every worker a right to paid annual leave, notwithstanding the clarity of the wording appearing to exclude that purpose?

3   Are all workers employed in the road transport area of activity necessarily excluded from the scope of the Working Time Directive?

4   If not, what test should national courts apply in determining whether workers employed in the road transport sector are covered by the Directive and which are not.

At the time of writing no date has been fixed for the hearing of this case by the European Court of Justice. Until this reference has been determined, it is submitted that the better view is that all workers in the excluded sectors of activity are excluded from the scope of the Regulations.[15]

REGULATION 13—THE ENTITLEMENT TO ANNUAL LEAVE

8–13   The basic entitlement to annual leave is contained in Regulation 13. This provides that:

---

[15] For a more detailed analysis of the excluded sectors see Chap. 12.

(1) Subject to paragraphs (5) [accrual of annual leave during the first leave year of employment] and (7) [qualifying period for exercising the right to annual leave], a worker is entitled in each leave year to a period of leave determined in accordance with paragraph (2).

(2) The period of leave to which a worker is entitled under paragraph (1) is—

(a) in any leave year beginning on or before November 23, 1998, three weeks;

(b) in any leave year beginning after November 23, 1998 but before November 23, 1999, three weeks and a proportion of a fourth week equivalent to the proportion of the year beginning on November 23, 1998 which has elapsed at the start of that leave year; and

(c) in any leave year beginning after November 23, 1999, four weeks.

8–14 Under this Regulation therefore a worker is entitled to a basic three weeks' paid annual leave up to November 23, 1999 and to four weeks' paid annual leave thereafter. The right to annual leave is expressed as an individual entitlement enforceable by way of a complaint to an employment tribunal. The fact that the right is expressed as an individual entitlement has a number of consequences, including:

(a) The employer cannot lawfully require workers to do anything which would effectively deny them that entitlement nor impose any detriment on the workers for asserting the entitlement **and** must take any necessary measures to ensure that the workers can take up that entitlement; but

(b) If workers want to work during time when they are entitled not to do so, the employer can allow them to do so; and

(c) It is for workers to exercise their right to annual leave, so that if they do not do so through no fault of the employer, then they will lose that right.

8–15 Unlike other provisions of the Regulations, such as the limits on working time and the record keeping obligations, the health and safety authorities have no jurisdiction to enforce the provisions on annual leave. The right to paid leave has therefore been treated as a private law matter to be enforced by individual workers rather than an issue pertaining to public health and safety and legally there is no requirement on an employer to ensure that a worker exercises these rights.

Although both the Regulations and the Directive create one new right—to paid leave—for the purposes of implementing the right in practice, it is more convenient to consider the two parts of this entitlement separately. Firstly, the entitlement to take time off from work, and secondly the right to be paid in respect of that time.

THE RELATIONSHIP BETWEEN STATUTORY AND CONTRACTUAL RIGHTS TO ANNUAL LEAVE

8–16 The right to paid annual leave operates as a statutory minimum floor of rights and does not reduce any more favourable contractual entitlements which are contained in a worker's contract with the employer. Regulation 16(4) specifically provides that the right to be paid for statutory annual leave "does not affect any right of a worker to remuneration under his contract".

Regulation 17 provides that:

> "Where during any period a worker is entitled to a rest period, rest break or *annual leave* both under a provision of these Regulations and under a separate provision (including a provision of his contract), he may not exercise the two rights separately, but may, in taking a rest period, break or leave during that period, take advantage of whichever right is, in any particular respect, the more favourable." [our emphasis]

8–17   As a result of this provision, a worker can "pick and choose" between contractual and statutory rights to paid leave and elect to exercise whichever is the more favourable in any respect. This is a concept which is not uncommon in the context of employment protection legislation and has traditionally applied to rights such as the right to maternity leave, recently having been extended to the new right to parental leave.[16] However, in the context of the annual leave provisions it has meant that even those employers who traditionally provided contractual rights to paid leave have not been unaffected by the Regulations, and those contractual rights must now be interpreted in the context of the statutory provisions. So, for example, an employer whose holiday policy provided for no payments of holiday pay on termination of employment, or for no holiday to be taken during the first year of employment, could face claims under the Regulations from workers seeking to rely upon the more favourable statutory rules.

However, Regulation 17 does specify that a worker cannot choose to exercise both statutory **and** contractual rights to paid leave and this is reinforced by Regulation 16(5) which provides that:

> "Any contractual remuneration paid to a worker in respect of a period of leave goes towards discharging any liability of the employer to make payments under this Regulation in respect of that period; and conversely, any payment of remuneration under this Regulation in respect of a period goes towards discharging any liability of the employer to pay contractual remuneration in respect of that period."

8–18   This Regulation was the subject of scrutiny by the Manchester Employment Tribunal in the case of *Barton v. SCC Limited*[17] In this case the worker were provided with 29 days paid leave a year, well in excess of the statutory entitlement. However the payment for holiday days was calculated in part by reference to the workers' attendance records. As a result the workers were paid less than their "normal week's pay" (calculated in accordance with the Employment Rights Act 1996) for certain holiday periods and they claimed that the employer had therefore failed to comply with its obligations under the Regulations. The employer argued that the additional holiday pay that the employees received in respect of the periods of leave over and above the statutory entitlement should be set off against the statutory entitlement. The tribunal did not agree and found that payments made in respect of additional contractual leave periods should not be taken into account in assessing whether the worker has received proper payment for a particular period of statutory leave. The

---

[16] The Maternity and Parental Leave etc Regulations 1999, S.I. 1999 No. 3312.
[17] Case number 2403475 and others: October 6, 1999.

correct approach was to focus on the period in question and assess whether the worker had received payments in respect of that period which complied with the Regulations.

Interestingly, the tribunal also found that it was for the worker to choose which weeks she or he took as statutory leave and which as contractual leave.

8–19 A worker cannot claim **both** contractual holiday pay **and** statutory paid leave for the same day of absence, but must choose to exercise one or the other. In many cases the division between contractual and statutory leave will not be clear in practice and provided that a contractual holiday scheme complies with the minimum requirements of the Regulations then worker and employer may not need or wish to distinguish between them. However, in some circumstances an employer may wish to distinguish between the two if it is providing contractual provisions that are more generous than the statutory. Take the example of the employer who has in the past prevented a worker from accruing holiday during periods of long sickness absence or absence beyond the ordinary maternity leave period and wishes to continue to do so. Under the Regulations, it is submitted that the entitlement to statutory leave is unaffected by absences from work. Although the Regulations do not deal explicitly with this point, for the purposes of calculating whether a worker has sufficient service to qualify for the entitlement to annual leave under Regulation 13(7),[18] Regulation 13(8) states that:

> "a worker has been continuously employed for thirteen weeks if his relations with his employer have been governed by a contract during the whole or part of each of those weeks."

8–20 This would suggest that provided the worker is still governed by a contract with her or his employer, then she or he will still have the right to statutory leave notwithstanding the fact that she or he is absent from work[19] and that the decisive factor is therefore the contractual relationship rather than the availability and indeed ability of the individual worker to provide services during that period. An employer who wishes to provide in the contract of employment that annual leave will not continue to accrue whilst a worker is off on long-term sick or on additional maternity leave may need to distinguish between statutory leave and additional contractual leave in the contract. It is submitted that there is no reason (subject to any arguments under the Disability Discrimination Act in relation to disability related absences) why an employer should not provide in the contract that annual leave or indeed entitlement to other benefits will not accrue during such a period. Indeed, the Maternity and Parental Leave etc. Regulations 1999 which specify the provisions of an employee's contract that remain in force during any period of additional maternity or parental leave[20] make no mention of holiday entitlement but refer instead to provisions such as notice period, trust and confidence, disciplinary or grievance procedures and confidentiality. This is in contrast with the situation during the period of ordinary maternity leave when, in accordance with section 71 of the Employment Rights Act 1996 and Regulation 9 of the Maternity and Parental Leave etc. Regulations 1999 an employee is entitled to the benefit of her normal terms and conditions of employment with the exception of remuneration.

---

[18] See para. 8–28 below.

[19] See however the decision of the London (North) Employment Tribunal dated November 3, 1999 in *R. C. Warnes v. Situsec Contractors Limited*, Case Number 6003949/99 (unreported) on the issue of *exercising* the entitlement to paid leave during periods of extended sickness absence, considered in more detail below.

[20] Regulation 17 S.I. 1999 No. 3312.

During a period of ordinary maternity leave therefore contractual leave entitlement will continue to accrue. However an employer could provide in the contract that during periods of additional maternity leave or parental leave, holiday over and above the statutory entitlement will not accrue. For these purposes the employer may wish to specify that the first 20 days of paid leave taken by a worker in any leave year (including bank holidays) will be treated as the worker's statutory leave entitlement and that any additional days granted by the employer will be subject to special rules. These rules could potentially include, for example, provisions that additional entitlement could be "bought out" by the employer, and that there would be no accrual during periods of extended absence for whatever reason and no entitlement to payment of untaken holiday on termination.

BANK HOLIDAYS

8–21   The eight days of the year which in the United Kingdom are commonly known as "Bank", "Public" or in many cases "Statutory" holidays are indeed somewhat of a misnomer as there is no statutory right to be absent from work on these days, much less to be paid for such absence. The Regulations themselves make no reference whatsoever to "Bank" holidays and certainly do not grant the right to take those days as paid holiday. However, in its Guidance issued shortly prior to the entry into force of the Regulations,[21] the DTI stated that as with other contractual leave, "bank" holidays

> "can be used to discharge an employer's responsibility for providing the statutory leave under these Regulations. [Where a worker is paid for a public holiday this will count towards their entitlement to annual leave.]"

It is submitted that this view is correct and that an employer can set off "bank" holidays against the statutory period of paid leave if the worker is paid for the bank holidays. However if an employer wishes to insist that a worker takes a bank holiday as paid leave and that this will count towards the annual statutory leave entitlement it may be preferable to specify this explicitly in the contract. A worker will not then be able to argue that she or he has not had the necessary period of notice from the employer requiring him or her to take leave at a particular time under Regulation 15.[22]

THE LEAVE YEAR

8–22   The "leave year" is fundamental to the exercise of the right to annual leave which is expressed as being a right to a certain amount of holiday "in any leave year".[23]

Regulation 13 (3) deals with the issue of the leave year and specifies that:

> "A worker's leave year, for the purposes of this Regulation, begins
>
> (a) On such date during the calendar year as may be provided for in a relevant agreement; or
> (b) Where there are no provisions of a relevant agreement which apply—

---

[21] Working Time Regulations: Regulatory Guidance.
[22] See para. 8–52 below.
[23] Regulation 13(2).

(i) If the worker's employment began on or before October 1, 1998, on that date and each subsequent anniversary of that date; or

(ii) If the worker's employment begins after October 1, 1998, on the date on which that employment begins and each subsequent anniversary of that date."

In many cases the contract of employment will establish the "leave year" or as it is more commonly known the "holiday year" and these arrangements will be unaffected by the Regulations. If however no holiday year is specified in the contract, the default arrangements apply so that:

(i) If the worker started work for the employer before the date on which the Regulations came into force (*i.e.* before October 1, 1998) the leave year starts on October 1, 1998 and the leave year will therefore run from 1 October to 30 September each year; and

(ii) If the worker starts work with the employer after October 1, 1998, the worker's leave year starts on the date on which employment begins.

8–23 If the employer does not specify the leave year in the contract or a "relevant agreement" therefore it could be faced with different leave years for different workers depending on the date the worker joined the Company which could, administratively, prove very difficult to manage.

The Government indicated prior to the implementation of the Regulations that it anticipated that most employers and workers would agree when the leave year begins and this indication appears to have been accurate. Most contracts of employment will stipulate the commencement and end of the holiday year. If the definition of the holiday year is contained in a workforce agreement, collective agreement or a contract of employment or other contractually binding document, that would be sufficient for the purposes of the Regulations. The position is less clear however if the provisions on holiday are contained in a set of holiday rules such as, for example, an employee handbook, which are not contractually binding. Such a handbook may not amount to a "relevant agreement" for the purposes of the Regulations and therefore there is always the risk that the default provisions would apply in that scenario.

The start of the leave year differs slightly for workers employed in agriculture when, in accordance with Schedule 2 of the Regulations, the leave year begins:

"on 6 April each year or such other date as may be specified in an agricultural wages order, unless a relevant agreement states otherwise."

8–24 It is still possible to specify the commencement of the leave year in a relevant agreement for agricultural workers, but it is the default provisions that differ in respect of such workers as Regulation 13(4) provides that the default provisions contained in Regulation 13(3) do:

"not apply to a worker to whom Schedule 2 applies (workers employed in agriculture) except where, in the case of a worker partly employed in agriculture, a relevant agreement so provides."

It is necessary therefore for a relevant agreement to specify that the default provisions will apply in relation to the agricultural workers, otherwise they will not.[24]

---

[24] For a more detailed consideration of Schedule 2 and agricultural workers see Chap. 17.

WHAT IS A WEEK'S LEAVE?

8–25 The annual leave entitlement is expressed in terms of weeks and the actual amount of time to which the worker will be entitled by way of paid leave in those weeks will be determined by reference to how many days or hours he or she normally works in a seven day period. For a worker working five days a week, the four weeks' paid leave amounts to a total of 20 days' annual leave. A part-timer working three days a week would have a right to 12 days' paid annual leave. In the case of those whose working time is set in terms of hours, their annual leave can also be expressed in terms of hours by multiplying the number of hours in the working week by four. In the case of those who work irregular hours, the workers would have a right to annual leave that allows them to be away from the place of work for four weeks and for each such week to receive pay equivalent to what they might reasonably expect for a normal working week (see below). A week's leave is not however defined in the Regulations or in the Directive. The DTI Guidance[25] states that a week's leave should be:

> "equivalent to the time a worker would work in a week ... where a worker works irregular hours, the worker would have a right to annual leave that would allow them to be away from their place of work for a week ... if a part-time worker's working time is set in terms of hours, then their annual leave might be expressed in terms of hours too. In the case of a worker working 24 hours a week the leave entitlement would be 72 hours" [during the transitional period until November 23, 1998]

8–26 The position is not clear however where, for example, a worker regularly works additional days of overtime. There is no definition of a "week" in relation to the provision of annual leave and it is unclear as to whether the week merely includes the basic contractual hours or the number of days actually worked by the worker. If, for example, a worker has a basic four day working week but regularly works a fifth day as overtime, it is not clear how much annual leave they would be entitled to. It is submitted that the answer may lie in granting the worker sufficient leave to enable them to be away from work for four weeks and looking instead at the question of payment during that week.

The view taken by the Engineering Employers' Federation[26] is that because the entitlement to pay during annual leave is calculated according to the formula of a week's pay laid down in sections 221–224 of the Employment Rights Act 1996, which excludes non-contractual overtime, then any overtime which is not contractual should be excluded for the purposes of calculating the length of a week's paid leave.

For the purpose of calculating leave entitlement for workers with irregular or unusual working hours, it is useful to distinguish between the right to time off and the right to be paid for that time off.[27] If a worker does not have regular working hours and wishes to take, for example, a day off work by way of annual leave then it is submitted that the real issue for the employer is not how much time that worker may take off, as it is clear that they would be entitled not to attend for work on that particular day (subject to serving the employer with the requisite period of notice and provided that the employer does not serve a "counter" notice),[28] but rather how much

---

[25] Working Time Regulations: Regulatory Guidance.
[26] Implementing the Working Time Regulations—a Practical Guide 1998.
[27] See para. 8–44 below.
[28] See Regulation 15 below.

the employer is required to pay the worker in respect of that day, and we consider this in more detail below.

8–27 The principle of pro rating of holiday entitlement for part-time workers should apply not only to statutory but also to any additional contractual holiday provisions. If it does not, then an employer may face claims of indirect sex discrimination from female part-time workers or claims under the Part-time Workers (Prevention of Less Favourable Treatment) Regulations 2000.[29] Under these Regulations, which came into force on July 1, 2000, a part-time worker is entitled to receive the same pay and other benefits as "comparable" full-time workers but calculated pro rata according to the number of weekly hours worked by the part-time worker in comparison with the comparable full-time worker. So a part-time worker who works 75 per cent of the time that a full-time worker would work would be entitled to 75 per cent of the contractual holiday entitlement.

THE QUALIFYING PERIOD

8–28 One of the most controversial steps taken by the Government in introducing the Regulations was to make the right to paid leave subject to a qualifying period. Under Regulation 13(7) the right to take paid annual leave "does not arise until a worker has been continuously employed for 13 weeks."

It is submitted that the correct interpretation of this provision is **not** that a worker does not accrue annual leave during the first 13 weeks of the contract, but rather that the worker cannot take leave at any time during that period. Temporary workers on contracts for less than 13 weeks would therefore in effect be excluded from the right to paid annual leave provided that their contract terminates within a 13-week period. The 13-week qualifying period was introduced by the Labour Government and is not contained in the Directive. The previous Conservative Government initially suggested that there should be a 49 week qualification period[30] which would have been reduced to 48 weeks after November 1999, so that an employer could minimise the disruption to its business by preventing workers from exercising their right to annual leave until they had been with the company for 49 weeks.

8–29 The qualifying period has to date been the subject of perhaps more litigation than any of the other provisions relating to annual leave. Indeed the very validity of a 13-week qualifying period has now been challenged in the request for judicial review of Regulation 13(7) brought by the entertainment union BECTU in *R. v. Secretary of State for Trade & Industry ex p. BECTU* (unreported). In this case BECTU argued that the exclusion of workers with less than 13 weeks' service was contrary to the Working Time Directive. The High Court, by consent, referred the case to the ECJ for a preliminary hearing on two questions:

(1) Is the expression "in accordance with the conditions for entitlement to and granting of, such leave laid down by national legislation and/or practice" in Article 7 of [the Directive] to be interpreted as permitting a Member State to enact national legislation under which:

(a) a worker does not begin to accrue rights to the paid annual leave contained in Article 7 or to derive any benefits consequent thereon, until

---

[29] S.I. 2000 No. 51.
[30] Consultation Document on measures to implement provisions of the E.C. Directive on the organisation of working time.

he has completed a qualifying period of employment with the same employer; but

(b) once that qualifying period has been completed his employment during the qualifying period is taken into account for the purposes of computing his leave entitlement?"

(2) If the answer to question 1 is "yes" what are the factors that the national court should take into account in order to determine whether a particular qualifying period of employment with the same employer is lawful and proportionate? In particular, is it legitimate for a Member State to take into account the cost for employers of conferring the rights on those workers who are employed for less than the qualifying period?

Pending the decision of ECJ in the *BECTU* case however, the 13-week qualifying period remains in force.

8-30 There was initially some doubt as to whether employment prior to October 1, 1998 could count towards the 13-week period, or whether to qualify for the right to annual leave under the Regulations, a worker had to have 13 weeks' continuous employment beginning on or after the October 1, 1998. The Regulations themselves are silent on this issue and the employment tribunals initially did little to resolve the confusion. In *Orme v. Office Angels Limited*[31] the Manchester Employment Tribunal held that the 13-week qualifying period commenced on October 1, 1998, the date when the Regulations came into force. This case involved a temporary worker who worked for an employment agency as a clerical assistant at a number of different institutions. She began working for the agency on June 10, 1998 in accordance with a written "temporary worker's agreement". This agreement was amended with effect from October 1, 1998 and the new agreement included a right to statutory holiday leave. The applicant continued to work under this agreement until November 18, 1998 when she resigned and returned to Australia. She claimed that she had been continuously employed between June and November 1998 for a period of approximately 22 weeks and was therefore entitled to holiday pay under Regulation 13.

The Manchester Employment Tribunal considered that the Temporary Worker's Agreement was a "relevant agreement" for the purposes of the Regulations **and** that the applicant was only entitled to holiday pay after she had accrued 13 weeks' service from October 1, 1998. In reaching its conclusion the tribunal gave as its reasons the fact that:

"the Working Time Regulations 1998 were not retrospective. The Regulations were operative from October 1, 1998 ... the tribunal was satisfied that the applicant was continuously engaged under a contract as provided by [Regulation 13(7)] between October 1 and November 18 (a 7-week period). The tribunal did not consider that it was appropriate to retrospectively consider the period between June 10, 1998 and September 30, 1998 in this calculation. To do so would give retrospective effect to both the 1998 Working Time Regulations and to the [Temporary Worker's Agreement]."

8-31 Moreover, the applicant was not entitled to carry over any entitlement that she might have had prior to October 1, 1998 and was therefore not entitled to holiday pay.

However just a few weeks after this decision, the Southampton Employment

---

[31] Case No. 2405570/98: 17.02.99.

Tribunal took a different view in the unreported case of *Wellicome v. Kelly Services (UK) Limited.*[32] This case also concerned a temporary worker who was issued with a new contract shortly before the Working Time Regulations came into force. Under his new contract, Mr Wellicome was entitled to 15 days' holiday with immediate effect, rising to 20 days' holiday in November 1999. The agreement specifically stated that the entitlement to annual leave would include bank holidays, but that holiday would accrue at the rate of 0.29 days for each week that Mr Wellicome worked for the agency.

Mr Wellicome had been working for the agency for more than 13 weeks prior to October 1, 1998. His revised contract stated that the holiday year would end on the second Sunday in January. The tribunal held that because Mr Wellicome had accrued 13 weeks' service prior to October 1, 1998, when the Regulations came into force on that date he was entitled to a full three weeks' paid leave in respect of that holiday year. This meant, in effect, that Mr Wellicome would have been entitled to three weeks' paid leave for the period from October 1, 1998 until the end of the holiday year on the second Sunday in January 1999.

8–32 It is submitted that the better view is that employment prior to October 1, 1998 can be taken into account in assessing whether a worker has sufficient continuous employment to qualify for the right to paid annual leave under the Regulations and that the view taken by the Southampton tribunal in *Wellicome* is to be preferred.

The *Wellicome* case is however also interesting for a number of other reasons. Firstly because it suggests that once a worker has 13 weeks' service then he or she is entitled to the full amount of annual leave. Applying this principle a worker could in theory work for an employer for 13 weeks and then take four weeks' annual leave, subject to serving the appropriate notice on the employer. The worker would be entitled to be paid for all of that leave. Of course it would be open to an employer to serve a "counter-notice" denying the worker's request to take annual leave at that particular time under Regulation 15(2)(b). However if the employer did not serve a counter-notice then the worker could in theory take four weeks' paid leave and then resign from his or her position with the employer. The Regulations themselves make no provision for the worker to repay excess holiday pay to the employer although it would be open to the employer to enter into a "relevant agreement" to require the worker to compensate the employer under Regulation 14(4).

The tribunal in the *Wellicome* case also held that an accrual provision which provided that the worker accrued holiday at the rate of 0.29 days per week was void and unenforceable. It fell foul of Regulation 35 which provides that:

(1) Any provision in an agreement (whether a contract of employment or not) is void insofar as it purports—

    (a) to exclude or limit the operation of any provision of these Regulations..."[33]

However, it is submitted that the same effect as an accrual clause can be achieved by means of a contractual restriction on when leave can be taken.

---

[32] Case No. 3100333/99: 25.03.99.
[33] See Chap. 14 for a more detailed analysis of Regulation 35.

CONTINUITY OF SERVICE

8–33   The Regulations themselves provide little guidance as to what will amount to continuity of service. Regulation 13(8) merely states that:

> "a worker has been continuously employed for 13 weeks if his relations with his employer have been governed by a contract during the whole or part of each of these weeks."

The key issue therefore seems to be whether the relations were governed by a contract during the period in question. It is noticeable that in contrast with the provisions of the Employment Rights Act 1996 relating to the calculation of a week's pay (which have been explicitly incorporated into the Regulations) the provisions of the Employment Rights Act 1996 governing continuity of employment (Part IX) have not been incorporated. It will therefore be for a tribunal to decide on a case by case basis whether an individual has continuity of employment and whether the continuity provisions contained in the ERA will be taken into account.

8–34   Regulation 13(8) does not link continuity to an obligation on the part of the worker to carry out work for the employer. So, for example, a worker on a contract in which he or she only provides services during term time, will continue to accrue paid holiday during school holidays notwithstanding the fact that he or she was not providing any services at that time. Similarly, workers who are registered with employment agencies and who have signed a contract with the agency at the time they register, could continue to accrue holiday even if they are not providing services to the agency if the contract between them and the agency remains in place. It is submitted therefore that a provision in such a contract which includes words to the effect of "these terms and conditions will apply on each and every occasion that the worker provides services" may create continuity for the purposes of the entitlement to annual leave.

Periods of unpaid leave will not break continuity of employment for these purposes. In *Stewart v. Heron Recruitment Limited* (unreported)[34] an agency sought to argue that a two week period of unpaid leave did not count towards the applicant's period of continuous employment. This argument was rejected by the Sheffield Employment Tribunal on the basis that the contract between the parties had remained in existence during the period of absence and the applicant's relations with her employer were therefore governed by a contract during the period of unpaid leave.

If the employer or the agency wishes to avoid continuity therefore, they would need to terminate the existing contract at the end of an assignment and then issue a new one at the beginning of the new assignment. Not only that but the employer or the agency would need to ensure that there was a sufficient break between the two contracts so that there was at least one complete week which was governed by a contract. It is submitted that it would not be sufficient to terminate a contract on a Wednesday, for example, and then enter into a new contract the following Wednesday because the worker would then be governed by a contract during part of both of those weeks and would therefore have continuity.

---

[34] Case No. 2800141/99.

Accrual of Holiday During Periods of Sickness and Other Absences

8–35   The Regulations do not deal specifically with the issue of accrual of annual leave during periods of sickness. However, as discussed above, as the annual leave entitlement appears to a worker would depend solely on continuity the right to annual leave during periods of sickness absence. Any contractual provisions stating that annual leave does not accrue during periods of sickness would be void in respect of the statutory element of leave, although would, it is submitted, be enforceable in respect of any enhanced contractual leave.

8–36   As the entitlement to annual leave appears to depend purely on the existence of a contract between the employer and worker at any given time, statutory annual leave will be unaffected during periods of absence such as maternity or parental leave, or sickness.[35]

Not only that, but in theory a worker who is on long-term sick leave but remains an employee to enable him or her to benefit from the provisions of the employer's permanent health insurance policy, could also potentially claim a right to paid annual leave in respect of each holiday year. However in the case of *R. C. Warnes v. Situsec Contractors Limited* (unreported),[36] the London (North) Tribunal found that a worker who was on sick leave did not fall within the ambit of Regulation 13 and could not take annual leave. Mr Warnes had been employed by Situsec since November 7, 1990. He became sick in February 1998 and was off work from then until the tribunal heard the case in October 1999. Mr Warnes worked in the construction industry and his terms and conditions of employment were set out in the Building & Civil Engineering Joint Agreement on Holidays and Pay which laid down a number of rules governing holiday entitlement. These included a rule that if an employee was absent from work on sick leave, the employer would continue to contribute towards holiday pay entitlement for a period of up to 10 weeks and that the employee must take set periods of leave at Christmas and Easter but could then negotiate with the employer when the balance of the leave was to be taken.

Mr Warnes had already received from his employer a payment representing his holiday during the 10 weeks' accrual period which was the maximum to which he was entitled under the Joint Agreement. However, he argued that notwithstanding the fact that he was off work sick his entitlement to leave continued to accrue and that he was therefore entitled to be paid in respect of bank holidays and other leave which he was required to take at specified times. His employer argued that whilst he was off sick he was not entitled to take leave but his entitlement to accrue holiday pay continued. They argued that they had paid him the full amount of the holiday pay to which he was entitled under the terms of his contract and that there was therefore no additional money owing to him.

8–37   The tribunal noted that Regulation 13(9) provides that annual leave can only be taken in the leave year to which it relates and that it may not be replaced by a payment in lieu except when the worker's contract is terminated. The tribunal also noted that:

"the operation of the limits and entitlements set out in the Regulations is governed by the definition of working time which . . . appears in Regulation 2 . . . the purpose of the Working Time Regulations is to secure the health of workers

---

[35] See para. 8–20 above.
[36] Case No. 6003949/99: 13.11.99.

and to ensure that they can and do take adequate breaks from work. The Regulations provide for workers to take periods of leave from work with pay. We do not see how a person who is absent from work through sickness can fall within the ambit of Regulation 13. Mr Warnes is not at work. How can he take leave from it?"

The tribunal went on to say that the right to annual leave was defined by reference to the definition of working time. It found that Mr Warnes was not a person who was at his employer's disposal, carrying out his duties or receiving training and was therefore not working. This interesting analysis by the tribunal would appear to suggest that the right to take annual leave is dependent upon the worker being at work and providing services (and thus satisfying the definition of "working time") at the time they wish to take the leave. Moreover, the tribunal stated that as Regulation 13:

"unambiguously proscribes payment in lieu of leave except where a worker's contract of employment is terminated"

and as the applicant's contract in this case had not been terminated he was not entitled to any payment in respect of untaken periods of leave.

8-38   If this analysis is followed by other tribunals, it would indicate that any worker who is not available to provide services for reasons such as, for example, long-term sickness absence, additional maternity leave or parental leave is not entitled to exercise his or her statutory right to annual leave, nor to be paid in respect of that period. So, for example, an employee who was on an extended period of additional maternity leave and was approaching the end of the leave year, would, following the *R. C. Warnes v. Situsec* reasoning lose that right to annual leave as he or she would not be able to take it during the leave year, and would not be able to carry it forward, unless of course there was a relevant agreement with his or her employer which entitled him or her to do so.

The same principles would apply to a worker who was on long-term sickness absence and in receipt of permanent health insurance, although when the worker ceased to be an employee (for example if she or he reached normal retirement age) then she or he may be able to claim a payment in lieu of untaken leave in the leave year in which the employment terminates, in accordance with the provisions of Regulation 14.

TRANSITIONAL PROVISIONS

8-39   Article 18(1)(b)(ii) of the Directive gives Member States the option to make use of a three-year transitional period up to November 23, 1999 during which workers need only be granted three weeks' paid annual leave. This option was taken up by the United Kingdom in implementing the Directive and Regulation 13(2) provides that:

"the period of leave to which a worker is entitled is

    (a) in any leave year beginning on or before November 23, 1998, three weeks;

    (b) in any leave year beginning after November 23, 1998 but before November 23, 1999, 3 weeks and a proportion of a fourth week equivalent to the proportion of the year beginning on November 23, 1998 which has elapsed at the start of that leave year; and

    (c) in any leave year beginning after November 23, 1999, 4 weeks."

8–40 By way of example, for a worker whose leave year begins on 1 January, entitlement to holiday for 1999 would be calculated on the assumption that he or she would be entitled to three weeks' paid leave (pro-rata) for the period 1 January to 22 November (326 days) and to four weeks' annual leave (pro-rata) for the period 23 November to 31 December (39 days). This would give a total of 3.11 weeks holiday. For workers working a five-day week this would amount to 15.53 days annual leave which could be rounded up to 16 days in accordance with Regulation 13(6).

Regulation 13(6) provides that:

"where by virtue of paragraph 2(b) [entitlement in leave year spanning November 23, 1998] or (5) [entitlement during first year of engagement] the period of leave to which a worker is entitled is or includes a proportion of a week, the proportion shall be determined in days and any fraction of a day shall be treated as a whole day."

In calculating annual leave therefore a portion of a day will be rounded up and treated as a whole day's entitlement. However, the rounding up provisions only apply where leave entitlement is being calculated in respect of a leave year which spans November 23, 1998, and where entitlement is being calculated during the first year of employment, where employment began after the commencement of the leave year. They do not apply for example when calculating entitlement to a payment in lieu of untaken leave on termination unless of course the termination was during the first year of employment so that Regulation 13(5) applies.

EXERCISING THE ENTITLEMENT TO ANNUAL LEAVE

8–41 Regulation 13(9) provides that:

"leave to which a worker is entitled under this Regulation may be taken in instalments, but

    (a) It may only be taken in the leave year in respect of which it is due, and

    (b) It may not be replaced by a payment in lieu except where the worker's employment is terminated".

Annual leave can therefore be taken in instalments, but must be taken in the leave year in respect of which it is due. If a worker chooses not to take their leave during a particular leave year then he or she loses his or her entitlement. This would not however prevent the parties agreeing contractually to permit the carrying forward of annual leave, but if a worker of his or her own volition does not take holiday during a particular leave year, he or she will lose it and cannot claim a payment in lieu. Moreover the reasoning adopted by the London (North) Employment Tribunal in *R. C. Warnes v. Situsec Contractors Limited*[37] would suggest that a worker is not able to take periods of annual leave whilst she or he is not actually working for the employer and will therefore lose the entitlement unless the employer allows him or her to carry it forward to the next leave year.

---

[37] See above (para. 8–36).

8–42 Regulation 9(b) provides that the right to annual leave cannot be replaced by a payment in lieu except upon termination of the employment. It is therefore not possible for employers and workers to agree to "buy out" annual leave. The right in the Regulations is to time off work as holiday, which is paid, not merely to holiday pay to compensate for the fact that no holiday has been taken. This would not however appear to prevent an employer from compensating a worker who did not take all of his or her annual leave in one year, by providing him or her with additional contractual leave the next year. However, a worker who did insist on taking his or her statutory leave in one year and who did not get additional contractual leave the next year could complain that he or she had suffered a detriment for exercising an entitlement under the Regulations, if one of his or her colleagues was provided with additional contractual leave for not exercising their right to statutory leave.

A difficulty may also arise if a worker who is approaching the end of his or her leave year and has not taken all his or her paid leave, asks the employer to "buy out" the paid leave. If the employer did buy-out the paid leave, the worker could issue proceedings in the tribunal claiming that she or he had been denied his or her entitlement to paid leave under the Regulations. Employers would therefore find themselves in a situation where they may have to enter into a Compromise Agreement with the worker to prevent them taking proceedings for paid leave, or waiting until the three month time limit for issuing proceedings in an employment tribunal has expired, *i.e.* until three months have elapsed from the end of the leave year, before making the payment. This was emphasised by the London (North) tribunal in *Miah v. La Gondola Limited* (unreported)[38] where a worker had asked his employers to "buy out" a week's leave by paying him an extra week's salary. The employer agreed to do this. A few weeks later however, Mr Miah resigned and left the company. The tribunal found that he had not taken any leave that year but had accrued eight days' leave in the leave year in which his employment terminated. He was therefore entitled to eight days' holiday pay. Not only that but the payment made by his employer could not count towards that entitlement.

8–43 The tribunal in this case clearly considered that the right granted by the Regulations is an independent right to time off work, and that even though that right may be replaced by a payment in lieu on termination of employment, a payment made in lieu prior to the termination of employment can not discharge the employer's obligation towards the worker. The situation may have been different however, if La Gondola Limited had waited a few weeks until Mr Miah resigned before making the payment.

PAYMENT FOR ANNUAL LEAVE

8–44 It is submitted that the correct approach to take in analysing entitlements under the annual leave provisions is to look firstly at the right of the worker to take time off and, secondly, the right of the worker to be paid for that time off. In terms of enforcing the Regulations however, it is the right to payment for annual leave which in practice is most relevant. The entitlement to annual leave can only be enforced by way of complaint to an employment tribunal (Regulation 30). The only remedies available to the tribunal are to make a declaration that the worker has been denied his or her entitlement under the Regulations or to make an award of compensation.[39] The tribunal cannot however order the employer to allow the worker to take time off

---

[38] Case No. 6001720/1999: 29.06.99.
[39] For a more detailed analysis of the enforcement and remedies provisions of the Regulation see Chap. 14.

work. In theory therefore an employer could deny a worker any entitlement to paid leave and the worker's only remedy would be compensation from the tribunal in respect of that leave.

Implicitly therefore, in implementing the Directive in the United Kingdom, the Government could be said to have acknowledged that in enforcement terms the right to take annual leave can be replaced by a payment in lieu. It is submitted that this may be open to challenge for not providing a worker with adequate remedies for non-compliance with the Directive, which specifically states that annual leave may not be replaced by an allowance in lieu, except where the employment relationship is terminated.

8–45   Regulation 16 sets out the provisions governing the payments to workers during periods of annual leave. Regulation 16(1) provides that:

> "the worker is entitled to be paid in respect of any period of annual leave to which he is entitled under Regulation 13, at the rate of a week's pay in respect of each week of leave."

Regulation 16(2) provides that for the purpose of calculating the amount of a week's pay, sections 221–224 of the Employment Rights Act 1996 shall apply, subject to some modifications. The effect of this is as follows:

1. For workers whose remuneration does not vary according to the number of hours that he or she works (such as for example, workers who are paid a flat rate salary and are expected to work overtime without receiving any payment for that overtime) the amount of a week's pay will be the amount which is payable by the employer under the contract of employment in respect of that week if the worker works during his or her normal working hours.

2. For workers whose remuneration varies according to the number of hours that they work, the provisions are slightly more complicated. For those who have regular working hours, pay will be the contractual salary that they would normally receive for that normal working week. This may include payments such as shift premiums provided that such payments are contractual. However, non-contractual payments will not be taken into account in calculating the normal week's pay. This was confirmed by the EAT in the case of *Spence v. City of Sunderland Council* (unreported)[40] in which car park attendants employed by Sunderland Council claimed that the six hours' overtime that was regularly made available to them each week was not guaranteed. The applicants in that case were required to work a basic 39 hours per week but regularly worked six hours' overtime and claimed that their normal working hours were therefore 45 hours per week. However the tribunal rejected their claim and took the view that overtime can only be counted as part of "normal working hours" (as defined in section 234 of the Employment Rights Act 1996) if it is obligatory on both sides, *i.e.* if the employer is obliged to provide it and the employee is required to work it. This decision was upheld by the EAT who confirmed that even though the additional hours had been worked regularly over a period of time the employer had not committed itself to providing overtime by way of a contractual obligation but had deliberately retained flexibility to alter working arrangements in the event of changes in the working conditions. As

---

[40] EAT case No. 1255/98: 30.07.99.

such, overtime hours did not form part of the worker's "normal working hours".

3. If normal working hours vary from week to week, and workers are paid by reference to the number of hours worked, the payment for annual leave will be the average hourly rate of pay over the 12 weeks prior to the date on which the annual leave commences, divided by the average weekly working hours over the same period.

4. If there are no normal working hours and workers are paid by reference to the number of hours worked, the annual leave payment will be the average pay received over the 12 weeks worked prior to the commencement of the leave period.

8–46 For workers who have no normal working hours therefore, payment in respect of annual leave will be calculated by reference to the number of hours worked over the 12 weeks prior to the commencement of the annual leave period. Workers on annualised hours contracts or whose workload varies during the course of the year will therefore receive a higher payment in respect of annual leave if they take their leave at the end of a particularly busy period when their average earnings would be higher. Similarly a worker without normal working hours could receive a higher payment for annual leave if annual leave were taken following the payment of an annual bonus. It would of course be open to the employer to refuse a request for annual leave at these periods and to require a worker to take annual leave at a time when his or her normal week's pay would be lower.

A practice which is fairly widespread in certain industries is to include an amount in respect of holiday pay in a worker's hourly rate of pay. It is submitted that, provided the worker is made aware that the hourly rate specifically includes an amount in respect of holiday pay, and the employer has not just designated part of the existing hourly rate as holiday pay following the implementation of the Working Time Regulations, then this should not fall foul of the Regulations. This was the view of the Brighton Employment Tribunal in *Johnson v. Northbrook College* (unreported)[41] in which a part-time lecturer was paid an hourly rate which specifically included an amount in respect of holiday pay. Ms Johnson had a contract with Northbrook College which applied 52 weeks of the year. However she was not required to work during all of that period so did have time off work. Following the implementation of the Working Time Regulations, the College increased the hourly rate of pay to part-time lecturers to include an element of holiday pay. When Ms Johnson took time off however she did not get paid for that time off, because the paid holiday was built in to her general hourly rate.

8–47 Ms Johnson argued that the provisions in the contract contravened Regulation 13(9)(b) because they constituted an attempt on the part of the College to replace her right to annual leave with a payment in lieu. However, the Tribunal found that although the Regulations did outlaw payments in lieu of holiday leave, in this case Ms Johnson was entitled to take leave, and it was therefore open to the employer to pay her in respect of that leave by way of an increased amount included in her hourly rate of pay.

The Southampton Employment Tribunal took a similar view in *Tompkins v. Kurn* (unreported)[42] in which an increase in a worker's hourly rate of pay was held to have

---

[41] Case No. 3102727/99: 25.10.99.
[42] Case No. 3102571/99: 25.10.99.

discharged the respondent's obligation to pay that worker holiday pay, as the worker had actually taken four weeks' holiday. It is however difficult to reconcile this decision with that of *Barton v. SCC Limited* [43] where the tribunal stated that the correct approach was to look at the particular week of leave and ask what payments were made during that week. Had the tribunal applied that reasoning in the *Johnson* and *Tompkin* cases the applicants would have been entitled to additional compensation in respect of annual leave because they received no payments whatsoever in the weeks in which they actually took the leave.

What does seem clear from the above cases is that if the intention is that an hourly rate should include an amount in respect of holiday pay, that must be made clear at the outset of the arrangement and ideally should be specified in the contract between the worker and the employer.

PAYMENT IN LIEU OF ANNUAL LEAVE

8–48   The general principle contained in both the Directive and in the Regulations is that the right to annual leave cannot be replaced by a payment in lieu. However, the Regulations do contain specific provisions dealing with payments during the first and last years of employment.

Where a worker joins a company part way through an annual leave year, he or she is entitled to a proportion of the annual leave entitlement which is equivalent to that proportion of the annual leave year that she or he is working for the employer. Regulation 13(5) provides that:

> "Where the date on which a worker's employment begins is later than the date on which (by virtue of a relevant agreement) his first leave year begins, the leave to which he is entitled in that leave year is a proportion of the period applicable under paragraph (2) equal to the proportion of that leave year remaining on the date on which his employment begins."

So, for example, a worker who joins the company six months through the annual leave year specified in a relevant agreement would be entitled from November 1999 to 10 days' annual leave although he or she would not be able to exercise that right until he or she had actually been working for the company for 13 weeks (subject to the challenge to the 13 week qualifying period contained in the *BECTU* case referred to in paragraph 8–29). In calculating leave entitlement during this period however any fractions of days will be rounded up in accordance with Regulation 13(6).

8–49   The same principles regarding accrual apply on termination of employment with two important differences. The first is that the rounding-up provisions do not apply for the purposes of calculating entitlement to annual leave in the last leave year of the employment. The second is that Regulation 13(9) provides that the right to annual leave can be replaced by a payment in lieu on termination of employment. This is clearly designed to deal with the situation where a worker leaves without having taken the paid leave that he or she has accrued.

Regulation 14 provides that:

> (ii) Where the proportion of leave taken by the worker is less than the proportion of the leave year which has expired his employer shall make him a payment in lieu of leave in accordance with paragraph (iii).

---

[43] See para. 8–18 above.

(iii) The payment due under paragraph (ii) shall be:

    (a) such sum as may be provided for the purposes of this Regulation in a relevant agreement; or

    (b) where there are no provisions in the relevant agreement which apply, a sum equal to the amount which would be due to the worker under Regulation 16 in respect of a period of leave determined according to the formula—

$$A \times B - C,$$

where A is the period of leave to which the worker is entitled under Regulation 13(1);
B is the proportion of the worker's leave year which expired before the termination date; and
C is the period of leave taken by the worker at the start of the leave year until the termination date."

8–50 Worker and employer can therefore agree in a relevant agreement the amount of holiday pay to be paid upon termination. In the absence of any provision in a relevant agreement however then default provisions apply. However the Regulations do not specify a minimum amount of payment on termination of employment. Theoretically therefore it would be possible to agree in a relevant agreement that holiday pay upon termination would be a nominal amount such as £1 per day. This may be particularly relevant to cases of termination for gross misconduct. Many holiday rules and disciplinary policies have traditionally provided that where employees are dismissed for gross misconduct, they forfeit any right to payment in lieu of accrued but untaken holiday. The Regulations do not cover this point however and technically therefore, a worker who is dismissed for gross misconduct would retain his or her right to paid annual leave. Unless the amount of the payment was determined in a relevant agreement the payment would be calculated in accordance with the statutory formula.

The DTI in its Regulatory Guidance[44] gives the following example of how this provision will work in practice:

"in the case of a worker who works 5 days a week (*i.e.* 3 × 5 days' leave during the leave year) whose employment terminated 6 months into the leave year (*i.e.* half a leave year has expired) and has taken only 3 days leave. The calculation would be:

$$(15 \times 0.5) - 3 = 4.5$$

Therefore the employer should pay the worker the equivalent of 4½ days' pay."

This example would of course now need amending to reflect the higher rate of annual leave entitlement so that the correct figure would be $(20 \times 0.5) - 3 = 7$.

8–51 Regulation 14(4) gives the opportunity for the employer to recoup excess annual leave from the worker where the worker leaves having taken more than his or her accrued annual leave entitlement:

"a relevant agreement may provide that, where the proportion of leave taken by the worker exceeds the proportion of the leave year which has expired, he shall

---

[44] Working Time Regs: Regulatory Guidance.

compensate his employer, whether by a payment, by undertaking additional work or otherwise."

It is therefore open to the employer in a relevant agreement to provide for a worker to repay overpaid holiday. If there is no such provision in a relevant agreement, then the tribunal will not imply one. Indeed, tribunals have stressed the importance of Regulation 14(4) in determining that contractual holiday provisions which provide that statutory holiday accrues on a weekly or monthly basis are not enforceable and that once a worker has accrued 13 weeks' service he or she is entitled to the full amount of their annual leave, because it is open to the employer to recover excess leave taken under Regulation 14(4).

It is not possible to exclude the right to payment in lieu of accrued but untaken statutory holiday payments in a relevant agreement but merely to specify the amount of the payment. If an employer did not wish to make payments for annual leave on termination (for example in cases of summary dismissal or where the worker leaves without working his or her notice period) it is submitted that they would need to ensure that there was in place a relevant agreement which includes a provision for payment of a nominal sum upon termination.

NOTICE PROVISIONS

8–52   One of the ways in which the Government tried to soften the blow of the new rights to annual leave to employers was to include in Regulation 15 a set of fairly detailed notice provisions which effectively give the employer the right to tell the worker when she or he will take paid leave.

Regulation 15(1) states that a worker can take statutory leave on the day she or he chooses by giving notice to the employer that she or he wishes to take leave on a particular day. The notice must be given to the employer at least twice as many days in advance of the first day upon which the worker wishes to take holiday as the number of days or part days to which the notice relates. (Regulation 15(4)) So, a worker who wishes to take two days' paid leave would have to give the employer four days' notice. A worker who wishes to take a week's paid leave would have to give two weeks' notice, etc.

However Regulation 15(2) provides that the employer can give the worker notice either to take statutory leave or not to take it by giving the worker a period of notice equivalent to the number of days or part days to which the notice relates. So if the employer wishes the worker to take leave of one week at Christmas it must give the worker one week's prior notice. For workers who are required to take holiday at certain times of the year, for example during factory shut down or during school or university holidays, it is submitted that a provision in a contract of employment or handbook, or alternatively a written notice confirming the dates of such holiday should be sufficient for the purposes of Regulation 15. An employer therefore only has to give half as much notice to a worker either to take annual leave or not to take it, as the worker has to give to the employer. This has been criticised as being unduly weighted in favour of the employer. For example a worker who knew that she was getting married in June could give notice to her employer in January that she wished to take two weeks' honeymoon beginning on 1 June. The employer could in theory serve a notice on her at any time up to two weeks' before 1 June, *i.e.* as late as 16 May requiring her not to take leave during that period.

8–53   Similarly if a worker's normal hours of work vary such that there are periods of the year where he or she carries out substantially less work than others, the employer, to reduce the amount of payment for annual leave to which the worker would be entitled in accordance with the provisions of the Employment Rights Act 1996 relating to calculation of a "normal week's pay", could in theory serve notice on the worker to take annual leave at the end of a quiet period when their average wages over the previous 12 weeks would be lower.

Where an employer serves notice on the worker that he or she is to take leave at a particular time, there is no provision for the worker to actually serve a counter-notice saying that he or she does not wish to take leave at that particular time.

The Regulations do not provide that the notice need be in writing, although both employers and workers would be well-advised to ensure that any notices were in written form, for evidential purposes. If an employer wishes bank holidays to count towards statutory leave entitlement they would also be well advised to include a specific provision in the contract stating the dates upon which the bank holidays will be taken and preferably also stating that the bank holidays will count towards the worker's period of statutory paid leave.

It is open to the worker and the employer to agree to vary the notice provisions in a relevant agreement and it would not be uncommon, for example, for a contract to provide that a worker has to give one week's notice of a period of leave of just one day. This would not be unlawful. Similarly, a worker could be required under a relevant agreement to give a longer period of notice than is required by the Regulations.

CHAPTER NINE

Provisions Relating to Night Work and Night Workers

INTRODUCTION

9–01 The Working Time Directive[1] acknowledges that certain categories of workers—night workers and shift workers—are entitled to receive special protection in respect of the organisation of their working time. In the case of night workers, the rationale behind these additional protections is set out in the preamble to the Directive, which states that "research has shown that the human body is more sensitive at night to environmental disturbances and also to certain burdensome forms of work organisation and that long periods of night work could be detrimental to the health of workers and can endanger safety at the workplace".[2] Accordingly, the Directive recognises the "need to limit the duration of periods of night work, including overtime, and to provide for employers who regularly use night workers to bring this information to the attention of the competent authorities if they so request".[3] The preamble also stresses[4] the importance of free health assessments for night workers and the importance of the transfer of night workers to suitable day work if they suffer from health problems. Further, the level of safety and health protection in the work place "should be adapted to the nature of the work and ... the organisation and functioning of protection and prevention services and resources should be efficient".[5]

Prior to the introduction of the Directive, Regulation of night-time working in Member States was typically a piecemeal affair, with specific Regulation of certain industries or specific classes of employee.[6] In particular, many Member States had blanket prohibitions on night work by female workers. These restrictions were eventually challenged under the Equal Treatment Directive.[7] In *Republic of France v. Stoeckel*[8] the ECJ held that legislative measures prohibiting night work by women but not men were unlawful, constituting sex discrimination. Similarly, in the United Kingdom, statutory restrictions on the working hours of women in factories and mines (including night work) were abolished by the Sex Discrimination Act 1986.

9–02 In 1990, the ILO adopted a revised Protocol on female night workers and a specific Night Work Convention (1990, No. 171) and a Night Work Recommendation (1990, No. 178). These last two measures apply to all workers, male

---

[1] Directive 93/104/E.C.
[2] Directive 93/104/E.C., preamble, para. 11.
[3] Directive 93/104/E.C., preamble, para. 12.
[4] Directive 93/104/E.C., preamble, para. 13.
[5] Directive 93/104/E.C., preamble, para. 14.
[6] A useful analysis of the approach of Member States to working time, and of the International Labour Organisation's Conventions in this area, is found in "Legal and contractual limitations to Working Time in the European Union" Blanpain; Köhler and Rojot, second revised and updated edition, office for official publications of the European Communities/Teeters.
[7] E.C./76/207.
[8] [1993] C.M.L.R. 673.

and female. They do not seek to directly regulate the length of night-time working but deal with issues such as health assessments, the transfer of night workers to day work on health grounds and consultation with worker representatives over the planning of night-time working. As we have seen, some of these issues are dealt with in the Directive which itself states (preamble, paragraph 9) that "account should be taken of the principles of the International Labour Organisation with regard to the organisation of working time, including those relating to night work".

This chapter examines the nature and effect of the limits on night-time work introduced by the Directive and the Regulations, and the rights conferred on night workers. Where appropriate, differences between the Directive and the Regulations will be highlighted and the compatibility of the domestic and community provisions explored.

OVERVIEW OF THE PROVISIONS OF THE DIRECTIVE AND THE REGULATIONS

9–03   Articles 8 to 12 of the Directive require Member States to take measures necessary to ensure that:

- Normal hours of work for night workers do not exceed an average of eight hours in any 24-hour period[9];

- Night workers whose work involves special hazards or heavy physical or mental strain do not work more than eight hours in any period of 24 hours during which they perform night work[10];

- Night workers are entitled to a free health assessment before their assignment and thereafter at regular intervals[11];

- Night workers suffering from health problems recognised as being connected with the fact that they perform night work are transferred whenever possible to day work to which they are suited[12];

- Employers who regularly use night workers bring this information to the attention of the competent authorities if they so request[13];

- Night workers have safety and health protection appropriate to the nature of their work[14]; and

- Appropriate protection and prevention services or facilities with regard to the safety and health of night workers are equivalent to those applicable to other workers and are available at all times.[15]

9–04   Under Article 10, Member States are given the option to make the work of certain categories of night workers subject to certain guarantees, under conditions laid down by national legislation and/or practice, in the case of workers who incur risks to their safety or health linked to night-time working.

These provisions are transposed into domestic law primarily by Regulations 6 and 7

---

[9] Art. 8(1).
[10] Art. (2).
[11] Art. 9(1)(a).
[12] Art. 9(1)(b).
[13] Art. 11.
[14] Art. 12(1).
[15] Art. 12(2).

of the Working Time Regulations. Regulation 6 contains the applicable limits on night-time working. Regulation 7 governs the provision of health assessments and the transfer of night workers to day work in specified circumstances.

As with other provisions of the Regulations, many of these limits and entitlements can be excluded or modified by way of agreement, albeit in some cases only on a collective basis. Additionally, in the event of "special cases", the limits on working hours in Regulation 6(1) and (7) are excluded under the derogations in Regulation 21.

Young workers

9–05   In general terms, the provisions in respect of night workers apply to young workers in the same way as to adult workers. There is no separate concept of a "young night worker". The only specific provision in respect of young workers in Regulations 6 and 7 is in Regulation 7(2) which obliges employers to provide assessments of "health and capacities" (as opposed simply to health assessments) if the young worker is assigned to work during the restricted period of 10.00 p.m. to 6.00 a.m. This "restricted period" should not be confused with the definition of "night time" under Regulation 2(1) and plays no part in determining whether the young worker is a "night worker".

DEFINITIONS: "NIGHT TIME" AND "NIGHT WORKER"

9–06   "Night work" is, unsurprisingly, work carried out during "night time".[16] The two main definitions for the purposes of Regulations 6 and 7 are those of "night time" and "night worker".

"Night Time"

9–07   As with many of the provisions of the Regulations, the definition of "night time" in Regulation 2(1) includes a default definition which the employer and the workforce are free to substitute with their own agreed definition, subject to the observance of certain minimum standards.

Regulation 2(1) defines "night time" as a period of at least seven hours which must include the period from midnight to 5.00 a.m. Although not expressly defined as such by the Regulations, it would appear that the period should be one of *consecutive* hours. The default night-time period is from 11.00 p.m. to 6.00 a.m. However, a relevant agreement (*i.e.* a contract of employment or a collective or workforce agreement) may substitute an alternative period as being night time, provided that the agreed period is at least seven hours long and contains the period of 12.00 a.m. to 5.00 a.m. For example, a relevant agreement could define "night time" as 10.00 p.m. to 5.00 a.m., or midnight to 7.00 a.m., or even 7.00 p.m. to 7.00 a.m.

Employers may wish to disapply the default definition of "night time" for two very different reasons. On the one hand, the default period may create anomalies in the application of Regulations 6 and 7 to different categories of workers. The employer may also wish to extend the scope of the night work provisions to a wider class of employees than would otherwise be caught, in order to improve health and safety protection. On the other hand, the employer might, by careful alteration of the night-time definition, prevent workers from falling within the ambit of the limits on night-time working at all. For example, a worker who works between 9.00 p.m. and 2.00 a.m. would count as a night worker if the default definition of night time were

---

[16] Regulation 2(1).

applied. As will be seen, if a worker works three hours of working time during night time as a normal course, he or she will be classed as a night worker under the Regulations. If, however, night time was redefined as being 12.00 a.m. to 7.00 a.m., the worker would not work three hours of working time during night time. The night work provisions would not apply. The employer must of course obtain the agreement of the worker (whether on an individual basis or under a collective or workforce agreement) to disapply the Regulations in this way. However, the worker may be prepared to so agree in order to continue with certain patterns of working which are financially advantageous (for example because of receipt of night-shift premiums).

"Night Worker"

9–08   Under Regulation 2(1), a "night worker" is one who:

(a) As a normal course, works at least three hours of his daily working time during night time, or

(b) Is likely, during night time, to work at least such proportion of his annual working time as may be specified for the purposes of these Regulations in a collective agreement or a workforce agreement.

It should be noted that these are alternative provisions. A worker will be classed as a night worker if he satisfies either of them. The existence of a collective or workforce agreement satisfying part (b) of the definition does not affect the operation of part (a) of the definition.

Part (a) of the definition therefore operates as a minimum standard which we shall refer to as the "standard" night worker definition.

Part (b) of the definition allows a wider (but not more restrictive) definition of night worker to be adopted. This shall be referred to as the "expanded night worker definition".

The standard night worker definition

9–09   Under the standard definition, a night worker is someone who works at least three hours of his daily working time during night time as a normal course. The concepts of "daily working time" and "night time" are discussed above. The key phrase here is "as a normal course", which is also the qualifying condition under the Directive.[17]

Regulation 2(1) expressly provides that the phrase "as a normal course" includes a worker who works at least three hours of working time during night time on the majority of days on which he works. There is no corresponding provision in Article 2(4)(a) of the Directive. It is submitted however that although the wording of the Directive and Regulations differ, there is no real incompatibility. It is clear from Regulation 2(1) that the additional words are simply an interpretative clarification, which leaves the scope of the definition unqualified.

The term "as a normal course" is clearly intended to have a wide application and would seem to include those who work at least three hours of night-time work on a regular or frequent basis, for example under an alternating or rotating shift pattern. Those who only work the requisite hours during night time on an infrequent, irregular or ad hoc basis would not qualify.

9–10   This approach was confirmed by the Northern Ireland High Court in the

---

[17] See Art. 2(4)(a).

case of *R. v. Attorney General for Northern Ireland ex p. Burns*.[18] Mrs Burns was a production operative and from January 1993 to September 1995 worked on an alternating shift system under which she worked a night shift (from 9.00 p.m. to 7.00 a.m.) every third week. From September 1995 she worked a cycle of 15 eight-hour shifts, five of which involved her working at least three hours during the period 11.00 p.m. to 6.00 a.m. Mrs Burns had unsuccessfully applied for jobs on the day shift and eventually, in September 1996, she began a lengthy period of sick leave occasioned by severe stress as a result of night-shift working. This forced her to resign from her employment in February 1997, although she did ask to be considered for day work.

The Working Time Directive was due to be implemented by Member States by November 23, 1996. The United Kingdom Government failed to do so. Mrs Burns considered that if they had been implemented in domestic law the provisions of the Directive would have been of benefit to her. The Directive gave night workers a right to be transferred to alternative day work in certain circumstances.[19] Her argument was that had the Directive been implemented she would have been able to avail herself of the right to be transferred to day work against her employer. Under the *Francovich* principle, individuals who suffer loss as a result of a Member State's failure to implement the provisions of a Directive have a right of action under community law against the Member State. Mrs Burns brought a *Francovich*-type claim against the United Kingdom Government by way of judicial review proceedings. As part of her claim, she sought a declaration that she was a "night worker" within the meaning of that term in the Directive.

9–11   The Northern Ireland High Court held that Mrs Burns was indeed a night worker under the Directive. The requirement that three hours of daily working time should be worked during night time "as a normal course" meant no more than that this should be a regular feature of the employment. In reaching this conclusion, the Court rejected the Government's argument that the phrase "as a normal course" limited the concept of night worker to those who work night shifts exclusively or predominantly.[20]

The attitude taken by the Government in these proceedings is rather interesting. Although the proceedings concerned the Directive rather than the Regulations, the Government's arguments as to the meaning of "as a normal course" conflicted with the interpretation offered in the DTI's guidance on the Regulations. The guidance indicated that the Regulations would apply to a worker who worked the required proportion of working time during night time under an alternating or rotating shift pattern, *i.e.* exactly the type of working pattern involved in the *Burns* case.

Qualification as a night worker under the standard definition therefore depends on the frequency and degree to which "working time" coincides with "night time". In identifying their night workers, employers must bear in mind the potentially wide ambit of the definition of "working time". For example, if "on-call" hours constitute working time, and are "worked" during night time, the "on-call" worker may be classed as a night worker.

9–12   Indeed, whether on-call workers can be classed as night workers, simply by virtue of being on-call during night-time hours, is one of the issues considered by the European court of Justice in the *SIMAP* case. The case concerns the working time of

---

[18] [1999] I.R.L.R. 315 N.I.H.C.Q.B.

[19] Art. 9(1)(b) and see below.

[20] Although Mrs Burns obtained her declaration that she was a night worker, her claim was ultimately unsuccessful. The High Court was not convinced, on the evidence before it, that if Mrs Burns had been able to have recourse to domestic rules implementing Art. 9(1)(b), she would have been able to require her employer to transfer her to day work and thus would have been able to continue in her employment.

Spanish doctors and raises a number of key questions regarding the application and operation of the Directive. In particular, the ECJ asked to consider whether the hours spent by the doctors on-call are to be classed as "working time" and, in particular, whether it makes any difference if the on-call system involves the worker being present at the place of work. Advocate General Saggio suggested in his opinion[21] that only on-call hours spent at the employer's premises count as working time. In his view, on-call hours spent away from work (*e.g.* at the worker's home) do not count as working time. Under this type of on-call arrangement, if the worker is called upon by the employer to work, only the hours actually worked will count as working time. Following the decision of the ECJ in the *SIMAP* case employers may need to reassess the scope of the night worker definition although there is clearly room for further argument as to whether on-call hours are worked during the night "as a normal course".

As we have seen in the context of the limit on average weekly working time, the Government made significant changes to the Regulations by the Working Time Regulations 1999. In particular, so called "voluntary" overtime no longer counts towards the 48-hour average weekly working time limit under Regulation 4. If "without being required to do so by the employer", the worker does work the duration of which is not "measured or predetermined or can be determined by the worker himself", such time does not count for the purposes of the average weekly working time limit in Regulation 4(1).[22] Regulation 20(2) also states that the limits on night-time working in Regulation 6(1), 6(2) and 6(7) shall not apply to such voluntary overtime. This does not, however, affect the operation of the definitions in Regulation 2. If the voluntary overtime would count as working time apart from Regulation 20(2), it must be taken into account for determining the identity of a night worker.

"Expanded definition" of night worker

9–13   The expanded night worker definition allows a collective or workforce agreement to identify a proportion of annual working time which, if likely to be worked at night, will qualify the worker as a night worker. Note that the worker does not have to actually to meet the threshold set out in the agreement—it is sufficient if he is likely to do so. As yet there is no guidance as to the degree of probability necessary to satisfy this condition. Indeed it is possible that the probability of an individual employee working the required proportion of annual working time during night time might fluctuate during the relevant year. It is submitted that the likelihood of the employee satisfying the threshold should be judged at the start of the year in question. Otherwise, there is a risk that the worker would become a night worker during the relevant year, placing the employer retrospectively in breach of the limits on night work under Regulation 6. There is no reported decision on the interpretation of this provision, however.

The expanded definition cannot be more restrictive than the core definition. Whatever the proportion of annual working time specified in the agreement, a worker will still be a "night worker" if he works at least three hours of his daily working time during night time as a normal course.

Strictly speaking, the collective or workforce agreement cannot simply designate certain workers or groups of worker as night workers—it must define a proportion of annual working time which, if worked during night time, would make the worker a "night worker". It is submitted that any classification by worker or group would

---

[21] Given on December 16, 1999.
[22] Regulation 20(2) introduced by Regulation 4 of the 1999 Regulation.

simply "voluntarily"—and without legal effect—extend the scope of the Regulations, since the strict definition of "night worker" under the Regulations would not be satisfied. The employer would be free to argue at a later stage that the workers concerned are not in fact night workers under either the standard or expanded definitions. From the employer's perspective, there is little to be lost by such an approach.

9–14   There is some uncertainty as to whether the expanded definition of night worker in the Regulations is compatible with that in the Directive. The expanded definition in Article 2(4) of the Directive provides that a night worker is "any worker who is likely during night time to work *a certain proportion of his annual working time, as defined* at the choice of the Member State concerned:

> (i) by *national legislation*, following consultation with the two sides of industry;
> or
>
> (ii) by collective agreements or agreements concluded between the two sides of industry at national or regional level." (our emphasis).

The Regulations themselves do not define any proportion of annual working time, but allow the relevant proportion to be set by collective or workforce agreements. The latter do not have to be "between the two sides of industry at collective or regional level". The Regulations therefore envisage agreements between employers and their workforces whereas the Directive contemplates agreements between the two sides of industry only at national and regional level. It is suggested that the constraints on the level of collective bargaining are consistent with the purpose of the Directive as a health and safety measure, from which derogations (whether legislative or negotiated) should be tightly controlled. However, the strict wording of the Directive is at odds with the general practice of collective bargaining in the United Kingdom and with the concept of workforce agreements introduced by the Regulations.[23] It is arguable that the Government has incorrectly transposed Article 2(4) of the Directive.

The effect of extending by agreement the application of the night worker provisions

9–15   As we have seen above, the Regulations contain standard or default definitions of night time and night worker. Employers are free to extend the scope of the night worker provisions by:

> (i) Widening the definition of night time, by means of a relevant agreement;
>
> (ii) Widening the definition of night workers by means of a collective or workforce agreement.

Employers who expand the application of the night-work provisions in this way should only do so after careful thought, since doing so will voluntarily extend the scope of the employer's obligations to his workers. The rights (and therefore the legal remedies) of individual workers against the employer will be based on the increased obligations and not the minimum or default provisions of the Regulations. Further,

---

[23] Indeed this difference is recognised in Art. 17(3) of the Directive which allows derogations from certain provisions of the Directive by means of "collective agreements concluded between the two sides of industry at the appropriate collective level" in Member States in which there is no statutory system ensuring the conclusion of such agreements at national or regional level. This derogation is not available however in respect of Art. 2 (Definitions).

breaches of the night work provisions in Regulations 6 and 7 are enforceable by the Health and Safety Authorities by way of criminal prosecution. By extending the application of Regulations 6 and 7, employers are voluntarily assuming a higher burden of criminal liability than that which ordinarily would apply. They are in effect re-writing health and safety legislation to adopt more onerous burdens. It seems rather surprising that the Regulations operate in this way, effectively criminalising breaches of measures which employers might adopt by way of "best practice".

LIMITS ON HOURS OF WORK OF NIGHT WORKERS[24]

9–16   There are two separate limits on the hours of work of night workers. The first limit (discussed below) applies to all night workers. The second limit, discussed in paragraph 9–27 below applies only where the work carried out by night workers involves "special hazards or heavy physical or mental strain". As will be seen, the two limits are very different in nature.

Limits on average normal hours of work

9–17   The Regulation of average normal hours of work for night workers under Regulation 6 follows a similar pattern to the Regulation of average working time under Regulation 4(1). First, Regulation 6(1) sets a limit:

> "a night worker's normal hours of work in any reference period which is applicable in his case shall not exceed an average of eight hours for each 24 hours."

This essentially mirrors the restriction in Article 8(1) of the Directive. It is vital to note that Regulation 6(1) does not limit the normal hours of night work, but rather the normal hours of work of night workers, regardless of whether these hours are worked in night time or day time.

Regulation 6(2) sets the employer's health and safety obligation in respect of this limit—the employer shall "take all reasonable steps, in keeping with the need to protect the health and safety of workers, to ensure that [the limit] is complied with".

The relevant aspects of the limit are as follows:

- The "normal hours of work" of night workers;
- The applicable reference period; and
- The calculation of the average normal hours of work of night workers.

These will be considered in turn.

Normal hours of work

9–18   It is important to note that the limit in Regulation 6(1) is a limit on "normal hours of work" rather than a limit on "working time".

For this reason, it is difficult to understand why Regulation 20(2)—the "voluntary overtime" derogation introduced by the 1999 Regulations—states that Regulation 6(1) and (2) do not apply to work which the worker is not required by the employer to perform and which is not measured or predetermined or can be determined by the

---

[24] Regulation 6.

worker himself. Regulation 6(1) and (2) are concerned with normal hours of work and not with working time. It is submitted that the amendment is ultimately without effect, as far as the Regulation of normal hours of work of night workers is concerned.

The expression "normal hours of work" is used in the Directive but is not defined. In particular it is not clear how normal hours of work differ from working time and whether overtime hours are to be included or excluded from normal hours. The preamble to the Directive indicates that normal hours should be included—reference is made to the "need to limit the duration of periods of night work, including overtime".[25] However, Article 8 itself makes no mention of overtime (contrast the limit on working time in Article 4—"the average working time for each seven-day period, including overtime, shall not exceed 48 hours").

9–19 Some clarification on this point was provided by the ECJ decision in *SIMAP*, in which the meaning of "normal hours of work" was at issue. Question 4(c) asks the court to determine whether on-call hours (either those spent physically at the workplace or those spent under a contact system at the worker's home) are to be classed as "normal hours". The Court's decision is that on-call hours will only qualify as "normal hours" of work to the extent that they fall within the definition of working time. The rationale for this approach is not altogether clear.

It is clear however that under the Regulations, "normal hours of work" do not include overtime hours, unless these are guaranteed by the employer. Under Regulation 6(6) the starting point for identifying normal hours of work is to determine whether or not section 234 of the ERA 1996 (ERA) applies to the night worker. If so, the night worker's "normal hours of work" for the purpose of the Regulations will be his "normal working hours" for the purposes of the ERA 1996.

Section 234 of the ERA 1996 applies "where an employee is entitled to overtime pay when employed for more than a fixed number of hours in a week or other period". In such a case, the normal hours of work will be the fixed number of hours (section 234(2) of the ERA), save that where

(a) The contract of employment fixes the number or minimum number of hours of employment in a week or other period (whether or not it also provides for the reduction of that number or minimum in certain circumstances); and

(b) That number or minimum number of hours exceeds the number of hours without overtime" (section 234(3) ERA)

the normal working hours are that number or minimum number of hours, and not the number of hours without overtime.

9–20 Essentially, this means that overtime is discounted (unless it is "contractual" or "guaranteed", *i.e.* obligatory on employer and worker) and normal hours are those fixed or determined by the contract whether or not these are in fact worked.

Where section 234 of the ERA 1996 does *not* apply, for example in the case of salaried staff who are not paid overtime, then "normal hours of work" for the purposes of the Regulations must be determined by construction of the contract of employment. An express statement of normal working hours in the contract will usually be conclusive, even where the worker's actual hours of work are longer, unless a variation of the contractual provision can be proven. Where the contract of employment leaves the question of working hours open, the "normal hours" will have to be identified by what happens in practice during the employment.

If normal hours of work are to be determined in this way—*i.e.* without reference to

---

[25] Directive 93/104/E.C., preamble, para. 12.

overtime, unless guaranteed—then the night-work limit essentially applies to the contractual or scheduled hours of work. The benefit to the employer from this approach is that the normal hours of work are identifiable in advance and the employer can check compliance with the Regulations when planning or scheduling work.

The applicable reference period

9–21 A number of different reference periods may apply for the purposes of the limit specified in Regulation 6(1):

(a) In the case of a worker who has worked for his employer for less than 17 weeks, the reference period is the period that has elapsed since he started work for his employer (Regulation 6(4)). For example, if a worker had only worked for his employer for three weeks, the reference period for Regulation 6(1) would be three weeks;

(b) Thereafter, the Regulations provide for a "rolling" reference period of 17 weeks, (Regulation 6(3)(b)), in default of any provision to the contrary in a relevant agreement (see (c) and (d) below);

(c) A relevant agreement may set a reference period of consecutive periods of 17 weeks (Regulation 6(3)(a));

(d) An alternative reference period may be set under a workforce or collective agreement (Regulation 23). No maximum limit on the length of such alternative reference period is specified.

9–22 Regulation 23 allows collective or workforce agreements to modify or exclude the application of, *inter alia*, Regulation 6(1) to (3), *i.e.* the limit itself, the employer's duty in respect of that limit and the reference period. However, Regulation 23 does not allow Regulation 6(4), the reference period for new employees, to be modified or excluded. (This position is to be contrasted with the ability under Regulation 23(b) to substitute a period of up to 52 weeks as the reference period for the average weekly working time of "new" workers under Regulation 4(4).) However, as the limit itself can be modified or excluded for "new" workers, this apparent quirk in the drafting would appear to be of no consequence.

Article 8 of the Directive does not in itself contain any calculation for the average normal hours of work of night workers. It makes no reference to the reference period over which this average is to be taken, and Article 16 leaves the reference period in such cases to be determined either by Member States after consultation of the two sides of industry or by collective agreements or agreements "concluded between the two sides of industry at national or regional level". In the case of Member States (such as the United Kingdom) in which there is no statutory system ensuring the conclusion of collective agreements or agreements concluded between the two sides of industry at national or regional level, derogations are permitted from Article 8 and 16 by way of collective agreements "between the two sides of industry at the appropriate collective level".[26]

---

[26] John Fairhurst argues in *The Working Time Directive: A Spanish Inquisition*, that the averaging process for normal hours under the Directive should exclude any 24 hour period in which the worker does not work. The rationale is that otherwise night workers would not receive any additional protection over and above the 48-hour limit on average weekly working time. However, the Regulation clearly proceed on the basis that only the 24-hour rest period should be excluded from the calculation, and not any additional days on which the worker does not work.

9–23   Article 16 provides that if the minimum weekly rest period of 24 hours required by Article 5 falls within that reference period, it shall not be included in the calculation of the average. It is not clear from the Directive whether the 24-hour rest period is to be discounted in full or only those hours of the rest period actually taken as rest, although the wording of the Regulations seems to adopt the latter view (see above).

Calculating average normal hours of work

9–24   Regulation 6(5) provides that the formula for calculating a night worker's average normal hours of work is as follows:

$$\frac{A}{B-C}$$

Where:

A is the number of hours during the reference period which are normal working hours for that worker;

B is the number of days during the reference period; and

C is the total number of hours during the reference period comprised in rest periods spent by the worker in pursuance of his entitlement under Regulation 11, divided by 24.

Assume that a night worker normally works 12 hours for four days a week and has an entitlement to a weekly rest period of 24 hours. The normal hours of work over the 17 weeks are $4 \times 12 \times 17$, *i.e.* 816 hours. There are 119 days during the reference period. There are seventeen 24-hour rest periods over the 17-week reference period. The calculation is therefore:

$$\frac{816}{119-17}$$

which produces an average of eight hours in each 24-hour period.

9–25   It can be seen that the calculation involves taking an average over the whole of the week (making allowance for the weekly rest period) rather than the particular number of days in the week in which the night worker works. Further, unlike the averaging process for the weekly working time limit, no adjustments have to be made for days of absence through sickness or annual leave.

It would appear however that only the hours of rest actually taken by the worker under the entitlement to weekly rest under Regulation 11 will count towards the value of **C** in the above calculation. So, if the worker forgoes the entitlement or if the entitlement to weekly rest is modified or excluded, that will have to be taken into account in the calculation of average normal hours under Regulation 6(5). Employers may have to keep records of weekly rest periods (or at least of those occasions where the weekly rest period is not taken) for the purposes of the calculation in Regulation 6(5) even though there is no separate obligation under the Regulations to keep records in respect of rest periods.

If the limit in Regulation 6(1) is breached or likely to be breached, the employer will need to consider whether the limit is excluded by operation of any of the "special cases" in Regulation 21 and, if not, take steps to reduce the normal working hours or modify or exclude the limit or reference period by way of collective or workforce agreement.

Derogations and flexibilities

9–26   As the same derogations and flexibilities apply to the limit on normal hours of night workers and the limit on night work involving special hazards, these will be considered below.

Limits on work involving special hazards or heavy physical or mental strain

Nature of the limit

9–27   Regulation 6(7) provides that "an employer shall ensure that no night worker employed by him whose work involves special hazards or heavy physical or mental strain works for more than eight hours in any 24-hour period during which the night worker performs night work".

It is essential to note that, in respect of this limit:

(a)   The limit applies to actual working time and not "normal hours of work";

(b)   There is no averaging process or reference period—the limit of eight hours applies on any day where the worker performs, during night time, work involving "special hazards";

(c)   The employer's duty is to ensure that the limit is observed, and not simply take all reasonable steps to ensure observance of the limit;

(d)   The limit only applies to any 24-hour period during which the night worker performs night work (as defined above). In the case of a worker employed on alternate day and night shifts, the limit in Regulation 6(7) would restrict only the length of the night shifts; and

(e)   Application of the limit is not triggered by a specific proportion of work involving special hazards or heavy physical or mental strain. It appears therefore that if any of the night worker's work falls into this category, the limit in Regulation 6(7) will apply. Further, it would seem that there is no requirement for any of the work involving special hazards, etc., to be carried out at night time before the limit applies. The limit is expressed to apply each time the night worker performs night work, regardless of whether the night worker actually performs any work involving special hazards or heavy physical or mental strain during night time.

However, the limit in Regulation 6(7) is not as absolute as may first appear. The limit is excluded altogether where the unmeasured working time or the "special cases" derogations apply. Further, the limit can be modified or excluded by a collective or workforce agreement, as will be seen below.

Additionally, where working time consists of work which the worker is not required by the employer to perform, and where it is not measured, predetermined or where the duration of the work can be determined by the worker himself, such time does not count towards the limit in Regulation 6(7).[27] The validity of this approach is extremely questionable. The Directive does not allow for this type of derogation.

---

[27] Regulation 20(2) introduced by Regulation 4 of the 1999 Regulation.

Definition of "Special Hazards or Heavy Physical or Mental Strain"

9–28   Work involves "special hazards or heavy physical or mental strain" where:

(a)   It is recognised in a risk assessment made by the employer under Regulation 3 of the Management of Health and Safety At Work Regulations 1992 as involving *a significant risk* to the health and safety of workers employed by him; or

(b)   It is identified as such in a collective agreement or workforce agreement which takes account of the specific effects and hazards of night work.

Neither of these provisions are straightforward. Firstly, it will be noted in respect of (a) above that Regulation 6(7) is triggered where the employer's risk assessment identifies the work as involving "*a significant risk*" to the health and safety of workers, not the identification of that work as involving "special hazards or heavy physical or mental strain". On the other hand, for a collective or workforce agreement to trigger the application of Regulation 6(7), it must classify the work as involving "special hazards or heavy physical or mental strain".

9–29   Further, the wording of Regulation 6(8)(b) suggests that a collective or workforce agreement must do something more than identify work as involving special hazards, namely "take account of the specific effects and hazards of night work". It is not at all clear what is required in this respect. In particular, it is not clear whether these words mean that specific provision has to be made in the collective or workforce agreement for the protection of night workers.

The Directive itself provides that "work involving special hazards or heavy physical or mental strain shall be defined by national legislation and/or practice or by collective agreements or agreements concluded between the two sides of industry, taking account of the specific effects and hazards of night work". It is submitted that in fact the proper reading of the Directive is that it is the definition of work as involving special hazards, *etc.*, which must take account of the specific effects and hazards of night work, whether this definition is by national legislation, practice or collective agreements.

It is submitted that there is no requirement under the Directive for a collective or workforce agreement to take account of the specific effects and hazards of night work except as regards the classification of work as involving special hazards or heavy physical or mental strain. The Regulations appear to have been drafted on a misreading of Article 2(4)(b).

Nature of the night work limits: enforcement by workers

9–30   We have seen that in *Barber v. RJB Mining (UK) Limited*,[28] the High Court gave contractual effect to the weekly working time limit in Regulation 4. In doing so, the Court rejected the employer's argument that Regulation 4(1) and Regulation 4(2) should be read together. Regulation 4(1) sets out the working time limit and Regulation 4(2) imposes the obligation (enforceable by the Health and Safety Authorities) to take all reasonable steps to ensure compliance with that limit. The High Court held that Regulation 4(1), the limit itself, was a free-standing contractual right incorporated into every contract of employment, entitling workers to enforce the limit directly by way of declaration, injunction, or proceedings for breach of contract. The decision in *Barber* was a surprising one and remains questionable. It is

---

[28] [1999] I.R.L.R. 308. Also see para. 6–12.

suggested that the proper interpretation of Regulation 4(1) (in its form at the time of the *Barber* case) is that the limit on average weekly working time is a statutory limit which overrides any contrary provisions of the contract of employment. However, simply because the legislative provision governs the operation of the contract does not mean that it must be regarded as part of the contract itself, creating contractual obligations and indeed contractual remedies in the event of breach. In any event it is submitted that the amendments to Regulation 4(1) by the Working Time Regulations 1999 undermine the conclusion in Barber that the weekly working time limit has contractual effect (see above).

9–31   However, it is clear that the same interpretation as adopted in the *Barber* case could be applied to the night work limits in Regulation 6. In particular, the structure of Regulation 6(1) and (2) is identical to the structure of Regulations 4(1) and 4(2); one paragraph sets out the limit, the other imposes a duty enforceable by the Health and Safety Executive in respect of that limit. Further, if the duty in Regulation 6(1) were contractual, there would seem to be no logical basis on which Regulation 6(7) should not be contractual as well. If the setting of a mandatory limit on working hours is sufficient to create a contractual term, then Regulation 6(7) is no different from Regulation 6(1) or Regulation 4(1).

Derogations and flexibilities in respect of Regulation 6(1) and (7)

9–32   Exclusion or modification of the limits in Regulation 6(1) and Regulation 6(7) can result either from automatic exclusion by virtue of the Regulations or under collective or workforce agreements.

Automatic exclusions by virtue of the Regulations themselves

9–33   The limits on the average normal working hours of night workers and the limit on work involving special hazards or heavy physical and mental strain are automatically excluded in the following circumstances:

- In the case of workers whose working time is not measured or pre-determined or can be determined by the worker himself—*i.e.* where the unmeasured working time derogation in Regulation 20 applies; or

- If any of the "special cases" set out in Regulation 21 apply.

The effect of "special cases" on the limit on the normal hours of night workers should be contrasted with its effect on the average weekly working time limit. While in the case of weekly working time, the "special cases" extend the reference period to 26 weeks, the limits in respect of night work are excluded altogether if any of the special cases apply.

The scope of these exceptions is considered below.

Exclusion or modification by agreement

9–34   Under regulation 23, a collective or workforce agreement can modify or exclude:

- The limit on the normal hours of night workers in Regulation 6(1) and the employer's duty in relation thereto in Regulation 6(2);

- The reference period over which the normal working hours of night workers are averaged (Regulation 6(3)); and

- The limit on the daily working time of night workers whose work involves special hazards or heavy physical or mental strain (Regulation 6(7)).

Compensatory rest

9–35   However, where the limit is:

(a) Excluded by "special cases" or modified or excluded through a collective or workforce agreement; *and*

(b) The worker is "accordingly required by the employer to work during a period which would otherwise be a rest period or rest break"

the employer is obliged, by virtue of Regulation 24, to allow the night worker to take an equivalent period of compensatory rest. In exceptional cases where, for objective reasons, this is not possible the employer is obliged to afford the worker "such protection as may be appropriate to safeguard the worker's health and safety".

PROVISION OF HEALTH ASSESSMENTS—REGULATION 7

9–36   Regulation 7 imposes various obligations on employers to afford the opportunity of free health assessments to those engaged in or about to be assigned to night work.

Requirement that health assessment is free

9–37   The health assessment must be free to the worker. Clearly, this means that the worker must not have to pay for the assessment. Further (if the assessment takes place in working hours), the worker must not lose any pay and is entitled to be reimbursed for expenses (*e.g.* travelling expenses) incurred when taking the assessment.

The timing of health assessments

9–38   Regulation 7(1)(a)(i) provides that an employer shall ensure that a night worker is given the opportunity of a free health assessment before being assigned to night work, unless the worker has had a health assessment on an earlier occasion and the employer has no reason to believe that that assessment is no longer valid.

The employer is also obliged to ensure that each night worker has the opportunity of free health assessments at regular intervals after being assigned to night work. The obligation to provide health assessments is therefore a continuing one. The DTI's guidance suggests that, at the very least, health assessments should be provided on an annual basis. However, the obligation applies in respect of each individual night worker and the employer must have regard to the individual circumstances of each such worker. While employers may set up a regular assessment programme in respect of night workers, individual night workers may require more frequent assessments if, for example, suffering from or at risk of a particular medical problem which could affect their ability to carry out night work, or as a result of the specific nature of their work.

Purpose of the assessment

9–39   The purpose of the assessments is not stated expressly in the Regulations (or indeed the Directive). However, it can be inferred from Regulation 7(5) that the purpose of the health assessment is to determine whether the worker is fit to perform the night work to which he or she is to be, or has been, assigned.

Assessment of risks affecting night workers

9–40   The first stage in the assessment is for the employer to identify any particular risks associated with the work in question and, in particular, its performance during night time. Employers have an existing obligation under the Health and Safety At Work Regulations 1992 to identify hazards to health and safety in the workplace, assess the extent to which these might harm the worker and identify appropriate action required to control and reduce such exposure.

The Government's view is that the nature of workplace hazards is unlikely to change according to the time or day at which work is performed. While that is true, it is submitted that account must be taken of the fact that the worker's susceptibility to risk may be increased during night-time hours. Particular medical conditions may be affected by the fact that work is performed at night (examples are given in the DTI guidance). Further, individual workers who have worked for night hours for long periods, or indeed have only just commenced night work, may suffer increased susceptibility to risk.

Procedure for health assessments

9–41   The Regulations do not make any express provision as to how the health assessments required by Regulation 7(1) are to be carried out. It should be noted however that the obligation is to provide a "health assessment" rather than a "medical assessment". A health assessment does not necessarily involve examination of the worker by a medical professional.

Guidance provided by the DTI suggests that the first stage of the health assessment might involve workers completing a "screening" questionnaire. The guidance suggests the following in relation to such questionnaires:

- The questionnaire should be compiled with guidance from a qualified health care professional familiar with the nature of the employer's business and issues associated with working at night. This may be the employer's Occupational Health Department;

- The questionnaire should explain its purpose, the nature of the work to which the individual is being assigned and ask whether the worker suffers from any medical condition or is undergoing any medical treatment which might affect a fitness to work at night;

- Responses to such questionnaires should be screened by individuals trained to interpret the information to identify individuals with conditions that may be affected by night work;

- The questionnaire should be adapted for regular updating;

- In cases where the screening process raises doubts about an individual's fitness to work at night, the worker should be referred to a suitably qualified health care professional for further assessment and an opinion on his or her fitness to carry out the work to which they are or are about to be assigned. Such assessment and opinion could be provided through the employer's Occupational Health Department, through consultation with the worker's own general practitioner or through an external provider; and

- Employers will need to ensure that those who are conducting such medical assessments should be aware of the purpose for which the assessment is required and are familiar with the employer's business, the relevant working environment and the nature of and duration of the night work in question.

9–42   The DTI's guidance includes a sample questionnaire. The health assessment process must comply with medical confidentiality and specifically with the employer's obligation under the Access to Medical Reports Act 1988. Regulation 7(5) expressly provides that no person shall disclose any assessment to any person other than the worker to whom it relates "unless the worker has given his consent to the disclosure *or* the disclosure is confined to a statement that the worker is fit ... to take up an assignment or ... to continue to undertake an assignment".

Additional provisions for "Young Night Workers"

9–43   In the case of "young" night workers, the obligation is to provide the opportunity of an assessment of "health and capacities". It is not clear what additional burdens are imposed by the word "capacities" as this is undefined.

Further, the obligation arises if the young worker is to be assigned to work during a "restricted period" of 10.00 p.m. to 6.00 a.m.

TRANSFER TO SUITABLE DAY WORK

Obligation to transfer

9–44   Under Regulation 7(6), "where a registered medical practitioner advises an employer that a worker is suffering from health problems which the practitioner considers to be connected with the fact that the worker performs night work" the employer shall transfer the worker to suitable day work, where possible.

The opinion of the registered medical practitioner does not, therefore, of itself give rise to any absolute right to transfer. It must also be shown that it is possible for the employer to transfer the worker to day work to which the worker is suited (Regulation 7(6)(b)).

It is submitted that the question of whether it is possible for the employer to transfer the worker to suitable day work is likely to be interpreted restrictively against employers. For example, it is likely that employers will be required not simply to examine whether there are any vacancies for day work but also to investigate the possibility of a day worker and a night worker swapping roles.

The provisions of the Disability Discrimination Act 1995, and in particular the duty to make reasonable adjustments, may also be relevant in such circumstances.

OTHER HEALTH AND SAFETY PROVISIONS IN RESPECT OF NIGHT WORKERS

9–45   Articles 10 to 12 of the Working Time Directive contain further provisions in respect of general health and safety issues relating to night workers. Not all of these Articles have direct counterparts in the Regulations.

Article 10 provides that Member States may "make the work of certain categories of night workers subject to certain guarantees, under conditions laid down by national legislation and/or practice, in the case of workers who incur risks to their safety or health linked to night time working". This opportunity has not been taken up by the United Kingdom Government.

Article 11 provides that Member States shall take measures necessary to ensure "that an employer who regularly uses night workers brings this information to the attention of the competent authorities if they so request". This provision is included indirectly in the Regulations. Regulation 28(5) extends the enforcement provisions of the HSWA 1974 to the enforcement of the "relevant requirements" of the Regulations (as defined in Regulation 28(i)). The enforcement provisions under the 1974 Act include a requirement to provide upon request such information requested by an enforcing authority which it is reasonable to expect the employer to have and this will include the identity of night workers and other information relevant to them.

9–46 Article 12 of the Directive provides that Member States shall take the measures necessary

> "to ensure that night workers have safety and health protection appropriate to the nature of their work and that appropriate protection and prevention services or facilities with regard to the safety and health of night workers and shift workers are equivalent to those applicable to other workers and are available at all times."

The United Kingdom Government has taken the view that these requirements are already in place under existing health and safety at work legislation and see no need for provisions specific to night workers.

CHAPTER TEN

Shift Work

INTRODUCTION

10–01 The European Commission's Explanatory Memorandum to the proposed Working Time Directive included statistics relating to the proportion of workers in each member state who carried out shift work. The United Kingdom and Spain were found to have the highest percentage of shift workers overall with 29 per cent of workers in both Member States undertaking regular or occasional shift work. The Explanatory Memorandum also included statistics relating to the proportion of workers who carried out shift work within the manufacturing sectors in the Member States. The data revealed that the United Kingdom manufacturing sector had far and away the highest proportion, with 64 per cent of workers undertaking regular or occasional shift work, followed by Italy with 46 per cent.

The Explanatory Memorandum suggested a strong empirical link between working patterns and workers' health. Quoting from a number of surveys, the Explanatory Memorandum highlighted evidence that shift and night workers displayed a higher incidence of health problems, such as cardio-circulatory complaints, gastro-intestinal illnesses, appetite disturbances, sleeping problems, greater recourse to medicines, alcohol and tobacco and, during night shifts in particular, an increased risk of serious work accidents.

The initial drafts of the Directive therefore required Member States to take measures necessary to ensure that the scheduling and total length of breaks for rotating shift workers took account of the "more demanding nature of these forms of working time".[1] Ultimately this provision did not survive to the final text of the Directive.

10–02 The initial drafts of the Directive also contained a provision which prohibited the working of two consecutive full-time shifts where this involved night work.[2] Again, this provision did not survive to the final text. The only specific protection afforded to shift workers in the final text is contained in Article 12, which requires member states to take measures necessary to ensure that night workers and shift workers have "health and safety protection appropriate to the nature of their work" and further that "appropriate protection and prevention services and facilities. . . are equivalent to those applicable to other workers and are available at all times".

However, not even this provision has been included in the Regulations. The Government expressed its view in the DTI Consultation Document[3] that such measures had already been given effect through the Management of Health and Safety at Work Regulations 1992.

---

[1] Art. 7(4) of the draft Directive.
[2] Art. 7(2) of the draft Directive.
[3] Measures to Implement the Provision of the E.C. Directive in Organisation of Working Time and the Protection of Young People at Work URN 98/645.

The only other provision which potentially relates to shift workers is the general provision contained in Article 13 of the Directive which sets out the principle of the humanisation of work and which has been implemented by Regulation 7 of the Regulations.[4]

SHIFT WORK UNDER THE WORKING TIME DIRECTIVE

10–03 Shift work is subject to the Directive's general requirements on minimum daily and weekly rest periods and maximum daily and weekly working hours. However, such provisions are, in certain circumstances, less favourable to shift workers.

The original resolution on the adaption of working time which was adopted by the Commission on December 18, 1979 emphasised the need for increasing flexibility in the workforce in the use of part-time, temporary and shift workers, whilst also providing social protection. This principle is incorporated into the Directive, which in the preamble states "in view of the question likely to be raised by the organisation of working time within an undertaking, it appears desirable to provide for flexibility in the application of certain provisions of this Directive, whilst ensuring compliance with the principles of ensuring the safety and health of workers." The Commission recognised that the requirement for a minimum daily rest period of 11 consecutive hours per 24-hour period (Article 3) and to a minimum uninterrupted rest period of 24 hours per each seven-day period (Article 5) clearly pose practical difficulties for many patterns of work. Consequently, Article 17 (2.3) of the Directive permits derogation from both Articles 3 and 5 in the case of:

(a) Shift work activities, each time the worker changes shift and cannot take daily and/or weekly rest periods between the end of one shift and the start of the next one;

(b) Activities involving periods of work split up over the day, particularly those of cleaning staff.

SHIFT WORK UNDER THE WORKING TIME REGULATIONS

10–04 The relevant provisions relating to shift workers are contained in Regulation 22, which states as follows:

22(1) Subject to Regulation 24—

(a) Regulation 10(1) does not apply in relation to a shift worker when he changes shift and cannot take a daily rest period between the end of one shift and the start of the next one;

(b) Paragraphs (1) and (2) of Regulation 11 do not apply in relation to a shift worker when he changes shift and cannot take a weekly rest period between the end of one shift and the start of the next one; and

(c) Neither Regulation 10(1) nor paragraphs (1) and (2) of Regulation 11 apply to workers engaged in activities involving periods of work split over the day as may be the case for cleaning staff.

---

[4] See Chap. 7, para. 7–20.

22(2) For the purpose of this Regulation –

"shift worker" means any worker whose work schedule is part of shift work; and "shift work" means any method of organising work in shifts whereby workers succeed each other at the same work stations according to a certain pattern, including a rotating pattern, and which may be continuous or discontinuous, entailing the need for workers to work at different times over a given period of days or weeks.

10–05 Regulation 22 literally copies out Article 17 of the Directive. Furthermore, the definition of shift worker and shift work contained in Regulation 22(2) is identical to the definition set out in Article 2, paragraphs 5 and 6 of the Directive.

The definition of shift work is unnecessarily convoluted. The lack of clarity is compounded by the fact that the Government has merely copied out the wording of the Directive without any explanation. The Conservative Government expressed the view in the first Consultation Document[5] that unless workers succeed each other at the same workstation and in accordance to a certain pattern, they could not be defined as "shift workers" under this definition. Accordingly, the provision of cover for shift workers would not result in the classification of that worker as a shift worker unless that cover was according to a certain pattern. Furthermore, if workers do not succeed each other "at the same work stations" because the pattern of production is such that the various stages of production are timed to coincide with the starting and finishing times for each group of workers, such pattern would not be classified as "shift work". A strict reading of the definition could therefore potentially exclude many workers who would otherwise be regarded as shift workers. The succeeding Labour Government made no reference to the potential difficulty posed by the definition in its own consultation document and merely confirmed that it was the same as the definition contained in the Directive.[6]

10–06 It should be noted that the general requirements contained in the Regulations relating to minimum daily rest periods (Regulation 10(1)) and minimum weekly rest periods (Regulation 11) still apply to shift work. Regulation 22 only enables derogation in circumstances where it is not possible for a shift worker to take his weekly or daily rest entitlement between the end of one shift and the start of the next. The derogation is not available simply because an individual is a "shift worker". The same is true in the case of a worker whose activities involve periods of work split up over the day.

There are clearly situations where shift working patterns would preclude employees from receiving the minimum daily rest period of 11 consecutive hours. The two-shift system is the most common shift pattern in the United Kingdom with statistics showing approximately a million and a half employees working such patterns in Spring 1999.[7] Under this shift pattern workers might, for example, work an early shift from 6.00 a.m. to 2.00 p.m. and a late shift from 2.00 p.m. to 10.00 p.m. It is common for such shifts to involve alternating arrangements where a late shift is followed by an early shift and vice versa. Obviously, where such changeover takes place, the worker will not receive his full entitlement to 11 consecutive hours within a 24-hour cycle.

The other situation which is likely to conflict with the minimum daily and weekly rest requirements involve split shifts, where workers have to attend for two or more

---

[5] "A Consultation Document on Measures to Implement Provisions of the E.C. Directive on the Organisation of Working Time" (1997).
[6] See postscript on the SIMAP case.
[7] New Labour Force Survey questions on working patterns—January 2000 Labour Market Trends.

shifts per day, separated by a break. The example contained in both the Directive and the Regulations of where such a pattern applies is that of cleaning. It is clearly more difficult to provide a rest period of 11 consecutive hours where there are two shifts or more within a 24-hour period.

10–07   Regulation 22 therefore enables a shift worker (or a worker whose work is split over the day) to change from a late shift one day to an early shift the following day, even though there may not be 11 consecutive hours between such a shift, or from a shift pattern in one week to another shift pattern the following week even though he would not be receiving a period of 24 consecutive hours of weekly rest between each shift.

The derogation contained in Regulation 22 is subject to Regulation 24, which states that where a worker is not afforded the minimum rest entitlement because he is a shift worker or, alternatively, because his activities are split over a day, he should be allowed wherever possible to take an equivalent period of compensatory rest.[8]

---

[8] See Chap. 11.

CHAPTER ELEVEN

Compensatory Rest

INTRODUCTION

11–01 Regulation 24, which deals with the issue of compensatory rest, reduces the impact of a number of the exceptions set out in Part III of the Regulations. It does this by providing that

> "where ... any provision of these Regulations is excluded by Regulation 21 [special cases] or 22 [shift workers] or is modified or excluded by means of a collective agreement or a workforce agreement [Regulation 23] and the worker is accordingly required by his employer to work during a period which would otherwise be a rest period or rest break—
>
> (a) His employer shall wherever possible allow him to take an equivalent period of compensatory rest; and
>
> (b) In exceptional cases in which it is not possible, for objective reasons, to grant such a period of rest, his employer shall afford him such protection as may be appropriate in order to safeguard the worker's health and safety."

11–02 This wording reproduces more or less exactly the provisions of Article 17(3) of the Directive on which it is based. However in one respect Regulation 24 goes further than Article 17(3) by emphasising the need in exceptional cases to give such protection "as may be appropriate in order to safeguard the worker's health and safety". This may be due to the influence of Article 13—the Article which introduces the humanisation principle and requires work to be adapted to the individual worker. Article 13 specifically refers to "safety and health requirements, especially as regards breaks during working time". In any event Regulation 24 makes it clear that where—exceptionally—compensatory rest is not available the health and safety of the individual worker must be the prime concern in giving him or her appropriate protection.

The requirement that any modification or exclusion of the Regulations must usually be balanced by "an equivalent period of compensatory rest" clearly limits quite considerably the impact of the exceptions in Regulations 21 to 23. However, because of certain defects in the drafting of Regulation 24, the precise scope of Regulation 24 is unclear and a number of problems arise.

Under Regulation 24 compensatory rest need only be granted if due to the application of one of the specified derogations the worker has to work during a period "which would otherwise be a rest period or a rest break". As discussed above, the term "rest period" is defined in Regulation 2(1) to mean "a period which is not working time other than a rest break or leave to which the worker is entitled under these Regulations". "Rest break" is undefined, but presumably means a break to which the worker would be entitled under Regulation 12.

On a literal reading, therefore, any time at which a worker is working would otherwise be a rest period, and the worker would be entitled to compensatory rest in respect of that period. However, the purpose of Regulation 24 is to protect the health and safety of those workers who are not permitted to take up the rest entitlements that they would have but for the derogations contained in the Regulations. It seems clear therefore that Regulation 24 should primarily be read as requiring an employer to grant compensatory rest only where a worker has not received what would otherwise be their entitlements under Regulations 10, 11 and 12.[1] On this basis it would only be possible to determine whether a worker was entitled to compensatory rest at the end of the applicable reference period (*i.e.* 6 hours, a working day or 7 or 14 days as the case may be). It is submitted that this is the case even where a worker is not granted their entitlements at the time at which they should be granted under any provision of the worker's contract, although obviously in such circumstances the worker may have a contractual remedy.

It should also be noted that in relation to rest breaks, there may be a fine line between an agreement which defines the detail of a worker's entitlement, as permitted by Regulation 12(2), and one that modifies the application of Regulation 12(1) as permitted by Regulation 23(a). It is only in the latter case that the worker would be entitled to compensatory rest.

What is Meant by "An Equivalent Period of Compensatory Rest"?

11–03   There is no definition of "compensatory rest" in either the Directive or the Regulations and as a result it can be very difficult to assess how and when such rest should be provided. For example, if a worker is only allowed 10 hours rest in a 24-hour period (and so is denied the 11-hour daily rest period guaranteed by Regulation 10), it is not clear whether "equivalent compensatory rest" amounts to the one hour he has missed or to a full consecutive 11-hour period. The original DTI guidance suggested that an "equivalent" period of rest "should be as long as the period of rest to which the worker was entitled" (*i.e.* the full 11 hours). However in many shift systems this would be completely unworkable, as the following illustration shows.

Example

11–04   A company wishes to introduce a 6-day shift system whereby certain employees will work from 8.00 a.m. until 10.30 p.m. on Mondays whilst on Tuesdays to Saturdays they will work from 6.30 a.m. until 12 noon. A lunch and evening meal break are to be provided during the Monday shift. Although the average 48-hour limit will not be exceeded under this system, the workers involved will only receive eight consecutive hours of rest between the Monday and Tuesday shifts. If equivalent compensatory rest is a full consecutive 11-hour period there will be great difficulties as there is just not sufficient time within the weekend to allow for Saturday's daily rest period (11 hours), the weekly rest period (24 hours) plus a further 11 hours by way of compensatory rest. However, if the period of compensatory rest is just three hours then there is no problem as on Tuesdays to Saturdays there is a daily rest period of 181/2 hours which compensates for the longer shift on Mondays.

---

[1] If a worker who is not in fact covered by any of Regulations 10, 11 or 12 is nevertheless granted those entitlements as if he was so covered, this is strictly speaking compensatory rest, but there will be no issue concerning the application or interpretation of Regulation 24 in such cases.

The practical difficulties of insisting on full periods of rest being given in lieu of any missed hours has no doubt influenced the DTI to change its mind on this issue. In its revised guidance it now states that compensatory rest is "a period of rest the same length as the period of rest, *or part of a period of rest*, that the worker has missed . . .the principle is that everyone gets his or her entitlement of 90 hours rest a week on average, although some rest may come slightly later than normal".

However it is submitted that neither of the two approaches suggested by the DTI are strictly accurate. Regulation 24 requires an employer to grant an "equivalent period" of compensatory rest, wording taken from the Directive. On a purposive view, the period of rest should be equivalent in both qualitative as well as quantitative terms. On this basis, one would look at the quality of the compensatory rest period, including factors such as the worker's degree of freedom to utilise that time, how frequently the compensatory period was interrupted, the proximity of the period in time to the time when rest should have been granted and the excess fatigue which gave rise to the compensatory rest entitlement caused by the working pattern of the worker, as well as the duration of that period. This approach is consistent with the principle of humanisation contained in Article 13 of the Directive.[2]

However, the suggested approach would render it very difficult for employers to determine how to comply with their obligations under Regulation 24. Given that an employer may face criminal sanctions for breach of the compensatory rest provisions,[3] this is clearly undesirable, and further clarification of Regulation 24 from either the Government or the courts is needed as a matter or urgency. In the meantime, the competing interests of health and safety and legal certainty will in most cases be best balanced through the medium of collective bargaining.

This further supports the view that an entitlement to compensatory rest may only be assessed at the end of the relevant reference period, as this would enable consideration to be given to the entire pattern and duration of rest granted throughout that period in order to determine what the principle of equivalence required in a particular case.

WHEN MUST THE COMPENSATORY REST BE TAKEN?

11–05 The Regulations do not state when the compensatory rest must be given, although the original version of the DTI Guidance suggested that this should occur "within a reasonable time from the date the entitlement to rest was modified". It went on to suggest that this should usually be possible within a couple of weeks for rest breaks and daily rest and a couple of months for weekly rest.

It is submitted that this is the correct approach. The determination of what is reasonable should be made in the light of the purpose of the Directive and the employer's implied contractual duty of care to his employees in respect of their health and safety. If one adopts the approach suggested above, the timing of the compensatory rest will be relevant in determining whether an "equivalent" period of compensatory rest has been granted.

On this view, compensatory rest breaks should be granted as soon as possible following the end of the working day, or 6 hour period, in which a full rest break was not granted. A compensatory rest break of 20 minutes granted a week after a working day of six hours without a break would arguably not compensate the worker for the

---

[2] The Irish Organisation of Working Time Act 1997 provides that an employee must be granted a rest period that "in all the circumstances can reasonably be regarded as equivalent to" the rest period to which he would have been entitled but for the relevant derogation (s.6(2)).
[3] Regulations 28 and 29.

added fatigue, and the added risk to his health and safety, caused by the original omission.

In determining what is a reasonable time within which to grant compensatory rest, courts may take note of the provisions of Regulation 27, which requires compensatory rest breaks and daily rest to be granted to young workers within three weeks in certain circumstances.

A worker who is ordinarily entitled to more than 11 hours' rest per day may receive compensatory rest as a matter of course. Similarly, if a worker is granted two days off a week, he will routinely receive compensatory rest on the second day off, as he is only entitled to 24 hours' weekly rest under the Regulations.

This approach would mean that an employer will generally be unable to extend a worker's holiday entitlement to compensate for those rest periods which have been missed.

PARTICULAR PROBLEMS OF NIGHT SHIFTS

11–06 Where the night shift rules have been modified or excluded, Regulation 24 can present real problems. Take for example a shift system which has been sanctioned by collective agreement and which involves five nine hour night shifts from 10.00 p.m. to 7.00 a.m. on Mondays to Fridays. The work involves heavy physical strain. In this case, the night work rules have clearly been modified because normally such shifts could only be eight hours long.[4] However, despite this modification, the worker still receives his daily and weekly rest breaks. This raises the question whether there is any need to grant him any compensatory rest at all in this situation. Under Regulation 24 compensatory rest need only be granted if the worker has to work during a period "which would otherwise be a rest period or a rest break". If this phrase refers merely to the daily and weekly rest periods granted by the Regulations then there is no problem in this example as the worker clearly does not work through these periods at any time. However the term "rest period" is defined in Regulation 2 to mean "a period which is not working time other than a rest break or leave to which the worker is entitled under these Regulations".[5] As the above shift system clearly eats into time in which, but for the modifications, would not be working time, then arguably on a literal interpretation of the Regulations, some form of compensatory rest must be given. This would appear to be a drafting error in the Regulations and it is suggested that Regulation 4 urgently needs amendment to ensure that it is only if the entitlement to daily and weekly rest is affected that the compensatory rest rules come into play.

EXCEPTIONAL CASES

11–07 Regulation 24 provides that where in "exceptional cases" it is not be possible for "objective reasons" to grant compensatory rest the employer must provide "such protection as may be appropriate in order to safeguard the worker's health and safety". The Government, in its public consultation on the draft Regulations, took the view that "exceptional circumstances will be rare but will also be self-evident". They gave two examples. The first situation concerned a worker who left his job before compensatory rest has been or could be provided. The second was where a business closed down completely before the rest could be given. It has to be said in these cases that it is hard to see how any protection can be given and there is an

---

[4] See Regulation 6(7).
[5] "Rest break" is not defined but presumably refers to the 20-minute rest granted by Regulation 12.

argument that in such exceptional cases as long as the employer is complying with the general law on health and safety he has no further obligations. The original DTI guidance gave little help on this issue, merely suggesting that the flexibility provided by the "exceptional circumstances" provision was not something that could be used on a routine basis and that in most cases compensatory rest would have to be granted. It is suggested that where the exception does apply it may be prudent to give additional periods of holiday (possibly to be taken within a certain fairly short period) to ensure that Regulation 24 is satisfied.

ENFORCEMENT

11–08   Employers who have modified or excluded the rules on night work and who fail to grant equivalent periods of compensatory rest (or who in exceptional circumstances do not afford their workers adequate protection) commit an offence. Otherwise the Regulation is enforced by individual complaint to the employment tribunal. The fact that some criminal liability does arise under this Regulation makes the uncertainties and difficulties associated with Regulation 24 particularly serious and gives force to the call for Regulation 24 to be amended as quickly as possible to deal with these problems.

ADMINISTRATIVE BURDEN

11–09   Although there is no record keeping obligation in respect of the compensatory rest provisions, in practice it may require a great deal of work to set up systems which comply with the rules on compensatory rest. In addition it may be necessary to create mechanisms to record periods which would normally be rest breaks or rest periods so that compensatory entitlements can be calculated. Such information would also be very useful in case of any dispute between employer and worker as regards entitlements under the Regulations.

CHAPTER TWELVE

Exclusions

12–01   When the Department of Trade and Industry published the draft Working Time Regulations, on April 5, 1998, together with its Consultation Paper,[1] they made provision for all of the exclusions and derogations available under Articles 1 and 17 respectively of the Working Time Directive. This came as a surprise considering that the derogations from the Directive had been negotiated by the former Conservative Government which, unlike the Labour Government, implementing the Directive, had been vehemently opposed to the Directive's application to the United Kingdom.[2]

The Labour Government sought to justify inclusion of the derogations in the draft Regulations in its Consultation Paper[3] as follows:

> "... there is no reason to deny either business or workers the opportunity of taking up derogations which the Directive allow[s] so as to preserve flexibilities and freedom to organise work as they wish. The conditions attaching to such derogations will always provide protections for the workers concerned."

When the final form Regulations were laid before Parliament on July 30, 1998 all of the exclusions and derogations had survived the consultation process. These are found in Part III of the Working Time Regulations 1998[4] headed "Exceptions". However, a distinction must be made between the exclusions (which relate to economic sectors and activities to which it seems the Regulations do not, at present, apply) and the exceptions (which allow for certain entitlements and limits to be disapplied or to operate differently in respect of workers engaged in certain types of activity).

Below we look, firstly, at the excluded sectors and activities and then, secondly, at the exceptions to the otherwise general application of the Regulations.

1. EXCLUDED SECTORS AND ACTIVITIES

12–02   Workers employed in certain sectors and activities are it would seem totally excluded from the application of the Regulations at present. These sectors and activities are found in Article 1(3) of the Directive and transposed into United Kingdom law by Regulation 18 of the Working Time Regulations.

---

[1] URN 98/645.

[2] One famous example of the former Conservative Government's negative approach to the Directive and its implementation in the U.K. can be found in para. 1.6 on p. 2 of its 1997 Department of Trade and Industry Consultation Document ("A Consultation Document on Measures to Implement Provisions of the E.C. Directive on the Organisation of Working Time ('the Working Time Directive')" which states "When the Directive no longer applies [sic], it will be the intention of the Government to repeal the legislation and remove those entitlements and obligations so that employers and employees are once again free to determine these matters for themselves."

[3] At p. 43.

[4] S.I. 1998 No. 1833.

Regulation 18

12–03   Regulation 18 states:

"Excluded Sectors

18. Regulations 4(1) and (2), 6(1), (2) and (7), 7(1), and (6), 8, 10(1), 11(1)
   and (2), 12(1), 13 and 16 do not apply—

   (a) to the following sectors of activity-

      (i) air, rail, road, sea, inland waterway, and lake transport;
      (ii) sea fishing;
      (iii) other work at sea; or

   (b) to the activities of doctors in training; or
   (c) where the characteristics peculiar to certain specific services such as
      the armed forces or the police, or to certain specific activities in the
      civil protection services inevitably conflict with the provisions of
      these Regulations."

Article 1(3) of the Directive

12–04   Article 1(3) of the Directive, which Regulation 18 implements, states:

"3. This Directive shall apply to all sectors of activity, both public and private,
within the meaning of Article 2 of Directive 89/391/EEC, without prejudice to
Article 17 of this Directive [Derogations], *with the exception of air, rail, road,
sea, inland waterway and lake transport, sea fishing, other work at sea and the
activities of doctors in training* (our emphasis)."

It can be seen that Regulation 18 reflects Article 1(3) of the Directive, almost
verbatim and, it would seem, excludes workers from the entirety of the Regulations if
they are carrying out certain activities or are employed in certain economic sectors.
The only exception from the otherwise wholesale exclusion of the Regulations in the
contexts mentioned are the provisions of the Regulations which relate specifically to
young workers.[5]
Total employment, including self-employment, in the E.U. in the sectors and
activities excluded from the Directive was about 5.6 million in 1996, according to one
source.[6] That is about 4 per cent of total employment in the E.U.

The excluded sectors of transport activity

12–05   Those working in the air, rail, road, sea, inland waterway and lake
transport sectors are excluded from the provisions of the Working Time Regulations
by Regulation 18(a)(1). This is an exhaustive list and, as such, only the sectors of
transport activity specified in it are excluded from the Regulations. Of the reported
total 5.6 million workers excluded from the Regulations, 3.5 million are in the road

---

[5] The provisions of the Regulation which relate specifically to young workers and whose application is not
  excluded by Regulation 18 are:
  ● health assessments for night workers: Regulation 7(2)
  ● daily rest: Regulation 10(2)
  ● weekly rest: Regulation 11(3)
  ● rest breaks: Regulation 12(4).
[6] Employment in Europe 1996 as cited in the House of Commons Select Committee on European
  Legislation Fourth Report 1997.

transport industry. Notably this is the only industry where there is other relevant Community legislation on working time.[7]

It is not clear whether the exclusion provided by Regulation 18(a)(1) is intended to apply to all workers employed in the transport sectors specified or only mobile workers in those sectors. For example, are office workers or other non-mobile workers who work for a rail transport provider at a railway station excluded? Are workers employed in the movement of goods or people between two of the excluded forms of transport excluded? Arguably such workers are employed in the transport sector but the answer to these, and other such similar questions, will ultimately be for employment tribunals and the courts to determine. The ultimate arbiter of the question will, of course, be the ECJ.[8] Although the position is, at present, uncertain some assistance can perhaps be gleaned from Government and European Commission views on the issue.

In an answer to a written question from a Member of the European Parliament on the extent of the transport exclusion, given on behalf of the European Commission on March 29, 1996, Padraig Flynn, the former European Employment and Social Affairs Commissioner said:

"This exception makes no distinction between "mobile" and "non-mobile" staff [in the transport sector]"[9]

12–06 The former Conservative Government of the United Kingdom agreed with Mr Flynn and took the view that workers employed in any transport business (within the excluded categories), even if not mobile, are excluded from the Directive and accordingly the Regulations. The former Government's Consultation Document[10] stated:

"... any employee whose work has a clear enough connection with a sector excluded from the Directive's coverage (*e.g.* retail staff who work in an airport) ... should also be outside the scope of implementing legislation."

This perhaps takes the exclusion too far. Why should, for example, a worker employed by a retailer to work at their branch in a railway station be excluded from the Regulations when a colleague working at a branch in a city centre would not be? There is no logical reason for such a distinction. Retailers are not transport providers and it is submitted that the mere location of work in a railway station or airport, for example, is not sufficient for the Regulation 18(a) exclusion to apply. The worker must be employed by an organisation in one of the excluded transport sectors.

In the context of its proposals to extend the Working Time Directive to cover the presently excluded sectors and activities,[11] the European Commission expressed the view that:

---

[7] Regulation 3820/85 sets limits on daily driving periods and provides for breaks and rest periods but is beyond the scope of this book.

[8] In *Bowden v. Tuffnells Parcels Express Ltd* (6.4.2000 EAT 622/99) the EAT has referred, to the ECJ, the question of whether or not all workers employed in the road transport sector of activity are necessarily excluded from the application of the Regulation If they are not, the EAT asks what test should be applied to determine which of those workers are excluded from the application of the Regulation and which are not.

[9] [1996] O.J. C173/65.

[10] At para. 3.3. on p. 12.

[11] Commission "White Paper on Sectors and Activities Excluded from the Working Time Directive" (COM (97) 334).

"The way in which the exclusions are drafted has been interpreted as implying that all workers in the transport ... sectors are excluded from the scope of the Directive, even those who perform sedentary tasks. The Commission considers that this should be *clarified* (our emphasis) as there is no objective reason why 'non-mobile' employees should be treated differently in comparison to employees carrying out similar tasks in other industries. The test should relate to the nature of the activity, not the definition of the 'sector' in which the employee works."

12–07 Here the Commission does not say that the excluded sectors, as drafted, are *correctly* interpreted as implying that all workers in the transport sectors are excluded from the scope of the Directive. The Commission merely says that the excluded sectors *have been* interpreted as such and that this needs clarifying. In any event even if the Commission had expressed a view as to the correct interpretation, that would not be binding on a court or tribunal or, indeed, on the European Court of Justice. It might, however, have some persuasive impact. European Court case law could clarify the extent of the exclusions as presently drafted, just as additional legislation would.

The Economic and Social Committee, an E.U. advisory body which provides opinions on proposed legislation,[12] stated:

"The ESC agrees with the Commission when it states openly that a large number of workers particularly those in the road, rail, inland waterway, sea and air-transport sectors, were excluded for no objective reason in 1993 and should be covered ... These workers are engaged in occupations which can be equated with work in other industries currently covered...."

This opinion assumes that the Commission considers that all workers in the excluded sectors (both mobile and non-mobile) are excluded from the application of the Directive.

The present Government's view may be different. The Labour Government's Consultation Paper[13] stated:

"a. Only certain specified transport sectors of activity are excluded ... The movement of goods or people between any of [them] (as might occur, for example, in docks and harbours) ... is not explicitly covered by [the] exclusions.
b. The terms of the exclusions carry no implication that the mere location of work activity in, for example, a transport facility (such as a port, railway station, airport, road transport terminal or the like) is sufficient to make workers carrying it out subject to exclusion."

That seems a sensible approach to the exclusion.

12–08 The Department of Trade and Industry has, of course, produced non-statutory guidance on the Working Time Regulations. The original guidance[14] which has since been revised followed the same line as the Labour Government's Consultation Paper and stated[15]:

"Excluded sectors

---

[12] In its opinion, CES 460/98, on the Commission's White Paper mentioned above in note 11.
[13] At para. 42 on p. 16.
[14] URN 98/894.
[15] At para. 1.2.3.

The Regulations . . . do not apply to workers who are employed in the following sectors:

- Air transport;
- Rail transport;
- Road transport;
- Sea transport;
- Inland waterway and lake transport."

The exclusions relate specifically to the sectors specified. Employers will need to consider whether particular workers fall within a sector or not. The location of the work, for example in a port, railway station, or airport, will not necessarily mean that those doing it are excluded. Furthermore, neither will workers involved in the movement of goods or people to or from a mode of transport (for example, in docks or loading/unloading onto/from road vehicles) necessarily be excluded. Where workers are directly involved in the operation of the sector, such as baggage handlers and signal and maintenance staff, they are more likely to be excluded from the Regulations, but where they are not (e.g. construction workers at an airport) the exclusion is not likely to apply.

There are sound reasons for maintaining that some "own account" transport operations (for example, a retail chain operating a fleet of vehicles to deliver goods to its own stores) are excluded from the Regulations on the basis that they fall within the road transport sector. Such operations will often be almost identical to those undertaken by businesses operating for hire, which are clearly excluded.

The European Commission has announced its intention to bring forward proposals to extend rights to provide rest and limit working hours for workers in these sectors.

12–09 The revised DTI guidance which was published on March 31, 2000 adopts a similar view of the transport exclusion. Section 1 of the guidance states:

The Regulations . . . do not apply to workers who are employed in the following sectors regardless of what job they do:

- Air transport;
- Rail transport;
- Road transport;
- Sea transport;
- Inland Waterway and lake transport.

12–10 To be considered to be in a transport sector, an employer must be directly involved in the business of transport. For example, if you work in a road haulage, delivery or distribution firm, you are in the road transport sector and the Regulations will not apply to you, even if you are not a driver. Similarly, if you work for a railway operator, you are in the rail sector and excluded. However, if you work for a retailer in a station or sell petrol at a garage the Regulations will apply to you.

Also, you may work in a transport operation for an employer, not wholly in a transport sector. If this is part of an identifiable transport function ("own account" transport services), such as a transport division of a retail chain that delivers goods to its stores, then it is part of the transport sector."

12–11 In *Bowden v. Tuffnells Parcels Express Limited* (see below), Ms Bowden, and two other appellants are all employed by Tuffnells Parcels Express Limited. Tuffnells Parcels Express Limited is a parcel delivery service with depots in various parts of the United Kingdom delivering goods by road. All three appellants work at one of the company's depots in offices above the loading bays from which the company's delivery vans operate. The van drivers are not allowed into the offices and the appellants do not have any contact with the vans. Indeed, they cannot contractually be required to work with any transport. None of the appellant employees have a contractual entitlement to paid holidays. All three complained to an employment tribunal that their employer had failed to pay them in respect of the period of annual leave to which they were entitled under Regulation 13 of the Working Time Regulations. The employment tribunal dismissed the workers' complaints. It decided that they were denied the right to paid annual leave by operation of Regulation 18(a)(i) of the Regulations. The tribunal also relied, at least in part, on the DTI guidance to the Regulations referred to above.

The EAT thought that Regulation 18(a)(i) of the Regulations was a curious exception, because Regulation 13 confers rights on workers and so it might have been expected that any exceptions to the application of those rights would refer to classes of workers rather than sectors of activity. The EAT said that, "if one has to translate the exception of 'sectors of activity' to fit the generality from which the exception is to be made, then one has to read the exception as if referring to workers in the described 'sectors of activity'."

The EAT was unable to detect anything in the Regulations or the Directive to limit the reference to the road transport sector of activity so as to mean anything less than the whole undivided sector of activity of that description. The EAT found that the blunt language of Article 1(3) of the Directive does not admit of broad or narrow construction but simply of construction, and no warrant appears for sub-dividing by reference to activities within a given sector. The EAT therefore found no error of law in the tribunal's conclusion, but it did not feel able to approve the tribunal's reasoning.

The EAT did not think it proper to consider the DTI guidance which itself correctly states that it "should not be regarded as a complete or authoritative statement of the law".

12–12   The EAT did not feel it could resolve the issues before it with complete confidence without guidance from the European Court of Justice. Accordingly, the EAT stayed the Appeal pending the ruling of the ECJ on four questions. The questions that the EAT has referred to the ECJ are as follows:—

1. Given that the informed view of responsible bodies is needed if a legislative provision is to achieve a certain effect is likely to be consistent only with a view that the provision before amendment does not have that effect, and given also the previously expressed views of the Economic and Social Committee, the European Parliament, the Commission and the Council's common position paper on the subject of the exceptions to Article 1(3) of the Directive suggesting that, as yet, there is an exception from the benefits of the Directive of all who work in the road transport sector of activity but that such an exception has been and is entirely unjustified, how far, if at all, are we enabled to infer from such non-legislative materials either: (a) that, as yet, the proper construction of the wording of Article 1(3) is one which excludes all such persons; or (b) that such a reading would not represent a just and purposive construction of the Article?

2. Whatever the conclusion is to question 1, if, in the course of our task of interpreting our national laws in the light of the wording and purpose of the Directive, we encounter what we take to be a broad purpose ("Every worker in the European Community shall have a right ... to annual paid leave ...")

but also, given no less prominence in the very same provision, a wording ("...shall apply to all sectors of activity...with the exception of...road... transport...") which appears to be significantly destructive of that broad purpose, at all events on the facts before us, are we entitled (and, if so, by reference to what principles) to apply our national laws to the facts of the particular case before us so as to give effect to that broad purpose notwithstanding the clarity of the wording appearing to exclude that purpose on such facts?

3. To raise similar issues in a less abstract way, are all workers employed in the road transport sector of activity referred to in Article 1(3) necessarily excluded from the scope of the Directive?

4. If all such workers are not necessarily excluded, what test should the national court apply in order to determine which workers employed in the road transport sector of activity are excluded by Article 1(3) and which are not?

12–13 It may be some time before the ECJ gives its decision. In the meantime, whilst the above discussion demonstrates that contradictory views exist, a strong argument can be made that all workers in the specified transport sectors are presently excluded and not only mobile workers in those sectors. The basis for this argument is that the Directive at present makes a distinction between excluded sectors and excluded "activities"; the transport exclusions refer to sectors of activity not to the workers (which it does in the context of the junior hospital doctor exclusion). However at the risk of over-emphasising this, the extent of the transport exclusion will ultimately be for the courts, employment tribunals and European Court to determine. The case presently pending before the ECJ on the extent of the road transport exclusion is eagerly awaited. In the meantime the very cautious might take the view that non-mobile workers employed by employers in the excluded transport sectors are not excluded from the Regulations and all should take the view that those who work for employers outside of the excluded transport sectors, even if their place of work is at a transport facility such as an airport, are not excluded from the Regulations.

The other excluded sectors of activity

12–14 Those working in sea fishing and those engaged in "other work at sea" are also excluded from the provisions of the Working Time Regulations, by Regulation 18(a). The term, "other work at sea," according to the first version of the non-statutory Government guidance, essentially means offshore work in the oil and gas industry. However, the revised guidance is more expansive regarding what is meant by the phrase "other work at sea". The current guidance says that the phrase "applies to offshore work rather than work in the oil industry generally". It goes on to say, "If you work partly onshore but mostly offshore the Regulations will not apply to you". According to one source, in 1993, in the E.U. Member States there were about 270,000 sea-going fishermen and a small number of land-based workers engaged in the sea fishing sector. The best estimate of numbers employed in "other work at sea" is about 45,000, well over half of whom are based in the United Kingdom working on offshore operations.

The discussion above, about the extent of the exclusions in respect of the specified transport sectors, applies equally to the sea-fishing exclusion. As such it remains, to some extent, unclear whether land-based workers in the sea-fishing sector are excluded from the Regulations. In the case of "other work at sea" the reference is implicitly to activities at sea, so the problem of defining the extent of the exclusion is less likely to arise except in the case of those who work partly onshore and partly at sea.

Junior hospital doctors

12–15 Regulation 18(b) excludes the activities of doctors in training from the application of the Regulations. It is well-known that it was the former Conservative Government who pushed for this exclusion from the Directive. There are, reportedly, approximately 270,000 junior hospital doctors in the E.U. Around half of these are in Germany where legislation on working time already existed prior to the Working Time Directive. The first version of the Government's non-statutory guidance stated[16] that:

> "The Regulations ... do not apply to the activities of doctors in training—in effect covering the NHS training grades: pre-registration house officer, house officer, senior house officer, registrar, senior registrar and specialist registrar."

However, the revised guidance appears to be silent on the issue of who is a junior hospital doctor, although that is perhaps not problematic; one would assume that the distinction between a doctor in training and a fully registered and qualified medical practitioner can fairly easily be drawn. Because the reference in the Regulations is to the activities of doctors in training as opposed to an entire sector it is less likely that there will be problems in defining the scope of the exclusion.

The police, armed forces and civil protection services

12–16 Article 1(3) of the Working Time Directive refers to Framework Directive 89/391/EEC on measures to encourage improvements in the safety and health of workers. This reference means that "certain specific activities such as the armed forces or the police, or ... certain specific activities in the civil protection services" may lawfully be excluded from the application of the Working Time Regulations but only to the extent that "the characteristics" of those activities "inevitably conflict" with the requirements of the Framework Directive. Accordingly, Regulation 18(c) in true "copy-out drafting" style excludes from Regulation, under the Working Time Regulations, those working in "certain specific service activities such as the armed forces or the police" or "certain specific activities in the civil protection services" but only to the extent that such work inevitably conflicts with the provisions of the Working Time Regulations.

The example given in the former Conservative Government's Consultation Document[17] of such activities was "[the] armed forces fighting a campaign". The Labour Government's Consultation Paper,[18] perhaps less than helpfully, stated:

> "The extent to which those in the armed forces, police or other civil protection services are excluded from entitlements and limits provided for in the Regulations

[16] At para. 1.2.3.
[17] At para. 3.1 on p. 11.
[18] At para. 42 on p. 16.

will be the same as under the Framework Directive on Health and Safety at Work."

The first version of the DTI guidance on the Regulations, perhaps also less than helpfully, stated that:

"The Regulations ... do not apply to activities of specific services, such as the police or the armed forces, or specific activities of the civil protection services, where particular characteristics of the service or the activities inevitably conflict with provisions of the Regulations. It will be for such services to identify the activities which conflict with the Regulations".

12–17 Somewhat confusingly, civil protection services are defined in Regulation 2(1) of the Working Time Regulations as including "the police, fire brigades and ambulance services, the security and intelligence services, customs and immigration officers, the prison service, the coastguard, and lifeboat crew and other voluntary rescue services". As such, when Regulation 18(c) is properly construed, the police are potentially excluded from the application of the Regulations twice!

That minor point of confusion aside, the exclusion provided for in Regulation 18(c) only applies if there is an inevitable conflict between the provisions of the Regulations and the operational demands of the services or certain of their activities.

Regulations 38 and 41 of the Working Time Regulations 1998 make further provision for members of the armed forces and the police service, respectively.

Proposals for reform

12–18 The European Commission's original proposal for a Directive on working time covered all economic sectors and activities. The Council of Ministers, however, decided to exclude certain sectors and activities from the scope of the Directive. The Sixteenth recital to the Directive sets out the rationale for this approach, thus:

"... given the specific nature of the work concerned, it may be necessary to adopt *separate measures* (our emphasis) with regard to the organisation of working time in certain sectors or activities which are excluded from the scope of this Directive."

Since the exclusion of the specified transport sectors from the Working Time Directive by the Council of Ministers in 1993 the European Commission has been pressing for progress on discussions on the Regulation of working time between the Social Partners in the presently excluded sectors. This is consistent with the undertaking given by the Commission to the European Parliament in negotiations during the Directive's second reading that it would take initiatives in respect of the sectors and activities excluded from the Directive.

Beginning in June 1995, former European Commissioners Flynn and Kinnock encouraged the Social Partners in the excluded sectors to come forward with agreed proposals on how best the principles of the Working Time Directive could be applied in their respective sectors. The Commission stimulated the debate in July 1997 when it published its White Paper with the stated aim of finding the best ways of ensuring the protection of health and safety, with regard to working time, of workers excluded from the Working Time Directive.[19]

---

[19] COM (97) 334.

12–19 In April 1998 the Commission opened the second formal phase of consultations on the content of future legislation to extend the principles of the Working Time Directive by adopting and sending to the Social Partners a consultative document which confirmed the Commission's view that legislation is required to ensure the protection of transport sector workers' health and safety. The Social Partners were given a deadline of September 30, 1998 to reach an agreement on the possible content of such legislation.

By the end of September 1998 the Social Partners in the railway and maritime sectors had signed agreements on working time which were swiftly converted into proposals to the Council of Ministers for E.U. legislation. However, the Social Partners in the road transport sector failed to reach an agreement by the September 1998 deadline.

The Commission's response was set out in a press statement on September 30, 1998, which stated that the Commission would "rapidly prepare" proposals for legislation covering working time in all sectors excluded from the Working Time Directive based on the strategy identified in the White Paper which had initiated the negotiations between the Social Partners.

12–20 On November 18, 1998 the Commission published its detailed proposals to extend working time protections to those not presently covered by the Working Time Directive.[20]

In summary, the Commission's proposals were:

- Amendment of the Working Time Directive to cover all non-mobile workers in the transport sectors, doctors in training and offshore workers;

- Amendment of the Working Time Directive to cover all mobile railway workers, with appropriate derogations to take account of the operational and safety requirements of the industry;

- Amendment of the Working Time Directive to give mobile workers in road, air and inland waterway transport and sea fishing:

    guaranteed adequate rest periods,
    a limit on the maximum number of hours worked each year,
    basic provisions on night workers,
    four weeks' paid annual leave;

- A new directive for mobile workers in road transport, covering all categories of haulage including self-employed drivers and dealing with the definition of working time, breaks, rest periods and night work limits; and

- A new directive on specific measures for maritime transport.

12–21 On May 25, 1999 the E.U. Social Affairs Council reached a unanimous political agreement[21] on the Commission's proposal for a Directive concerning the extension of the provisions of the Working Time Directive to all non-mobile workers in the currently excluded sectors and, in due course, trainee doctors. The agreement envisaged that mobile workers in the currently excluded sectors will be protected by a mixture of the existing Working Time Directive as amended and/or by sector specific legislation. Political agreement was also reached by the Council on two proposed Directives relating to seafarers: one to apply to E.U. registered ships, the other to

---

[20] COM (98) 662 final, November 18, 1998.
[21] Labour and Social Affairs council press release Nr. 5439/99 (Presse 164). 25.05.99.

non-E.U. registered ships using Community ports. The road transport sector was not covered by the agreement.

The Directive implementing the maritime sector Social Partner agreement concerning E.U. registered ships was adopted on June 21, 1999[22] and the Directive on the organisation of working time for seafarers on board ships using Community ports was adopted on December 13, 1999.[23]

The first of these Directives embodies the agreement under what was the Social Protocol[24] between the relevant Social Partners in the maritime sector. The Directive reflects the provisions of International Labour Organisation Convention No. 180 on seafarers' hours of work. It applies to E.U. registered ships and provides, amongst other things, for maximum working time of 14 hours in any 24-hour period and 72 hours in any seven-day period. The Directive must be implemented by Member States by June 30, 2002.

12–22 The second Directive applies similar requirements to non-E.U. registered ships using Community ports and must also be implemented by Member States before June 30, 2002.

On April 3, 2000 the Council and the European Parliament agreed a revised text of the Commission's proposal of November 18, 1998 to extend the Working Time Directive to cover the currently excluded sectors and activities[25] other than seafarers onboard seagoing ships.[26]

The revised text provides for a four-year implementation period for the application of the 48-hour working week to doctors in training. Once implemented the full application of the 48-hour working week will take place gradually over a five year transition period. During the first three years of the transition period, average weekly working hours must not exceed 58 and during the subsequent two years must not exceed 56.

12–23 In exceptional circumstances, Member States may apply to the commission for an extension of up to another two years and subsequently for a further extension of one year. During any extension period average weekly working time should not exceed 52 hours.

The Commission's proposal for a specific Directive on the organisation of working time for mobile road transport workers and self-employed drivers has failed to make any progress in the Council for some time.

2. EXCEPTIONS TO THE APPLICATION OF CERTAIN REGULATIONS

12–24 Apart from those workers who are presently excluded from the protections and limits set by the Regulations because of the wholesale exclusion of the sector or activity in which they work, others are excepted from the application of certain of the Regulations because an exception applies to them.

---

[22] Council Directive 99/63/E.C. of June 21, 1999 concerning the Agreement on the organisation of working time of seafarers concluded by the European Community Shipowners' Association (ECSA) and the Federation of Transport Workers' Unions in the European Union (FST).

[23] Directive 99/95/E.C. of the European Parliament and the Council of December 13, 1999 concerning the enforcement of provisions in respect of seafarers' hours of work on board ships calling at Community ports.

[24] New Articles 136 to 139 of the Treaty of Rome.

[25] The currently excluded sectors are "air, rail, road, sea, inland waterways and lake transport, sea fishing, other work at sea and the activities of doctors in training" (see Art. 17 Directive 93/104 and Regulation 18(a) and (b) Working Time Regulations).

[26] Two separate Directives relating to seafarers have been adopted see above and notes 24 and 25.

Regulation 19

12–25   Regulation 19 states:

"Domestic service

> 19. Regulations 4(1) and (2), 6(1), (2) and (7), 7(1), (2) and (6) and 8 do not apply in relation to a worker employed as a domestic servant in a private household."

Accordingly, the following parts of the Regulations do not apply to workers employed as domestic servants in private households:

- The limit of 48 hours on the average working week;

- Length of night work;

- Health assessments and transfer to day work; and

- Monotonous work.

Domestic servants are covered, however, by the provisions of the Regulations on daily and weekly rest, rest breaks and annual leave.

12–26   Generally, British health and safety legislation does not apply to domestic service in a private household. However, there is no specific domestic service exception to be found in the Working Time Directive which is, in fact, expressed to apply to all sectors of activity both public and private, within the meaning of Article 2 of the Framework Health and Safety Directive.[27] Article 2 of the Framework Directive states "This Directive shall apply to all sectors of activity, both public and private (industrial, agricultural, commercial, administrative, service, educational, cultural, leisure, etc) ...". However, the object of the Framework Directive is to introduce measures to encourage improvements in the safety and health of workers and domestic servants in private households are expressly excluded from the definition of worker in the Framework Health and Safety Directive by Article 3 of that Directive.

The Labour Government's Consultation Document simply explained this exception as being based on the fact that ordinary domestic health and safety law does not apply to domestic service.[28]

Regulation 20

12–27   Regulation 20 states:

> 20. "Unmeasured working time
>
> > (1) Regulations 4(1) and (2), 6(1), (2) and (7), 10(1), 11(1) and (2) and 12(1) do not apply in relation to a worker where, on account of the specific characteristics of the activity in which he is engaged, the duration of his working time is not measured or predetermined or can be determined by the worker himself, as may be the case for—
> >
> > > (a) managing executives or other persons with autonomous decision-taking powers;
> > > (b) family workers; or

---

[27] 89/391/EEC.
[28] See HSWA 1974, s.51.

(c) workers officiating at religious ceremonies in churches and religious communities.

(2) Where part of the working time of a worker is measured or predetermined or cannot be determined by the worker himself but the specific characteristics of the activity are such that, without being required to do so by the employer, the worker may also do work the duration of which is not measured or predetermined or can be determined by the worker himself, Regulations 4(1) and (2) and 6(1), (2) and (7) shall apply only to so much of his work as is measured or predetermined or cannot be determined by the worker himself."

Article 17(1) of the Directive

12–28 Article 17(1) of the Directive states:

"1. With due regard for the general principles of the protection of the safety and health of workers, Member States may derogate from Article 3, 4, 5, 6, 8 or 16 when, on account of the specific characteristics of the activity concerned, the duration of the working time is not measured and/or predetermined or can be determined by the workers themselves, and particularly in the case of:

(a) managing executives or other persons with autonomous decision-taking powers;
(b) family workers; or
(c) workers officiating at religious ceremonies in churches and religious communities."

Regulation 20 implements Article 17(1) of the Directive. The exception in Regulation 20(1) is from the provisions of the Regulations on rest breaks, daily and weekly rest periods, length of night work and maximum weekly working time but *not* annual leave or pattern of work. The exception provided for in Regulation 20(2) was added in late 1999.[29] It should be noted that the provisions of Regulations 10 (daily rest), 11 (weekly rests) and 12 (rest breaks) which are disapplied by Regulation 20(1) remain in force in the case of a worker only coming within Regulation 20(2).

12–29 The first limb of Regulation 20 provides that certain limits and entitlements contained in the Regulations do not apply to a worker where:

"On account of the specific characteristics of the activity in which he is engaged, the duration of his working time is not measured or predetermined or can be determined by the worker himself."

Regulation 20 then goes on to cite examples of workers who *may* (or may not) fall within this category, including "managing executives" and "other persons with autonomous decision-taking powers", "family workers" and "workers officiating at religious ceremonies in churches and religious communities".

In determining whether the exception provided for in Regulation 20(1) applies the key question is, of course, whether because of the specific characteristics of the activity

---

[29] By the Working Time Regulations 1999 S.I. 1999 No. 3372 Regulation 4.

concerned, the duration of the working time is not measured and/or predetermined or can be determined by the worker him or herself. As with much of the Working Time Regulations, the wording of Regulation 20 is taken almost word for word from Article 17(1) of the Working Time Directive.

There is no guidance in the Directive itself or indeed in the preparatory documents issued prior to its adoption as to who Article 17(1) is intended to cover. Proposals for the European level Regulation of working time had been in existence for some time prior to the adoption of the Working Time Directive in November 1993. However, Article 17 was not included in the original proposals but was introduced at a relatively late stage in June 1993 by way of a Council common position. The preparatory documents which preceded the adoption of the Directive do not give any explanation or discussion of the Article.

12–30   One view is that the phrase was introduced into the Working Time Directive as a means of allowing for a "common sense" derogation from the provisions of the Directive for individuals who are responsible for determining their own working time. However, in the absence of any detailed preparatory documents dealing with the issue it has been suggested as likely that the phrase was introduced without any detailed consideration as to precisely which workers it would ultimately cover. The question is in the end one for the United Kingdom courts and tribunals to determine on a case by case basis, subject to any rulings on the issue by the ECJ. Article 17 of the Directive does however provide that the derogation is to apply subject to the obligation to have "due regard to the general principles of the protection of the safety and health of workers". Adopting a purposive interpretation of Article 17(1) a court or tribunal may seek to take as restrictive an approach as possible to the question of who falls within the exception so as to maximise the coverage of the Directive. However the present Government's position on that phrase (expressed in its Consultation Document) was that it was satisfied by existing laws relating to health and safety and the common law duty of care owed by an employer.

In the Consultation Paper on implementation of the Working Time Directive, issued by the then Conservative Government in March 1997, the previous Government indicated that it wished the concept of a "managing executive" to be interpreted as widely as possible. This approach does not appear however to have been taken up by the present Labour Government, whose Consultation Document was silent on the issue of who the exception might apply to. Moreover, the issue does not appear to have been discussed in Parliament at the time the Regulations were introduced.

12–31   The original DTI guidance took a very restrictive approach to the question of who falls within the unmeasured working time exemption contained in what is now Regulation 20(1). The guidance suggested[30] that Regulation 20(1) covers:

> "workers who have complete control over the hours they work and whose time is not monitored or determined by their employer."

The original guidance went on to say that this may cover workers who can decide when they are to carry out their work, or who can adjust the time that they work as they see fit. Moreover it suggested that an indicator may be:

> "if the worker has discretion over whether to work or not on a given day without needing to consult their employer."

This interpretation is extremely restrictive and appears to run contrary to the very

---

[30] At para. 2.2.2.

principles of the employment relationship. It is difficult to envisage any employee (other than perhaps the owner of an owner-run business) who can decide whether to work on a given day without consulting their employer.

12–32 If employers adopt the approach taken in the original regulatory guidance, then even senior management workers are unlikely to fall within the unmeasured working time exception. However it is suggested that a worker may fall within this exception, notwithstanding the fact that he or she cannot decide whether to turn up for work or not on a particular day, provided that the worker has control over the additional hours that he or she works over and above their normal contracted hours. Senior managers will usually have some control over the number and timing of the additional hours that they work, although it is in our view unlikely that this alone would be sufficient to bring them within Regulation 20(1) as they would still be obliged to be at work during their normal contracted hours. It is possible however that some of the additional hours worked by senior managers, especially those undertaken at home, may not fall within the definition of "working time" contained in Regulation 2 of the Working Time Regulations.

It should be remembered that the Government's guidance does not have force of law and that it is only intended to give general guidance. However the re-issued guidance takes a less restrictive approach to the question of who falls within the unmeasured working time exception in Regulation 20(1). It states[31]:

> "The Regulations, apart from the entitlement to paid annual leave, do not apply if a worker can decide how long he or she works.
>
> A test, set out in the Regulations, states that a worker falls into this category if 'the duration of his working time is not measured or predetermined, or can be determined by the worker himself'.
>
> An employer needs to consider whether a worker passes this test. Workers such as senior managers, who can decide when to do their work, and how long they work, are likely to pass the test. Those without this freedom to choose are not."

12–33 A literal interpretation of the Regulations could lead one to the conclusion that anyone who is expected to work an unquantified number of additional hours as are necessary to fulfil the requirements of the job would fall within the exemption because their working hours cannot be measured. However, Article 17 itself provides that the exemption must be applied bearing in mind the general need to have regard to the health and safety of workers. It may therefore be that in interpreting the Regulations purposefully in line with the Directive, a Court or tribunal would seek to include as many workers as possible within the protection granted by the Regulations.

In late 1999 the Government reviewed the unmeasured working time exception and added Regulation 20(2) with effect from December 17, 1999. The effect of Regulation 20(2) is to modify the affect of the Regulations on certain workers who have control over some of the time that they work so that the 48-hour week and their length of night work provisions to operate only on that part of the work that is measured or predetermined, or that cannot be determined by the worker himself. All other provisions of the Regulations apply without modification to a worker coming within Regulation 20(2) and they will apply in relation to all his working time, not only that which is measured or predetermined or cannot be determined by the worker.

12–34 The application of Regulation 20(2) will depend upon the meaning of the

---

phrase "without being required to do so by the employer". The Government's view on the meaning of this phrase, at the time Regulation 20(2) was introduced, was:

> "The amendments are there for those who put in more hours than their employer requires of them, because they want to, not because they are paid[32] or required to. If a worker is required to work additional hours because of the demands of the job the amendment will not apply ... Simply put, unless the worker has voluntarily decided to put in extra hours the amendment will not apply. Therefore, the amendment will not apply to the teacher who must do marking after school, the cleaner who is required to work longer than usual after a function, the paramedic who is tending the injured after the end of a shift or the shop worker who is stocktaking after work."[33]

Even if one applies Regulation 20(2) in the light of the Government's view problems remain. A worker may not be directly required to work long hours in the sense of a direct instruction being given to him. But he may feel under pressure to do so to obtain promotion or because of a long hours culture. If that kind of pressure is construed as not being "required" to work long hours then the exception to the application of the 48-hour working week provision will apply and the Regulations would not achieve the changes to the long hours culture in the United Kingdom that many hoped they would.

12–35   The partly unmeasured working time exception is the subject of regulatory guidance. The revised DTI guidance states that the "exception is restricted to those that have the capacity to choose how long they work. The key factor for this exception is worker choice without detriment." The guidance goes on to say that the "exception does not apply to ... any time a worker is implicitly required to work, for example because of the loading or requirements of the job". Again, if this were applied then the exception would not embrace the large numbers of professional workers whose working time is defined, for practical purposes at least, by the task to be performed rather than the time taken to do it.

12–36   The expression "without being required to so by the employer" used in Regulation 20(2) seems very problematic. If the contract of employment states that in addition to 39 hours per week the worker must work "such additional hours as are required by the business" or "such additional hours as are necessary for the proper and efficient performance of your duties under the employment", then Regulation 20(2) is unlikely to apply.

Regulation 20(2) does not directly change the definition of what is "working time".[34] Regulation 20(2) would apply to time which is already classed as working time (*i.e.* time when the worker "is working, at the employer's disposal and carrying out his activities and duties"). The definition is difficult to apply in the case of white-collar workers who are generally required to work "such additional hours as are required from time to time to meet the needs of the business". Whether or not these additional hours count as working time is one of the most difficult questions in applying the working time definition. However, the definition of working time itself seems to require that the time must be worked at the employer's request or

---

[32] Note that Regulation 20(2) itself only refers to being "required" to work. The fact that the worker is paid is not relevant on the face of the Regulation. However if a worker is paid there is a strong chance that the working time is measured and so Regulation 20(2) would not apply.

[33] HC Official Report, First Standing Committee, November 2, 1999, cols 4, 5.

[34] See paras 3–18 *et seq.*

requirement, *i.e.*, it has to be time when the worker is at the employer's disposal. Regulation 20(2) seeks to exempt from the weekly working time limit unmeasured "working time" which the worker works "without being required to do so by the employer". But if the time worked is working time in the first place, that suggests that the employer has required the worker to carry it out. It is difficult to see what Regulation 20(2) achieves.

In any event, employers will still have the duty under Regulation 9 to keep records, which are adequate to show that the working time limit is complied with. It seems to us that even under Regulation 20(2) the employer still has to keep records of additional hours worked by white-collar staff over and above their contractual hours. As ever, each slice of working time worked outside contractual hours would have to be examined in isolation to determine whether or not it was classed as working time. It is arguably even more important as a result of Regulation 20(2) for an employer to keep records which show whether or not any additional hours were expressly or implicitly required by the employer. Employers who seek to interpret the revised Regulations as allowing them to dispense with record keeping (relying simply on the contract of employment) may still face prosecution and may also find themselves in difficulties if the worker alleges that the working time limit has been breached and the employer has no records to rebut this allegation.

Further, it is not clear whether Article 18 of the Directive permits Member States to derogate from the weekly working time limit in respect of part of a worker's working time rather than all of it.

Finally, it is difficult to see why Regulation 20(2) refers to Regulation 6(1) and 6(2). This night-work limit applies only to "normal hours of work" and not to working time at all. Normal hours of work cannot be anything other than hours which are "measured or predetermined or cannot be determined by the worker himself". Regulation 20(2) seems to be a fertile area for litigation.

Regulation 21

12–37 Regulation 21 states:

"Other special cases

21. Subject to Regulation 24, Regulations 6(1), (2) and 7, 10(1), 11(1) and (2), and 12(1) do not apply in relation to a worker:

(a) where the worker's activities are such that his place of work and place of residence are distant from one another or his different places of work are distant from one another;

(b) where the worker is engaged in security and surveillance activities requiring a permanent presence in order to protect property and persons, as may be the case for security guards and caretakers or security firms;

(c) where the worker's activities involve the need for continuity of service or production, as may be the case in relation to—

(i) services relating to the reception, treatment or care provided by hospitals or similar establishments, residential institutions and prisons;

(ii) work at docks or airports;

(iii) press, radio, television, cinematographic production, postal and telecommunications services, and civil protection services;

   (iv) gas, water and electricity production, transmission and distribution, household refuse collection and incineration;

   (v) industries in which work cannot be interrupted on technical grounds;

   (vi) research and development activities;

   (vii) agriculture;

(d) where there is a foreseeable surge of activity, as may be the case in relation to:

   (i) agriculture;

   (ii) tourism;

   (iii) postal services;

(e) where the workers' activities are affected by—

   (i) an occurrence due to unusual and unforeseeable circumstances, beyond the control of the worker's employer;

   (ii) exceptional events, the consequences of which could not have been avoided despite the exercise of all due care by the employer; or

   (iii) an accident or the imminent risk of an accident."

Article 17(2) of the Directive

12–38   Article 17(2) of the Directive states, almost word for word with Regulation 21:

"2. Derogations may be adopted by means of laws, Regulations or administrative provisions or by means of collective agreements or agreements between the two sides of industry provided that the workers concerned are afforded equivalent periods of compensatory rest or that, in exceptional cases in which it is not possible, for objective reasons, to grant such equivalent periods of compensatory rest, the workers concerned are afforded appropriate protection:

2.1 from Articles 3, 4, 5, 8 and 16:

(a) in the case of activities where the worker's place of work and his place of residence are distant from one another or where the worker's different places of work are distant from one another;

(b) in the case of security and surveillance activities requiring a permanent presence in order to protect property and persons, particularly security guards and caretakers or security firms;

(c) in the case of activities involving the need for continuity of service or production, particularly:

   (i) services relating to the reception, treatment and/or care provided by hospitals or similar establishments, residential institutions and prisons;

   (ii) dock or airport workers;

   (iii) press, radio, television, cinematographic production, postal and telecommunications services, ambulance, fire and civil protection services;

   (iv) gas, water and electricity production, transmission and distribution, household refuse collection and incineration plants;

    (v) industries in which work cannot be interrupted on technical grounds;

    (vi) research and development activities;

    (vii) agriculture;

  (d) where there is a foreseeable surge of activity, particularly in:

    (i) agriculture;

    (ii) tourism;

    (iii) postal services;

2.2 from Articles 3, 4, 5, 8 and 16:

  (a) in the circumstances described in Article 5(4) of Directive 89/391/EEC;

  (b) in cases of accident or imminent risk of accident;

2.3 from Articles 3 and 5:

  (a) in the case of shift work activities, each time the worker changes shift and cannot take daily and/or weekly rest periods between the end of one shift and the start of the next one;

  (b) in the case of activities involving periods of work split up over the day, particularly those of cleaning staff."

So, again, with some very slight amendments we have "copy-out" drafting. Regulation 21(a) to (d) can conveniently be called the special circumstances exceptions and Regulation 21(e) can be termed the *force majeure* exception.

12–39 The special circumstances exceptions provide an exception to the provisions of the Regulations on length of night work, rest breaks and daily and weekly rest but **not** annual leave or maximum weekly working time. Accordingly these provisions do not apply to the following categories of worker:

- In the case of activities where the worker's place of work and place of residence are distant from one another or where the worker's different places of work are distant from one another;

- In the case of security and surveillance activities requiring a permanent presence in order to protect property and persons, particularly security guards and caretakers or security firms;

- In the case of activities involving the need for continuity of service or production particularly:

  (a) services relating to the reception, treatment and/or care provided by hospitals or similar establishments, residential institutions and prisons;

  (b) dock or airport workers;

  (c) press, radio, television, cinematographic production, postal and communications services, ambulance, fire and civil protection services;

  (d) gas, water and electricity production, transmission and distribution, household refuse collection and incineration plants;

  (e) industries in which work cannot be interrupted on technical grounds;

  (f) research and development activities; and

  (g) agriculture.

- Where there is a foreseeable surge of activity as may be the case in:

    (a) agriculture;

    (b) tourism; and

    (c) postal services.

Distance between home and work

12–40 Regulation 21(a) provides for an exception from the specified Regulations where the worker's activities are such that his or her place of work and place of residence are distant from one another. On this exception, the original DTI guidance,[35] stated:

> "This may apply to workers where because of the distance from home it is desirable for them to work longer hours for a short period to complete the task more quickly or where continual changes in the location of work make it impractical to set a pattern of work."

The revised guidance states that the exception will apply where:

> "A worker works far away from where he or she lives and wants to work longer hours over fewer days to complete a task more quickly, or he or she constantly has to work in different places making it difficult to work to a set pattern."

It has been noted by several commentators that the wording of Regulation 21 suggests that the distance must be due to the "worker's activities" and that this may mean that, for example, a travelling sales representative would be likely to be covered by the exception while a non-mobile worker who simply chose to live some distance from his or her place of work may not be covered by the exception.

Security and surveillance

12–41 Where a worker is engaged in security and surveillance activities requiring a permanent presence in order to protect property and persons that worker is excepted from the specified Regulations. Regulation 22(b) gives examples of where this *may* (or may not) be the case, being security guards, caretakers and security firms. On this special circumstance exception the original DTI guidance,[36] stated: "This *may*[37] apply to security and surveillance work where there is a need for round-the-clock presence to protect property or a person". The revised guidance is more robust, saying that the exception will apply where: "The work involves security or surveillance to protect property or individuals".

Continuity of service or production

12–42 The exception provided for by Regulation 21(c) applies in respect of workers engaged in activities which involve the need for continuity of service as *may* be the case in relation to, amongst other activities, research and development. It should be noted that the wording of Regulation 21 suggests that it is the worker's activities rather than the employer's activities that must involve the need for continuity.

    The exception is not in respect of research and development activities or the other six example activities given in Regulation 21(c) *per se*. The examples are a

---

[35] At para. 2.2.3.
[36] At para. 2.2.3.
[37] Our emphasis.

non-exhaustive list of activities which *may* involve the need for continuity of service or production round the clock. Whether this is the case will depend upon evidence of the need for continuity of service or production rather than the question of whether the worker is engaged on one of the listed activities in Regulation 21(c).

The "copy-out" style of drafting adopted by the Regulations is not particularly helpful to an employer attempting to ascertain whether or not its workers fall within the scope of the "need for continuity of service or production exception". In the end it will be for the courts and employment tribunals to determine whether a particular worker employed in one of the example activities given in Regulation 21(c) is excepted because there is a need for continuity of service or production round the clock. The ultimate arbiter of the extent of the exception will be the ECJ but as yet that court has not had an opportunity to provide any guidance. Furthermore, at present there are no cases pending before the ECJ, from any E.U. Member State on the application of the exception in practice.

12–43 Paragraphs 2.2.2, 3.2.2, 5.2.2 and 6.2.2 of the original DTI guidance dealt with the "need for continuity of service or production exception". The relevant part of paragraph 6.2.2 read:

> "6.2.2 Special circumstances
> The entitlement[s] to a rest break [daily and weekly rest periods and the limits on length of night work do] not apply to workers in a range of circumstances. For these situations, the Regulations list a number of examples. The entitlement does not arise where:
> c. a worker's "activities involve the need for continuity of service or production". This applies where there is a need for round-the-clock activity. The Regulations cite a list of examples, as set out in the Working Time Directive ...
> Again it is important to note that these examples are only illustrations and it is the characteristics of a worker's activity which determine whether the entitlement arises. In seeking to use any of the above flexibilities, it is for the employer to take a view as to whether the conditions are satisfied in each individual worker's situation."

The revised guidance is less detailed, simply saying that the exception will apply where the job "requires round-the-clock staffing such as hospitals, residential institutions, prisons, media production companies, public utilities or industries where work cannot be interrupted".

12–44 In conclusion what is clear is that *merely* being engaged in one of the example activities given in Regulation 21(c) will not bring a worker within the exception. However, if the characteristics of a worker's activity involve the need for continuity of service or production round the clock then there will be a basis on which to rely on the exception. Evidence of the need for continuity of service or production should be kept and maintained in case of challenge before an employment tribunal or investigation by an enforcement authority.

Foreseeable surge of activity

12–45 The fourth special circumstance exception is set out in Regulation 21(d). The exception applies where there is a foreseeable surge of activity, as may be the case in agriculture, tourism and postal services. Again these are examples of sectors where there may be a surge in activity. Other sectors may experience such a surge and if so there will be a basis on which to apply the exception.

Compensatory rest

12–46   The special circumstances exceptions are subject to the condition[38] that:

(i)   The workers concerned are wherever possible allowed equivalent periods of compensatory rest; or

(ii) In exceptional cases in which it is impossible, for objective reasons, to grant such equivalent periods of compensatory rest, the workers concerned are afforded such protection as may be appropriate in order to safeguard the workers' health and safety.

This is discussed in detail in Chapter 11.

The Regulation 21(e) derogation—*force majeure*

12–47   Regulation 21(e) is the so-called *force majeure* exception. As with the special circumstances exceptions the provisions of the Regulations on length of night work, rest breaks and daily and weekly rest but **not** annual leave or maximum weekly working time are excluded from application to certain workers. The workers who fall within the exception are those whose activities are affected by:

• An occurrence due to unusual and unforeseeable circumstances beyond the employer's control or to exceptional events, the consequences of which could not have been avoided despite the exercise of all due care; or

• In cases of accident or imminent risk of accident.

Again the exception is subject to the compensatory rest provisions of Regulation 24 which are discussed in Chapter 11.

---

[38] See Regulation 24.

CHAPTER THIRTEEN

Collective and Workforce Agreements

INTRODUCTION

13–01 Regulation 23 creates a useful exception to the rules on working time, allowing certain parts of the Regulations to be modified—or even completely excluded—by means of agreement between the employer and the workforce. It provides as follows:

"A collective agreement or workforce agreement may—

(a) modify or exclude the application of Regulations 6(1) to 6(3) and (7),[1] 10(1),[2] 11(1) and (2)[3] and 12(1),[4] and
(b) for objective or technical reasons or reasons concerning the organisation of work, modify the application of Regulation 4(3) and (4)[5] by the substitution, for each reference to 17 weeks, of a different period, being a period not exceeding 52 weeks,

in relation to particular workers or groups of workers."

13–02 At first sight this wording appears to offer considerable scope for avoiding the minimum standards set by the Regulations. Employers who can secure the collective agreement of their workers are apparently permitted to contract out of the rules on night work, rest periods and rest breaks and to adjust the reference period for calculating weekly working time to their advantage. However, Regulation 23 has to be read in conjunction with Regulation 24 (discussed in detail in Chapter 11), which deprives the exception of much of its force. Under Regulation 24, if a worker is required, by virtue of arrangements made under Regulation 23, to work during what

---

[1] Regulation 6 regulates the length of night work. Regulation 6(1) limits a night worker's normal hours of work to an average of eight hours in each 24 hours, Regulation 6(3) specifies the reference periods which apply in the case of a night worker and Regulation 6(7) places further restrictions on the working hours of certain night workers (*e.g.* those whose work involves heavy physical strain) by limiting their working hours to no more than eight hours in any 24-hour period. Note that Regulation 6(3) was not included in the draft version of Regulation 23.

[2] Regulation 10(1) governs daily rest and entitles an adult worker to a rest period of no less than 11 consecutive hours in each 24-hour period.

[3] Regulation 11(1) deals with weekly rest periods and gives an adult worker the right to an uninterrupted rest period of no less than 24 hours in each 7-day period. Under Regulation 11(2) the employer can change the entitlement under Regulation 11(1) slightly, so that the worker becomes entitled to two continuous rest periods of at least 24 hours in each 14-day period or one continuous rest period of at least 48 hours in each 14-day period.

[4] Regulation 12(1) entitles an adult worker to a rest break where his daily working time is more than six hours.

[5] These provisions specify the applicable reference periods to be used for calculating whether a worker's weekly working time exceeds the average of 48 hours laid down in Regulation 4(1).

would otherwise be a rest period or a rest break then he must be allowed "wherever possible" to take "an equivalent period of compensatory rest". If—exceptionally— this is not possible, he must be given appropriate protection "in order to safeguard [his] health and safety".

Regulation 24 therefore places a significant limitation on the changes that can be made under Regulation 23. As a result, although Regulation 23 will allow employers a welcome degree of flexibility in arranging working patterns, it is unlikely to undermine to any great extent the principle of a universally accepted floor of rights.

THE NEED FOR A COLLECTIVE OR WORKFORCE AGREEMENT

13–03   Regulation 23 only applies if the employer can reach agreement with his workers by means of either a workforce agreement or a collective agreement. This reflects Article 17(3) of the Working Time Directive which permits "derogations" (*i.e.* exceptions) to be made from certain aspects of the Directive[6] as long as this is done by collective agreement or by an agreement "concluded between the two sides of industry".

The collective agreement is a familiar concept to English law and presents few difficulties in this context. The standard definition, contained in section 178 of the Trade Union and Labour Relations (Consolidation) Act 1992 (TULR(C)A), is adopted by the Regulations. The agreement must therefore be made between one or more trade unions and one or more employers or employers' associations and must relate to at least one of the matters listed in section 178(2) of the TULR(C)A, including the terms and conditions of employment. In addition, any trade union which is a party to such an agreement must be independent within the meaning of section 5 of the TULR(C)A. (A certificate of independence granted by the Certification Officer is conclusive proof of this status.)

"Workforce agreements" on the other hand are a new type of agreement between the employer and the workforce.[7] In essence such agreements are similar to collective agreements except that instead of there being trade union involvement, the employer negotiates directly with the workforce or with specially elected worker representatives. This means that the flexibility permitted by Regulation 23 is not dependent upon a unionised workplace—reflecting the reality that by the mid-1990s less than half of all workplaces recognised a union.

13–04   Detailed rules governing workforce agreements are found in Schedule 1 of the Regulations and are discussed in detail below. However it is important to emphasise at the outset that a workforce agreement cannot be used if any of the terms and conditions of the workers concerned are already covered by a collective agreement. This is clear from Schedule 1 paragraph 2 which defines those workers who can be covered by a workforce agreement to exclude "any worker whose terms and conditions of employment are provided for, wholly or in part, in a collective agreement". This means that no worker can be covered by both a collective agreement and a workforce agreement. (Apparently this prohibition applies even where just one term of the worker's employment is covered by a collective agreement.) On the other hand it will be possible for a collective agreement and a workforce agreement to co-exist in the same workplace. So, for example, if an existing collective agreement only covers part of the workforce it may be possible for the employer to negotiate a

---

[6] Derogations are permitted from Art. 3 (daily rest), 4 (breaks), 5 (weekly rest period), 8 (length of night work) and 16 (reference periods) which correspond to the provisions in Regulation 23.
[7] They have since been used in the Maternity and Parental Leave etc. Regulations S.I. 1999 No. 3312.

workforce agreement with the remainder. Whether worker representatives are as effective at negotiating as their trade union counterparts remains to be seen. Unlike trade union officials, they have no right to time off work for training for their role and without the backing and support of a national union may be less successful in their dealings with employers.[8]

What is Meant by a Workforce Agreement?

13–05 Under Regulation 2(1) a workforce agreement is an agreement between "an employer and workers employed by him or their representatives in respect of which the conditions set out in Schedule 1 ... are satisfied". It is worth noting that under this definition there is no place for industry-wide workforce agreements. Such agreements are only valid if they are made between an individual employer and some or all of the workforce. This contrasts with collective agreements which will be effective under Regulation 23 even if they are made at regional or national level between a number of employers and the relevant unions.

Schedule 1 lays down five conditions which must be satisfied if the workforce agreement is to be valid:

1. The agreement must be in writing. This is not the case with collective agreements which strictly speaking do not need to be in written form, although in practice they almost invariably will be.

2. The agreement must be for a specified period of no more than five years. Again this contrasts with collective agreements where there is no such restriction. Note that although the draft Regulations required the employer to determine the terms during which worker representatives would serve there is no such requirement in the final Regulations. However there seems nothing to prevent the employer setting a term if he so wishes.

3. The workforce agreement must cover all relevant members of the workforce or all relevant members of "a particular group" within the workforce (although as noted above workers who have any terms or conditions governed by a collective agreement will automatically be excluded from the scope of the workforce agreement). "A particular group" is defined to mean workers "who undertake a particular function, work at a particular workplace or belong to a particular department or unit within the employer's business". The Regulations in their draft form did not allow workforce agreements to be made on behalf of a section of the workforce—a limitation that was subject to much criticism and which could have made them unworkable in some organisations. The reference to particular groups of workers in the final Regulations is therefore to be welcomed and means, for example, that a multi-site employer will be able to negotiate separate workforce agreements at each workplace. It will also allow employers to negotiate with workers who belong to a particular department or unit within the business. However care will have to be exercised where staffing at such units is predominantly race or gender imbalanced. Any difference in

---

[8] The lack of a right to paid time off for training is surprising and contrasts with the position of health and safety representatives and employee representatives in the context of consultation on collective redundancies and the transfer of an undertaking.

conditions between the different units might then give rise to a discrimination claim.

4. In general the agreement must be signed by all the duly elected representatives of the workforce (or the representatives of a particular group of workers if the agreement is to be limited to such a group). However a concession is made to small businesses by paragraph 1(d)(ii) of Schedule 1. This provides that if an employer has 20 or fewer workers[9] the agreement may be signed either by the worker representatives or by a *majority of the workers employed by him*. This provision purports to give the small employer the option of negotiating directly with the workforce, so avoiding the need for an election.[10] At the same time any worker who does not wish to sign up to a workforce agreement (for whatever reason) is protected from any resulting victimisation or dismissal by Regulations 31 and 32 (although if a majority of his colleagues sign the agreement it will clearly be binding on him).

    Note that problems will arise where an employer with 20 or fewer workers wants to negotiate directly with a *particular group* within the workforce. Unless that group numbers 11 or more the agreement cannot possibly be signed by "the majority of those employed by him". This would appear to be a drafting oversight and reflects the fact that the draft Regulations did not take groups of workers into account. The result is that in such a case an election will be inevitable.

5. The draft Regulations stipulated that the commencement date in the workforce agreement could not precede the date of signature. This provision is omitted from the Regulations in their final form, although on normal contractual principles a workforce agreement cannot be effective unless and until it is signed by both parties. Until this occurs a worker will be entitled to rely on his normal entitlements under the Regulations and will be protected from any victimisation or dismissal which follows such reliance.[11] It is suggested that this will still be the case even where the workforce agreement purports to be retrospective.

6. Before the agreement is signed a copy of it must be given to all those workers who will be governed by it. In addition "such guidance as those workers might reasonably require in order to understand it fully" must also be provided. This provision appears to require written guidance notes—a meeting to go through the provisions of the agreement would not suffice. Again such a requirement does not apply where a collective agreement is used to take advantage of Regulation 23.

THE ELECTION OF WORKER REPRESENTATIVES

13–06   As noted above, if the employer wants to negotiate a workforce agreement, worker representatives will have to be elected unless the small employer exception, discussed above, applies. The requirements governing such elections are found in

---

[9] Note that workers of associated employers are *not* included in this calculation.

[10] Note that under the draft Regulation every employer had the choice of dealing with his workers directly rather than negotiating with workers' representatives. In restricting this option to small businesses the final Regulation acknowledge the practical difficulties involved in negotiating with large numbers of people.

[11] see Regulation 31 and 32.

Schedule 1 paragraph 3 of the Regulations. Where these requirements are not fulfilled the election, and any subsequent workforce agreement, will be invalid, leaving it open to a worker to refuse to comply with the workforce agreement and to insist on his normal entitlement under the Regulations. In such a case the worker would be protected from unfair dismissal or action short of dismissal for refusing to comply with the workforce agreement (see Regulations 31 and 32).

The election requirements are:

1. The employer must determine the number of representatives to be elected. The original DTI Guidance document suggested that the number be "sufficiently large to be representative of the workers concerned, though not so large as to make negotiations unwieldy". The revised Guidance is silent on the point.

2. The candidates for election must be members of the workforce or members of a particular group within the workforce who are to be covered by the agreement.[12] As noted above any worker whose terms and conditions are already covered by a collective agreement will not qualify. The time for determining who is a member of the workforce would appear to be the date of the election. (See Schedule 1 paragraph 2 which pinpoints this date as the relevant time for determining if the election requirements have been satisfied.)

3. No worker who is eligible to be a candidate can be unreasonably excluded from standing for election. This raises the question of what amounts to a *reasonable* exclusion. Presumably it will not be sufficient that a potential candidate is "impossible to deal with" or is "a member of the awkward squad". On the other hand would it be reasonable to exclude someone who has little employment experience and has only just joined the firm? Given the uncertainty, employers should be wary of excluding candidates, although there is nothing to stop them encouraging workers whom they consider suitable to stand.

4. All members of the workforce (or of a particular group within the workforce) who are to be covered by the workforce agreement must be entitled to vote. As noted in (2) above, this entitlement does not apply to any worker already covered by a collective agreement. Similarly the relevant date for determining who is a member of the workforce would seem to be the date of the election (see Schedule 1 paragraph 2).

5. Those voting must be able to vote for as many candidates as there are representatives to be elected. This appears to allow for a range of voting systems including transferable voting systems where workers place their favoured candidates in order of preference so that if their first choice does not do well enough, their subsequent preferences can be taken into account. At the very least it must cover a system in which votes for each candidate have equal weight in the final count.

6. The election must ensure that so far as reasonably practicable those voting do so in secret and the votes given at the election are fairly and accurately

---

[12] As noted above, a group is defined by reference to a particular function, workplace, department or unit within the employer's business; see Schedule 1 para. 2.

counted. The original DTI Guidance document stated that it would be rare for secret balloting to be impossible. In addition it suggested that an employer might wish to enlist an independent body to verify the count. Again, the revised Guidance does not address these issues.

13–07 A number of questions are left unresolved by Schedule 1. In the first place it is not clear who is to bear the costs of the election. In practice it is likely that this will fall on the employer's shoulders, at least if this is the only way to achieve the flexible work patterns needed by the organisation. However there seems to be no reason in principle why the workforce should not bear part or all of the cost—however unlikely they are in practice to do so.

Secondly, Schedule 1 does not stipulate whether such elections have to be held during the working day. Again in principle there seems no reason why the employer cannot insist that any workplace ballot be held outside normal working hours and of course a postal ballot would avoid such issues altogether. However in practice it may speed the process if the ballot takes place during the working day.

Thirdly, the Schedule does not deal with the situation where only two candidates put themselves forward for two posts. A literal reading of Schedule 1 suggests that an election must always be held—even where to do so would be both a futile and expensive exercise. It remains to be seen whether the courts would adopt such a strict interpretation.

13–08 Finally, it does seem possible to use one election for a number of purposes where this would be easier from an administrative point of view. So for example the same ballot could elect worker representatives for the purposes of both the Working Time Regulations and also the Maternity and Parental Leave Regulations 1999. However it should be made clear to those voting that the representatives are being elected for both purposes.[13] Care would also need to be taken to ensure that the election requirements under both sets of Regulations were followed (although under the Maternity and Parental Leave Regulations they are the same). An employer would be ill-advised to assume that existing representatives (such as health and safety representatives) can automatically become worker representatives for the purposes of the Working Time Regulations without a fresh election. It is thought unlikely that a court would regard such individuals as having been "duly elected" under the Regulations not least because their original election is unlikely to satisfy the requirements of Schedule 1.[14]

THE SCOPE OF REGULATION 23

13–09 An agreement which falls within Regulation 23 can exclude or modify a number of important provisions in the Regulations, although as noted above this is subject to Regulation 24, which places significant limits on the employer's flexibility.

The provisions covered by Regulation 23(a) are the restrictions on night work (including the protection of night workers who encounter special hazards or who are subject to heavy physical or mental strain),[15] the requirement for adult workers to

---

[13] This was regarded as essential in the original DTI guidance although the revised version does not deal with the point.

[14] This contrasts with the election of employee representatives for the purpose of consultation on proposed redundancy dismissals or the transfer of an undertaking. In certain circumstances the employer can choose to consult representatives even if they were elected for other purposes (see TULR(C)A, s.188(1B)(b)(i) and the Collective Redundancies and Transfer of Undertakings (Protection of Employment) (Amendment) Regulation 1999, Regulation 10(2A)(b)(i)).

[15] see Regulation 6(1) to (3) and 6(7).

have daily and weekly rest periods[16] and the requirement for rest breaks for adult workers where daily working time is more than six hours.[17]

Equally important are the matters which are *not* covered by Regulation 23(a). These include the rules on paid holiday entitlement, the requirements relating to health assessments for night workers and the transfer of night workers to day work. The rules relating to young workers—including the provisions entitling young workers to rest periods and rest breaks—are also excluded with the result that in practice it may not be worthwhile negotiating an agreement under Regulation 23 if there are significant numbers of young workers in the workplace.

13–10 It is important to note that Regulation 23 agreements cannot be used to amend or exclude the requirement that weekly working time must not exceed an average of 48 hours (although this can be achieved at individual rather than collective level by an "opt-out" agreement between the worker and the employer in accordance with Regulation 5). However, Regulation 23(b) does allow modification of the 17-week *reference period* used to calculate average weekly working time. This power to modify is subject to two limitations:

1. The modified reference period must not exceed 52 weeks. (Although Regulation 23(b) does not say so expressly there seems no reason why the reference period cannot be reduced to less than 17 weeks if the parties so wish, although it is unlikely to be in the employer's interests to do so.)

2. The modification must be done for "objective or technical reasons or reasons concerning the organisation or work". These words are exactly the same as those used in Article 17(4) of the Directive and ultimately their meaning will have to be tested in the courts.[18] The phrase is potentially very wide and could have a significant impact particularly in industries or organisations where there are seasonal fluctuations in the workload. (Of course it may be that such organisations qualify for a 26-week reference period under Regulation 4(5) in any event. Even so a reference period of 52 rather than 26 weeks could still make a significant difference to the calculation of average weekly working time.) Article 17(4) of the Directive, on which Regulation 23(b) is based, explicitly states that any lengthening of the reference period beyond six months must be subject to "compliance with the general principles relating to the protection of the safety and health of workers". Although these words do not appear in Regulation 23, public sector workers may be able to rely on them directly in United Kingdom tribunals to show a breach of the Directive if such a long reference period leads to intolerable working hours at certain times of the year.[19]

13–11 It should be noted that Article 17(4) of the Directive provides that the

---

[16] see Regulation 10(1), 11(1) and 11(2).

[17] see Regulation 12(1).

[18] The words are very similar to the "economic, technical or organisational" defence to a claim for unfair dismissal under Regulation 8(2) of TUPE and it may be that cases interpreting that Regulation will be influential in this context.

[19] It is interesting to note that Regulation 23(a) places no limitation on the power to amend the relevant reference period which applies in the case of a night worker under Regulation 6(3). In theory therefore it would be possible to negotiate a reference period in respect of night work which exceeds the 52-week maximum allowed in connection with weekly working time. In practice however such a long reference period is likely to be impractical and contrary to the spirit of Regulation 6(2) which specifically refers to "the need to protect the health and safety of workers".

European Council must reconsider the issue of derogations from the normal 17-week reference period used to calculate average weekly working time before November 23, 2003. The Council must do this "on the basis of a Commission proposal accompanied by an appraisal report". It is therefore possible that the provisions of Regulation 23(b) may not apply indefinitely.

THE ADMINISTRATIVE BURDEN

13–12 The aim of Regulation 23 is to give businesses a degree of flexibility so that if employer and workforce can agree on sensible modifications to the Working Time Rules, these will be allowed, so long as compensatory rest periods are granted wherever possible in accordance with Regulation 24. Where collective bargaining mechanisms already exist within a workplace, it would normally be possible to reach a Regulation 23 agreement without introducing any new systems. However, where there is no tradition of collective bargaining and where it is therefore necessary to hold elections for employee representatives, the financial and administrative burden on employers could be high, particularly where large numbers of workers are involved. (As indicated above, although the Regulations do not deal with the issue, the costs of an election are likely to fall on the employer.) Even where the same election is used to elect representatives for a number of other purposes (such as health and safety or parental leave) the cost of organising even one election could be considerable both in financial terms and in terms of management time.

As stated above, a workforce agreement cannot last for more than five years. This apparently means that, even though the workforce agreement may be working successfully, new elections must be held and the draft of a new agreement must be circulated and then signed at least once in every such five year period. In contrast where collective agreements are used under Regulation 23 no time limit is imposed and such agreements can continue indefinitely.

PARTICULAR PROBLEMS

13–13 One of the greatest practical difficulties in negotiating a flexible working pattern by means of a Regulation 23 agreement will be ensuring that Regulation 24 is also complied with and that "equivalent periods of compensatory rest" are given. This means that organisations will only have limited room for manoeuvre and the need to monitor particular patterns of work to ensure that appropriate rest is given may become a very onerous task.

Another difficulty with Regulation 23 relates to collective agreements. There is an argument that a collective agreement must be incorporated into the contracts of individual workers if it is to qualify for the Regulation 23 exemption. This point arises because, elsewhere in the Regulations, "relevant agreements" (which can be used to modify a number of working time provisions) are defined to include "any provision of a collective agreement which forms part of a contract between [the worker] and his employer" (see Regulation 2(1)). By contrast neither Regulation 23 nor the definition of collective agreement in Regulation 2(1), say anything about incorporation and it is arguable therefore that, for the purposes of Regulation 23, such agreements do not have to be as contractually binding as between the worker and his employer. A cautious employer may nonetheless want to ensure that any collective agreement negotiated to take advantage of Regulation 23 is incorporated into the contracts of the individual workers concerned. The same point arises in relation to workforce agreements, although the precise legal status of these new agreements is not yet clear. If worker representatives sign such agreements as *agents* for the workforce then, in contrast to collective agreements, a binding contract between worker and employer will be created automatically on signature without the need for express incorporation into individual contracts. However, until this issue has been resolved, it would again be prudent to incorporate workforce agreements into individual contracts of employment to avoid any problems.[20]

13–14 Finally, Regulation 23 does not deal with the situation where the parties wish to renegotiate the collective or workforce agreement (*e.g.* because the order pattern changes and it is necessary to move to a different shift system). In the case of a collective agreement this should present little difficulty as the agreement can no doubt be varied in the usual way (normally by written agreement between the parties). It will then be binding on the relevant members of the workforce.[21] Arguably the same applies in respect of a workforce agreement so that a variation can be reached by written agreement between the employer and the worker representatives who signed the original agreement.[22] Presumably in such a situation a copy of the changes, together with appropriate guidance material, would have to be circulated to the workers concerned before signature. In addition it would seem that the amended agreement must expire no later than five years after the original agreement was signed. However there may be situations where it is advisable to hold new elections and negotiate a completely fresh agreement—such as where substantial changes are proposed and there has been a significant turnover of staff since the last elections were held. If this is done there can be no question of the new agreement being invalid.

---

[20] Note that under Regulation 16 of the Maternity and Parental Leave etc Regulation 1999 a collective or workforce agreement must be incorporated into the individual contract of employment if it is to be effective in supplanting the Parental Leave Scheme set out in Schedule 2 to the regs.

[21] For this reason employment contracts should incorporate collective agreements "from time to time in force", so that any amendments automatically form part of the individual worker's contract.

[22] Note that the DTI's guidance on the operation of workforce agreements in the context of parental leave states that "employers and employees can seek to renegotiate the terms and conditions of a workforce or collective agreement". There is no reference to any requirement for a fresh election in such a case.

CHAPTER FOURTEEN

Enforcement

INTRODUCTION

14–01   Part IV of the Regulations deals with, essentially, the issues of enforcement of the Regulations. Prior to the publication of the draft Regulations it had been a matter of debate amongst commentators how the provisions of the Working Time Directive would be enforced in the United Kingdom and whether the existing employment tribunal system would be utilised for that purpose.

The resulting Regulations not surprisingly confirmed that the existing system of employment tribunals would be a key measure in enforcing the rights and obligations concerning working time and that, in particular, the employment tribunal would be the primary port of call for individual complaints. The issue then was whether claims by employees for breach of their rights could be fitted in within the existing scheme of complaints whether by way of a complaint for unfair dismissal, discrimination or otherwise. Again it appears that this is what the Government has sought to do. The key protections, against unfair dismissal and against detriment, are similar to those that have been seen and which exist in relation to health and safety issues, pregnancy and trade union affiliation.

However, at present,[1] the right to complain of unfair dismissal is confined to 'employees' whereas the Regulations confer protection on the wider category of 'workers'. A worker who is not an employee may however bring a claim relating to detriment under s.45A of the ERA 1996 if he is dismissed for one of the reasons specified in that section.

14–02   The third area of enforcement is institutional. It was assumed by many that the HSE would bear the brunt of enforcing the Regulations on this basis. This is indeed the case save where Local Authority Environmental Health Departments are specifically made responsible. Further, the guidance issued alongside the Regulations confirms that enforcement will be in line with the Health & Safety Commission's (HSC) Enforcement Policy Statement.

In this section we will address each Regulation in turn.

REGULATION 28—ENFORCEMENT

14–03   Regulation 28 confirms that the method for institutional enforcement of obligations is the same as the methods for enforcement of other obligations pursuant to the Health & Safety at Work etc. Act 1974 (HSWA).

---

[1] The Secretary of State does however have power to extend this protection to the wider category of workers pursuant to s.23 of the Employment Relations Act 1999.

Provisions

14–04 Sub-section 1 defines certain "relevant requirements", in other words the obligations of employers in relation to which the enforcement provisions of the HSWA 1974 will apply. These are the employer's duties in relation to:

- Regulation 4(2) (compliance with the 48-hour limit);

- Regulation 6(2) (compliance with the eight-hour limit for night workers);

- Regulation 6(7) (compliance with the absolute eight-hour limit for those night workers involved with special hazards or who have a physical or mental strain);

- Regulation 7(1) and (2) (health assessments for night workers and young workers);

- Regulation 7(6) (transfer of night workers);

- Regulation 8 (pattern of work);

- Regulation 9 (the maintenance of records); and

- Regulation 24 (compensatory rest).

Paragraph 2 of Regulation 28 makes it clear that it is the duty of the HSE to make adequate arrangements for enforcement of the relevant requirements (save under paragraph 3) where responsibility is passed to the local authority where workers are employed in premises in respect of which the local authority is responsible under the Health & Safety (Enforcing Authority) Regulations 1998. In general, the HSE is responsible for enforcing the working time limits where they apply in factories, building sites, mines, farms, fairgrounds, quarries, chemical plants, nuclear installations, schools and hospitals. Local authorities are responsible for retailing, offices, hotels and catering, sports, leisure and consumer services.

14–05 Paragraph 3 also confirms that where a local authority has duties, performance is in accordance with the guidance issued by the HSC. It is now clear from the guidance that this means the HSC's Enforcement Policy Statement.

Paragraph 5 of Regulation 28 defines those provisions of the HSWA which will apply in relation to the enforcement of the relevant requirements. These are:

- Section 19;

- Section 20 sub-sections 1, 2(a)-(d) and (j)-(m), 7 and 8;

- Sections 21, 22(a), 23(1), (2) and (5), 24 and 26; and

- Section 28 insofar as it relates to information obtained by an inspector in pursuance of a requirement imposed under section 20(2)(j) or (k).

Finally, Regulation 28(6) confirms that any function of the HSC under the HSWA is equally exercisable in relation to the enforcement of the relevant requirements under the Working Time Regulations.

Issues for employers

14–06 Of course, the criminal sanctions and strict liability imposed by the HSWA mean that the Working Time Regulations are ignored at the employer's peril. Whilst of course it is open to an employer to assess the potential claims made by individual employees and balance that against its commercial objectives, the risk of imprisonment and/or a fine arising from by an HSE inspection cannot be so readily ascertained. Employers need to be particularly concerned that their records are kept up-to-date and accurate in the event of any inspection. Further, of course, the employer cannot afford simply to be only concerned about the impact of the Regulations in the event that there is a dispute with the employees. Whilst employees may be more than happy to flout the Regulations for financial or other reasons, the HSE and/or local authority environmental health departments will not have the same agenda.

The HSE and the local authorities who will be responsible for institutional enforcement are of course concerned regarding where funding for such enforcement will come from. Many local authorities are already under considerable strain in relation to their existing duties and it is possible that this lack of resources could mean that institutional enforcement takes some time to get off the ground. Spot checks may be unlikely but the provisions of the Regulations will have to be dealt with in scheduled inspections under the existing law. Employers however cannot afford to be lax.

REGULATION 29—OFFENCES

Provisions

14–07   Paragraph 1 confirms that an employer who fails to comply with any of the relevant requirements set out above is guilty of an offence. Accordingly paragraph 2 confirms that certain paragraphs of section 33(1) of the HSWA apply to the exercise of powers by an inspector. In brief it will also be an offence for an employer to:

- Contravene any requirement imposed by an inspector under section 20 HSWA 1974;

- Prevent or attempt to prevent any other person from appearing before an inspector or from answering any question to which an inspector may require an answer under section 20(2);

- Contravene any requirement or prohibition imposed by an improvement or prohibition notice;

- Intentionally obstruct an inspector in the exercise or performance of his duties;

- Use or disclose any information in contravention of section 28; or

- Make any statement which is known to be false or recklessly to make a statement which is false where the statement is made in purported compliance with a requirement to furnish information or for the purpose of obtaining an issue of a document.

Regulation 29(3) deals with the penalties for failure to comply with any of the relevant requirements under paragraph 1. Accordingly these are:

- On summary conviction, a fine not exceeding the current statutory maximum (currently £20,000); or

- On conviction or indictment, to a fine (unlimited).

14–08 Regulation 29(4) deals with where the employer is guilty of an offence as a result of the provisions of section 33(1) of the HSWA 1974. Depending on the offence the penalty may be a fine or an imprisonment which, if convicted on indictment, could be up to two years.

Regulation 29(5) applies certain provisions of the HSWA to the offences set out above. These relate to when offences are due to the fault of another person or are offences by bodies corporate, and to the power of the court to order the cause of offence to be remedied. The interesting effect of this provision is to make it clear that where a corporate employer has breached the relevant requirements but it can be proved that breach has been committed with the consent or connivance of or is attributable to the neglect of any director, manager, secretary or other similar officer, that such an individual can be guilty alongside the body corporate and punished accordingly.

Issues for employers

14–09 The fact that there are criminal consequences of successful enforcement action means that not only the body corporate but also the individual managers, directors and other officers of the company need to be conscious of the requirements placed upon them by the Regulations. Whilst convictions of individuals may be relatively rare a period of imprisonment cannot be traded off against a commercial benefit.

REGULATION 30—REMEDIES

Provisions

14–10 In contrast, Regulation 30 deals with individual complaints. Regulation 30 gives a new cause of action to a worker (and not merely an employee) enabling that worker to bring a complaint before an employment tribunal that his individual rights under the Working Time Regulations have been breached because the employer has refused to permit him to exercise those rights. This cause of action relates to:

- Regulation 10(1) or (2) (daily rest);

- Regulation 11(1)-(3) (weekly rest);

- Regulation 12(1) and (3) (rest breaks);

- Regulation 13(1) (annual leave);

- Regulation 24 (compensatory rest);

- Regulation 25(3) (special provision for armed forces);

- Regulation 27(2) (young workers—*force majeure*);

- Failure to pay the whole or any part of any amount due under Regulation 14(2) (payment in lieu of leave) or 16(1) (payment in respect of annual leave).

14–11 Regulation 30(2) provides that the employment tribunal cannot consider a complaint under Regulation 30 unless it is presented before the end of the period of three months beginning with the date on which it is alleged that the exercise of the rights should have been permitted, payment should have been made or, in the case of a rest period or leave extending over more than one day, the date on which it should have been permitted to begin. As with other tribunal claims where the tribunal considers that it was not reasonably practicable for the complaint to be presented within that period then the tribunal can accept jurisdiction if a complaint is presented within such further period as the tribunal considers reasonable. It should be noted that where the armed forces are concerned and the person concerned has made a complaint in respect of that matter, the time limit is extended to six months.

As the "reasonably practicable" test is applied to this time limit it is likely that the time limit will be applied strictly by the tribunal system. Employees and other workers must beware the fact that, in contrast with the discrimination legislation, the clock starts ticking at the beginning of the "continuing act" and not at the end.

14–12 Regulation 30(3) provides the type of remedy, that is it provides for a declaration and/or an award of compensation. Regulation 30(4) confirms that the amount of compensation is such as the tribunal considers just and equitable in all the circumstances having regard to:

- The employer's default; and
- The loss sustained by the worker.

Not surprisingly where the complaint relates to a failure to pay amounts due, the tribunal's remedy is limited to an order to pay the worker the amount which it finds is due to him.

Issues for Employers

14–13 This provision comes as little of a surprise. An existing system is being used. However, these measures differ from the majority of those contained in the ERA 1996 in that the complainant need not establish that he is in fact an employee before being entitled to bring his complaint. Employers historically only experienced claims from non-employees through the employment tribunal system when issues of discrimination had been raised. The difference of course is that it is very rare for a "worker" to bring a claim for discrimination. The claims that are seen are often in the field of harassment. These claims under the Regulations will be very different. They will mean that employers need to be much more conscious of the contractual terms that they have with their various workers and not merely with the employees. As workers may often work on behalf of more than one employer then the duties in some respects become more onerous as record keeping is more difficult.

REGULATION 31—RIGHT NOT TO SUFFER DETRIMENT

Provisions

14–14 Regulation 31 inserts a new section 45A into the Employment Rights Act 1996 (ERA) and then goes on to make certain consequential amendments to the ERA 1996 to reflect the insertion.

The new section 45A provides that a worker (not merely an employee) has a right not to be subjected to any detriment (whether by act or omission) by his employer on the ground that the worker has:

- Refused or proposed to refuse to comply with a requirement which the employer imposed or proposed to impose in contravention of the Regulations;

- Refused or proposed to refuse to forgo a right conferred on him by those Regulations;

- Failed to sign a workforce agreement or enter into or agree to vary or extend any other agreement with his employer which is provided for in the Regulations;

- Performed or proposed to perform any functions or activities as a representative of members of the workforce or a candidate in any election to become such a representative;

- Brought proceedings against the employer to enforce rights conferred by the Regulations; or

- Alleged that the employer had infringed such a right.

14–15 The new section 45A(2) confirms that it is not necessary where the worker has brought proceedings or alleged that his rights have been infringed for the worker actually to have the right or for the right to have been infringed provided that the claim to the right and the claim that it has been infringed are made in good faith. This is akin to the provisions relating to the assertion of statutory rights already found within the ERA 1996. Similarly the new section 45A(3) makes it clear that where a worker is alleging that a right has been infringed that the worker need not specify the right provided it is reasonably clear to the employer what the right claimed might be.

Finally section 45A(4) confirms that it does not apply where the worker is an employee and the detriment amounts to dismissal covered by Part X of the ERA.

Regulation 31 then goes on to amend section 48(1) of the ERA 1996 by providing that a worker may make a complaint to an employment tribunal in relation to detriment and amends section 49 to provide for a remedy. It should be noted that where the worker is not an employee but the detriment is the termination of his contract the compensation which he can receive cannot exceed that that would be payable if he had been an employee and had brought a claim of unfair dismissal. The rest of Regulation 31 deals with consequential amendments.

Issues for Employers

14–16 Regulation 31 therefore covers the situation where the employer has not refused the worker his rights but has then sought to penalise the worker for insisting upon his rights. It brings workers who are not employees within the scope of the ERA. Alongside Regulation 30 it provides for the only remedies for non-employee workers.

It is notable that the only remedies are a declaration and/or compensation and not, in the case of termination, reinstatement or re-engagement. Accordingly, there may be some scope for argument that the Regulations have failed to provide an effective remedy as required by European law. There were a number of changes to this Regulation in the passage of time between draft and the issue of the actual Regulation. In particular the limitation on compensation in the event of termination of a worker's contract was introduced. Presumably this is to ensure that workers are not in a more advantageous position than employees given that employees cannot bring a claim for detriment if the circumstances are such that they have a claim for unfair dismissal.

REGULATION 32—UNFAIR DISMISSAL

Provisions

14–17 Regulation 32(1) inserts a new section 101A into the ERA. In essence the provision provides that any employee who is dismissed shall be regarded as automatically unfairly dismissed if the reason or the principal reason for the dismissal is that the employee:

- Refused or proposed to refuse to comply with a requirement which the employer imposed in contravention of the Working Time Regulations;

- Refused or proposed to refuse to forgo a right conferred by the Regulations;

- Failed to sign a workforce agreement or to enter into or agree to vary or extend any other agreement with his employer provided for in the Regulations;

- Performed or proposed to perform any functions or activities as a representative of members of the workforce or a candidate in an election for such a representative.

14–18 These provisions therefore are akin to the provisions inserted by Regulation 31 in relation to detriment. The provisions covering circumstances where proceedings have been brought or the employee has alleged that a right has been infringed are covered by further amendments to the ERA providing, in particular, that the right of employees not to be unfairly dismissed for asserting statutory rights should be extended to cover assertion of rights under the Working Time Regulations.

Further, Regulation 32(3) amends section 105 of the ERA to confirm that where the reason for selection for dismissal for redundancy purposes was one of those specified above then the dismissal will be automatically unfair.

The Regulation then goes on to make certain consequential amendments but in particular amendments in relation to section 202(2) where disclosure of information is restricted on grounds of national security. Further, sections 237(1)(a) and 238(2)(a) of the Trade Union and Labour Relations (Consolidation) Act 1992, specifying cases where an employee can complain of unfair dismissal notwithstanding industrial action, are extended to also cover claims arising under this Regulation.

Issues for employers

14–19 Employers should note that, in a similar vein to the protections in health and safety cases and the protections for asserting statutory rights, there is no qualifying period of service for such a complaint. In other words an employee who, upon starting work, refuses to sign an individual consent to work in excess of 48 hours cannot be dismissed. Given recent developments in case law, providing that employment begins the moment the offer is accepted then it is highly likely that insistence upon a waiver as part of an offer of employment could in itself not be relied upon as good grounds for dismissal (even though the refusal to enter into such a waiver would in fact be a breach of contract).

As mentioned earlier the remedies for unfair dismissal are capped. Although there will be the availability of the remedies of reinstatement and re-engagement in unfair dismissal cases there is a query whether the cap in itself (the primary remedy) prevents there being an effective remedy for the purposes of European law.

REGULATION 33—CONCILIATION

14–20 This Regulation very simply extends section 18(1) of the ERA to ensure that claims brought pursuant to Regulation 30 of the Regulations (the freestanding right) are within the ambit of ACAS conciliation. This is not surprising given the fact that it is a claim that is being brought through the employment tribunal system, even though it can be brought by those other than employees. Of course the claims of unfair dismissal and detriment which have been inserted into the ERA are, by virtue of the consequential amendments, included within the scope of conciliation.

REGULATION 34—APPEALS

14–21 In a similar vein section 21 of the ERA relating to the jurisdiction of the Employment Appeal Tribunal is extended to cover the Working Time Regulations. In other words, in any case where there is a complaint to the employment tribunal then there is an appeal available to the Employment Appeal Tribunal.

REGULATION 35—RESTRICTIONS ON CONTRACTING OUT

14–22 This provides that any provision in an agreement (whether a contract of employment or not) is void insofar as it purports to exclude or limit the operation of the provision of the Regulations (save insofar as the Regulations provide for such an agreement) or to preclude a person from bringing proceedings before an employment tribunal unless there has been an agreement to so refrain through ACAS or there is a valid compromise agreement. The provisions for compromise agreements are identical to those for compromise agreements in other employment cases. The terms are of course extended now to cover the amendments to section 203 of the ERA pursuant to the Employment Rights (Dispute Resolution) Act 1998 insofar as the relevant independent adviser is concerned.

It should however be noted that this does not mean that an employer and an employee cannot contract out of the Regulations by virtue of a workforce agreement, an individual consent, a relevant agreement or a collective agreement anticipated by the Regulations themselves. It will only be in circumstances where those agreements are not valid (either because the Regulations do not allow or the agreement is improper) that such an agreement would be void under Regulation 35.

CONCLUSION

14–23 So the scheme for enforcement does not bring many surprises but ensures that alongside the scheme of individual remedies there is a form of institutional enforcement. That of course is vital to ensure that the Regulations are effective. Many employees/workers may not be prepared to bring complaints despite the apparent protections afforded but the possibility of criminal sanction imposes a burden on employers that cannot be ignored.

CHAPTER FIFTEEN

Workers in the Armed Forces and Young Workers

INTRODUCTION

15–01 Regulations 25 to 27 deal specifically with working in the armed forces and what are described as "young workers".

REGULATION 25

15–02 Regulation 25 permits derogation from certain of the requirements of the Directive in relation to the armed forces. It reads as follows:

(1) Regulation 9 does not apply in relation to a worker serving as a member of the Armed Forces

(2) Regulations 10(2) and 11(3) do not apply in relation to a young worker serving as a member of the Armed Forces

(3) In the case where a young worker is accordingly required to work during a period which would otherwise be a rest period, he shall be allowed an appropriate period of compensatory rest.

The effect of Regulation 25(1) is to disapply the requirement for records, set out in Regulation 9, to workers (young or adult) serving as members of the armed forces, naval, military and air forces of the Crown. Regulation 9 requires employers to keep records to show that the limits relating to maximum weekly working time, length of night work and the provisions relating to health assessments and transfers are being complied with.

15–03 Regulation 25(1) did not feature in the published draft Regulations, appearing for the first time in the finalised Regulations. The effect of the derogation is that whilst the armed forces must (subject to Regulation 18(c)) comply with the various limits contained in the Regulations, they are exempt from the requirement to keep records to demonstrate that the various limits are being complied with. The Government stated in the Consultation Document[1] that record keeping was necessary to provide evidence to ensure that the limits were being observed and that, "in the event of a dispute between a worker and employer it would be important that the enforcing authority has documentary evidence to inform their investigation and enable a proper assessment to be made without the need for a full hearing in court". Therefore, in the absence of such records it is suggested that, if the armed forces were

---

[1] Measures to Implement the Provision of the E.C. Directive in Organisation of Working Time and the Protection of Young People at Work URN 98/645.

ever challenged for failing to comply with the limits, such a challenge would be difficult to defend.

Regulation 25(2) provides that entitlement to daily rest periods and weekly rest periods do not apply to young workers serving as members of the armed forces. This takes advantage of Article 10(4) of the Young Workers' Directive, which permits derogation in respect of daily and weekly rest entitlement provided that there are "objective grounds for doing so" and provided that "[any adolescent worker concerned] is granted appropriate compensatory rest".

15–04 The derogation contained in Article 10(4) of the Young Workers' Directive[2] is only permitted in specified cases and these are set out as follows:

- work performed in the shipping or fisheries sectors;

- work performed in the context of the armed forces or the police;

- work performed in hospitals or similar establishments;

- work performed in agriculture;

- work performed in the tourism industry or in the hotel, restaurant and café sector;

- activities involving periods of work split up over the day.

15–05 Interestingly, the Conservative Government did not recommend any derogation from young workers' weekly and daily rest entitlement in any of the cases specified above in its Consultation Document on measures to implement the provisions of the Young Workers' Directive.[3] However, the succeeding Labour Government stated in its own Consultation Document[4] that "in the considered opinion of the Ministry of Defence, failing to provide for this derogation for the armed forces would seriously affect their ability to maintain combat effectiveness. Accordingly the MOD assesses that there are the requisite 'objective grounds' to take up the derogation".

Regulation 25(2) was therefore introduced, which permits derogation from the daily and weekly rest entitlement only for young workers who perform work in the context of the armed forces. It should also be noted that Regulation 25(3) provides that in any instance where the derogation is applied "appropriate compensatory rest" must be provided.

REGULATION 26

Young workers employed on ships

15–06 Regulation 26 provides that Regulations 7(2), 10(2), 11(3) and 12(4) do not apply in relation to a young worker whose employment is subject to Regulation under section 55(2)(b) of the Merchant Shipping Act 1995.

This meant that young workers who worked in the crew of sea-going ships would not benefit from the special entitlement to health assessments and transfers in relation to night work; daily and weekly rest; and rest breaks. The Government indicated in the

---

[2] Council Directive 94/33/E.C. on the protection of young people at work.
[3] A Consultation Document on Measures to Implement Provisions of the E.C. Directive on the Organisation of Working Time (1997).
[4] Measures to Implement Provisions of the E.C. Directives on the Organisation of Working Time and the Protection of Young People at Work URN 98/645.

Consultation Document[5] that the Department of Environment, Transport and the Regions would be bringing forward Regulations to implement the Young Workers' Directive[6] for young workers employed on ships, in consultation with the Ministry of Agriculture, Fisheries & Food. The resulting Regulations, the Merchant Shipping & Fishing Vessels Health & Safety (Employment of Children & Young Persons) Regulations 1998 (S.I. 1998 No. 2411), came into force on October 30, 1998 and implement the provisions of the Young Workers' Directive in respect of young workers employed in the fishing and shipping sectors.

REGULATION 27

Young workers—*force majeure*

15–07   Regulation 27 reads as follows:

(1) Regulations 10(2) and 12(4) do not apply in relation to a young worker whose employer requires him to undertake work which no adult worker is available to perform and which—

(a) is occasioned by either—

(i) an occurrence due to unusual and unforeseeable circumstances, beyond the employer's control, or

(ii) (exceptional events, the consequences of which could not have been avoided, despite the exercise of all due care by the employer)

(b) is of a temporary nature; and

(c) must be performed immediately;

(2) Where the application of Regulation 10(2) or 12(4) is excluded by paragraph (1), and a young worker is accordingly required to work during a period which would otherwise be a rest period or rest break, his employer shall allow him to take an equivalent period of compensatory rest within the following three weeks.

15–08   Regulation 27 transposes Article 13 of the Young Workers' Directive,[7] which permits derogation from a young worker's entitlement to a daily rest period and to rest breaks in the event of *force majeure*. It does not permit derogation from a young worker's entitlement to minimum weekly rest periods. It should also be noted that all the relevant conditions allowing this derogation to apply must be satisfied before it can be relied upon by the employer. Furthermore, the employer must allow an equivalent period of compensatory rest to be taken by the young worker within the following three weeks of the derogation taking place.

The scope for using this derogation is very limited. The Government stated in the Consultation Document[8] that "it is not a derogation that could possibly be used to

---

[5] Measures to Implement Provisions of the E.C. Directives in the Organisation of Working Time and the Protection of Young People at Work URN 98/645.
[6] 94/33/E.C. on the protection of young people at work.
[7] Council Directive 94/33/E.C. on the protection of young people at work.
[8] Measures to Implement the Provisions of the E.C. Directive on Organisation of Working Time and the Protection of Young People at Work (URN 98/645).

deal with anything other than unique ('one off') crises that allow for no other reasonable response". Examples of the circumstances in which the derogation might be taken up were "responding to the aftermath of a terrorist act, or the effect of a completely unexpected outbreak of illness among a work force".

CHAPTER SIXTEEN

Special Classes of Person

INTRODUCTION

16–01　As with most Regulations there are a number of general provisions dealing with different classes of individuals. The Working Time Regulations makes provision in respect of a number of classes of persons as set out in this section.

REGULATION 36

16–02　This Regulation deals with agency workers who are not otherwise "workers" as defined within the Regulations. Regulation 2 defines a worker as:

"... an individual who has entered into or works under (or, where the employment has ceased, worked under)—

    (a) A contract of employment; or

    (b) Any other contract, whether express or implied and (if it is express) whether oral or in writing, whereby the individual undertakes to do or perform personally any work or services for another party to the contract whose status is not by virtue of the contract that of a client or customer of any profession or business undertaking carried on by the individuals; and any reference to a worker's contract shall be construed accordingly";

The definition of a worker in Regulation 2 is the same definition of a worker under the Employment Rights Act 1996.[1] This deals with both those who work under a contract of employment and the second limb which is workers under other sorts of contract. Those who work under a contract of employment are employees.[2] For the purposes of the 1996 Act a contract of employment means a contract of service or apprenticeship.

16–03　It will be important in order to establish responsibility, to determine precisely what is the relationship between the organisation and the individual providing work to it. A fundamental point to understand is that a worker does not need to be employed under a written contract of employment in order to qualify as a worker. Contracts of employment can be oral or implied from a consistent course of dealing. Furthermore, what the parties decide to call the relationship is not conclusive in law.

16–04　The modern approach of the courts is to consider all relevant factors and features of the contractual relationship. The test was first propounded by MacKenna J. in *Ready Mixed Concrete (South East) Limited v. Minister of Pensions and National*

---

[1] 1996 s.230(3).
[2] s.230(1).

Insurance.[3] The case concerned a lorry driver who used his own lorry to deliver ready mixed concrete for the company. However, under the terms of his contract, he wore the company's uniform and his lorry carried the company livery. He was required to drive exclusively for the company and had agreed to carry out company instructions "as if he were an employee". The question arose as to whether the driver was a contractor or an employee for the purpose of the National Insurance Act 1965. MacKenna J. set out three key questions:

1. Did the driver undertake to provide his own work and skill in return for remuneration?

2. Was there a sufficient degree of control to enable the driver fairly to be called an employee?

3. Were there any other factors *inconsistent* with the existence of a contract of employment?

If a person is not a worker within the meaning of Regulation 2, can they be brought into the ambit of the Working Time Regulations by virtue of Regulation 36?

REGULATION 36(1)

16–05   Regulation 36(1) says that where an individual is supplied by a person (the agent) to do work for another person (the principal) under an arrangement between the agent and principal, but where that individual is not a "worker" within the meaning of Regulation 2 (because there is no worker's contract between the individual and the agent or the principal), nor is the individual a party to a contract under which he undertakes to work for another party to the contract, whose status is that of client or customer of any professional business undertaken or carried on the individual, then in such circumstances the individual carrying out the work is an agency worker.

Where Regulation 36(1) applies, such an individual is to be covered by the Regulations in general, and is to be treated as if there was a worker's contract between the individual and the agent or the principal. That is to be determined by looking at who is responsible for paying the worker in respect of the work.[4]

16–06   Regulation 36(2) is not easy to construe. In essence it attempts to allow a person to identify who is to be responsible under the Regulations for the agency worker by deeming them to be a worker within the meaning of Regulation 2. The question is who is the other party to the deemed worker's contract? As mentioned above, the first point is to look at who is responsible for paying the worker and whether that person is the agent or the principal. But what if it is neither the agent or the principal?

Here it is suggested there is some confusion. Regulation 36(2)(b) states in essence that if neither the agent nor the principal is "responsible" for paying the agency worker in respect of the work, then, to determine who the deemed employer is one has to look at whichever of the agent or the principal actually pays the worker. This is discussed further below.

16–07   Returning to Regulation 36(1) a number of issues seem to arise.

The first question arises in relation to Regulation 36(1)(a). This says that this

---

[3] [1968] 2 Q.B. 497.
[4] Regulation 36(2).

Regulation applies in any case where an individual, an agency worker, is supplied by the agent to do work for a principal under a contract or other arrangements made between the agent and the principal. However, does this require that the agent has the contract with the principal to supply a specific person or can it be any person? What if, for example, the agent has arrangements with a number of other companies who themselves provide agency workers (some of the workers indeed may have set up those companies for the specific purpose of hiring themselves out to do contract work). The principal asks the agent to provide several individuals to carry out short-term contract work and the agent merely asks company A to provide someone, company B to provide say two people and company C to provide another person. Are these arrangements in which no particular agency worker is supplied by an agent to do work for the principal covered? Will the courts construe this narrowly to look at these precise terms of the agreement between the agent and the principal? Is the agent truly supplying "an individual" as required by Regulation 36(1)? The answer is not at all clear. On the other hand the courts have shown themselves willing to construe legislation purposively and of course in relation to domestic legislation based on European law must do so (see above).

The second point to note arises as a result of the drafting of Regulation 36(1)(c) which says that the Regulation only applies where the agency worker is not a party to a contract under which he, the agency worker, undertakes to do work for another party to the contract whose status is that of a client or customer of any professional business undertaking carried on by the individual. In other words, if an individual sets up a business for the purpose of hiring himself out to do contract work and there is a contract between the individual's business and another business, the terms of which are that the individual will be doing work for the second business, this Regulation will not apply. The reason for that is that the business requiring the work to be done is clearly a customer of an undertaking carried on by the individual who is in essence agreeing to perform the work.

Is that person nevertheless a worker within the meaning of Regulation 2? It would seem not. Regulation 2 excludes arrangements whereby an individual undertakes to perform work for another party where that other party is a customer of any profession or business undertaking carried on by the individual. It would seem therefore that those individuals who undertake work for a party through the mechanism of their of their own limited company are excluded from the ambit of the Regulations entirely.

16–08   Turning now to Regulation 36(2) in more detail, as mentioned above this attempts to identify who the deemed employer of an agency worker should be. The deemed employer will be either the agent or the principal who is "responsible" for paying the agency worker in respect of the work being done or, if neither of them is "responsible", then it is whichever of them pays the agency worker in respect of the work. This would appear to be straightforward unless the parties to these agency arrangements can construct circumstances in which neither the agent nor the principal is responsible for paying the worker and that neither of them in fact pay the worker. Say for example an agent provides an agency worker to a principal but the principal, being say a company in a group of companies, allows the agency worker to go and work for another group company and that group company begins paying the individual agency worker. It may be that neither the agent nor the principal are responsible for paying the agency worker and that neither of them in fact pay the agency worker. Looking at the Regulations purposively it may be that the court could construe the original principal as the agent and the company for whom the agency worker is in fact working as the new principal in order to make at least one party liable under the Regulations, but there is at least scope for argument here.

Identifying Agency Workers and the Self-Employed

16–09 The question of whether a worker is an employee or an independent contractor (who are outwith the Regulations) frequently arises if the worker in question has been supplied by an employment agency. The difficulty is that an agency worker performs work pursuant to a three party contract. The agency contracts with the worker to provide that worker for a client company. The worker performs the work for the client but is paid by the agency who are in turn paid a fee by the client company. The worker frequently works under a contract which states that there is no entitlement to holiday or sick pay and that there is no obligation on the agency to provide, or on the worker to perform, any work. The worker would not be paid during any period in which there was no work provided. It is clear that agency workers do not become the employees of the client company without some conclusive evidence of a change in their status, such as the formal offer and acceptance of permanent employment by the worker with the company.

The courts have traditionally held that agency contracts also do not constitute a contract of service between the agency and the worker. Agency employment contracts usually lack the mutual obligations to provide or do work which are one of the key features of a contract of service. Similarly, the agency rarely exercises any control over the worker.

16–10 This view was confirmed by the EAT in *Wickens v. Champion Employment*.[5] The EAT had to consided whether the "temporaries" on the agency's books were employees of the agency. The agency was not bound to find work for the temps, nor conversely was the temp bound to accept a booking made by the agency on his behalf. If work was not offered or accepted, there would be no pay. However, there was no evidence that the temps were carrying on business on their own accounts. Despite this, the EAT concluded that the contracts between the agency and the temps did not create a relationship that had the elements of continuity and care associated with a contract of employment. The vital elements missing were the obligation of an agency to provide work and the obligation upon the temps to accept a booking. The EAT pointed out that in order to find that there was no contract of employment, it did not need to be shown that the temp was in business on his or her own account. The test did not include as a necessary element the question of whether the individual carries on a separate business.

Wickens was followed by *Ironmonger v. Movefield Limited*[6] in which the EAT again confirmed that there was no contract of employment between the employment agency and the agency worker. The contract in question bore no resemblance to a contract of employment. There was no written contract and the agency exercised no control over the agency worker. Notice of termination could be given by the hiring party, there was no pension provision or holiday pay and, again, there was no obligation on the agency to find work. However, the EAT, whilst accepting that there was no contract of employment thought that this did not necessarily mean that the agency worker was self-employed. The EAT agreed with the observation of Cooke J. in the earlier case of *Construction Industry Training Board v. Labour Force Limited*[7] when he said that the contracts of agency workers were neither contracts of services nor contracts for services but fell within an entirely different category of *sui generis* contracts which had a unique identity.

16–11 In this context it is worth noting the case of *Costain Building and Civil*

[5] [1984] I.C.R. 365.
[6] [1988] I.R.L.R. 461.
[7] [1970] 3 All E.R. 200.

Engineering Limited v. (1) Mr D. R. Smith and (2) Chanton Group Plc.[8] As the EAT pointed out, this appeal raises important questions as to whether an agency worker, in this case in the construction industry, was an employee of the building contractor.

Mr Smith was registered on the books of a number of agencies in the business of supplying labour to building contractors. One of those agencies was Chanton. Mr Smith had been registered with Chanton for about 10 years.

In June 1998 Chanton told Mr Smith that Costain needed a site engineer to work at the site of a new supermarket being built in Essex. Mr Smith and Chanton had no written agreement but there was an oral agreement between them under which Chanton would pay to Mr Smith £13 per hour. Chanton received that money from Costain.

Mr Smith was eventually told by Chanton that Costain had said that they did not want him to work on site again. Consequently Mr Smith claimed that he had been unfairly dismissed and moreover that the dismissal was automatically unfair under section 100(1)(b) of the ERA 1996.

The employment tribunal came to this conclusion:

"Weighing up all the facts that we have found and having considered the submissions made to us we find the Applicant was not a self employed person but was an employee of Costain at the material times."

The tribunal identified 6 factors which were inconsistent with a contract of service between Mr Smith and Costain. These were as follows:

- The method of payment;

- The applicant's tax treatment by the Inland Revenue (self employed);

- His relationship with Costain was not permanent;

- The Applicant was not issued with a Disciplinary Code, received no holiday pay, had no pension and there was no provision for notice;

- The applicant delivered invoices for payment to him by Chanton;

- The applicant's dismissal was brought about by Costain informing Chanton that they would not require the applicant's services.

Although the tribunal addressed each of these points they dismissed them and found for Mr Smith.

16–12   Costain, before the EAT, argued that the tribunal had made a fundamental error of law when considering the relationship between the applicant, Mr Smith, and Costain. The factors which the tribunal had found as inconsistent with an employment contract were indeed inconsistent with an employment contract and they should not have been dismissed in the way that the tribunal had done. The tribunal seemed to have been swayed by its concern that Costain was attempting to evade its employment responsibilities by treating Mr Smith as self employed. Mr Smith argued that, first the tribunal had made no error of law but secondly, and in one sense rather worryingly, that the Employment Rights Act should be applied "purposively" in order to grant protection to agency workers who can be denied the protection of employment law through the device of agency work.

The EAT considered both sets of arguments and pointed out that it can be difficult

---

[8] EAT, 29.11.99 (141/99).

to determine whether an agency worker is an employee or independent contractor. However, in this case the EAT found that the tribunal erred in law in finding that Mr Smith was an employee of Costain. They pointed out that there were two relevant contracts in this case. There was a contract between the agency, Chanton, and the building company, Costain. There was also a contact between Chanton and Mr Smith. There was no contract of employment between Costain and the applicant.

Importantly the EAT said that what was clear from the case was that Mr Smith chose to operate as a self employed agent because he was paid free of tax. He submitted invoices to Chanton. He received no holiday or sick pay. He had no notice provision and was provided with no benefits associated with being an employee. The EAT criticised the tribunal for focusing on what they considered to be the use of a "device" by Costain to avoid its statutory duties. This meant that the tribunal lost sight of the facts which clearly indicated that Mr Smith was not employed by Costain. The EAT found no need to apply the law purposively.

The EAT also said that if one considers the test of "service" then again Mr Smith can be shown not to have been an employee of Costain. Costain were specifically seeking an site engineer for a temporary period and they went to an agency to supply them with such a person. Costain did not identify Mr Smith, Costain did not request Mr Smith. So far as Costain were concerned the identity of the site engineer was immaterial. They simply needed someone to fill a vacancy for 4 weeks. Although Mr Smith was required to work site hours and he had an obligation to perform the work, either Mr Smith or Costain could terminate the arrangement without notice and without any further obligation. The fact that Costain had a supervisory role in relation to Mr Smith is not inconsistent with agency work, indeed, mere supervision is inconsistent with employment status.

One other issue which the EAT dealt with was the argument on behalf of Mr Smith that his appointment as a health and safety representative under the Safety Representatives and Safety Committees' Regulations 1997 elevated him to the status of employee. The EAT dismissed the argument out of hand saying that in order to be appointed as a health and safety representative under those Regulations the individual concerned had to be an employee in the first place.

Also of interest in this context is the case of *MHC Consulting Services v. Tansell*[9] which concerned the right of an individual to bring a complaint of disability discrimination under the DDA 1995 in relation to a chain of contracts to supply workers.

Mr Tansell offered computer services through his own company called Intelligents Limited. He was the sole shareholder and one of four directors.

His name was placed with several agencies including MHC Consulting Services which is an employment agency specialising in placing computer personnel with third parties.

MHC had an agreement with Abbey Life Assurance Co Limited to supply personnel to them as and when needed. Mr Tansell was interviewed pursuant to that agreement by Abbey Life and was found to be acceptable. Following the interview MHC and Intelligents entered into a contract under which Intelligents would supply Mr Tansell for use by Abbey Life. Therefore Mr Tansell went to work for Abbey Life (but not be employed by them). In that context he was clearly under their control. Monies were paid by Abbey Life to MHC who in turn paid monies to Intelligents. Mr Tansell received a salary from Intelligents. The money Mr Tansell received was less than the sum paid by MHC to Intelligents.

---

[9] [1999] I.R.L.R. 677.

When Abbey Life rejected Mr Tansell's services Mr Tansell argued that that was by reason of his disability. MHC withdrew him from the site and therefore he sought to complain that he had been discriminated against contrary to the DDA by Abbey Life and/or MHC.

Section 12 of the DDA says that it is unlawful for a principal, in relation to contract work, to discriminate against a disabled person. A principal for the purposes of the DDA is a person who makes work available for doing by individuals who are employed by another person, who supplies them under a contract made with the principal. The Sex Discrimination Act and the Race Relations Act have a similar definition of contract worker. Furthermore the approach is not dissimilar to that of Regulation 36(1) except that section 12 of the DDA seems to require that the individual providing work to the Principal should be employed by someone. Regulation 36(1) does not require this.

The Employment Tribunal held that section 12 of the DDA requires a direct contractual relationship between the employer and the principal. Therefore, Mr Tansell could not have a claim against Abbey Life. In this case the direct contractual relationships were between MHC and Abbey Life and between MHC and Intelligents. However, since it was Intelligents who was the employer (and therefore within section 12 the person supplying Mr Tansell) but the end user was Abbey Life (the Principal), the fact that there was no direct contractual relationship between Intelligents (or Mr Tansell directly) and Abbey Life, meant that there could be no claim by Mr Tansell against Abbey Life.

MHC and Mr Tansell appealed and the EAT allowed both appeals. It said that if there is an unbroken chain of contracts between an individual and the end user then the end user is the principal within the meaning of section 12 of the DDA. This is a highly purposive approach because section 12 seems to be prescriptive in that it seems clear from the wording of the statute that there must be a contract between the employer and the user of the individual concerned. It is clear that in this case there was no contract between the employer (Intelligents) and the end user (Abbey Life). Not surprisingly this case is going to the Court of Appeal. There is no reason why the "clash of contracts" approach, and a highly purpose interpretation would not be adopted in relation to Regulation 36(1) also.

REGULATION 37

16–13 This Regulation brings within the ambit of the Regulations those in Crown employment, meaning employment under or for the purposes of a Government department or any officer or body exercising on behalf of the Crown functions conferred by statutory provision.

The only exemption is that the Crown cannot be criminally liable for any offences under Regulation 29 (see above). The most that can be hoped for is a declaration by the High Court (or the Court of Session) that an act or omission is unlawful.

REGULATION 38

16–14 This Regulation applies to members of the Armed Forces and anyone employed by an association established for the purposes of Part XI of the Reserve Forces Act 1996.

Regulation 38 ensures that no complaint can be presented to an employment tribunal by a member of the Armed Forces as defined by this Regulation under

Regulation 30 (see above), unless that person has already made a complaint regarding the same matter to an officer under the relevant procedures in that particular branch of the Armed Forces and that complaint has not been withdrawn.

Regulation 38(3) states that a complaint is to be treated as having been withdrawn if, under the relevant procedure, the individual failed to submit the complaint to the Defence Counsel.

Regulation 38(4) ensures that even if a complaint has been presented, to an employment tribunal, the internal service redress procedures can continue.

For the purposes of this Regulation, "service redress procedures" means those procedures referred to in section 180 of the Army Act 1955, section 180 of the Air Force Act 1955 and section 130 of the Naval Discipline Act 1957, but excludes those which relate to the making of a report on a complaint to Her Majesty.

REGULATION 39

16–15 Regulation 39 ensures that the Regulations apply to House of Lords staff as they apply to other workers. For the purposes of these Regulations a member of the House of Lords staff is the only person who is employed under a "worker's contract" with the Corporate Officer of the House of Lords. (See above for the meaning of "worker's contract".)

REGULATION 40

16–16 Likewise Regulation 40 ensures that the Regulations apply generally to a member of the House of Commons staff. For the purposes of the Regulations a member of the House of Commons staff is anyone who has been appointed by the House of Commons Commission or is a member of the Speaker's personal staff.

REGULATION 41

16–17 It is well known that police officers are not employees for the purposes of rights under the Employment Rights Act and other employment rights. They are, it should be noted, "workers" for the purposes of discrimination legislation (in particular the Sex Discrimination Act 1975, Race Relations Act 1976 and Disability Discrimination Act 1996).

REGULATION 41(1)

16–18 States that a police officer who holds the office of constable or who has been appointed as a police cadet shall be treated as an employee working under a worker's contract for the purposes of the Regulations.

It should be noted that for the most part police officers, where they are taken to be employed, are employed by the Chief Constable and proceedings are issued against that officer, not against the relevant Police Force.

REGULATION 41(2)

16–19 States that where, in the Regulations, there is reference to a "workforce agreement" (see above generally), then that workforce agreement can be provided in respect of constables or police cadets by an agreement between the "relevant officer" and a "joint branch board".

A joint branch board is a board constituted in accordance with the Police Federation Regulations 1969 (Regulation 7(3)), or the equivalent Regulation in the Police Federation (Scotland) Regulations 1985.

The "relevant officer" is determined by the identity of the complainant.

For a member of the Police Force or a special constable or police cadet, the relevant officer is the Chief Constable. However, for police members of the National Criminal Intelligence Service and the National Crime Squad, the relevant officer is the Director General of the National Criminal Intelligent Service or the Director General of the National Crime Squad as the case may be.

REGULATION 42

16–20   This is a "sweeping up" provision in relation to non-employed trainees, which states that anyone who is receiving relevant training, but is not under a contract of employment, will nevertheless be regarded as a worker and a person providing the training shall be regarded as the employer. This again is an example of the scope of the provisions.

REGULATION 43

16–21   This deals with agricultural workers and states that provisions of Schedule II shall have effect in relation to workers employed in agriculture.

CHAPTER SEVENTEEN

Workers Employed in Agriculture

17–01 Schedule 2 contains fairly limited provisions in relation to workers employed in agriculture. Agricultural workers who fall within the definition of "worker" contained in the Regulations are in principle covered by the Regulations just as any other worker would be.[1] However the situation is complicated by the fact that the employment of such individuals is also regulated by Agricultural Wages Orders (AWOs). These AWOs (which in England and Wales are issued under the Agricultural Wages Act 1948 and in Scotland under the Agricultural Wages (Scotland) Act 1949) impose minimum standards of pay and conditions throughout the industry and may well overlap to some extent with the Regulations. So for example the Agricultural Wages Order 2000 which came into effect on June 1, 2000 and which covers England and Wales contains provisions relating to holiday pay and rest breaks.[2]

It is essential that the relationship between the Regulations and the AWOs is unambiguous and to this end the Government has adopted the policy that in cases of inconsistency the provisions which are most generous to the worker will apply (see Regulation 17). This ensures maximum protection for the worker and at the same time avoids the risk that the provisions relating to agricultural workers fall short of the standards required by the Directive. The disadvantage of this approach is that the agricultural employer will sometimes have to perform two different calculations under two separate pieces of legislation to be sure that he is operating within the law. This is particularly so in the case of holiday pay where account must be taken of both the Regulations and the current AWO to determine the appropriate level of pay.

17–02 As far as Schedule 2 is concerned, this simply gives further clarification in the area of holiday pay by providing that the practical arrangements for taking leave and determining the start of the leave year will be determined by the relevant AWO and not by the Regulations. However if the AWO fails to give a start date for the leave year, the leave year will have to begin on 6 April. (See Schedule 1 paragraph 1(a).) The only exception to this relates to workers who are "partly employed in agriculture" (*i.e.* employed by the same employer in both agricultural and non-agricultural work[3]). If the start of the leave year and the arrangements for taking leave are covered by a relevant agreement then it is the terms of that agreement and not the AWO that will apply (see Schedule 2 paragraphs 1 and 2). The scope of Schedule 2 is therefore very limited and anyone investigating the rights of agricultural workers in this area should always refer to the relevant AWO as well as the Regulations before proceeding.

---

[1] This is clear from the fact that certain aspects of the Regulation can be modified for specified types of agricultural worker under Regulation 21.
[2] See ss.14 and 16, AWO 2000 (No. 1).
[3] See Regulation 2.

CHAPTER EIGHTEEN

Record Keeping

INTRODUCTION

18–01 One of the main administrative burdens placed on employers by the Regulations is the obligation relating to record keeping. While the limits on working time themselves oblige employers to monitor and review levels of working time to ensure compliance with applicable limits, the obligation to keep and maintain records relating to working time extends that burden considerably. However, the extent of the additional burden imposed by the Regulations is often exaggerated.

Regulation 9 obliges employers to keep records adequate to demonstrate compliance with the limits on weekly working time, length of night work and the health assessment obligations in respect of night workers. In addition to these requirements, certain records must be kept in relation to workers who have opted out of the weekly working time limit. This latter requirement has been greatly reduced following the abolition of the requirement to keep records of the working time of opted-out workers.

The Regulation 9 obligation

18–02 Regulation 9 provides that:

"An employer shall

(a) keep records which are adequate to show whether the limits specified in Regulations 4(1) and 6(1) and (7) and the requirements in Regulations 7(1) and (2) are being complied with in the case of each worker employed by him in relation to whom they apply; and

(b) retain such records for two years from the date on which they were made."

The record keeping obligation therefore arises in respect of:

- The limit on the average working week;

- The limit on the average normal hours of work of night workers;

- The limit on actual daily hours of work in the case of night workers whose work involves special hazards or heavy physical and mental strain; and

- The duty to provide health assessments and assessments of health and capacities for young workers.

18–03 After some general comments on the nature of duties, each of these will be examined in turn to identify the nature of the records which will be required. How the record keeping obligation in respect of average weekly working time might be discharged in practice is considered later in the Chapter (see paragraph 18–15), which discusses the sample working time records set out in the Appendices.

General observations

18–04 As stated above, the extent of the record keeping obligation imposed by Regulation 9 is often exaggerated. For example, in respect of the weekly working time limit, a common misconception is that employers are required to keep records of the work time of each of their workers on a daily basis and be able to calculate at any given date the average weekly working time over the preceding 17 weeks. The proper reading of Regulation 9 is that it requires employers to keep records which are sufficient to show that the limit of 48 hours average weekly working time has not been exceeded, which is a lesser burden.

It should also be noted that there is no obligation to keep separate or specific records expressly relating to the Regulations. Existing record keeping arrangements will be sufficient provided that these contain the information which the employer needs to demonstrate compliance with the various requirements of the Regulations. However, while records required by the Regulations may be kept for other purposes and kept on several different record keeping or information gathering systems, it will obviously be important for employers to be able to collate that information easily for the purposes of monitoring working time and working patterns.

The obligation to keep records is imposed by the Regulations on the employer. While this obligation cannot be delegated by the employer to the worker, the keeping of records will undoubtedly involve a large degree of "self-reporting" by workers. Employers will have to put in place appropriate reporting systems (*e.g.* timesheets) and also ensure that workers keep and maintain the relevant records.

18–05 It is suggested that employers should consider amending their disciplinary rules and contracts of employment to ensure that any failure by the worker to maintain the records requested by the employer, or the provision of false information, will be treated as disciplinary offences.

Records for the weekly working time limit

18–06 As stated above, the obligation under Regulation 9 is to keep records which are adequate to show that the average weekly working time limit (for those workers who have not opted out) does not exceed an average of 48 hours per week in the applicable reference period.

A worker's hours of work can be typically divided into two categories, namely "pre-determined" hours and "additional" hours. Pre-determined hours are likely to be recorded in existing documents, for example contracts of employment or work plans, shift rotas, etc. Employers can assume that such pre-determined hours are in fact worked (and will therefore count as working time) and do not need to put in place specific record keeping arrangements in respect of such hours. However, employers will wish to introduce record keeping arrangements to record occasions on which the worker is absent, either from holiday (because of sickness, holiday, maternity leave, etc) or on which the worker does not work part of their pre-determined hours on any day, (because of medical appointments, jury service, ante-natal classes, etc). Such records could be maintained by simply asking the worker to declare on a daily or weekly basis that they have worked their "pre-determined" hours or else to provide details to the contrary.

As a result of the requirement to make adjustments in the applicable calculations in the case of absence through sickness, maternity leave or annual leave, employers will also need to ensure that their workers report such absences. While these will probably be recorded under an employer's existing procedures, employers should note that the records required to be kept under Regulation 9 must be kept for two years from the date on which they are made.

18–07   Employers may have to introduce new record keeping procedures in order to comply with Regulation 9 in relation to additional hours over and above any fixed hours or normal hours of work. Where these are in the form of paid overtime, it is likely that these will already be recorded on payroll or other systems. Where not already recorded, employers will have to introduce systems requiring workers to report, on a daily or weekly basis, such additional hours.

The employer could streamline these record keeping obligations even further by setting a threshold level over which such additional hours are reported or recorded. Whether this route is available to employers would depend on the precise hours of work of the workers concerned and how close this is to the limit in Regulation 4(1). For example, a worker who works a basic 39-hour working week without overtime has an average of nine hours per week which can be worked by way of overtime or other "working time" without breaching the weekly working time limit. If it is the case that overtime for such a worker rarely exceeded five hours per week, the employer could satisfy the record keeping obligation under Regulation 9 by requiring the worker to document any week in which the amount of overtime or additional working time exceeds five hours. One disadvantage of this route is that, because no specific records will be kept of weeks where the total working time is less than this 44-hour threshold, the employer would have to assume (in the absence of any other records) that 44-hours had been worked in each week where the worker did not report hours in excess of the threshold. This might restrict the employer's overall flexibility in terms of the limit in Regulation 4(1).

Some categories of workers present particular problems for employers in terms of the record keeping obligation under Regulation 9:

Salaried staff

18–08   It is very common that contracts of employment for salaried staff will state that their normal hours of work are, for example, 37½ hours per week "plus such additional hours as are necessary for proper performance of the employee's duties". It may be the case that in practice such employees regularly begin work earlier than normal office hours, work late in the evenings, do not take their lunch hours and carry out work at home on evenings or weekends. Employers will need to introduce specific record keeping systems to detect such additional hours of working time, either by way of a timesheet or some other record.

However, as discussed above, these additional hours may not necessarily be "working time". It is therefore important that employers ensure that records of these additional hours accurately reflect what is in fact working time or at least contain information sufficient to examine the true nature of the additional hours worked. It is suggested when introducing timesheets or other systems to "self-report" additional working time, employers should give proper guidance to the worker on the circumstances in which time should be recorded and the details required. Employers may also wish to consider, as a preliminary step to the introduction of such record keeping arrangements, carrying out a review period during which employees keep a detailed record of their working hours which record not just the time spent on a particular activity but also the nature of the activity and the reasons why it is performed out of "normal" hours. This may assist employers in compiling guidance to workers on what will and will not count as working time.

Sales persons

18–09 Sales persons who spend all or a large part of their time "in the field" may spend the vast majority of their time away from the employer's premises. For that reason, the employer will clearly not be able to keep records of the working time of such workers unless these are self-reported. Again, it is suggested that employers give guidance on the information to be recorded.

Workers with more than one job

As discussed above, where a worker has more than one job, the time spent by that worker in each job will count towards the limit in Regulation 4(1). Each employer will therefore need to ask the worker to report the hours worked each week in any other employment.

18–10 There is no prescribed format for the records required to be kept in relation to Regulation 4(1). The amount of detail will depend upon the employer's preference. Some employers may wish to keep fairly detailed records of time spent by their workers while others may wish to keep the amount of information to be reported to a minimum. There is clearly a risk that the more detailed the information required to be provided by the worker, the more likely it is that any new systems of record keeping introduced in order to meet the requirements of the Regulations will face resistance from workers. It is likely that record keeping systems introduced to meet the Regulations will detect unauthorised absences and poor time-keeping. Issues of inefficiency may also be raised where a worker appears to be taking much longer than his/her colleagues to perform certain types of work or carry out similar workloads. If working time records are used when addressing such issues in a disciplinary context, this may create mistrust and undermine the co-operation necessary to ensure that records are kept. Employers should also bear in mind that a worker who is subject to disciplinary sanctions for lateness or failure to keep the records may find it easier to sustain an allegation of inconsistent treatment where records show that other workers have not been subject to such sanctions in identical cases.

Records for the limits on night work

18–11 As the "normal hours of work" of night workers will typically be fixed by the contract of employment, it is likely that records will already exist, whether in the form of contracts of employment or work schedules. Employers should therefore ensure that such records are kept for the requisite two-year period and also ensure that all of the workers who work on those particular systems are identifiable.

The limit in Regulation 6(7), however, relates to actual working time. Because of the strict requirements of this limit employers should ensure that there are records identifying all workers whose work involves special hazards or heavy physical or mental strain and the actual working time of such workers during night time.

Records of health assessments

18–12 The process of providing health assessment to workers, whether in the form of questionnaires or medical examinations, should in itself generate sufficient documentation to identify the workers, the date of the assessment and the fact that the health assessment has been provided. Employers should ensure that these records are kept for two years.

Records for workers who have opted out of the weekly working time limit

18–13   Originally Regulation 5(4) required that, in relation to workers who had opted out of the 48-hour average working week, an employer should "maintain up-to-date records which:

"(i)   identify each of the workers whom he employs who has agreed that the limit specified in Regulation 4(1) should not apply in his case;

(ii)   sets out any terms on which the worker agreed that the limit should not apply; and

(iii)   specify the number of hours worked by him for the employer during each reference period since the agreement came into effect (excluding any period which ended more than two years before the most recent entry in the records)".

However, it will be noted that (iii) above required records to be kept of the actual working time of such workers in each applicable reference period. This essentially meant that employers were obliged to keep a daily record of the actual working time of those workers who are subject to the opt-out. It will be appreciated that this was a more onerous record keeping obligation than that which applies where there is no "opt-out", where the obligation is simply to keep records which are sufficient to show compliance with the limit. This came as a surprise (and a source of frustration) to many employers, who wrongly assumed that once the individual opt-out agreement was in place they had no duty to keep records at all in respect of weekly working time.

18–14   As the individual agreement to exclude Regulation 4(1) must be in writing, the record keeping obligations in (i) and (ii) were met if the employer kept a copy of the "opt-out" for at least two years.

However, in a major shift of policy, the Government bowed to business pressure and removed this requirement entirely, along with the duty to record the terms of the opt-out. The only record keeping obligation in respect of opted-out workers is now found in Regulation 4(2) (as amended) which contains the duty to keep up-to-date records of all workers who have opted out.

THE RECORDING OF WEEKLY WORKING TIME

18–15   This section explains, by reference to the specimen records in Appendices 10 to 17, how compliance with the weekly working time limit might be recorded.

The specimen records are of two kinds:

- A record of working time to be maintained by the worker ("Worker Records"); and

- A further record to be completed by management on which the data from the individual records is compiled to demonstrate compliance under the Regulations ("Management Records").

Some more general documentation, such as a working time monitoring form and a record keeping policy, are also included in the Appendices.

Employee records

18–16 These forms are necessary because the individual worker needs to provide information to the company about his/her working time. The first issue which arises is what counts as "working time".

As explained in Chapter 3, paragraph 3–03, the definition of working time set out in the Working Time Regulations is not entirely straightforward. It may be appropriate to give guidance to worker (whether on the worker's record keeping forms and/or in a Working Time Record Keeping Policy) as to the sorts of time which will count as "working time" and should therefore be recorded by the worker.

It is possible to agree an expanded definition of working time with workers but before this is done, we would recommend that employers consider whether any such agreement would place any workers beyond the 48-hour working time limit.

It is not necessary for individual workers to record every moment of their working time. For instance, a worker's normal or contractual hours of work would count as working time and, as these are pre-determined, the company can assume that these hours are being worked (unless informed to the contrary) without requiring the worker to give detailed records of the type of activity being carried on within these hours. It may be more appropriate to place the emphasis in terms of record keeping on the "additional hours" of work over and above the normal or contractual hours.

18–17 Furthermore, in the case of part-time workers (for example someone working 20 hours a week) it may be clear that the 48-hour average weekly working time limit would never be exceeded. Again, for such workers it would be unnecessary to keep detailed records of the precise composition of their working time.

These factors must be balanced against the fact that workers may be tempted to include as much time as possible on their working time records. The employer may at a later date want to argue whether or not this time counts as working time. It would only be able to advance such an argument with any degree of force if it was aware of the nature of the activity concerned and why it was being performed at that time.

The different formats of the specimen worker's records are as follows:

Record of time at work excluding lunch breaks[1]

18–18 This form requires workers to indicate the time which they arrive at work and the time at which they leave, as well as the length of any lunch break which they take. This gives a simple record of their time on the premises. This may be a useful guide to the worker's working time although it obviously assumes that all of the time spent on the employer's premises would be working time. Provided this does not regularly show the working time of 48 hours or more a week then this method of record keeping may be appropriate. As a rough guide as to whether this is likely to be an appropriate record keeping system, the limit of 48 hours per week equates to 9½ hours per day (excluding a lunch break of one hour) over a five-day week, *e.g.* 9.00 a.m. to 7.30 p.m. or 8.00 a.m. to 6.30 p.m. If workers are working at home or travelling in the course of their duties, this method of record keeping may be inappropriate and the forms would have to be adapted.

Record of additional hours[2]

18–19 The basis for this record is that workers will (most weeks) work their normal contractual hours, all of which are likely to count as working time. The form

---

[1] Appendix 10.
[2] Appendix 11.

asks employees to confirm that these hours have been worked or to give details of the number of hours not worked, for example because of absences for sickness, holiday, medical appointments, etc.

In section B of the form, the employees are asked to declare any working time over and above their contractual hours of work. In order to monitor the nature of this additional time I would recommend that the additional columns (requesting details of the activity carried out, the reason for it being carried out at the time and whether the activity was carried out with management knowledge or instruction) are included as these will be a guide to whether this does in fact fall within the definition of working time.

Assumed number of hours per week[3]

18–20   Under the Regulations, workers can work up to 48 hours per week for 17 weeks without breaching the limit. This equates to 816 hours over 17 weeks. If the employee has contractual hours of, say, 37½ hours per week this would allow an additional 10.5 hours per week to be worked without breaking the limit or, more accurately 178 hours 30 mins over 17 weeks.

To simplify the record keeping requirements, the company might therefore assume that an employee is working, say, 42 or 45 hours of working time per week unless the worker notifies the company that they are working more. This would still allow 102 or 51 additional hours to be worked in the 17 weeks of the reference period.

18–21   The advantage of this system is that it is relatively straightforward and requires little by way of detailed information from employees on their working hours. However, if the employee is absent from work for three days out of five, it would be inappropriate to assume that they are working 42 or 45 hours working time that week. For absences of this sort, there would therefore need to be a statement of the actual hours worked. Furthermore, the reference period over which the weekly working time limit is to be calculated must be extended to take account of any absences from holiday, sickness or maternity leave. Such an extension of the reference period therefore requires the keeping of records of the number of hours of working time worked in each day for which the reference period is extended.

The disadvantage of this approach would be that it may well reduce the amount of flexibility in terms of additional hours of working time that can be worked. For example if the company assumes (unless told to the contrary) that 45 hours working time per week is being worked, and an employee only works 38 hours, seven hours of available working time would have been "lost". It is therefore important that the assumed number of hours being worked is set carefully.

Supplementary working time form[4]

18–22   As explained above, in the case of absences for sickness, holiday and maternity leave, the reference period is extended. It is necessary for the employer to keep a specified record in respect of working time for these days. For this reason, we would suggest that a supplementary working time form should be issued to workers in respect of the days in which the reference period is extended.

The supplementary Working Time Form includes a reference to the number of hours that can be worked in the extension to the reference period without breaching

---

[3] Appendix 12.
[4] Appendix 13.

the weekly working time limit. Employers will not wish to find out after the event that the limit has been breached—they need to take steps to ensure that the limit is observed in the first place.

It is unreasonable to expect workers to decide when the reference period is being extended and for how many days. For this reason, there is no alternative to this form being issued centrally once the period by which the reference period is to be extended is identified. A prompt for this is included in the records which are to be kept by the worker.

Record of work carried out for other employers[5]

18–23 Under a Regulations, working time spent by an employee in a second job will count towards his/her working time with the main employer. Workers who have second jobs should be asked to declare on a weekly basis the number of hours worked that week for the other employer and the number of hours expected to be worked in the following week. The management records (see below) would need to be adapted to allow for these hours to be taken into account.

Management records

18–24 The purpose of these records is to compile information from the individual forms to demonstrate that the limit is being complied with. The detail of the form depends on the precise reference period which has been adopted by the employer.

The weekly working time limit can be calculated over a number of different reference periods, as follows:

Rolling reference period[6]

18–25 The Regulations themselves provide for a 17-week rolling reference period. This means that the working time for any given week and the preceding 16 weeks are added together and must not exceed 816 hours.

Obviously, the Regulations have been in place since October 1, 1998 and therefore, on the basis of the rolling reference period, it is, strictly, incorrect (where record keeping systems are introduced at a later date) to start the record from a particular week without taking account of what has happened over the preceding 16 weeks. However, it may well be that no records or no sufficient records exist on working time over the previous 16 weeks and therefore there will be no option but to start the form from a given date and ignore what has happened in the preceding 17 weeks.

After the first 17-week period, this record becomes more complex. It needs to record that week's working time, working time over the previous 16 weeks, any absences for that week and absences over the preceding 16 weeks (so that the extension to the reference period can be determined) and the number of hours worked in the reference period. This record also includes a calculation of working time for the following week and the following three weeks, which may be useful in terms of planning ahead. There is no need to actually average out weekly working time over the reference period and state what the average is. The key question is whether the working time in the reference period has exceeded 816 hours (*i.e.* 17×48 hours).

---

[5] Appendix 14.
[6] Appendix 15.

Fixed reference period[7]

18–26 The Regulations allow the reference period to be fixed into successive 17 weeks periods. One advantage of that is that peaks in working time are cleared "out of the system" more quickly as the reference period has a defined start date and finish date. Another benefit is that the record keeping requirements are more straightforward. There is no need to keep a running total or a calculation of working time over the previous 16 weeks. The employer would simply keep a record of working time over the 17 weeks of the fixed reference period and can easily determine how much working time is left in the relevant period.

New workers[8]

Over the first 17 weeks of employment, a worker cannot work an average of more than 48 hours a week over the number of weeks for which they have been employed by the company (unless they have signed an opt-out).

Other specimen documents[9]

18–27 A draft working time record keeping policy and a monitoring form are also included in the Appendices. The purpose of the policy is to explain the record keeping system in force, what is required from the employee and what sort of time should be recorded as "working time". Given the difficulties caused by the definition of working time, the monitoring form is suggested as a means of clarifying the type of activities carried out by individual workers and the reason for these being carried out outside of the pre-determined hours of work. This information may allow the guidance to workers on this issue, in the working time record keeping policy, to be clarified.

---

[7] Appendix 16.
[8] Appendix 17.
[9] Appendices 18 and 19.

Appendices

PART I
STATUTORY MATERIALS

Council Directive 93/104/EC [1993] O.J. L307/18

COUNCIL DIRECTIVE 93/104/EC of 23 November 1993 concerning certain aspects of the organisation of working time

A–01 THE COUNCIL OF THE EUROPEAN UNION,

Having regard to the Treaty establishing the European Community, and in particular Article 118a thereof,

Having regard to the proposal from the Commission,[1]

In cooperation with the European Parliament,[2]

Having regard to the opinion of the Economic and Social Committee,[3]

Whereas Article 118a of the Treaty provides that the Council shall adopt, by means of directives, minimum requirements for encouraging improvements, especially in the working environment, to ensure a better level of protection of the safety and health of workers

Whereas, under the terms of that Article, those directives are to avoid imposing administrative, financial and legal constraints in a way which would hold back the creation and development of small and medium-sized undertakings

Whereas the provisions of Council Directive 89/391/EEC of 12 June 1989 on the introduction of measures to encourage improvements in the safety and health of workers at work[4] are fully applicable to the areas covered by this Directive without prejudice to more stringent and/or specific provisions contained therein

Whereas the Community Charter of the Fundamental Social Rights of Workers, adopted at the meeting of the European Council held at Strasbourg on 9 December 1989 by the Heads of State or of Government of 11 Member States, and in particular points 7, first subparagraph, 8 and 19, first subparagraph, thereof, declared that:

"7. The completion of the internal market must lead to an improvement in the living and working conditions of workers in the European Community. This process must result from an approximation of these conditions while the improvement is being maintained, as regards in particular the duration and organisation of working time and forms of employment other than open-ended contracts, such as fixed-term contracts, part-time working, temporary work and seasonal work.

8. Every worker in the European Community shall have a right to a weekly rest period and to annual paid leave, the duration of which must be progressively harmonised in accordance with national practices.

---

[1] [1990] O.J. C254/4.
[2] [1991] O.J. C72/95 and Decision of 27 October 1993 (not yet published in the Official Journal).
[3] [1991] O.J. C60/26.
[4] [1989] O.J. L183/1.

19. Every worker must enjoy satisfactory health and safety conditions in his working environment. Appropriate measures must be taken in order to achieve further harmonisation of conditions in this area while maintaining the improvements made.";

Whereas the improvement of workers' safety, hygiene and health at work is an objective which should not be subordinated to purely economic considerations

Whereas this Directive is a practical contribution towards creating the social dimension of the internal market

Whereas laying down minimum requirements with regard to the organisation of working time is likely to improve the working conditions of workers in the Community

Whereas, in order to ensure the safety and health of Community workers, the latter must be granted minimum daily, weekly and annual periods of rest and adequate breaks whereas it is also necessary in this context to place a maximum limit on weekly working hours

Whereas account should be taken of the principles of the International Labour Organisation with regard to the organisation of working time, including those relating to night work

Whereas, with respect to the weekly rest period, due account should be taken of the diversity of cultural, ethnic, religious and other factors in the Member States whereas, in particular, it is ultimately for each Member State to decide whether Sunday should be included in the weekly rest period, and if so to what extent

Whereas research has shown that the human body is more sensitive at night to environmental disturbances and also to certain burdensome forms of work organisation and that long periods of night work can be detrimental to the health of workers and can endanger safety at the workplace

Whereas there is a need to limit the duration of periods of night work, including overtime, and to provide for employers who regularly use night workers to bring this information to the attention of the competent authorities if they so request

Whereas it is important that night workers should be entitled to a free health assessment prior to their assignment and thereafter at regular intervals and that whenever possible they should be transferred to day work for which they are suited if they suffer from health problems

Whereas the situation of night and shift workers requires that the level of safety and health protection should be adapted to the nature of their work and that the organisation and functioning of protection and prevention services and resources should be efficient

Whereas specific working conditions may have detrimental effects on the safety and health of workers whereas the organisation of work according to a certain pattern must take account of the general principle of adapting work to the worker

Whereas, given the specific nature of the work concerned, it may be necessary to adopt separate measures with regard to the organisation of working time in certain sectors or activities which are excluded from the scope of this Directive

Whereas, in view of the question likely to be raised by the organisation of working time within an undertaking, it appears desirable to provide for flexibility in the application of certain provisions of this Directive, whilst ensuring compliance with the principles of protecting the safety and health of workers

Whereas it is necessary to provide that certain provisions may be subject to derogations implemented, according to the case, by the Member States or the two sides of industry whereas, as a general rule, in the event of a derogation, the workers concerned must be given equivalent compensatory rest periods,

HAS ADOPTED THIS DIRECTIVE:

SECTION 1: SCOPE AND DEFINITIONS

Article 1

Purpose and scope

A–02

1. This Directive lays down minimum safety and health requirements for the organisation of working time.

2.   This Directive applies to:

    (a)   minimum periods of daily rest, weekly rest and annual leave, to breaks and maximum weekly working time and

    (b)   certain aspects of night work, shift work and patterns of work.

3.   This Directive shall apply to all sectors of activity, both public and private, within the meaning of Article 2 of Directive 89/391/EEC, without prejudice to Article 17 of this Directive, with the exception of air, rail, road, sea, inland waterway and lake transport, sea fishing, other work at sea and the activities of doctors in training

4.   The provisions of Directive 89/391/EEC are fully applicable to the matters referred to in paragraph 2, without prejudice to more stringent and/or specific provisions contained in this Directive.

Article 2

Definitions

A–03   For the purposes of this Directive, the following definitions shall apply:

1.   working time shall mean any period during which the worker is working, at the employer's disposal and carrying out his activity or duties, in accordance with national laws and/or practice

2.   rest period shall mean any period which is not working time

3.   night time shall mean any period of not less than seven hours, as defined by national law, and which must include in any case the period between midnight and 5 a.m.;

4.   night worker shall mean:

    (a)   on the one hand, any worker, who, during night time, works at least three hours of his daily working time as a normal course and

    (b)   on the other hand, any worker who is likely during night time to work a certain proportion of his annual working time, as defined at the choice of the Member State concerned:

        (i)   by national legislation, following consultation with the two sides of industry or

        (ii) by collective agreements or agreements concluded between the two sides of industry at national or regional level

5.   shift work shall mean any method of organising work in shifts whereby workers succeed each other at the same work stations according to a certain pattern, including a rotating pattern, and which may be continuous or discontinuous, entailing the need for workers to work at different times over a given period of days or weeks

6.   shift worker shall mean any worker whose work schedule is part of shift work.

Section II: Minimum Rest Periods—Other Aspects of the Organisation of Working Time

Article 3

Daily rest

A–04   Member States shall take the measures necessary to ensure that every worker is entitled to a minimum daily rest period of 11 consecutive hours per 24-hour period.

Article 4

Breaks

A–05   Member States shall take the measures necessary to ensure that, where the working day is longer than six hours, every worker is entitled to a rest break, the details of which, including duration and the terms on which it is granted, shall be laid down in collective agreements or agreements between the two sides of industry or, failing that, by national legislation.

Article 5

Weekly rest period

A–06   Member States shall take the measures necessary to ensure that, per each seven-day period, every worker is entitled to a minimum uninterrupted rest period of 24 hours plus the 11 hours' daily rest referred to in Article 3.

The minimum rest period referred to in the first subparagraph shall in principle include Sunday.

If objective, technical or work organisation conditions so justify, a minimum rest period of 24 hours may be applied.

Article 6

Maximum weekly working time

A–07   Member States shall take the measures necessary to ensure that, in keeping with the need to protect the safety and health of workers:

1.   the period of weekly working time is limited by means of laws, Regulations or administrative provisions or by collective agreements or agreements between the two sides of industry

2.   the average working time for each seven-day period, including overtime, does not exceed 48 hours.

Article 7

Annual leave

A–08

1.   Member States shall take the measures necessary to ensure that every worker is entitled to paid annual leave of at least four weeks in accordance with the conditions for entitlement to, and granting of, such leave laid down by national legislation and/or practice.

2.   The minimum period of paid annual leave may not be replaced by an allowance in lieu, except where the employment relationship is terminated.

SECTION III: NIGHT WORK—SHIFT WORK—PATTERNS OF WORK

Article 8

Length of night work

A–09   Member States shall take the measures necessary to ensure that:

1.   normal hours of work for night workers do not exceed an average of eight hours in any 24-hour period

2.   night workers whose work involves special hazards or heavy physical or mental strain do not work more than eight hours in any period of 24 hours during which they perform night work.

      For the purposes of the aforementioned, work involving special hazards or heavy physical or mental strain shall be defined by national legislation and/or practice or by collective agreements or agreements concluded between the two sides of industry, taking account of the specific effects and hazards of night work.

Article 9

Health assessment and transfer of night workers to day work

A–10

1.   Member States shall take the measures necessary to ensure that:

     (a)   night workers are entitled to a free health assessment before their assignment and thereafter at regular intervals

     (b)   night workers suffering from health problems recognised as being connected with the fact that they perform night work are transferred whenever possible to day work to which they are suited.

2.   The free health assessment referred to in paragraph 1(a) must comply with medical confidentiality.

3.   The free health assessment referred to in paragraph 1(a) may be conducted within the national health system.

Article 10

Guarantees for night-time working

A–11   Member States may make the work of certain categories of night workers subject to certain guarantees, under conditions laid down by national legislation and/or practice, in the case of workers who incur risks to their safety or health linked to night-time working.

Article 11

Notification of regular use of night workers

A–12   Member States shall take the measures necessary to ensure that an employer who regularly uses night workers brings this information to the attention of the competent authorities if they so request.

Article 12

Safety and health protection

A–13   Member States shall take the measures necessary to ensure that:

1.   night workers and shift workers have safety and health protection appropriate to the nature of their work

2.   appropriate protection and prevention services or facilities with regard to the safety and health of night workers and shift workers are equivalent to those applicable to other workers and are available at all times.

Article 13

Pattern of work

A–14   Member States shall take the measures necessary to ensure that an employer who intends to organise work according to a certain pattern takes account of the general principle of adapting work to the worker, with a view, in particular, to alleviating monotonous work and work at a predetermined work-rate, depending on the type of activity, and of safety and health requirements, especially as regards breaks during working time.

SECTION IV: MISCELLANEOUS PROVISIONS

Article 14

More specific Community provisions

A–15   The provisions of this Directive shall not apply where other Community instruments contain more specific requirements concerning certain occupations or occupational activities.

Article 15

More favourable provisions

A–16   This Directive shall not affect Member States' right to apply or introduce laws, Regulations or administrative provisions more favourable to the protection of the safety and health of workers or to facilitate or permit the application of collective agreements or agreements concluded between the two sides of industry which are more favourable to the protection of the safety and health of workers.

Article 16

Reference periods

A–17   Member States may lay down:

1.   for the application of Article 5 (weekly rest period), a reference period not exceeding 14 days

2.   for the application of Article 6 (maximum weekly working time), a reference period not exceeding four months.
     The periods of paid annual leave, granted in accordance with Article 7, and the periods of sick leave shall not be included or shall be neutral in the calculation of the average

3.   for the application of Article 8 (length of night work), a reference period defined after consultation of the two sides of industry or by collective agreements or agreements concluded between the two sides of industry at national or regional level.
     If the minimum weekly rest period of 24 hours required by Article 5 falls within that reference period, it shall not be included in the calculation of the average.

Article 17

Derogations

A–18

1.   With due regard for the general principles of the protection of the safety and health of workers, Member States may derogate from Article 3, 4, 5, 6, 8 or 16 when, on account of the specific characteristics of the activity concerned, the duration of the working time is not measured and/or predetermined or can be determined by the workers themselves, and particularly in the case of:

     (a)   managing executives or other persons with autonomous decision-taking powers
     (b)   family workers or
     (c)   workers officiating at religious ceremonies in churches and religious communities.

2.   Derogations may be adopted by means of laws, Regulations or administrative provisions or by means of collective agreements or agreements between the two sides of industry provided that the workers concerned are afforded equivalent periods of compensatory rest or that, in exceptional cases in which it is not possible, for objective reasons, to grant such equivalent periods of compensatory rest, the workers concerned are afforded appropriate protection:

2.1. from Articles 3, 4, 5, 8 and 16:

(a)   in the case of activities where the worker's place of work and his place of residence are distant from one another or where the workers' different places of work are distant from one another
(b)   in the case of security and surveillance activities requiring a permanent presence in order to protect property and persons, particularly security guards and caretakers or security firms
(c)   In the case of activities involving the need for continuity of service or production, particularly:

(i)   services relating to the reception, treatment and/or care provided by hospitals or similar establishments, residential institutions and prisons
(ii)   dock or airport workers
(iii)   press, radio, television, cinematographic production, postal and telecommunications services, ambulance, fire and civil protection services
(iv)   gas, water and electricity production, transmission and distribution, household refuse collection and incineration plants
(v)   industries in which work cannot be interrupted on technical grounds
(vi)   research and development activities
(vii)   agriculture

(d)   where there is a foreseeable surge of activity, particularly in:

(i)   agriculture
(ii)   tourism
(iii)   postal services

2.2. from Articles 3, 4, 5, 8 and 16:

(a)   in the circumstances described in Article 5(4) of Directive 89/391/EEC;
(b)   in cases of accident or imminent risk of accident

2.3. from Articles 3 and 5:

(a)   in the case of shift work activities, each time the worker changes shift and cannot take daily and/or weekly rest periods between the end of one shift and the start of the next one
(b)   in the case of activities involving periods of work split up over the day, particularly those of cleaning staff.

3.   Derogations may be made from Articles 3, 4, 5, 8 and 16 by means of collective agreements or agreements concluded between the two sides of industry at national or regional level or, in conformity with the rules laid down by them, by means of collective agreements or agreements concluded between the two sides of industry at a lower level.
      Member States in which there is no statutory system ensuring the conclusion of collective agreements or agreements concluded between the two sides of industry at national or regional level, on the matters covered by this Directive, or those Member States in which there is a specific legislative framework for this purpose and within the limits thereof, may, in accordance with national legislation and/or practice, allow derogations from Articles 3, 4, 5, 8 and 16 by way of collective agreements or agreements concluded between the two sides of industry at the appropriate collective level.
      The derogations provided for in the first and second subparagraphs shall be allowed on condition that equivalent compensating rest periods are granted to the

workers concerned or, in exceptional cases where it is not possible for objective reasons to grant such periods, the workers concerned are afforded appropriate protection.

Member States may lay down rules:

— for the application of this paragraph by the two sides of industry, and
— for the extension of the provisions of collective agreements or agreements concluded in conformity with this paragraph to other workers in accordance with national legislation and/or practice.

4. The option to derogate from point 2 of Article 16, provided in paragraph 2, points 2.1. and 2.2. and in paragraph 3 of this Article, may not result in the establishment of a reference period exceeding six months.

However, Member States shall have the option, subject to compliance with the general principles relating to the protection of the safety and health of workers, of allowing, for objective or technical reasons or reasons concerning the organisation of work, collective agreements or agreements concluded between the two sides of industry to set reference periods in no event exceeding 12 months.

Before the expiry of a period of seven years from the date referred to in Article 18(1)(a), the Council shall, on the basis of a Commission proposal accompanied by an appraisal report, re-examine the provisions of this paragraph and decide what action to take.

Article 18

Final provisions

A–19

1. (a) Member States shall adopt the laws, Regulations and administrative provisions necessary to comply with this Directive by 23 November 1996, or shall ensure by that date that the two sides of industry establish the necessary measures by agreement, with Member States being obliged to take any necessary steps to enable them to guarantee at all times that the provisions laid down by this Directive are fulfilled.

(b) (i) However, a Member State shall have the option not to apply Article 6, while respecting the general principles of the protection of the safety and health of workers, and provided it takes the necessary measures to ensure that:

— no employer requires a worker to work more than 48 hours over a seven-day period, calculated as an average for the reference period referred to in point 2 of Article 16, unless he has first obtained the worker's agreement to perform such work,
— no worker is subjected to any detriment by his employer because he is not willing to give his agreement to perform such work,
— the employer keeps up-to-date records of all workers who carry out such work,
— the records are placed at the disposal of the competent authorities, which may, for reasons connected with the safety and/or health of workers, prohibit or restrict the possibility of exceeding the maximum weekly working hours,
— the employer provides the competent authorities at their request with information on cases in which agreement has been given by workers to perform work exceeding 48 hours over a period of seven days, calculated as an average for the reference period referred to in point 2 of Article 16.

Before the expiry of a period of seven years from the date referred to in (a), the Council shall, on the basis of a Commission proposal accompanied by an appraisal report, re-examine the provisions of this point (i) and decide on what action to take.

(ii) Similarly, Member States shall have the option, as regards the application of Article 7, of making use of a transitional period of not more than three years from the date referred to in (a), provided that during that transitional period:

— every worker receives three weeks' paid annual leave in accordance with the conditions for the entitlement to, and granting of, such leave laid down by national legislation and/or practice, and
— the three-week period of paid annual leave may not be replaced by an allowance in lieu, except where the employment relationship is terminated.

(c)   Member States shall forthwith inform the Commission thereof.

2.   When Member States adopt the measures referred to in paragraph 1, they shall contain a reference to this Directive or shall be accompanied by such reference on the occasion of their official publication. The methods of making such a reference shall be laid down by the Member States.

3.   Without prejudice to the right of Member States to develop, in the light of changing circumstances, different legislative, regulatory or contractual provisions in the field of working time, as long as the minimum requirements provided for in this Directive are complied with, implementation of this Directive shall not constitute valid grounds for reducing the general level of protection afforded to workers.

4.   Member States shall communicate to the Commission the texts of the provisions of national law already adopted or being adopted in the field governed by this Directive.

5.   Member States shall report to the Commission every five years on the practical implementation of the provisions of this Directive, indicating the viewpoints of the two sides of industry.

The Commission shall inform the European Parliament, the Council, the Economic and Social Committee and the Advisory Committe on Safety, Hygiene and Health Protection at Work thereof.

6.   Every five years the Commission shall submit to the European Parliament, the Council and the Economic and Social Committee a report on the application of this Directive taking into account paragraphs 1, 2, 3, 4 and 5.

Article 19

A–20   This Directive is addressed to the Member States.

Done at Brussels, 23 November 1993.

For the Council

The President

M. SMET

Council Directive 1999/63/EC
[1999] O.J. L167/33

COUNCIL DIRECTIVE 1999/63/EC of 21 June 1999 concerning the Agreement on the organisation of working time of seafarers concluded by the European Community Shipowners' Association (ECSA) and the Federation of Transport Workers' Unions in the European Union (FST).

A–21   THE COUNCIL OF THE EUROPEAN UNION,

Having regard to the Treaty establishing the European Community, and, in particular Article 139(2) thereof,

Having regard to the proposal from the Commission,

Whereas:

(1)   following the entry into force of the Treaty of Amsterdam, the provisions of the Agreement on social policy annexed to the Protocol 14 on social policy, annexed to the Treaty establishing the European Community, as amended by the Treaty of Maastricht, have been incorporated into Articles 136 to 139 of the Treaty establishing the European Community

(2)   management and labour ("the social partners"), may in accordance with Article 139(2) of the Treaty, request jointly that agreement at Community level be implemented by a Council decision on a proposal from the Commission

(3)   the Council adopted Directive 93/104/EC of 23 November 1993 concerning certain aspects of the organisation of working time[1]; whereas sea transport was one of the sectors of activity excluded from the scope of that Directive

(4)   account should be taken of the relevant Conventions of the International Labour Organisation with regard to the organisation of working time, including in particular those relating to the hours of work of seafarers

(5)   the Commission, in accordance with Article 3(2) of the Agreement on social policy, has consulted management and labour on the possible direction of Community action with regard to the sectors and activities excluded from Directive 93/104/EC;

(6)   after that consultation the Commission considered that Community action was desirable in that area, and once again consulted management and labour at Community level on the substance of the envisaged proposal in accordance with Article 3(3) of the said Agreement

(7)   the European Community Shipowners' Association (ECSA) and the Federation of Transport Workers' Unions in the European Union (FST) informed the Commission of their desire to enter into negotiations in accordance with Article 4 of the Agreement on social policy

(8)   the said organisations concluded, on 30 September 1998, an Agreement on the working time of seafarers this Agreement contains a joint request to the Commission to implement the Agreement by a Council decision on a proposal from the Commission, in accordance with Article 4(2) of the Agreement on social policy

---

[1] [1993] O.J. L307/18.

(9) the Council, in its resolution of 6 December 1994 on certain aspects for a European Union social policy: a contribution to economic and social convergence in the Union[2] asked management and labour to make use of the opportunities for concluding agreements, since they are close to social reality and to social problems

(10) the Agreement applies to seafarers on board every seagoing ship, whether publicly or privately owned, which is registered in the territory of any Member State and is ordinarily engaged in commercial maritime operations

(11) the proper instrument for implementing the Agreement is a Directive within the meaning of Article 249 of the Treaty it therefore binds the Member States as to the result to be achieved, whilst leaving national authorities the choice of form and methods

(12) in accordance with the principles of subsidiarity and proportionality as set out in Article 5 of the Treaty, the objectives of this Directive cannot be sufficiently achieved by the Member States and can therefore be better achieved by the Community this Directive does not go beyond what is necessary for the attainment of those objectives

(13) with regard to terms used in the Agreement which are not specifically defined therein, this Directive leaves Member States free to define those terms in accordance with national law and practice, as is the case for other social policy Directives using similar terms, providing that those definitions respect the content of the Agreement

(14) the Commission has drafted its proposal for a Directive, in accordance with its communication of 20 May 1998 on adapting and promoting the social dialogue at Community level, taking into account the representative status of the signatory parties and the legality of each clause of the Agreement

(15) the Commission informed the European Parliament and the Economic and Social Committee, in accordance with its communication of 14 December 1993 concerning the application of the Agreement on social policy, by sending them the text of its proposal for a Directive containing the Agreement

(16) the implementation of the Agreement contributes to achieving the objectives under Article 136 of the Treaty,

HAS ADOPTED THIS DIRECTIVE:

Article 1

A–22   The purpose of this Directive is to put into effect the Agreement on the organisation of working time of seafarers concluded on 30 September 1998 between the organisations representing management and labour in the maritime sector (ECSA and FST) as set out in the Annex hereto.

Article 2

Minimum requirements

A–23
1. Member States may maintain or introduce more favourable provisions than those laid down in this Directive.

2. The implementation of this Directive shall under no circumstances constitute sufficient grounds for justifying a reduction in the general level of protection of workers in the fields covered by this Directive. This shall be without prejudice to the rights of Member States and/or management and labour to lay down, in the light of

---

[2] [1994] O.J. C368/6.

changing circumstances, different legislative, regulatory or contractual arrangements to those prevailing at the time of the adoption of this Directive, provided always that the minimum requirements laid down in this Directive are adhered to.

Article 3

Transposition

A–24

1. Member States shall bring into force the laws, Regulations and administrative provisions necessary to comply with this Directive by 30 June 2002, or shall ensure that, by that date at the latest, management and labour have introduced the necessary measures by agreement, the Member States being required to take any necessary measure to enable them at any time to be in a position to guarantee the results imposed by this Directive. They shall forthwith inform the Commission thereof.

2. When Member States adopt the provisions referred to in the first paragraph, these shall contain a reference to this Directive or shall be accompanied by such reference at the time of their official publication. The methods of making such reference shall be laid down by the Member States.

Article 4

Addressees

A–25   This Directive is addressed to the Member States.

Done at Luxembourg, 21 June 1999.

For the Council

The President

L. SCHOMERUS

ANNEX

A–26   EUROPEAN AGREEMENT

on the organisation of working time of seafarers

Having regard to the Agreement on social policy annexed to the Protocol on social policy attached to the Treaty establishing the European Community and in particular Articles 3(4) and 4(2) thereof

Whereas Article 4(2) of the Agreement on social policy provides that agreements concluded at European level may be implemented at the joint request of the signatory parties by a Council Decision on a proposal from the Commission

Whereas the signatory parties hereby make such a request,

THE SIGNATORY PARTIES HAVE AGREED THE FOLLOWING:

Clause 1

A–27

1. The Agreement applies to seafarers on board every seagoing ship, whether publicly or privately owned, which is registered in the territory of any Member State and is ordinarily engaged in commercial maritime operations. For the purpose of this Agreement a ship that is on the register of two States is deemed to be registered in the territory of the State whose flag it flies.

2.   In the event of doubt as to whether or not any ships are to be regarded as seagoing ships or engaged in commercial maritime operations for the purpose of the Agreement, the question shall be determined by the competent authority of the Member State. The organisations of shipowners and seafarers concerned should be consulted.

Clause 2

A–28   For the purpose of the Agreement:

(a)   the term "hours of work" means time during which a seafarer is required to do work on account of the ship

(b)   the term "hours of rest" means time outside hours of work this term does not include short breaks

(c)   the term "seafarer" means any person who is employed or engaged in any capacity on board a seagoing ship to which the Agreement applies

(d)   the term "shipowner" means the owner of the ship or any other organisation or person, such as the manager or bareboat charterer, who has assumed the responsibility for the operation of the ship from the shipowner and who on assuming such responsibility has agreed to take over all the attendant duties and responsibilities.

Clause 3

A–29   Within the limits set out in Clause 5, there shall be fixed either a maximum number of hours of work which shall not be exceeded in a given period of time, or a minimum number of hours of rest which shall be provided in a given period of time.

Clause 4

A–30   Without prejudice to Clause 5, the normal working hours' standard of seafarer is, in principle, based on an eight-hour day with one day of rest per week and rest on public holidays. Member States may have procedures to authorise or register a collective agreement which determines seafarers' normal working hours on a basis on less favourable than this standard.

Clause 5

A–31

1.   The limits on hours of work or rest shall be either:

(a)   maximum hours of work which shall not exceed

(i) fourteen hours in any 24-hour period and
(ii) 72 hour in any seven-day period or

(b)   minimum hours of rest which shall not be less than:

(i) ten hours in any 24-hour period and
(ii) 72 hours in any seven-day period.

2.   Hours of rest may be divided into no more than two periods, one of which shall be at least six hours in length and the interval between consecutive periods of rest shall not exceed 14 hours.

3.   Musters, fire-fighting and lifeboat drills, and prescribed by national laws and Regulations and by international instruments shall be conducted in a manner that minimises the disturbance of rest periods and does not induce fatigue.

4.   In respect of situations when a seafarer is on call, such as when a machinery space is unattended, the seafarer shall have an adequate compensatory rest period if the normal period of rest is disturbed by call-outs to work.

5.   With regard to paragraphs 3 and 4, where no collective agreement or arbitration award exists or if the competent authority determines that the provisions in the

agreement or award are inadequate, it would be for the competent autority to determine such provisions to ensure that the seafarers concerned have sufficient rest.

6. With due regard for the general principles of the protection of the health and safety of workers, Member States may have national laws, Regulations or a procedure for the competent authority to authorise or register collective agreements permitting exceptions to the limits set out in paragraphs 1 and 2. Such exceptions shall, as far as possible, follow the standards set out but may take account of more frequent or longer leave periods, or the granting of compensatory leave for watchkeeping seafarers or seafarers working on board ship on short voyages.

7. A table shall be posted, in an easily accessible place, with the shipboard working arrangements, which shall contain for every position at least:

   (a) the schedule of service at sea and service in port and
   (b) the maximum hours of work or the minimum hours of rest required by the laws, Regulations or collective agreements in force in the Member States.

8. The table referred to in paragraph 7 shall be established in a standardised format in the working language or languages of the ship and in English.

Clause 6

A–32 No seafarer under 18 years of age shall work at night. For the purpose of this Clause, "night" means a period of at least nine consecutive hours, including the interval from midnight to five a.m. This provision need not be applied when the effective training of young seafarers between the ages of 16 and 18 in accordance with established programmes and schedules would be impaired.

Clause 7

A–33
1. The master of a ship shall have the right to require a seafarer to perform any hours of work necessary for the immediate safety of the ship, persons on board or cargo, or for the purpose of giving assistance to other ships or persons in distress at sea.

2. In accordance with paragraph 1, the master may suspend the schedule of hours of work or hours or rest and require a seafarer to perform any hours or work necessary until the normal situation has been restored.

3. As soon as practicable after the normal situation has been restored, the master shall ensure that any seafarers who have performed work in a scheduled rest period are provided with an adequate period of rest.

Clause 8

A–34
1. Records of seafarers' daily hours of work or of their daily hours of rest shall be maintained to allow monitoring of compliance with the provisions set out in Clause 5. The seafarer shall receive a copy of the records pertaining to him or her which shall be endorsed by the master, or a person authorised by the master, and by the seafarer.

2. Procedures shall be determined for keeping such records on board, including the intervals at which the information shall be recorded. The format of the records of the seafarers' hours of work or of their hours of rest shall be established taking into account any available international guidelines. The format shall be established in the language provided by Clause 5, paragraph 8.

3. A copy of the relevant provisions of the national legislation pertaining to this Agreement and the relevant collective agreements shall be kept on board and be easily accessible to the crew.

Clause 9

A–35 The records referred to in Clause 8 shall be examined and endorsed at appropriate intervals, to monitor compliance with the provisions governing hours of work or hours of rest tht give effect to this Agreement.

Clause 10

A–36
1. When determining, approving or revising manning levels, it is necessary to take into account the need to avoid or minimise, as far as practicable, excessive hours of work, to ensure sufficient rest and to limit fatigue.

2. If the records or other evidence indicate infringement of provisions governing hours of work or hours of rest, measures, including if necessary the revision of the manning of the ship, shall be taken so as to avoid future infringements.

3. All ships to which this Agreement applies shall be sufficiently, safely and efficiently manned, in accordance with the minimum safe manning document or an equivalent issued by the competent authority.

Clause 11

A–37 No person under 16 years or age shall work on a ship.

Clause 12

A–38 The shipowner shall provide the master with the necessary resources for the purpose of compliance with obligations under this Agreement, including those relating to the appropriate manning of the ship. The master shall take all necessary steps to ensure that the requirements on seafarers' hours of work and rest arising from this Agreement are complied with.

Clause 13

A–39
1. All seafarers shall possess a certificate attesting to their fitness for the work for which they are to be employed at sea.

   The nature of the health assessment to be made and the particulars to be included in the medical certificate shall be established after consultation with the shipowners and seafarers organisations concerned.

   All seafarers shall have regular health assessments. Watchkeepers suffering from health problems certified by a medical practitioner as being due to the fact that they perform night work shall be transferred, wherever possible, to day work to which they are suited.

2. The health assessment referred to in paragraph 1 shall be free and comply with medical confidentiality. Such health assessments may be conducted within the national health system.

Clause 14

A–40 Shipowners shall provide information on watchkeepers and other night workers to the national competent authority if they so request.

Clause 15

A–41 Seafarers shall have safety and health protection appropriate to the nature of their work. Equivalent protection and prevention services or facilities with regard to the safety and health of seafarers working by day or by night shall be available.

Clause 16

A–42 Every seafarer shall be entitled to paid annual leave of at least four weeks, or a proportion thereof for periods of employment of less than one year, in accordance with the conditions for entitlement to, and granting of, such leave laid down by national legislation and/or practice.

The minimum period of paid annual leave may not be replaced by an allowance in lieu, except where the employment relationship is terminated.

Brussels, 30 September 1998.

Federation of Transport Workers' Unions in the European Union (FST)

European Community Shipowners' Association (ECSA)

The Working Time Regulations 1998 No. 1833

Made: July 30, 1998

Laid before Parliament: July 30, 1998

Coming into force: October 1, 1998

A–43 The Secretary of State, being a Minister designated for the purposes of section 2(2) of the European Communities Act 1972 in relation to measures relating to the organisation of working time[1] and measures relating to the employment of children and young persons,[2] in exercise of the powers conferred on him by that provision hereby makes the following Regulations—

PART I

GENERAL

1. Citation, commencement and extent

A–44

(1) These Regulations may be cited as the Working Time Regulations 1998 and shall come into force on 1st October 1998.

(2) These Regulations extend to Great Britain only.

2. Interpretation

A–45

(1) In these Regulations—

"the 1996 Act" means the Employment Rights Act 1996;
"adult worker" means a worker who has attained the age of 18;
"the armed forces" means any of the naval, military and air forces of the Crown;
"calendar year" means the period of twelve months beginning with 1st January in any year;
"the civil protection services" includes the police, fire brigades and ambulance services, the security and intelligence services, customs and immigration officers, the prison service, the coastguard, and lifeboat crew and other voluntary rescue services;
"collective agreement" means a collective agreement within the meaning of section 178 of the Trade Union and Labour Relations (Consolidation) Act 1992, the trade union parties to which are independent trade unions within the meaning of section 5 of that Act;
"day" means a period of 24 hours beginning at midnight;
"employer", in relation to a worker, means the person by whom the worker is (or, where the employment has ceased, was) employed;
"employment", in relation to a worker, means employment under his contract, and "employed" shall be construed accordingly;
"night time", in relation to a worker, means a period—

---

[1] S.I. 1997/1174.
[2] S.I. 1996/266.

(a) the duration of which is not less than seven hours, and
(b) which includes the period between midnight and 5 a.m.,

which is determined for the purposes of these Regulations by a relevant agreement, or, in default of such a determination, the period between 11 p.m. and 6 a.m.;
"night work" means work during night time;
"night worker" means a worker—

(a) who, as a normal course, works at least three hours of his daily working time during night time, or
(b) who is likely, during night time, to work at least such proportion of his annual working time as may be specified for the purposes of these Regulations in a collective agreement or a workforce agreement;

and, for the purpose of paragraph (a) of this definition, a person works hours as a normal course (without prejudice to the generality of that expression) if he works such hours on the majority of days on which he works;
"relevant agreement", in relation to a worker, means a workforce agreement which applies to him, any provision of a collective agreement which forms part of a contract between him and his employer, or any other agreement in writing which is legally enforceable as between the worker and his employer;
"relevant training" means work experience provided pursuant to a training course or programme, training for employment, or both, other than work experience or training—

(a) the immediate provider of which is an educational institution or a person whose main business is the provision of training, and
(b) which is provided on a course run by that institution or person;

"rest period", in relation to a worker, means a period which is not working time, other than a rest break or leave to which the worker is entitled under these Regulations;
"worker" means an individual who has entered into or works under (or, where the employment has ceased, worked under)—

(a) a contract of employment; or
(b) any other contract, whether express or implied and (if it is express) whether oral or in writing, whereby the individual undertakes to do or perform personally any work or services for another party to the contract whose status is not by virtue of the contract that of a client or customer of any profession or business undertaking carried on by the individual;

and any reference to a worker's contract shall be construed accordingly;
"worker employed in agriculture" has the same meaning as in the Agricultural Wages Act 1948 or the Agricultural Wages (Scotland) Act 1949, and a reference to a worker partly employed in agriculture is to a worker employed in agriculture whose employer also employs him for non-agricultural purposes;
"workforce agreement" means an agreement between an employer and workers employed by him or their representatives in respect of which the conditions set out in Schedule 1 to these Regulations are satisfied;
"working time", in relation to a worker, means—

(a) any period during which he is working, at his employer's disposal and carrying out his activity or duties,
(b) any period during which he is receiving relevant trainng, and
(c) any additional period which is to be treated as working time for the purpose of these Regulations under a relevant agreement;

and "work" shall be construed accordingly;
"Working Time Directive" means Council Directive 93/104/EC of 23rd November 1993 concerning certain aspects of the organisation of working time;
"young worker" means a worker who has attained the age of 15 but not the age of 18 and who, as respects England and Wales, is over compulsory school age (construed in accordance with section 8 of the Education Act 1996) and, as respects Scotland, is over school age (construed in accordance with section 31 of the Education (Scotland) Act 1980), and

"Young Workers Directive" means Council Directive 94/33/EC of 22nd June 1994 on the protection of young people at work.

(2) In the absence of a definition in these Regulations, words and expressions used in particular provisions which are also used in corresponding provisions of the Working Time Directive or the Young Workers Directive have the same meaning as they have in those corresponding provisions.

(3) In these Regulations—

(a) a reference to a numbered Regulation is to the Regulation in these Regulations bearing that number;

(b) a reference in a Regulation to a numbered paragraph is to the paragraph in that Regulation bearing that number; and

(c) a reference in a paragraph to a lettered sub-paragraph is to the sub-paragraph in that paragraph bearing that letter.

PART II

RIGHTS AND OBLIGATIONS CONCERNING WORKING TIME

3. General

A–46

The provisions of this Part have effect subject to the exceptions provided for in Part III of these Regulations.

4. Maximum weekly working time

A–47

(1) [Unless his employer has first obtained the worker's agreement in writing to perform such work],[3] a worker's working time, including overtime, in any reference period which is applicable in his case shall not exceed an average of 48 hours for each seven days.

(2) An employer shall take all reasonable steps, in keeping with the need to protect the health and safety of workers, to ensure that the limit specified in paragraph (1) is complied with in the case of each worker employed by him in relation to whom it applies [and shall keep up-to-date records of all workers who carry out work to which it does not apply by reason of the fact that the employer has obtained the worker's agreement as mentioned in paragraph (1)].[4]

(3) Subject to paragraphs (4) and (5) and any agreement under Regulation 23(b), the reference periods which apply in the case of a worker are—

(a) where a relevant agreement provides for the application of this Regulation in relation to successive periods of 17 weeks, each such period, or

(b) in any other case, any period of 17 weeks in the course of his employment.

(4) Where a worker has worked for his employer for less than 17 weeks, the reference period applicable in his case is the period that has elapsed since he started work for his employer.

(5) Paragraphs (3) and (4) shall apply to a worker who is excluded from the scope of certain provisions of these Regulations by Regulation 21 as if for each reference to 17 weeks there were substituted a reference to 26 weeks.

(6) For the purposes of this Regulation, a worker's average working time for each seven days during a reference period shall be determined according to the formula—

$$\frac{(A + B)}{C}$$

---

[3] Words substituted by S.I. 1999/3372 (Working Time Regulations, Regulation 3 (1)(a)).
[4] Words substituted by S.I. 1999/3371 (Working Time Regulations, Regulation 3(1)(b)).

where—

A is the aggregate number of hours comprised in the worker's working time during the course of the reference period;

B is the aggregate number of hours comprised in his working time during the course of the period beginning immediately after the end of the reference period and ending when the number of days in that subsequent period on which he has worked equals the number of excluded days during the reference period; and

C is the number of weeks in the reference period.

(7) In paragraph (6), "excluded days" means days comprised in—

(a) any period of annual leave taken by the worker in exercise of his entitlement under Regulation 13;

(b) any period of sick leave taken by the worker;

(c) any period of maternity leave taken by the worker; and

(d) any period in respect of which the limit specified in paragraph (1) did not apply in relation to the worker [by reason of the fact that the employer has obtained the worker's agreement as mentioned in paragraph (1)].[5]

5. Agreement to exclude the maximum

A–48

[. . .][6]

(2) An agreement for the purposes of [regulation 4][7]—

(a) may either relate to a specified period or apply indefinitely; and

(b) subject to any provision in the agreement for a different period of notice, shall be terminable by the worker by giving not less than seven days' notice to his employer in writing.

(3) Where an agreement for the purposes of [regulation 4][8] makes provision for the termination of the agreement after a period of notice, the notice period provided for shall not exceed three months.

[. . .][9]

6. Length of night work

A–49

(1) A night worker's normal hours of work in any reference period which is applicable in his case shall not exceed an average of eight hours for each 24 hours.

(2) An employer shall take all reasonable steps, in keeping with the need to protect the health and safety of workers, to ensure that the limit specified in paragraph (1) is complied with in the case of each night worker employed by him.

(3) The reference periods which apply in the case of a night worker are—

(a) where a relevant agreement provides for the application of this Regulation in relation to successive periods of 17 weeks, each such period, or

(b) in any other case, any period of 17 weeks in the course of his employment.

(4) Where a worker has worked for his employer for less than 17 weeks, the reference period applicable in his case is the period that has elapsed since he started work for his employer.

---

[5] Words substituted by S.I. 1999/3372 (Working Time Regulations, Regulation3(1)(c)).
[6] Paragraph (1) repealed by S.I. 1999/3372 (Working Time Regulations, 3(2)(a)).
[7] Words substituted by S.I. 1999/3372 (Working Time Regulations, 3(2)(b)).
[8] Words substituted by S.I. 1999/3372 (Working Time Regulations, 3(2)(b)).
[9] Paragraph (4) repealed by S.I. 1999/3372 (Working Time Regulations, 3(2)(a)).

(5) For the purposes of this Regulation, a night worker's average normal hours of work for each 24 hours during a reference period shall be determined according to the formula—

$$\frac{A}{B - C}$$

where—

A is the number of hours during the reference period which are normal working hours for that worker;

B is the number of days during the reference period, and

C is the total number of hours during the reference period comprised in rest periods spent by the worker in pursuance of his entitlement under Regulation 11, divided by 24.

(6) A night worker's normal hours of work for the purposes of this Regulation are his normal working hours for the purposes of the 1996 Act in a case where section 234 of that Act (which provides for the interpretation of normal working hours in the case of certain employees) applies to him.

(7) An employer shall ensure that no night worker employed by him whose work involves special hazards or heavy physical or mental strain works for more than eight hours in any 24-hour period during which the night worker performs night work.

(8) For the purposes of paragraph (7), the work of a night worker shall be regarded as involving special hazards or heavy physical or mental strain if—

    (a)   it is identified as such in—

        (i)   a collective agreement, or

        (ii)   a workforce agreement,

        which takes account of the specific effects and hazards of night work, or

    (b)   it is recognised in a risk assessment made by the employer under [Regulation 3 of the Management of Health and Safety at Work Regulations 1999][10] as involving a significant risk to the health or safety of workers employed by him.

7. Health assessment and transfer of night workers to day work

A–50

(1) An employer—

    (a)   shall not assign an adult worker to work which is to be undertaken during periods such that the worker will become a night worker unless—

        (i)   the employer has ensured that the worker will have the opportunity of a free health assessment before he takes up the assignment; or

        (ii)   the worker had a health assessment before being assigned to work to be undertaken during such periods on an earlier occasion, and the employer has no reason to believe that that assessment is no longer valid, and

    (b)   shall ensure that each night worker employed by him has the opportunity of a free health assessment at regular intervals of whatever duration may be appropriate in his case.

(2) Subject to paragraph (4), an employer—

    (a)   shall not assign a young worker to work during the period between 10 p.m. and 6 a.m. ("the restricted period") unless—

        (i)   the employer has ensured that the young worker will have the opportunity of a free assessment of his health and capacities before he takes up the assignment; or

        (ii)   the young worker had an assessment of his health and capacities before being assigned to work during the restricted period on an earlier occasion, and the employer has no reason to believe that that assessment is no longer valid; and

---

[10] Words substituted by S.I. 1999/3242 (Management of Health and Safety at Work Regulations, Schedule 2, paragraph 1).

(b) shall ensure that each young worker employed by him and assigned to work during the restricted period has the opportunity of a free assessment of his health and capacities at regular intervals of whatever duration may be appropriate in his case.

(3) For the purposes of paragraphs (1) and (2), an assessment is free if it is at no cost to the worker to whom it relates.

(4) The requirements in paragraph (2) do not apply in a case where the work a young worker is assigned to do is of an exceptional nature.

(5) No person shall disclose an assessment made for the purposes of this Regulation to any person other than the worker to whom it relates, unless—

(a) the worker has given his consent in writing to the disclosure, or
(b) the disclosure is confined to a statement that the assessment shows the worker to be fit—

(i) in a case where paragraph (1)(a)(i) or (2)(a)(i) applies, to take up an assignment, or
(ii) in a case where paragraph (1)(b) or (2)(b) applies, to continue to undertake an assignment.

(6) Where—

(a) a registered medical practitioner has advised an employer that a worker employed by the employer is suffering from health problems which the practitioner considers to be connected with the fact that the worker performs night work, and
(b) it is possible for the employer to transfer the worker to work—

(i) to which the worker is suited, and
(ii) which is to be undertaken during periods such that the worker will cease to be a night worker,

the employer shall transfer the worker accordingly.

8. Pattern of work

A–51

Where the pattern according to which the employer organises work is such as to put the health and safety of a worker employed by him at risk, in particular because the work is monotonous or the work-rate is predetermined, the employer shall ensure that the worker is given adequate rest breaks.

9. Records

A–52

An employer shall—

(a) keep records which are adequate to show whether the limits specified in Regulations 4(1) and 6(1) and (7) and the requirements in Regulations 7(1) and (2) are being complied with in the case of each worker employed by him in relation to whom they apply; and
(b) retain such records for two years from the date on which they were made.

10. Daily rest

A–53

(1) An adult worker is entitled to a rest period of not less than eleven consecutive hours in each 24-hour period during which he works for his employer.

(2) Subject to paragraph (3), a young worker is entitled to a rest period of not less than twelve consecutive hours in each 24-hour period during which he works for his employer.

(3) The minimum rest period provided for in paragraph (2) may be interrupted in the case of activities involving periods of work that are split up over the day or of short duration.

11. Weekly rest period

A–54

(1) Subject to paragraph (2), an adult worker is entitled to an uninterrupted rest period of not less than 24 hours in each seven-day period during which he works for his employer.

(2) If his employer so determines, an adult worker shall be entitled to either—

(a) two uninterrupted rest periods each of not less than 24 hours in each 14-day period during which he works for his employer; or
(b) one uninterrupted rest period of not less than 48 hours in each such 14-day period,

in place of the entitlement provided for in paragraph (1).

(3) Subject to paragraph (8), a young worker is entitled to a rest period of not less than 48 hours in each seven-day period during which he works for his employer.

(4) For the purpose of paragraphs (1) to (3), a seven-day period or (as the case may be) 14-day period shall be taken to begin—

(a) at such times on such days as may be provided for for the purposes of this Regulation in a relevant agreement; or
(b) where there are no provisions of a relevant agreement which apply, at the start of each week or (as the case may be) every other week.

(5) In a case where, in accordance with paragraph (4), 14-day periods are to be taken to begin at the start of every other week, the first such period applicable in the case of a particular worker shall be taken to begin—

(a) if the worker's employment began on or before the date on which these Regulations come into force, on 5th October 1998; or
(b) if the worker's employment begins after the date on which these Regulations come into force, at the start of the week in which that employment begins.

(6) For the purposes of paragraphs (4) and (5), a week starts at midnight between Sunday and Monday.

(7) The minimum rest period to which an adult worker is entitled under paragraph (1) or (2) shall not include any part of a rest period to which the worker is entitled under Regulation 10(1), except where this is justified by objective or technical reasons or reasons concerning the organisation of work.

(8) The minimum rest period to which a young worker is entitled under paragraph (3)—

(a) may be interrupted in the case of activities involving periods of work that are split up over the day or are of short duration; and
(b) may be reduced where this is justified by technical or organisation reasons, but not to less than 36 consecutive hours.

12. Rest breaks

A–55

(1) Where an adult worker's daily working time is more than six hours, he is entitled to a rest break.

(2) The details of the rest break to which an adult worker is entitled under paragraph (1), including its duration and the terms on which it is granted, shall be in accordance with any provisions for the purposes of this Regulation which are contained in a collective agreement or a workforce agreement.

(3) Subject to the provisions of any applicable collective agreement or workforce agreement, the rest break provided for in paragraph (1) is an uninterrupted period of not less than 20 minutes, and the worker is entitled to spend it away from his workstation if he has one.

(4) Where a young worker's daily working time is more than four and a half hours, he is entitled to a rest break of at least 30 minutes, which shall be consecutive if possible, and he is entitled to spend it away from his workstation if he has one.

(5) If, on any day, a young worker is employed by more than one employer, his daily working time shall be determined for the purpose of paragraph (4) by aggregating the number of hours worked by him for each employer.

13. Entitlement to annual leave

A–56

(1) Subject to paragraphs (5) and (7), a worker is entitled in each leave year to a period of leave determined in accordance with paragraph (2).

(2) The period of leave to which a worker is entitled under paragraph (1) is—

(a)   in any leave year beginning on or before 23rd November 1998, three weeks;

(b)   in any leave year beginning after 23rd November 1998 but before 23rd November 1999, three weeks and a proportion of a fourth week equivalent to the proportion of the year beginning on 23rd November 1998 which has elapsed at the start of that leave year; and

(c)   in any leave year beginning after 23rd November 1999, four weeks.

(3) A worker's leave year, for the purposes of this Regulation, begins—

(a)   on such date during the calendar year as may be provided for in a relevant agreement; or

(b)   where there are no provisions of a relevant agreement which apply—

(i)   if the worker's employment began on or before 1st October 1998, on that date and each subsequent anniversary of that date; or

(ii)   if the worker's employment begins after 1st October 1998, on the date on which that employment begins and each subsequent anniversary of that date.

(4) Paragraph (3) does not apply to a worker to whom Schedule 2 applies (workers employed in agriculture) except where, in the case of a worker partly employed in agriculture, a relevant agreement so provides.

(5) Where the date on which a worker's employment begins is later than the date on which (by virtue of a relevant agreement) his first leave year begins, the leave to which he is entitled in that leave year is a proportion of the period applicable under paragraph (2) equal to the proportion of that leave year remaining on the date on which his employment begins.

(6) Where by virtue of paragraph (2)(b) or (5) the period of leave to which a worker is entitled is or includes a proportion of a week, the proportion shall be determined in days and any fraction of a day shall be treated as a whole day.

(7) The entitlement conferred by paragraph (1) does not arise until a worker has been continuously employed for thirteen weeks.

(8) For the purposes of paragraph (7), a worker has been continuously employed for thirteen weeks if his relations with his employer have been governed by a contract during the whole or part of each of those weeks.

(9) Leave to which a worker is entitled under this Regulation may be taken in instalments, but—

(a)   it may only be taken in the leave year in respect of which it is due, and

(b)   it may not be replaced by a payment in lieu except where the worker's employment is terminated.

14. Compensation related to entitlement to leave

A–57

(1) This Regulation applies where—

(a)   a worker's employment is terminated during the course of his leave year, and

(b)   on the date on which the termination takes effect ("the termination date"), the proportion he has taken of the leave to which he is entitled in the leave year under Regulation 13(1) differs from the proportion of the leave year which has expired.

(2) Where the proportion of leave taken by the worker is less than the proportion of the leave year which has expired, his employer shall make him a payment in lieu of leave in accordance with paragraph (3).

(3) The payment due under paragraph (2) shall be—

(a) such sum as may be provided for for the purposes of this Regulation in a relevant agreement, or

(b) where there are no provisions of a relevant agreement which apply, a sum equal to the amount that would be due to the worker under Regulation 16 in respect of a period of leave determined according to the formula—

$$(A \times B) - C$$

where—

A is the period of leave to which the worker is entitled under Regulation 13(1);
B is the proportion of the worker's leave year which expired before the termination date, and
C is the period of leave taken by the worker between the start of the leave year and the termination date.

(4) A relevant agreement may provide that, where the proportion of leave taken by the worker exceeds the proportion of the leave year which has expired, he shall compensate his employer, whether by a payment, by undertaking additional work or otherwise.

15. Dates on which leave is taken

A–58

(1) A worker may take leave to which he is entitled under Regulation 13(1) on such days as he may elect by giving notice to his employer in accordance with paragraph (3), subject to any requirement imposed on him by his employer under paragraph (2).

(2) A worker's employer may require the worker—

(a) to take leave to which the worker is entitled under Regulation 13(1); or
(b) not to take such leave,

on particular days, by giving notice to the worker in accordance with paragraph (3).

(3) A notice under paragraph (1) or (2)—

(a) may relate to all or part of the leave to which a worker is entitled in a leave year;
(b) shall specify the days on which leave is or (as the case may be) is not to be taken and, where the leave on a particular day is to be in respect of only part of the day, its duration; and
(c) shall be given to the employer or, as the case may be, the worker before the relevant date.

(4) The relevant date, for the purposes of paragraph (3), is the date—

(a) in the case of a notice under paragraph (1) or (2)(a), twice as many days in advance of the earliest day specified in the notice as the number of days or part-days to which the notice relates, and
(b) in the case of a notice under paragraph (2)(b), as many days in advance of the earliest day so specified as the number of days or part-days to which the notice relates.

(5) Any right or obligation under paragraphs (1) to (4) may be varied or excluded by a relevant agreement.

(6) This Regulation does not apply to a worker to whom Schedule 2 applies (workers employed in agriculture) except where, in the case of a worker partly employed in agriculture, a relevant agreement so provides.

16. Payment in respect of periods of leave

A–59

(1) A worker is entitled to be paid in respect of any period of annual leave to which he is entitled under Regulation 13, at the rate of a week's pay in respect of each week of leave.

(2) Sections 221 to 224 of the 1996 Act shall apply for the purpose of determining the amount of a week's pay for the purposes of this Regulation, subject to the modifications set out in paragraph (3).

(3) The provisions referred to in paragraph (2) shall apply—

  (a)   as if references to the employee were references to the worker;
  (b)   as if references to the employee's contract of employment were references to the worker's contract;
  (c)   as if the calculation date were the first day of the period of leave in question; and
  (d)   as if the references to sections 227 and 228 did not apply.

(4) A right to payment under paragraph (1) does not affect any right of a worker to remuneration under his contract ("contractual remuneration").

(5) Any contractual remuneration paid to a worker in respect of a period of leave goes towards discharging any liability of the employer to make payments under this Regulation in respect of that period; and, conversely, any payment of remuneration under this Regulation in respect of a period goes towards discharging any liability of the employer to pay contractual remuneration in respect of that period.

17. Entitlements under other provisions

A–60

Where during any period a worker is entitled to a rest period, rest break or annual leave both under a provision of these Regulations and under a separate provision (including a provision of his contract), he may not exercise the two rights separately, but may, in taking a rest period, break or leave during that period, take advantage of whichever right is, in any particular respect, the more favourable.

PART III

EXCEPTIONS

18. Excluded sectors

A–61

Regulations 4(1) and (2), 6(1), (2) and (7), 7(1), and (6), 8, 10(1), 11(1) and (2), 12(1), 13 and 16 do not apply—

  (a)   to the following sectors of activity—

      (i)   air, rail, road, sea, inland waterway and lake transport;
      (ii)   sea fishing;
      (iii) other work at sea; or

  (b)   to the activities of doctors in training, or
  (c)   where characteristics peculiar to certain specified services such as the armed forces or the police, or to certain specific activities in the civil protection services, inevitably conflict with the provisions of these Regulations.

19. Domestic service

A–62

Regulations 4(1) and (2), 6(1), (2) and (7), 7(1), (2) and (6) and 8 do not apply in relation to a worker employed as a domestic servant in a private household.

20. Unmeasured working time

A–63

[(1)]¹¹ Regulations 4(1) and (2), 6(1), (2) and (7), 10(1), 11(1) and (2) and 12(1) do not apply in relation to a worker where, on account of the specific characteristics of the activity in which he is engaged, the duration of his working time is not measured or predetermined or can be determined by the worker himself, as may be the case for—

(a) managing executives or other persons with autonomous decision-taking powers;

(b) family workers; or

(c) workers officiating at religious ceremonies in churches and religious communities.

[(2)]¹² Where part of the working time of a worker is measured or predetermined or cannot be determined by the worker himself but the specific characteristics of the activity are such that, without being required to do so by the employer, the worker may also do work the duration of which is not measured or predetermined or can be determined by the worker himself, Regulations 4(1) and (2) and 6(1), (2) and (7) apply only to so much of his work as is measured or predetermined or cannot be determined by the worker himself.

21. Other special cases

A–64

Subject to Regulation 24, Regulations 6(1), (2) and (7), 10(1), 11(1) and (2) and 12(1) do not apply in relation to a worker—

(a) where the worker's activities are such that his place of work and place of residence are distant from one another or his different places of work are distant from one another;

(b) where the worker is engaged in security and surveillance activities requiring a permanent presence in order to protect property and persons, as may be the case for security guards and caretakers or security firms;

(c) where the workers activities involve the need for continuity of service or production, as may be the case in relation to—

    (i) services relating to the reception, treatment or care provided by hospitals or similar establishments, residential institutions and prisons;

    (ii) work at docks or airports;

    (iii) press, radio, television, cinematographic production, postal and telecommunications services and civil protection services;

    (iv) gas, water and electricity production, transmission and distribution, household refuse collection and incineration;

    (v) industries in which work cannot be interrupted on technical grounds;

    (vi) research and development activities;

    (vii) agriculture;

(d) where there is a foreseeable surge of activity, as may be the case in relation to—

    (i) agriculture;

    (ii) tourism; and

    (iii) postal services;

(e) where the worker's activities are affected by—

    (i) an occurrence due to unusual and unforeseeable circumstances, beyond the control of the worker's employer;

    (ii) exceptional events, the consequences of which could not have been avoided despite the exercise of all due care by the employer; or

---

¹¹ Paragraph number (1) was added by S.I. 1999/3372 (Working Time Regulations, Regulation 4).

¹² Paragraph number (2) was added by S.I. 1999/3372 (Working Time Regulations, Regulation 4).

(iii) an accident or the imminent risk of an accident.

22. Shift workers

A–65

(1) Subject to Regulation 24—

(a) Regulation 10(1) does not apply in relation to a shift worker when he changes shift and cannot take a daily rest period between the end of one shift and the start of the next one;

(b) paragraphs (1) and (2) of Regulation 11 do not apply in relation to a shift worker when he changes shift and cannot take a weekly rest period between the end of one shift and the start of the next one; and

(c) neither Regulation 10(1) nor paragraphs (1) and (2) of Regulation 11 apply to workers engaged in activities involving periods of work split up over the day, as may be the case for cleaning staff.

(2) For the purposes of this Regulation—

"shift worker" means any worker whose work schedule is part of shift work; and
"shift work" means any method of organising work in shifts whereby workers succeed each other at the same workstations according to a certain pattern, including a rotating pattern, and which may be continuous or discontinuous, entailing the need for workers to work at different times over a given period of days or weeks.

23. Collective and workforce agreements

A–66

A collective agreement or a workforce agreement may—

(a) modify or exclude the application of Regulations 6(1) to (3) and (7), 10(1), 11(1) and (2) and 12(1), and

(b) for objective or technical reasons or reasons concerning the organisation of work, modify the application of Regulation 4(3) and (4) by the substitution, for each reference to 17 weeks, of a different period, being a period not exceeding 52 weeks,

in relation to particular workers or groups of workers.

24. Compensatory rest

A–67

Where the application of any provision of these Regulations is excluded by Regulation 21 or 22, or is modified or excluded by means of a collective agreement or a workforce agreement under Regulation 23(a), and a worker is accordingly required by his employer to work during a period which would otherwise be a rest period or rest break—

(a) his employer shall wherever possible allow him to take an equivalent period of compensatory rest, and

(b) in exceptional cases in which it is not possible, for objective reasons, to grant such a period of rest, his employer shall afford him such protection as may be appropriate in order to safeguard the worker's health and safety.

25. Workers in the armed forces

A–68

(1) Regulation 9 does not apply in relation to a worker serving as a member of the armed forces.

(2) Regulations 10(2) and 11(3) do not apply in relation to a young worker serving as a member of the armed forces.

(3) In a case where a young worker is accordingly required to work during a period which

would otherwise be a rest period, he shall be allowed an appropriate period of compensatory rest.

26. Young workers employed on ships

A–69

Regulations 7(2), 10(2), 11(3) and 12(4) do not apply in relation to a young worker whose employment is subject to Regulation under section 55(2)(b) of the Merchant Shipping Act 1995.

27. Young workers: *force majeure*

A–70

(1) Regulations 10(2) and 12(4) do not apply in relation to a young worker where his employer requires him to undertake work which no adult worker is available to perform and which—

(a) is occasioned by either—

    (i) an occurrence due to unusual and unforseeable circumstances, beyond the employer's control, or

    (ii) exceptional events, the consequences of which could not have been avoided despite the exercise of all due care by the employer;

(b) is of a temporary nature; and

(c) must be performed immediately.

(2) Where the application of Regulation 10(2) or 12(4) is excluded by paragraph (1), and a young worker is accordingly required to work during a period which would otherwise be a rest period or rest break, his employer shall allow him to take an equivalent period of compensatory rest within the following three weeks.

PART IV

MISCELLANEOUS

28. Enforcement

A–71

(1) In this Regulation and Regulation 29—

"the 1974 Act" means the Health and Safety at Work etc. Act 1974;
"the relevant requirements" means the following provisions—

(a) Regulations 4(2), 6(2) and (7), 7(1), (2) and (6), 8 and 9; and

(b) Regulation 24, in so far as it applies where Regulation 6(1), (2) or (7) is modified or excluded, and

"the relevant statutory provisions" has the same meaning as in the 1974 Act.

(2) It shall be the duty of the Health and Safety Executive to make adequate arrangements for the enforcement of the relevant requirements except to the extent that a local authority is made responsible for their enforcement by paragraph (3).

(3) Where the relevant requirements apply in relation to workers employed in premises in respect of which a local authority is responsible, under the Health and Safety (Enforcing Authority) Regulations 1998, for enforcing any of the relevant statutory provisions, it shall be the duty of that authority to enforce those requirements.

(4) The duty imposed on local authorities by paragraph (3) shall be performed in accordance with such guidance as may be given to them by the Health and Safety Commission.

(5) The following provisions of the 1974 Act shall apply in relation to the enforcement of the

relevant requirements as they apply in relation to the enforcement of the relevant statutory provisions, and as if any reference in those provisions to an enforcing authority were a reference to the Health and Safety Executive and any local authority made responsible for the enforcement of the relevant requirements—

(a) section 19;

(b) section 20(1), (2)(a) to (d) and (j) to (m), (7) and (8); and

(c) sections 21, 22,[13] 23(1), (2) and (5), 24 and 26; and

(d) section 28, in so far as it relates to information obtained by an inspector in pursuance of a requirement imposed under section 20(2)(j) or (k).

(6) Any function of the Health and Safety Commission under the 1974 Act which is exercisable in relation to the enforcement by the Health and Safety Executive of the relevant statutory provisions shall be exercisable in relation to the enforcement by the Executive of the relevant requirements.

29. Offences

A–72

(1) An employer who fails to comply with any of the relevant requirements shall be guilty of an offence.

(2) The following provisions of section 33(1) of the 1974 Act shall apply where an inspector is exercising or has exercised any power conferred by a provision specified in Regulation 28(5)—

(a) paragraph (3), in so far as it refers to section 20;

(b) paragraphs (f) and (g);

(c) paragraph (h), in so far as it refers to an inspector;

(d) paragraph (j) in so far as it refers to section 28; and

(e) paragraph (k).

(3) An employer guilty of an offence under paragraph (1) shall be liable—

(a) on summary conviction, to a fine not exceeding the statutory maximum;

(b) on conviction on indictment, to a fine.

(4) A person guilty of an offence under a provision of section 33(1) of the 1974 Act as applied by paragraph (2) shall be liable to the penalty prescribed in relation to that provision by subsection (2), (2A) or (3) of section 33,[14] as the case may be.

(5) Sections 36(1), 37 to 39 and 42(1) to (3) of the 1974 Act shall apply in relation to the offences provided for in paragraphs (1) and (2) as they apply in relation to offences under the relevant statutory provisions.

30. Remedies

A–73

(1) A worker may present a complaint to an employment tribunal that his employer—

(a) has refused to permit him to exercise any right he has under—

(i) Regulation 10(1) or (2), 11(1), (2) or (3), 12(1) or (4) or 13(1);

(ii) Regulation 24, in so far as it applies where Regulation 10(1), 11(1) or (2) or 12(1) is modified or excluded; or

(iii) Regulation 25(3) or 27(2); or

(b) has failed to pay him the whole or any part of any amount due to him under Regulation 14(2) or 16(1).

(2) An employment tribunal shall not consider a complaint under this Regulation unless it is presented—

---

[13] Section 22 of the 1974 Act was amended by the Consumer Protection Act 1987 (c.43), Schedule 3, paragraph 2.

[14] Subsection (2A) of section 33 of the 1974 Act was inserted by the Offshore Safety Act 1992 (c.15), section 4(3).

(a) before the end of the period of three months (or, in a case to which Regulation 38(2) applies, six months) beginning with the date on which it is alleged that the exercise of the right should have been permitted (or in the case of a rest period or leave extending over more than one day, the date on which it should have been permitted to begin) or, as the case may be, the payment should have been made;

(b) within such further period as the tribunal considers reasonable in a case where it is satisfied that it was not reasonably practicable for the complaint to be presented before the end of that period of three or, as the case may be, six months.

(3) Where an employment tribunal finds a complaint under paragraph (1)(a) well-founded, the tribunal—

(a) shall make a declaration to that effect, and
(b) may make an award of compensation to be paid by the employer to the worker.

(4) The amount of the compensation shall be such as the tribunal considers just and equitable in all the circumstances having regard to—

(a) the employer's default in refusing to permit the worker to exercise his right, and
(b) any loss sustained by the worker which is attributable to the matters complained of.

(5) Where on a complaint under paragraph (1)(b) an employment tribunal finds that an employer has failed to pay a worker in accordance with Regulation 14(2) or 16(1), it shall order the employer to pay to the worker the amount which it finds to be due to him.

31. Right not to suffer detriment

A–74

(1) After section 45 of the 1996 Act there shall be inserted—

"45A.—Working time cases.

(1) A worker has the right not to be subjected to any detriment by any act, or any deliberate failure to act, by his employer done on the ground that the worker—

(a) refused (or proposed to refuse) to comply with a requirement which the employer imposed (or proposed to impose) in contravention of the Working Time Regulations 1998,
(b) refused (or proposed to refuse) to forgo a right conferred on him by those Regulations,
(c) failed to sign a workforce agreement for the purposes of those Regulations, or to enter into, or agree to vary or extend, any other agreement with his employer which is provided for in those Regulations,
(d) being—
    (i)   a representative of members of the workforce for the purposes of Schedule 1 to those Regulations, or
    (ii) a candidate in an election in which any person elected will, on being elected, be such a representative,

    performed (or proposed to perform) any functions or activities as such a representative or candidate,
(e) brought proceedings against the employer to enforce a right conferred on him by those Regulations, or
(f) alleged that the employer had infringed such a right.

(2) It is immaterial for the purposes of subsection (1)(e) or (f)—

(a) whether or not the worker has the right, or
(b) whether or not the right has been infringed,

but, for those provisions to apply, the claim to the right and that it has been infringed must be made in good faith.

(3) It is sufficient for subsection (1)(f) to apply that the worker, without specifying the right, made it reasonably clear to the employer what the right claimed to have been infringed was.

(4) This section does not apply where a worker is an employee and the detriment in question amounts to dismissal within the meaning of Part X, unless the dismissal is in circumstances in which, by virtue of section 197, Part X does not apply."

(2) After section 48(1) of the 1996 Act there shall be inserted the following subsection—

"(1ZA) A worker may present a complaint to an employment tribunal that he has been subjected to a detriment in contravention of section 45A."

(3) In section 49 of the 1996 Act[15] (remedies)—

    (a)   in subsection (2), for "subsection (6)" there shall be substituted "subsections (5A) and (6)", and

    (b)   after subsection (5), there shall be inserted—

"(5A) Where—
    (a) the complaint is made under section 48 (1ZA),
    (b) the detriment to which the worker is subjected is the termination of his worker's contract, and
    (c) that contract is not a contract of employment,

any compensation must not exceed the compensation that would be payable under Chapter II of Part X if the worker had been an employee and had been dismissed for the reason specified in section 101A."

(4) In section 192(2) of the 1996 Act (provisions applicable in relation to service in the armed forces), after paragraph (a) there shall be inserted—

"(aa) in Part V, section 45A, and sections 48 and 49 so far as relating to that section,".

(5) In sections 194(2)(c), 194(2)(c) and 202(2)(b) of the 1996 Act, for "sections 44 and 47" there shall be substituted "sections 44, 45A and 47".

(6) In section 200(1) of the 1996 Act (which lists provisions of the Act which do not apply to employment in police service), after "45,", there shall be inserted "45A,".

(7) In section 205 of the 1996 Act (remedy for infringement of certain rights), after subsection (1) there shall be inserted the following subsection—

"(1ZA) In relation to the right conferred by section 45A, the reference in subsection (1) to an employee has effect as a reference to a worker."

32. Unfair dismissal

A–75

(1) After section 101 of the 1996 Act there shall be inserted the following section—

"101A. Working time cases.

An employee who is dismissed shall be regarded for the purposes of this Part as unfairly dismissed if the reason (or, if more than one, the principal reason) for the dismissal is that the employee—

    (a) refused (or proposed to refuse) to comply with a requirement which the employer imposed (or proposed to impose) in contravention of the Working Time Regulations 1998,

    (b) refused (or proposed to refuse) to forgo a right conferred on him by those Regulations,

    (c) failed to sign a workforce agreement for the purposes of those Regulations, or to enter into, or agree to vary or extend, any other agreement with his employer which is provided for in those Regulations, or

    (d) being—

        (i) a representative of members of the workforce for the purposes of Schedule 1 to those Regulations, or

---

[15] Section 49 of the 1996 Act was amended by the Public Interest Disclosure Act 1998 (c.23), section 4.

      (ii)   a candidate in an election in which any person elected will, on being elected, be such a representative,

performed (or proposed to perform) any functions or activities as such a representative or candidate."

(2) In section 104 of the 1996 Act (right of employees not to be unfairly dismissed for asserting particular rights) in subsection (4)—

    (a)   at the end of paragraph (b), the word "and" shall be omitted, and
    (b)   after paragraph (c), there shall be inserted the words—

"and
(d) the rights conferred by the Working Time Regulations 1998."

(3) In section 105 of the 1996 Act (redundancy as unfair dismissal), after subsection (4) there shall be inserted the following subsection—

"(4A) This subsection applies if the reason (or, if more than one, the principal reason) for which the employee was selected for dismissal was one of those specified in section 101A."

(4) In sections 108(3) and 109(2) of the 1996 Act, after paragraph (d) there shall be inserted—

"(dd) section 101A applies,".

(5) In sections 117(4)(b), 118(3), 120(1), 122(3), 128(1)(b) and 129(1) of the 1996 Act, after "100(1)(a) and (b)," there shall be inserted "101A(d),".

(6) In section 202(2) (cases where disclosure of information is restricted on ground of national security)—

    (a)   in paragraph (g)(i), after "100" there shall be inserted ", 101A(d)", and
    (b)   in paragraph (g)(ii), after "of that section," there shall be inserted "or by reason of the application of subsection (4A) in so far as it applies where the reason (or, if more than one, the principal reason) for which an employee was selected for dismissal was that specified in section 101A(d)".

(7) In section 209(2) of the 1996 Act (which lists provisions excluded from the scope of the power to amend the Act by order), after "101," in paragraph (e) there shall be inserted "101A,".

(8) In sections 237(1A) and 238(2A) of the Trade Union and Labour Relations (Consolidation) Act 1992[16] (cases where employee can complain of unfair dismissal notwithstanding industrial action at time of dismissal), after "100" there shall be inserted ", 101A(d)".

(9) In section 10(5)(a) of the Employment Tribunals Act 1996[17] (cases where Minister's certificate is not conclusive evidence that action was taken to safeguard national security), after "100" there shall be inserted ", 101A(d)".

33. Conciliation

A–76

In section 18(1) of the Employment Tribunals Act 1996 (cases where conciliation provisions apply)—

    (a)   at the end of paragraph (e), the word "or" shall be omitted, and
    (b)   after paragraph (f), there shall be inserted the words—

---

[16] Subsection (1A) of section 237 and subsection (2A) of section 238 were inserted by the Trade Union Reform and Employment Rights Act 1993 (c.19), Schedule 8, paragraphs 76 and 77.
[17] Section 1(2) of the Employment Rights (Dispute Resolution) Act 1998 (c.8) provides for the Industrial Tribunals Act 1996 to be cited as the Employment Tribunals Act 1996.

"or

(ff) under Regulation 30 of the Working Time Regulations 1998,".

34. Appeals

A–77

In section 21 of the Employment Tribunals Act 1996 (jurisdiction of the Employment Appeal Tribunal)—

(a) at the end of subsection (1) (which confers jurisdiction by reference to Acts under or by virtue of which decisions are made) there shall be inserted—

"or under the Working Time Regulations 1998.";

(b) in subsection (2), after "the Acts listed" there shall be inserted—

"or the Regulations referred to".

35. Restrictions on contracting out

A–78

(1) Any provision in an agreement (whether a contract of employment or not) is void in so far as it purports—

(a) to exclude or limit the operation of any provision of these Regulations, save in so far as these Regulations provide for an agreement to have that effect, or

(b) to preclude a person from bringing proceedings under these Regulations before an employment tribunal.

(2) Paragraph (1) does not apply to—

(a) any agreement to refrain from instituting or continuing proceedings where a conciliation officer has taken action under section 18 of the Employment Tribunals Act 1996 (conciliation); or

(b) any agreement to refrain from instituting or continuing proceedings within section 18(1)(ff) of the Employment Tribunals Act 1996 (proceedings under these Regulations where conciliation is available), if the conditions regulating compromise agreements under these Regulations are satisfied in relation to the agreement.

(3) For the purposes of paragraph (2)(b) the conditions regulating compromise agreements under these Regulations are that—

(a) the agreement must be in writing,

(b) the agreement must relate to the particular complaint,

(c) the worker must have received advice from a relevant independent adviser as to the terms and effect of the proposed agreement and, in particular, its effect on his ability to pursue his rights before an employment tribunal,

(d) there must be in force, when the adviser gives the advice, a contract of insurance, or an indemnity provided for members of a profession or professional body, covering the risk of a claim by the worker in respect of loss arising in consequence of the advice,

(e) the agreement must identify the adviser, and

(f) the agreement must state that the conditions regulating compromise agreements under these Regulations are satisfied.

(4) A person is a relevant independent adviser for the purposes of paragraph (3)(c)—

(a) if he is a qualified lawyer,

(b) if he is an officer, official, employee or member of an independent trade union who has been certified in writing by the trade union as competent to give advice and as authorised to do so on behalf of the trade union, or

(c) if he works at an advice centre (whether as an employee or as a volunteer) and has been certified in writing by the centre as competent to give advice and as authorised to do so on behalf of the centre.

(5) But a person is not a relevant independent adviser for the purposes of paragraph (3)(c) in relation to the worker—

(a) if he is, is employed by or is acting in the matter for the employer or an associated employer,

(b) in the case of a person within paragraph (4)(b) or (c), if the trade union or advice centre is the employer or an associated employer, or

(c) in the case of a person within paragraph (4)(c), if the worker makes a payment for the advice received from him.

(6) In paragraph (4)(a), "qualified lawyer" means—

(a) as respects England and Wales, a barrister (whether in practice as such or employed to give legal advice), a solicitor who holds a practising certificate, or a person other than a barrister or solicitor who is an authorised advocate or authorised litigator (within the meaning of the Courts and Legal Services Act 1990); and

(b) as respects Scotland, an advocate (whether in practice as such or employed to give legal advice), or a solicitor who holds a practising certificate.

(7) For the purposes of paragraph (5) any two employers shall be treated as associated if—

(a) one is a company of which the other (directly or indirectly) has control; or

(b) both are companies of which a third person (directly or indirectly) has control;

and "associated employer" shall be construed accordingly.

35A.

A–79

[(1) The Secretary of State shall, after consulting persons appearing to him to represent the two sides of industry, arrange for the publication, in such form and manner as he considers appropriate, of information and advice concerning the operation of these Regulations.

(2) The information and advice shall be such as appear to him best calculated to enable employers and workers affected by these Regulations to understand their respective rights and obligations under them.][18]

PART V

SPECIAL CLASSES OF PERSON

36. Agency workers not otherwise "workers"

A–80

(1) This Regulation applies in any case where an individual ("the agency worker")—

(a) is supplied by a person ("the agent") to do work for another ("the principal") under a contract or other arrangements made between the agent and the principal; but

(b) is not, as respects the work, a worker, because of the absence of a worker's contract between the individual and the agent or the principal; and

(c) is not a party to a contract under which he undertakes to do the work for another party to the contract whose status is, by virtue of the contract, that of a client or customer of any profession or business undertaking carried on by the individual.

(2) In a case where this Regulation applies, the other provisions of these Regulations shall have effect as if there were a worker's contract for the doing of the work by the agency worker made between the agency worker and—

(a) whichever of the agent and the principal is responsible for paying the agency worker in respect of the work; or

(b) if neither the agent nor the principal is so responsible, whichever of them pays the agency worker in respect of the work,

and as if that person were the agency worker's employer.

---

[18] Added by S.I. 1999/3372 (Working Time Regulations, Regulation 5).

37. Crown employment

A–81

(1) Subject to paragraph (4) and Regulation 38, these Regulations have effect in relation to Crown employment and persons in Crown employment as they have effect in relation to other employment and other workers.

(2) In paragraph (1) "Crown employment" means employment under or for the purposes of a government department or any officer or body exercising on behalf of the Crown functions conferred by a statutory provision.

(3) For the purposes of the application of the provisions of these Regulations in relation to Crown employment in accordance with paragraph (1)—

(a) references to a worker shall be construed as references to a person in Crown employment; and
(b) references to a worker's contract shall be construed as references to the terms of employment of a person in Crown employment.

(4) No act or omission by the Crown which is an offence under Regulation 29 shall make the Crown criminally liable, but the High Court or, in Scotland, the Court of Session may, on the application of a person appearing to the Court to have an interest, declare any such act or omission unlawful.

38. Armed forces

A–82

(1) Regulation 37 applies—

(a) subject to paragraph (2), to service as a member of the armed forces, and
(b) to employment by an association established for the purposes of Part XI of the Reserve Forces Act 1996.

(2) No complaint concerning the service of any person as a member of the armed forces may be presented to an employment tribunal under Regulation 30 unless—

(a) that person has made a complaint in respect of the same matter to an officer under the service redress procedures, and
(b) that complaint has not been withdrawn.

(3) For the purposes of paragraph (2)(b), a person shall be treated as having withdrawn his complaint if, having made a complaint to an officer under the service redress procedures, he fails to submit the complaint to the Defence Council under those procedures.

(4) Where a complaint of the kind referred to in paragraph (2) is presented to an employment tribunal, the service redress procedures may continue after the complaint is presented.

(5) In this Regulation, "the service redress procedures" means the procedures, excluding those which relate to the making of a report on a complaint to Her Majesty, referred to in section 180 of the Army Act 1955, section 180 of the Air Force Act 1955 and section 130 of the Naval Disciplne Act 1957.[19]

39. House of Lords staff

A–83

(1) These Regulations have effect in relation to employment as a relevant member of the House of Lords staff as they have effect in relation to other employment.

(2) Nothing in any rule of law or the law or practice of Parliament prevents a relevant member of the House of Lords staff from presenting a complaint to an employment tribunal under Regulation 30.

---

[19] Each of the sections referred to in paragraph (5) was substituted by section 20 of the Armed Forces Act 1996 (c.46).

(3) In this Regulation "relevant member of the House of Lords staff" means any person who is employed under a worker's contract with the Corporate Officer of the House of Lords.

40. House of Commons staff

A–84

(1) These Regulations have effect in relation to employment as a relevant member of the House of Commons staff as they have effect in relation to other employment.

(2) For the purposes of the application of the provisions of these Regulations in relation to a relevant member of the House of Commons staff—

(a) references to a worker shall be construed as references to a relevant member of the House of Commons staff; and
(b) references to a worker's contract shall be construed as references to the terms of employment of a relevant member of the House of Commons staff.

(3) Nothing in any rule of law or the law or practice of Parliament prevents a relevant member of the House of Commons staff from presenting a complaint to an employment tribunal under Regulation 30.

(4) In this Regulation "relevant member of the House of Commons staff" means any person—

(a) who was appointed by the House of Commons Commission; or
(b) who is a member of the Speaker's personal staff.

41. Police service

A–85

(1) For the purposes of these Regulations, the holding, otherwise than under a contract of employment, of the office of constable or an appointment as a police cadet shall be treated as employment, under a worker's contract, by the relevant officer.

(2) Any matter relating to the employment of a worker which may be provided for for the purposes of these Regulations in a workforce agreement may be provided for for the same purposes in relation to the service of a person holding the office of constable or an appointment as a police cadet by an agreement between the relevant officer and a joint branch board.

(3) In this Regulation—

"a joint branch board" means a joint branch board constituted in accordance with Regulation 7(3) of the Police Federation Regulations 1969[20] or Regulation 7(3) of the Police Federation (Scotland) Regulations 1985,[21] and
"the relevant officer" means—

(a) in relation to a member of a police force or a special constable or police cadet appointed for a police area, the chief officer of police (or, in Scotland, the chief constable);
(b) in relation to a person holding office under section 9(1)(b) or 55(1)(b) of the Police Act 1997 (police members of the National Criminal Intelligence Service and the National Crime Squad), the Director General of the National Criminal Intelligence Service or, as the case may be, the Director General of the National Crime Squad; and
(c) in relation to any other person holding the office of constable or an appointment as a police cadet, the person who has the direction and control of the body of constables or cadets in question.

---

[20] To which there are amendments not relevant to these Regulations.
[21] To which there are amendments not relevant to these Regulations.

42. Non-employed trainees

A–86

For the purposes of these Regulations, a person receiving relevant training, otherwise than under a contract of employment, shall be regarded as a worker, and the person whose undertaking is providing the training shall be regarded as his employer.

43. Agricultural workers

A–87

The provisions of Schedule 2 have effect in relation to workers employed in agriculture.

Signatures

Ian McCartney
Minister of State,
Department of Trade and Industry

30th July 1998

SCHEDULE 1

WORKFORCE AGREEMENTS

1.

A–88

An agreement is a workforce agreement for the purposes of these Regulations if the following conditions are satisfied—

- (a) the agreement is in writing;
- (b) it has effect for a specified period not exceeding five years;
- (c) it applies either—

    - (i) to all of the relevant members of the workforce, or
    - (ii) to all of the relevant members of the workforce who belong to a particular group;

- (d) the agreement is signed—

    - (i) in the case of an agreement of the kind referred to in sub-paragraph (c)(i), by the representatives of the workforce, and in the case of an agreement of the kind referred to in sub-paragraph (c)(ii) by the representatives of the group to which the agreement applies (excluding, in either case, any representative not a relevant member of the workforce on the date on which the agreement was first made available for signature), or
    - (ii) if the employer employed 20 or fewer workers on the date referred to in sub-paragraph (d)(i), either by the appropriate representatives in accordance with that sub-paragraph or by the majority of the workers employed by him;

- (e) before the agreement was made available for signature, the employer provided all the workers to whom it was intended to apply on the date on which it came into effect with copies of the text of the agreement and such guidance as those workers might reasonably require in order to understand it fully.

2.

A–89

For the purposes of this Schedule—

"a particular group" is a group of the relevant members of a workforce who undertake a particular function, work at a particular workplace or belong to a particular department or unit within their employer's business;

"relevant members of the workforce" are all of the workers employed by a particular employer, excluding any worker whose terms and conditions of employment are provided for, wholly or in part, in a collective agreement;

"representatives of the workforce" are workers duly elected to represent the relevant members of the workforce, "representatives of the group" are workers duly elected to represent the members of a particular group, and representatives are "duly elected" if the election at which they were elected satisfied the requirements of paragraph 3 of this Scedule.

3.

A–90

The requirements concerning elections referred to in paragraph 2 are that—

(a) the number of representatives to be elected is determined by the employer;

(b) the candidates for election as representatives of the workforce are relevant members of the workforce, and the candidates for election as representatives of a group are members of the group;

(c) no worker who is eligible to be a candidate is unreasonably excluded from standing for election;

(d) all the relevant members of the workforce are entitled to vote for representatives of the workforce, and all the members of a particular group are entitled to vote for representatives of the group;

(e) the workers entitled to vote may vote for as many candidates as there are representatives to be elected;

(f) the election is conducted so as to secure that—

(i) so far as is reasonably practicable, those voting do so in secret, and

(ii) the votes given at the election are fairly and accurately counted.

SCHEDULE 2

WORKERS EMPLOYED IN AGRICULTURE

1.

A–91

Except where, in the case of a worker partly employed in agriculture, different provision is made by a relevant agreement—

(a) for the purposes of Regulation 13, the leave year of a worker employed in agriculture begins on 6th April each year or such other date as may be specified in an agricultural wages order which applies to him; and

(b) the dates on which leave is taken by a worker employed in agriculture shall be determined in accordance with an agricultural wages order which applies to him.

2.

A–92

Where, in the case referred to in paragraph 1 above, a relevant agreement makes provision different from sub-paragraph (a) or (b) of that paragraph—

(a) neither section 11 of the Agricultural Wages Act 1948 nor section 11 of the Agricultural Wages (Scotland) Act 1949 shall apply to that provision; and

(b) an employer giving effect to that provision shall not thereby be taken to have failed to comply with the requirements of an agricultural wages order.

3.

A–93

In this Schedule, "an agricultural wages order" means an order under section 3 of the Agricultural Wages Act 1948 or section 3 of the Agricultural Wages (Scotland) Act 1949.

EXPLANATORY NOTE

(This note is not part of the Regulations)

A–94

These Regulations implement Council Directive 93/104/EC concerning certain aspects of the organisation of working time ([1993] O.J. L307/18) and provisions concerning working time in Council Directive 94/33/EC on the protection of young people at work ([1994] O.J. L216/12). The provisions in the latter Directive which are implemented relate only to adolescents (those aged between 15 and 18 who are over compulsory school age); provisions in that Directive relating to children were implemented by the Children (Protection at Work) Regulations 1998 (S.I. 1998 No. 276). Provisions implementing that Directive in relation to adolescents employed on ships are to be included in separate Regulations to be made shortly after the date on which these Regulations are made, and adolescents employed on ships are accordingly excluded from the scope of these Regulations (Regulation 26).

Regulations 4 to 9 in these Regulations impose obligations on employers, enforceable by the Health and Safety Executive and local authorities; failure to comply is an offence. The obligations concern the maximum average weekly working time of workers (subject to provision for individual workers to agree that the maximum should not apply to them), the average normal hours of night workers, the provision of health assessments for night workers, and rest breaks to be given to workers engaged in certain kinds of work; employers are also required to keep records of workers' hours of work.

Regulations 10 to 17 confer rights on workers, enforceable by proceedings before employment tribunals. The rights are to a rest period in every 24 hours during which a worker works for his employer and longer rest periods each week or fortnight, to a rest break in the course of a working day, and to a period of paid annual leave.

Regulations 18 to 27 provide for particular Regulations not to apply, either in relation to workers engaged in certain kinds of work or where particular circumstances arise. There is also provision for groups of workers and their employers to agree to modify or exclude the application of particular Regulations.

The remaining Regulations make provison in relation to enforcement and remedies, and in respect of agency workers, Crown servants, Parliamentary staff, the police, trainees and agricultural workers. The Employment Rights Act 1996 is amended to include a right for workers not to be subjected to any detriment for refusing to comply with a requirement contrary to these Regulations or to forego a right conferred by them, and to provide that the dismissal of an employee on account of any such refusal is unfair dismissal for the purposes of the Act.

The Working Time Regulations 1999 No. 3372

A–95

[Now incorporated into the Working Time Regulations 1998 No. 1833.]

PART II
DEROGATIONS

Schedule of Derogations Permissible by Agreement under the Regulations

A–96

Provision	Individual Agreement	Collective Agreement	Workforce Agreement Complying with Conditions in Schedule 1	Comments
Weekly Working Time				
Definition of working time	Can specify additional period to be treated as working time	Can specify additional period to be treated as working time	Can specify additional period to be treated as working time	Employer can only **add** time to definition of working time in Regulation 2(1)
48 hour average limit on weekly working time	Worker can agree to work longer hours than those permitted by the limit	N/A	N/A	Agreement must be in writing. It can contain a notice period of up to 3 months (otherwise a 7 day notice period applies)
17 Week Reference Period	Can set reference period of successive 17 week periods	Can set reference period of successive 17 week periods Can extend reference period to max of 52 weeks for "objective or technical reasons or reasons concerning the organisation of work"	Can set reference period of successive 17 week periods Can extend reference period to max of 52 weeks for "objective or technical reasons or reasons concerning the organisation of work"	

Provision	Individual Agreement	Collective Agreement	Workforce Agreement Complying with Conditions in Schedule 1	Comments
Night Work				
Definition of night time	Can define as period of 7 hours including period 12 a.m. to 5 a.m.	Can define as period of 7 hours including period 12 a.m. to 5 a.m.	Can define as period of 7 hours including period 12 a.m. to 5 a.m.	
Definition of night worker		Can set a proportion of annual working time during night time which qualifies worker as night worker	Can set a proportion of annual working time during night time which qualifies worker as night worker	
Limit on average normal hours of night workers		Can modify or exclude limit	Can modify or exclude limit	Requirement to provide equivalent period of compensatory rest or afford other appropriate protection
17 week reference period	Can set reference period of successive 17 week periods	Can set reference period of successive 17 week periods Can set alternative reference period (no maximum)	Can set reference period of successive 17 week periods Can set alternative reference period (no maximum)	Collective or Workforce Agreements only—requirement to provide equivalent period of compensatory rest or afford other appropriate protection
8 hour daily limit for night workers whose work involves special hazards or heavy physical or mental strain		Can modify or exclude limit Can identify work as involving special hazards or heavy physical or mental strain	Can modify or exclude limit Can identify work as involving special hazards or heavy physical or mental strain	Requirement to provide equivalent period of compensatory rest or afford other appropriate protection

Provision	Individual Agreement	Collective Agreement	Workforce Agreement Complying with Conditions in Schedule 1	Comments
Daily Rest Period				
Entitlement to 11 hours consecutive daily rest		Can modify or exclude entitlement	Can modify or exclude entitlement	Requirement to provide equivalent period of compensatory rest or afford other appropriate protection
Weekly Rest Period				
Entitlement to **EITHER** weekly rest period of 24 hours in 7 day period **OR** 2 periods of 24 hours' or 1 period of 48 hours' rest in 14 days (**EMPLOYER'S CHOICE**)		Can modify or exclude entitlement	Can modify or exclude entitlement	Requirement to provide equivalent period of compensatory rest or afford other appropriate protection
Start of 7 or 14 day period	Can define the start of the 7 or 14 hour period	Can define the start of the 7 or 14 hour period	Can define the start of the 7 or 14 hour period	Collective or Workforce Agreements only—Requirement to provide equivalent period of compensatory rest or afford other appropriate protection
Rest Breaks				
Uninterrupted period of 20 minutes		Can modify or exclude entitlement Can define duration of break and terms on which granted, e.g. whether uninterrupted break, whether spent away from workstation	Can modify or exclude entitlement Can define duration of break and terms on which granted, e.g. whether uninterrupted break, whether spent away from workstation	Requirement to provide equivalent period of compensatory rest or afford other appropriate protection

Provision	Individual Agreement	Collective Agreement	Workforce Agreement Complying with Conditions in Schedule 1	Comments
Annual Leave				
Leave year	Can specify start of leave year	Can specify start of leave year	Can specify start of leave year	If not so specified, leave year starts 1st October or any subsequent date on which worker starts work for employer
Entitlement to pay in lieu of untaken leave entitlement on termination	Can specify what sum is to be paid in lieu or how sum is to be calculated Can make provision for employer to be compensated for annual leave taken in excess of pro rata entitlement on termination	Can specify what sum is to be paid in lieu or how sum is to be calculated Can make provision for employer to be compensated for annual leave taken in excess of pro rata entitlement on termination	Can specify what sum is to be paid in lieu or how sum is to be calculated Can make provision for employer to be compensated for annual leave taken in excess of pro rata entitlement on termination	Otherwise calculation is as set out in Regulations 14 or 16
Notices re exercise of leave entitlement	Can vary or exclude: —length of notice required from worker before leave taken —length of notice from employer to worker not to take leave or to take leave on certain dates	Can vary or exclude: —length of notice required from worker before leave taken —length of notice from employer to worker not to take leave or to take leave on certain dates	Can vary or exclude: —length of notice required from worker before leave taken —length of notice from employer to worker not to take leave or to take leave on certain dates	

PART III
PRECEDENTS

Specimen Individual Opt-Out of Regulation 4(1) (Long-Form)

3. AGREEMENT

A–97

2.1 I [*insert name of worker*] of [*insert worker's address*] understand that, unless I agree otherwise, Regulation 4(1) of The Working Time Regulations 1998 limits my Working Time (including overtime) to an average of 48 hours per week, calculated over the reference period defined in clause 4.2 below.

2.2 I agree with [*insert name of Company*] of [*insert address*] ("the Company") that this limit shall not apply to me and that my average weekly Working Time calculated over the period referred to above may therefore exceed an average of 48 hours per week. [However I do not consent to my weekly Working Time ever exceeding an average of [55] hours per calendar week].

EITHER

DURATION OF AGREEMENT

2.1 This Agreement will apply from [*insert date*] until [*insert date*] [although I may terminate it at any point during this period by giving [3] months written notice to the Company].

OR

2.1 This Agreement will apply from [*insert date*] and will remain in force indefinitely [unless I exercise my right to terminate it at any time by giving [3] months written notice to the Company].

RECORDS

I agree that whilst this Agreement is in force I will comply with any requirements of the Company to record the hours I have worked and will provide those records on a [regular] [monthly] basis to the Company [using the form supplied for this purpose]. I also agree that I will comply with all policies or requirements of the Company, in force from time to time in relation to the recording of Working Time].

DEFINITIONS

In this Agreement:—

6.1 "Working Time" has the meaning given to it in the Regulations referred to above. However to avoid any doubt, the following activities [do not] constitute Working Time [*specify activities*]; and

6.2 The reference period to be used for calculating my weekly Working Time shall be any [17] [26] week period during my employment by the Company] [each successive [17]

[26] week period beginning on [*insert date*]] [any [maximum of 52] week period during my employment by the Company] [each successive [maximum of 52] week period beginning on [*insert date*] as agreed in the [workforce] [collective] agreement entered into between the Company and the [elected workforce representatives] [*insert name of independent trade union*] on [*insert date*]]; or [the number of weeks for which I have worked for the Company if this is less than [17] [26] [maximum of 52 weeks]].

CONTRACT OF EMPLOYMENT

[I accept that the terms of this Agreement will form part of my contract of employment with the Company with effect from the date of signature of this Agreement].

Signed ....   Dated ....

[*Name of worker*]

Signed ....   Dated ....

[on behalf of the Company]

Specimen Individual Opt-Out of Regulation 4(1) (Short-Form)

A–98

1. Individual opt-out

Agreement to Opt Out of Regulation 4(1) of the Working Time Regulations 1998 About Maximum Weekly Working Time

2. I, [*name of worker*] of [*worker's address*] agree with [*name of employer*] of [*employer's address*] (the "**Employer**") that the limit in Regulation 4(1) of the Working Time Regulations 1998 shall not apply to me and that my average working time may therefore exceed 48 hours for each seven-day period (as defined by and calculated in accordance with the Working Time Regulations 1998).

3. This Agreement shall apply from [*date*] until [*date*].

4. I agree that I will comply with any and all policies of the employer, from time to time in force, which relate to its maintenance of records of my hours of work.

5. This agreement can be terminated by me giving three months' notice in writing to the employer.

Signed .... Dated ....

[*Name of worker*]

Signed .... Dated ....

[on behalf of the Employer]

Specimen Individual Opt-Out of Regulation 4(1) (Short-Form)

Specimen Workforce Agreement

A–99

BETWEEN

[   ] ('the Company')

and

The representatives of [   ] employed by the Company ('the Representatives')

6. **The parties to this Agreement confirm that**

    6.1 This Agreement is a Workforce Agreement within the meaning of the Working Time Regulations 1998 ('the Regulations').

    6.2 The Representatives were duly elected on [*date*] as representatives of [   ] employed by the company, being a particular group of relevant members of the workforce employed by the Company within the meaning of the Regulations.

    6.3 The Company understands that, for the purposes of Regulation 11 of the Regulations (weekly rest period), the relevant members of its workforce referred to above shall be entitled to one uninterrupted rest period of 48 hours in each 14-day period.

7. It is agreed that

    7.1 This Agreement shall apply to all those employed by the Company who are [   ] and who are relevant members of that particular group of the workforce at any time during the term of this Agreement.

    7.2 In respect of the employees referred to above, Regulation 10 of the Regulations (daily rest of 11 consecutive hours in each 24-hour period) shall not apply in any week in which such employees are on standby and call-out as agreed with the Company from time to time.

    7.3 Whenever paragraph 2.2 above applies to an employee, he shall be entitled in that week to an equivalent period of compensatory rest, that is to say a total of 77 hours rest, which need not be consecutive. The equivalent period of compensatory rest is to be reckoned in accordance with paragraphs 2.4 and 2.5.

    7.4 Subject to paragraph 2.5 below, any period during which the employee is not called out or on travelling time between the hours [4.00 p.m.] and [8.45 a.m.], Monday to Friday shall count towards the equivalent period of compensatory rest.

    7.5 For each [complete] hour [or part of an hour] an employee is called out after midnight and before [8.45 a.m.] Monday to Friday, the same amount of time occurring after [8.45 a.m.] on the next normal working day (Monday to Friday) shall be taken as an equivalent period of compensatory rest and shall be paid time in accordance with existing contractual arrangements.

8. This Agreement shall come into force on [*date*] and shall have effect until [*date*].

Signed ....   Dated ....

[For and on behalf of the Company]

Signed ....   Dated ....

[By the Representative]

Specimen Collective Agreement

A–100

THIS AGREEMENT is made on [*date*]

PARTIES:

(1) [   ] (Number   ) whose Registered Office is at [   ] ("the Company")
    and

(2) [   ] of [   ] ("the Union")

WHEREAS

The parties hereto are desirous of entering into a Collective Agreement to take advantage of permitted derogation from the Regulations.

THE PARTIES AGREE as follows:—

9. DEFINITIONS

9.2   In this Agreement the following words and expressions shall have the following meanings:

"the Regulations"	The Working Time Regulations 1998
"Worker"	Any worker covered by a contract of employment with the Company or under any other contract whether express or implied and (if it is express) whether oral or in writing whereby the worker undertakes to do or perform personally any work or services for the Company whose status is not by virtue of the contract that of a client or customer of any profession or business undertaking carried on by the individual. For the avoidance of doubt, a worker shall include an individual who works for the Company in circumstances in which he is or was introduced or supplied to do that work by a third person and the terms on which he is engaged to do the work are substantially determined not by him but by the Company, by the third person or by both of them. The definition shall further include an individual who is provided with work experience provided pursuant to a training course or programme or who is provided with training for employment (or with both) otherwise than under a contract of employment.
"Working Time"	Time in which a worker is working, is at the Company's disposal and carrying out his activities or duties. For the avoidance of doubt Working Time does not include lunch and tea breaks.
"Exceptional Circumstances"	Unusual events that vary from the day to day operation of the Company and which cannot be planned or arranged around [and which are agreed as being exceptional by a Union representative and the Company].

9.3   The headings in this Agreement shall not affect its interpretation or construction.

9.4   A reference to any statute or statutory provision includes any statutory modification or re-enactment of it.

9.5   Any reference in this Agreement to a clause or sub-clause is to the relevant clause or sub-clause of this Agreement unless otherwise stated.

9.6   Words importing one gender include the other gender.

10. GENERAL

10.2   The Parties to this Agreement confirm that it is a Collective Agreement within the meaning of the Regulations;

10.3   This Agreement is implemented in order to protect as far as possible the health and safety of all workers;

10.4   This Agreement is intended to be incorporated into individual workers' contracts of employment;

10.5   This Agreement is based on the Parties having a mutual interpretation of the Regulations;

10.6   This Agreement is intended by the Parties to be a legally enforceable contract as between themselves.

11. TERM

This Agreement will have effect from [date] and will remain in force until [date]. The Parties hereby notify their intention to enter into a subsequent collective Agreement following the expiry of this Agreement.

12. DAILY REST

12.2   Regulation 10 of the Regulations (which provides for a daily rest period of 11 consecutive hours in each 24-hour period in which a worker works for the Company is thereby excluded.

12.3   Each worker is normally entitled (but subject to 4.3 below) and obliged to take a period of 11 hours' rest in respect of each 24-hour period during which he works for the Company ("daily rest entitlement"). Each 24-hour period commences at the start of the worker's usual shift pattern.

12.4   Where due to the needs of the business a worker is not able to take the daily rest entitlement (in other words the worker works more than 13 hours in a 24-hour period) the worker will be entitled and obliged to take any remaining daily rest entitlement as soon as reasonably practicable and except in exceptional circumstances within 14 days of the 24 hour period within which the worker was unable to take the fully daily rest entitlement ("the fourteen-day period"):

12.5   Where due to exceptional circumstances it is not possible to allow a worker to take his full daily rest entitlement referred to in clause 4.2 above within the 14-day period the worker will be entitled to an obliged to take any remaining daily rest entitlement at the earliest opportunity thereafter [with Union agreement]:

12.6   Any daily rest entitlement which is taken in addition to a worker's normal rest period may only be taken with the agreement of the worker's immediate line manager [or another appropriate person]:

12.7   For the avoidance of doubt an example would be that on Monday 1st the worker works 14 hours (8.00 a.m. –10.00 p.m.) and therefore only takes 10 hours of his daily rest entitlement (from 10.00 p.m. to 8.00 a.m.). On Tuesday 2nd, the worker works 13 hours (8.00 a.m. to 9.00 p.m.) and therefore is able to take his full 11-hour daily rest entitlement (9.00 p.m.–8.00 a.m.) but no remaining daily rest entitlement which is carried over from Monday 1st. If on Wednesday 3rd the worker works 12 hours (8.00 a.m.—8.00 p.m.) he is able to take his one remaining hour of daily rest entitlement owing on that day and so this remaining daily rest entitlement is taken within the 14-day period.

13. WEEKLY REST

13.2 Regulation 11 of the Regulations, which provides for an uninterrupted rest period of not less than 24 hours in each 7-day period during which the worker works for the Company is hereby excluded.

13.3 Each worker is normally (subject to clause 5.4) entitled and obliged to take one period of 24 hours' rest in respect of each seven-day period in which he works for the Company ("weekly rest period"). Each seven-day period commences at 12 o'clock midnight between Sunday and Monday of any given week.

13.4 Where due to the needs of the business in any seven day period a worker is not able to take a weekly rest period then the worker will be entitled and obliged to take a 24-hour rest period as soon as reasonably practicable and except in exceptional circumstances by the end of the third seven-day period following the end of the seven-day period in which the worker was unable to take his entitlement to weekly rest.

13.5 Any weekly rest period may only be taken with the agreement of the worker's immediate line manager or supervisor.

13.6 Where, due to exceptional circumstances it is not possible to allow a worker to take his/her weekly rest period within the period referred to in clause 5.3 above the worker will be entitled to and obliged to take a period of rest equivalent to the missed weekly rest period (in addition to his weekly rest period for the week in question) at the earliest opportunity, subject to clause 5.4 above.

14. AVERAGING PERIOD

14.2 Pursuant to Regulation (23), the Parties hereby agree that in Regulations 4(3) and (4) any reference to 17 weeks should be substituted by a reference to 52 weeks because of objective and technical reasons concerning the organisation of work.

15. WEEKEND WORK

15.2 The Company may require workers to work weekends as and when required. A worker must comply with any such request unless he/she has opted out of weekend working as set out in 15.5 below.

15.3 Workers will be paid at overtime rates for all work performed during the weekend [how paid?] but there will be no payment in respect of any rest days.

15.4 The Company will not be entitled to require a worker to work on any bank holiday or during an annual shutdown or personal holiday unless by mutual agreement.

15.5 Any worker may opt out of weekend working by notifying the Company in writing of their decision not to work weekends on or before [1st November 1998]. Any worker who provides the Company with such a notice cannot be required to work weekends as specified in 7.1 above unless they specifically agree to do so. Where notice is not given before 1st November 1998, one month's notice in writing must be given to the Company to either opt out of weekend work or to elect to be available for weekend work if notice of opting out has already been given.

16. ALTERNATIVE EMPLOYMENT

16.2 Workers who work for an employer or perform any other work which can be defined as Working Time other than for the Company must notify the Company in writing of their alternative employment and of the number of hours worked. Unless such notification is given, the Company will assume that workers are not carrying out work for any other employer. [Any alternative employment must not interfere or affect the workers working relationship with the Company].

17. RIGHT TO RENEGOTIATE

The complete or partial invalidity or unenforceability of any provision of this Agreement for any purpose shall in no way affect

17.1 the validity of enforceability of such provision for any other purpose;

17.2 the remainder of such provision, or

17.3 the remaining provisions of this Agreement.

17.3 If it is shown to the satisfaction of both parties:

17.3.1 That this Agreement is in breach of the Regulations or that [the terms of it cannot be implemented without breaching the Regulations];

17.3.2 That more than 33 per cent of workers have opted-out of weekend working in accordance with clause 7.4.

Then this Agreement may be amended by recording in writing the amendment, such amendment to be signed by a representative of both parties to this Agreement.

Signed by

On behalf of the Company

Signed by

On behalf of the Union

Worker's Record: Specimen Weekly Working Time Record—Time Spent at Work

A–101

NAME:

DEPARTMENT:

WEEK COMMENCING:

DAY	DATE	TIME IN	TIME OUT	LUNCH BREAK (MINS)	TOTAL TIME AT WORK (EXCLUDING LUNCH BREAK)	ABSENT (INDICATE REASON)
MONDAY						
TUESDAY						
WEDNESDAY						
THURSDAY						
FRIDAY						
SATURDAY						
SUNDAY						
GRAND TOTAL						

I declare that the above information is correct.

Signed ....

Please note the information on the reverse of this form.

Purpose of this form

Under the Working Time Regulations 1998, your weekly "working time" should not exceed an average of 48 hours per week over [any 17 weeks] [successive 17-week periods]. The Company is also required to maintain records which are adequate to show that this limit is being complied with.

[You may agree with the Company that the weekly working time limit shall not apply to you by signing as opt-out agreement. If you do so, the Company is not obliged to keep records for your working time.]

"Working time" under the Regulations has a specific meaning and not all of the time which you spend at work may count as "working time" under this definition. However, the Company believes that a record of time spent at work (which takes account of lunch breaks) will be adequate to monitor compliance with the Regulations.

The Company may change its record keeping procedures in order to produce more detailed information, if it considers that to be necessary.

You are required to complete this form and send it, on a weekly basis, to your Manager/the Personnel Department. Failure to complete this form, or the provision of false information, will be treated as a serious disciplinary offence. Persistent failure to properly complete and submit this form, or the deliberate falsification of information, may result in dismissal.

This record should be retained by the Company for at least two years.

[Note: This information should be included in the form to explain its purpose to the worker.]

Worker's Record: Specimen Record of Additional Hours Weekly Working Time Record

A–102

NAME:

[DEPARTMENT:]

WEEK COMMENCING:

[Normal] [Basic] [Contractual] hours of work: [to   ], [Monday to Friday]

                                                [   ] hours per week

SECTION A—[Normal] [Basic] [Contractual] Hours of Work

Have you worked your [normal] [basic] [contractual] hours in full this week?   Yes/No

If Yes, go to Section B

If No, please give details below:

DAY AND DATE	NUMBER OF HOURS NOT WORKED	REASON (*e.g.* sickness, holiday, medical appointment, etc.)

SECTION B—Additional Working Time

Have you worked any hours in addition to your [basic] [normal] [contractual] hours of work?

☐ No—please complete Sections C and D overleaf

☐ Yes—please give details overleaf and complete Sections C and D

Section B (Continued)

DAY AND DATE	ADDITIONAL TIME WORKED (hrs/mins)	[BRIEF DETAILS OF ACTIVITY CARRIED OUT]	[BRIEF DETAILS OF WHY THIS ACTIVITY WAS CARRIED OUT AT THIS TIME	[PRIOR MANAGEMENT APPROVAL?]
MONDAY				
TUESDAY				
WEDNESDAY				
THURSDAY				
FRIDAY				
SATURDAY				
SUNDAY				
TOTAL				

SECTION C—Total hours worked this week

Total from Section A

Total from Section B

Total for Week   hours   mins

SECTION D—Declaration

I declare that information given above is correct:

Signed ....

Notes

This form should be submitted on a weekly basis to your Manager/the Personnel Department.

The information on this form is required to assist the Company to comply with its obligations under the Working Time Regulations 1998 to maintain records regarding your weekly working time. Failure to submit this form promptly, or to provide accurate information, will be treated as a serious disciplinary offence. Persistent failure to properly complete and submit this form, or the deliberate falsification of information, may result in dismissal.

This form is to be retained by the Company for at least two years.

Worker's Record: Specimen Weekly Working Time Record

A–103

[BASED ON ASSUMED [45] HOURS PER WEEK]

NAME:

DEPARTMENT:

WEEK COMMENCING:

SECTION A

Have you worked more than [45] hours of working time this week?   Yes/No

If yes, please specify total number of hours of working time worked this week?   ☐ **hours**

SECTION B

Have you been absent through sickness or holiday this week?   Yes/No

If no, please sign the form below
- **If yes: please indicate the number of days absent this week**   ☐ **days**
- Have you worked more than [*specify "average" no. of hours per day, e.g. 45 ÷ 5 = 9 hours*] working time on the days in which you have attended work this week?   Yes/No
- If you answered no to the last question, please specify the total number of hours worked this week: ☐ hours

Declaration

I declare that the information given above is correct.

Signed ....   Dated ....

Purpose of this form

Under the Working Time Regulations 1998, your weekly "working time" should not exceed an average of 48 hours per week in [any 17-week period] [successive 17-week periods]. This means that you can work up to 816 hours "working time" in any 17-week period.

Your [contractual/normal/basic] hours of work (which will count as "working time") are
[   ] per week, *i.e.* [A] hours over 17 weeks. You could therefore work up to
[   ] additional hours of working time in any 17 weeks without breaching the limit on average weekly working time set by the Regulations.

The Company is obliged to maintain records which are adequate to show that the weekly working time limit is being complied with. The Company cannot maintain these records unless you provide it with information about your weekly working time. In order to simplify this record keeping process, while ensuring compliance with the Regulations, the Company proposes to assume, unless you notify the Company to the contrary, that you have worked no more than [45] hours in any working week (Monday to Sunday).

Section A of this form requires you to declare whether or not you have worked more than [45] hours of "working time" in a given week and, if so, to state the number of additional hours worked. It is your responsibility to maintain records on a daily basis of the additional hours of working time which you work over and above your [contractual/normal/basic] hours of work to enable you to complete this form.

Section B requires you to notify the Company of the numbers of days absence for holiday or sickness in any given week. Where you have been absent, you are required to declare whether the number of hours worked by you on the days in that week when you have attended work exceed [9 (*i.e.* 45 divided by 5)] hours per day.

Absences due to holiday, sickness or maternity leave must be taken into account by the Company when calculating your average weekly working time over the relevant 17-week period. This is done by extending the reference period by the same number of working days as the number of days of absence. Where a reference period is extended to take account of those absences, the Company may request you to keep additional daily records of your working time.

You are required to complete this form and send it, on a weekly basis, to your manager/the Personnel Department. Failure to complete this form, or the provision of false information, will be treated as a serious disciplinary offence. Persistent failure to properly complete and submit this form or the deliberate falsification of information, may result in dismissal.

This record is to be retained by the Company for at least two years.

Worker's Record: Specimen Supplementary Working Time Record

A–104

To: [*Name*]

WORKING TIME REGULATIONS 1998

For the next [   ] days (beginning with [*insert date*]) on which you attend work, you are required to keep a record of your daily "working time". [The Company's Working Time Record Keeping Policy gives guidance on the meaning of "working time".]

Please enter the appropriate details in the box below and return the form to your Manager/the Personnel Department.

If at any time you consider it likely that your working time in this period will exceed [*insert identified limit for period of extension to reference period*] hours, you should inform your Manager immediately.

DAY NO	DATE	NUMBER OF HOURS		DAY NO	DATE	NUMBER OF HOURS
1				6		
2				7		
3				8		
4				9		
5				10		

Total hours of working time in the above period: [   ] hours [   ] minutes

I declare that the information given above is correct.

Signed ....   Dated ....

Purpose of this form

Under the Working Time Regulations, your weekly working time should not exceed an average of 48 hours per week in [any 17-week period] [successive 17-week periods]. The 17-week period is known as a "reference period". If you are absent through illness, maternity leave or holiday, the reference period is extended by an equivalent number of working days to ensure that your weekly working time is averaged out over a full reference period.

The Company's existing record keeping procedures will not provide information on daily working time in this extension to the reference period. It is therefore vital that you provide the information requested above. Please note that failure to submit this form promptly, or to provide accurate information, will be treated as a serious disciplinary offence. Persistent failure to submit this form, or the deliberate falsification of information, may result in dismissal.

This record is to be retained by the Company for at least two years.

Worker's Record: Specimen Record of Working Time in Other Employment

A–105

NAME:

WEEK COMMENCING:

Please state number of hours worked this week for any other employer ☐ hours

Please state number of hours you expect to work next week for any other employer ☐ hours

If it appears likely that you will work more than [   ] hours next week for any other employer, you must advise your Manager immediately.

I declare that this information is correct.

Signed ....   Dated ....

The purpose of this form

Under the Working Time Regulations 1998, hours of working time spent in your employment with another employer will count towards your working time with the Company for the purpose of the weekly working time limit.

You are required to notify the Company using this form on a weekly basis of the number of hours of working time worked for any other employer and the number of hours working time which you expect to work for any other employer in the following week.

It is important that this form is submitted to the Personnel Department/your Manager on a weekly basis. Failure to provide the information requested on this form or the provision of false information will be treated as a disciplinary offence. Persistent failure to provide this information, or the deliberate falsification of information will be treated as gross misconduct and may result in your dismissal.

[You may agree with the Company that the weekly working time limit shall not apply to you by signing an opt-out agreement. If you do so, the company is not obliged to keep records of your working time.]

This record is to be retained by the Company for at least two years.

Specimen Weekly Working Time Record—17-Week Rolling Reference Period (Management Record)

A–106

NAME:

Week Number	1	2	3	4	5	6	7	8	9	10	11	12	13	14	15	16	17	
Week Commencing (Date)																		
Total working time for week																		
Cumulative total (A)																		(A)
Working time (hrs) remaining in reference period (816-A)																		
Days absent this week																		
Cumulative days absent in reference period																		Extend reference period by this number of working days Issue Supplementary Working Time Form

Number of days by which reference period extended ☐ days

Working time in days for which reference period extended ☐ hours

Working time over entire reference period (A + B) ☐ hours

☐ mins (B)

☐ mins (should be less than 816 hours)

This record is to be retained by the Company for at least two years.

SPECIMEN WEEKLY WORKING TIME RECORD

NAME:

Week Number	[18]	[19]	[20]	[21]	[22]	[23]	[24]	[25]	[26]	[27]	[28]	[29]	[30]	[31]	[32]	[33]	[34]
Week commencing																	
Start of reference period (week no)																	
Working time in previous 16 weeks (A)																	(A)
Working time this week (B)																	(B)
Days absent this week																	
Days absent in previous 16 weeks																	
Extension of reference period (days) (Note 1)																	
Working time in extension (C)																	(C)
Total working time for reference period (A + B + C)																	
Working Time available next week (Note 2)																	
Working Time available over next three weeks (Note 3)																	

Notes

1. A supplemental Working Time form must be issued.
2. This is 816 hours less the total hours of working time in this week and the preceding 15 weeks.
3. This is 816 hours less the total hours of working time in this week and the preceding 13 weeks.

This record is to be retained by the Company for at least two years.

Specimen Weekly Working Time Record—Fixed 17-Week Reference Period (Management Record)

A–107

NAME:

Week Number	1	2	3	4	5	6	7	8	9	10	11	12	13	14	15	16	17
Week Commencing (Date)																	
Total working time for week																	
Cumulative total (A)																	
Working time (hrs) remaining in reference period (**816-A**)																	
Days absent in week																	
Cumulative days absent in reference period																	

Number of days by which reference period extended ☐ days

Supplementary Working Time Form issued on ☐ / /

Working time in days for which reference period extended ☐ hours ☐ mins (B)

Working time over entire reference period (A + B) ☐ hours ☐ mins (should be less than 816 hours)

This record is to be retained by the Company for at least two years.

Specimen Weekly Working Time Record—New Worker (Management Record)

A-108

Week Number	1	2	3	4	5	6	7	8	9	10	11	12	13	14	15	16	17	
Week Commencing (Date)																		
Total working time for week																		
Total working time to date (A)																		
Days absent in week																		
Cumulative days absent to date*																		
Working Time in Extended Reference Period (B)																		
Total Working Time in Reference Period (A + B)																		
Applicable limit on Working Time	48	96	144	192	240	288	336	384	432	480	528	576	624	672	720	768	816	

*Extend reference period by this number of days. Issue Supplementary Working Time Form to worker.

This record is to be retained by the Company for at least two years.

Specimen Working Time Record Keeping Policy

THE PURPOSE OF THIS POLICY

A–109   The Working Time Regulations 1998 ("the Regulations") introduced a number of limits on the amount of working time which employees may work and confer entitlements to in-work rest breaks, daily and weekly rest breaks and paid annual leave.

In addition, the Regulations oblige employers to maintain records which are adequate to show compliance with the limits on working time. The nature of these record keeping obligations means that employees are required to assist the Company to maintain the necessary records by providing information about their working time. Given the nature of your working time, it is impossible for the Company to maintain these records without your co-operation. The purpose of this Policy is:

- to explain the limits which apply to your working time;

- to outline the records which the Company proposes to keep;

- to explain what is required by you to assist the Company to maintain these records.

THE RELEVANT "WORKING TIME" LIMITS

A–110   The Working Time Regulations set a number of limits on working time. In particular, the Regulations state that weekly working time shall not exceed an average of 48 hours per week. The other limits set on working hours relate to night workers and are not relevant to your employment.

Definition of "Working Time"

A–111   The Regulations define "working time" as time where you are **working** and **carrying out your activities and duties** and **at your employer's disposal**. All three elements must be present for time to count as "working time".

In addition to this "core" definition, the Regulations also state that time spent on certain training courses counts as working time.

Employers can also agree with their workers that time not included in the definition given above will count as working time. The Company has not made any such agreements to date.

Examples of time which would count as working time under this definition are as follows:

- your normal hours of work (*i.e.* the hours stated in your Contract of Employment);

- travelling in the course of your work, for example to visit clients or customers;

- working lunches or meetings outside of your normal hours of work;

- time spent working at home with prior approval of your Manager.

Examples of time excluded from the definition are:

- time spent travelling between work and home;

- time spent working from home without prior management approval;
- attending social functions organised by the Company.

As is explained later in this document you will be required to keep records of your weekly working time. The Company considers that it will be difficult to give precise guidance as to exactly what types of activity will count as working time. In particular, the reason why the activity is being carried out at a particular time and whether prior management instruction or approval has been given for the work to be worked at this time will be relevant. In deciding how working time is to be recorded, the Company has to take account of these uncertainties.

The Weekly Working Time Limit

A–112   Under the Regulations, your weekly working time cannot exceed an average of 48 hours per week over 17 weeks. This does **not** mean that you cannot work more than 48 hours in any one week. The limit means that you cannot work more than 816 hours of working time in the 17-week period over which the average is taken.

The 17-week period over which working time is averaged out is known as a "reference period" [and is a rolling period, *i.e.* the calculation is made by adding your working time in any week to that over the previous 16 weeks and then calculating the average working time per week] **or** [The reference period has been fixed by your contract of employment/a workforce agreement/a collective agreement as successive 17-week periods commencing on [   ].

New Workers

In the first 17 weeks of your employment with the Company, a different reference period applies. Your working time is averaged over the number of weeks for which you have been employed by the Company. This means that:

- in the first week of your employment, your working time cannot exceed 48 hours;
- over the first two weeks of your employment, your working time cannot exceed 96 hours; and
- over the first three weeks of your employment, your working time cannot exceed 144 hours, and so on.

Extension of the Reference Period

A–113   In order to ensure that your working time is averaged over a full period of 17 weeks, the reference period is extended to take account of absences due to maternity leave, sickness or holiday. This is done by adding up the number of working days of absence in the 17-week reference period. Your working time in the equivalent number of working days immediately after the end of the reference period is then added on to the working time in the reference period itself. The total working time in the reference period and the extended period is then averaged over 17 weeks as before.

Opt-Out Agreements

A–114   The limit on weekly working time referred to above does not apply at all if you sign an opt-out agreement disapplying the limit.

Record Keeping

A–115   The Company is obliged by the Regulations to maintain certain records of your working time.

Non-Opted Out Workers

A–116 For these employees who have not opted-out of the weekly working time limit, the Company is obliged to maintain records which are adequate to show that the weekly working time limit is being complied with.

The Company believes that the following record keeping system will be sufficient to comply with its obligations to keep records which are adequate to show compliance with the weekly working time limit:

[Your Contract of Employment states that you will work a number of hours per week. These hours will fall within the definition of "working time".

You will be issued with a form which should be completed on a weekly basis and returned to your Manager/the Personnel Department. The form will ask you to confirm whether you have worked your contractual hours in full for the relevant week or, where (for example because of absences for illness and holiday) you have not worked these hours, to indicate the number of hours worked. You will also be asked to state how many additional hours (over and above your normal contractual hours) you have worked. Such hours may not necessarily count as working time. You should state on the form the reason for these hours being worked at this time and whether this was with prior management approval or instruction].

OR

[Your normal contractual hours per week are less than 48 hours and the Company believes that any additional hours worked are unlikely to take you above the 48-hour limit. [Many employees for example, work [*insert relevant figure*] hours per week which means that they could work an additional [*insert relevant figure*] hours over any 17 weeks without breaching the working time limit]. The Company therefore proposes to assume that employees are working no more than [42] [45] hours per week unless the employee notifies the Company to the contrary. You will be required on a weekly basis to indicate the amount of any absence for sickness or holiday in any particular week].

OR

[The Company proposes to keep a record of the time spent by you at work, excluding any lunch breaks. You will be asked to keep a record of the time that you arrive at work and the time you leave and the time which you take as a lunch break. This form should be returned to your Manager/the Personnel Department on a weekly basis].

As explained above, the reference period over which the weekly working time limit is calculated must be extended to take account of absences due to maternity leave, sickness or holiday. The Company's ordinary record-keeping procedures will not record working time in the days over which the reference period is extended. You will therefore be issued, where appropriate, with a supplementary working time record on which you will be asked to keep a record of your daily working time for the appropriate number of working days. The period over which this record is to be kept will be stated on the form.

Opted-Out Workers

A–117 For those employees who have opted-out from the weekly working time limit, the Company is obliged only to keep records identifying that the worker has opted out of the record. The Opt-Out Agreement used by the company satisfies this requirement.

YOUR OBLIGATIONS

A–118 The Company has a statutory obligation to keep the records described above. It can only comply with this obligation with your co-operation and assistance. You will be provided with forms on which to record details of your working time. These forms must be completed and submitted to your Manager/the Personnel Department promptly. Any failure to submit these forms promptly or the provision of false information, will be treated as a disciplinary offence. Any persistent failure to submit these forms or the deliberate falsification of information, may result in your dismissal.

If you have any queries about your obligations under this policy, you should contact your Manager/the Personnel Department.

Specimen Working Time Monitoring Form

THE PURPOSE OF THIS FORM

A–119 The Company is required under the Working Time Regulations 1998 to keep records which are adequate to show that the limit set by the Regulations in respect of your weekly working time are being complied with.

In order to keep these records, the Company needs to know what aspects of your time are likely to count as "working time" under the Regulations.

The Regulations define "working time" as time where you are *working* and *carrying out your activities and duties* and *at your employer's disposal*. All three elements must be present for time to count as "working time". Time spent on training courses may also count as "working time" under the Regulations.

Examples of time which *would count* as working time under this definition are as follows:

- your normal hours of work (*i.e.* the hours stated in your contract of employment);

- travelling in the course of your work, for example to visit clients or customers;

- working lunches or meetings outside of your normal hours of work;

- time spent working at home with the prior approval of your Manager.

Examples of time *excluded* from the definition are:

- time spent travelling between work and home;

- time spent working from home without prior management approval;

- attending social functions organised by the Company.

It is not clear whether other types of time would be classed as "working time" under the Regulations. This may depend on the type of activity being carried out, the reason why it is carried out at that time and whether you have agreed with, or been instructed by, your Manager to carry out work at this time.

The Company intends to implement a monitoring process over the next [   ] weeks/months to identify the nature of the activities which you are performing outside of your normal (*i.e.* contractual) hours of work. This review should give the Company a better understanding of the activities which you are performing and whether these should be classified as "working time".

Please complete the forms enclosed with this note and submit them to your Manager/the Personnel Department on a weekly/monthly basis.

Thank you for your co-operation.

NAME:

DEPARTMENT:

WEEK COMMENCING:

DATE	NUMBER OF HOURS OF ADDITIONAL WORK	NATURE OF ACTIVITY	REASON FOR PERFORMING THE ACTIVITY AT THIS TIME	PRIOR INSTRUCTION FROM MANAGER?	YES/NO	PLEASE STATE IDENTITY OF MANAGER

Index